A GAME OF INCHES

The Game Behind the Scenes

A GAME OF INCHES

*The Stories Behind the Innovations
That Shaped Baseball*

THE GAME BEHIND THE SCENES

Peter Morris

Ivan R. Dee

CHICAGO

www.ivanrdee.com

Library of Congress Cataloging-in-Publication Data:
Morris, Peter, 1962–
  A game of inches : the game behind the scenes: the stories behind the innovations
  that shaped baseball / Peter Morris.
        p. cm.
  Includes bibliographical references and index.
  ISBN-13: 978-1-56663-705-3 (cloth : alk. paper)
  ISBN-10: 1-56663-705-8 (cloth : alk. paper)
    1. Baseball—United States. 2. Baseball—United States—History.
3. Baseball—United States—Miscellanea. I. Title
  GV863.A1M654 2006
  796.357'640973—dc22
                                        2006007322

To Kim Schram, who soars

Contents

(iv) The Amenities

(v) Items Added for Spectators

CHAPTER 18: MONEY

(i) The Transition from Amateurism to Professionalism

(ii) Owners Grab the Reins

(iii) Players Seek a Bigger Share

(iv) Negotiations

(v) Contracts

(vi) Commercialization

CHAPTER 19: VARIANTS

CHAPTER 20: INCLUSION

(i) African Americans

CHAPTER 25: AS AMERICAN AS APPLE PIE

(i) Wrapping the Game in the Flag

(ii) Talking the Talk

CHAPTER 26: MISCELLANY

(i) Keeping Up Appearances

(ii) Rituals

(iii) Customs, Traditions, and Taboos

(iv) Legends and Shrines

Preface

THIS VOLUME picks up where the first one left off, moving away from the stories of how new slides and pitches and fielding tactics were unveiled on the playing field of baseball and instead chronicling the often unappreciated innovations that have taken place behind the scenes. Some of these are of obvious historical significance while others are much less momentous, yet each seems to me to have something to tell us about the essence of the game of baseball.

There is an old parable about several blind men who touch different parts of an elephant and reach seemingly irreconcilable conclusions about its totality. Similarly, baseball's rich history is too vast and amorphous to make sense of it from any single vantage point. Cumulatively, however, the stories of the origins of all of baseball's components can provide new insight because each of them has forced consideration of the same revealing question: Is this new thing worthy of being part of the national pastime?

Toward that end, as in the first volume, I have construed the story of an item's entry into baseball as being broader than just a list of names and dates and places. Of course nailing down these details is a vital part of the tale, and sometimes it is the whole story. But whenever possible I try to use these as a means of examining essential questions: Why was this new thing introduced when it was? What prevented it from entering earlier? Who felt that this new idea was a valuable addition and why? Who tried to keep it out and why? What underlying values were at stake? How was the battle fought and how was it won? Those are the questions that I find so fascinating because seeing how people have reacted to the prospect of something new in baseball brings us a little closer to an understanding of why baseball means so much to Americans.

I did my best to acknowledge my many debts in the first volume, so here I will simply repeat my gratitude to the many researchers who graciously contribute their insights, to Ivan Dee and his colleagues for all they have done to turn my dream for this book into reality, and to all the friends and family members who have provided me with such wonderful support.

P. M.

Haslett, Michigan
July 2006

A GAME OF INCHES

The Game Behind the Scenes

Chapter 13

BUILDING A TEAM

IF YOUR favorite major league team doesn't have much talent, at least it has a sizable group of people—the general manager and his assistants, the farm system director, a staff of scouts—who are exploring a variety of means of acquiring and developing new talent. In contrast, nineteenth-century clubs generally had one lone man who wore all these hats and many more. If this overworked individual found himself short a player in the National League's debut year of 1876, none of the methods of acquiring talent available to today's general manager were available. Not only were cell phones far in the future, but so were trades, player purchases, farm teams, drafts, scouts, and tryout camps. As a result, more often than not he would sign the first decent candidate at hand. It is small wonder that these men became known as "hustlers" (see **6.1.3**). This chapter describes the origins of all of the tools now available to general managers, with the exception of cell phones.

As important as the role of general manager is, there is no authoritative way to single out one man as the first to have this role. Early managers handled many of the functions of today's general manager, but the position has expanded enormously since then. As a result, it is not possible to pinpoint the first general manager.

Even determining the first man to hold this title is tricky. Bill James claimed that Billy Evans was the first man to hold the title of general manager, in 1927 (Bill James, *The New Bill James Historical Baseball Abstract*, 128). In fact a 1916 article reported, "Branch Rickey's official title with the St. Louis Browns is 'vice president and general manager'" (*Sporting News*, February 10, 1916). Moreover the title is a sufficiently generic one that it had been used earlier for different responsibilities. In 1879, for example, the *Chicago Tribune* reported that Jim White had brought in his brother-in-law to act as "General Financial Manager and Official Scorer" of the Cincinnati club (*Chicago Tribune*, May 11, 1879).

(i) Minor Leagues

Probably the most common recourse for plugging a hole is to call someone up from the minors. Baseball's farm system has a complex history, and it is noteworthy that other major sports such as football and basketball still have no equivalent. In order to understand how the farm system developed, it is necessary to review the origins of the minor leagues and the early attempts to forge a workable relationship between the minor and major leagues.

13.1.1 Minor League. Many sources list the International Association, which started play in 1877, as the first minor league. This is the ultimate example of the revisionism that can result when the victors write history. The International Association was a competitor to the National League that did very respectably in head-to-head competition. It had none of the characteristics of a minor league (see **18.4.1**).

The League Alliance was also formed in 1877 and had the important characteristic that its contracts were honored by the National League. But competition between the clubs was quite disorganized: "there was no rule to prescribe how many games League Alliance clubs should play to make a series, and therefore, although Indianapolis made the best record, the St. Paul Red Caps were credited with winning the championship" (*Reach's Official Base Ball Guide, 1884*, 25). This makes it hard to argue that it was a league in any meaningful sense. A New England League was operating in these same years and may deserve to be recognized as the first minor league, but more research is needed.

The Northwestern League of 1879 appears to have been the first circuit to function unquestionably as a league while also subordinating itself to the National League. Ted Sullivan, who had more firsthand knowledge of the nineteenth-century minor leagues than anyone else, wrote in 1905 that this was the first minor league (*Sporting News*, February 4, 1905).

The Northwestern League went defunct after one season, and the next three seasons saw only a few modest attempts at a minor league. The Eastern Championship Association was formed in 1881 by five clubs, but only three completed their schedules. The League Alliance was reconstituted in 1882 but with only two clubs (*Reach's Official Base Ball Guide, 1884*, 25–26).

In March 1883 the Northwestern League was revived and took the historic step of joining with the National League and American Association to sign the Tri-Partite Agreement. This accord bound the three leagues to honor one another's contracts, and the Northwestern League accepted a role as a subordinate league. For the 1883 campaign the Northwestern League was joined by the Inter-State Association. In subsequent years other leagues around the country proved willing to accept a lower place in the hierarchy in exchange for protection from player raids, and also affixed their signatures to the series of pacts that became known as the National Agreements (see 18.2.3). As a result, the minor leagues have existed continuously since 1883.

13.1.2 Climbing the Ladder. As soon as there were acknowledged "minor leagues," the major leagues became covetous of those leagues' best players. Moreover it seemed only fair to give the players in these circuits the opportunity to advance in their profession. Finding a satisfactory way of accomplishing this end would, however, prove extremely difficult.

In the 1885 National Agreement, minor league clubs were denied the right to reserve players. Presumably the expectation was that this would drive down the price of these players, but that didn't happen. Instead it gave the minor league clubs every incentive to dispose of their best players at season's end. The result was that the best minor leaguers acquired extravagant reputations, and by season's end it was acknowledged that "competition will be great, the price run up and clubs with deep purses will bag the game" (*Sporting Life*, September 9, 1885).

Less affluent clubs began to scout around for alternative methods of player acquisition. Louisville manager Jim Hart, for instance, was described as being "one of the wide-awake kind. Instead of waiting until the end of the season . . . he quietly slips off, pays as much for a release as it would cost him anyhow in the fall through bidding by different clubs, and captures the acknowledged best pitcher in the South" (*Sporting Life*, September 9, 1885). Other clubs experimented with rudimentary forms of the farm system.

All these efforts convinced players of the value of their services, and player costs continued to escalate. In 1889 the owners attempted to implement caps on player salaries, but this move led to the formation of the Players' League in 1890 and a costly war. When the Players' League folded after one season, and the American Association followed suit one year later, the National League owners were finally in position to implement a more comprehensive system for acquiring players.

The owners did not take long to take steps toward adopting a concept that had been proposed in Francis Richter's Millenium [sic] Plan. The idea was the draft system (described in the next entry), which was ostensibly designed to allow players to advance up the ladder. But it didn't escape notice that the new system would also mean savings for the major league owners: "The draft system under the new national agreement is going to knock chunks off base ball salaries once it gets into operation and the fight is over.

This is sure, because it will stop the competition between clubs which has driven prices up. Under it correspondence will show priority. First come will be first served" (*Williamsport Sunday Grit*, March 29, 1891).

13.1.3 Drafts. By 1892 the National League was again the only major league, and it worked in tandem with selected minor leagues to create the first comprehensive system by which players could advance to the major league.

The 1892 National Agreement established the first minor league classification system, under which each minor league was classified as either A or B. During the offseason, which ran from October 1 to February 1, a National League club could draft a minor leaguer and would pay the minor league club $1,000 for a Class A player or $500 for a Class B player. If more than one club selected the same player, the winner was drawn out of a hat. Class A clubs could also draft players from the B circuits.

The system led to the promotion of many players. For example, a note after the 1892 season indicated: "Baltimore has notified the Atlanta management that [it] has drafted [Jack] Wadsworth, and that he will play in that city this coming season" (*Atlanta Constitution*, February 19, 1893). The classification system was extended in the years that followed, and by 1896 it reached as low as Class F.

By then, however, problems with the system were becoming apparent. Johnny Evers and Hugh Fullerton reported that all too often major league clubs drafted "players from lower class leagues, not for themselves but for other clubs of lower rank with which secret agreements have been made" (John J. Evers and Hugh S. Fullerton, *Touching Second*, 50). As is discussed in the next entry, there was a price for such favors.

Eventually efforts were made to protect minor league clubs from losing an excessive number of players in the draft, but this rule too had unanticipated consequences. It soon became apparent that a major league club could help a minor league club by drafting a player the big club didn't want— effectively protecting a better player on the minor league team. These favors, naturally, were also done with the expectation of receiving something in return.

Such loopholes meant that the draft rarely functioned as it was designed to do. Nonetheless it remained the basic mechanism for player advancement until the farm system became prevalent.

Although this draft lost much of its importance with the advent of the farm system, it continues to this day and is now known as the Rule 5 draft. Blue Jays general manager Pat Gillick brought renewed attention to the Rule 5 draft in the 1980s by using it to acquire budding stars like George Bell. Clubs still use this draft and occasionally manage to pluck a gem from a rival's farm system.

13.1.4   Pick of the Club. As described in the preceding entry, the most commonly exploited flaw in the draft system was the opportunity it provided a major league club to place a minor league club in its debt. Naturally a major league club that did such a favor expected something in return, and the resulting arrangement became known as the "Pick of the Club."

For example, an 1895 note reported, "[Marty] Hogan has been farmed out to Indianapolis on satisfactory conditions. It was agreed between the two clubs that Hogan is to remain with the Hoosiers all season. Should he prove a success he can be reclaimed for the St. Louis team next season. Should there be another outfielder more valuable than Hogan, St. Louis will have first claim to him next season" (*Sporting Life*, May 18, 1895). And the following year: "Charley Reilly has been released to Syracuse by the Philadelphia Club under agreement that the Philadelphia Club have the right to draft any one Syracuse player, including Reilly himself, gratis, for the season of 1897. Nor will the Syracuse Club release any player to an outside club without first consulting the Philadelphia Club officials" (*Sporting Life*, March 7, 1896).

This ploy was extended in the ensuing years, and new variants were added. The *Chicago Tribune* offered several examples in 1906: "Sometimes a club owner is compelled to 'cover up' players in order to secure favorable training grounds, sometimes it is done to create friendly relations with a minor club and secure reliable tips on good material in other clubs of the same league suitable for future purchase or draft" (quoted in *Sporting Life*, March 24, 1906).

It proved exceedingly difficult to prevent these kinds of shady dealings. *Sporting Life* reported in 1905 that Charles Comiskey had "drafted a number of gentlemen from his faithful friend, Joe Cantillon. . . . Usually Commy drafts Joe's best men every fall, and then returns them back to him, but this time he says if the men make good they will stick" (*Sporting Life*, September 9, 1905). But with no definitive way to determine whether such promises were sincere, the abuses continued.

One such deal could have changed baseball history. The *Washington Post* reported in 1908 that Washington manager Joe Cantillon agreed to let Kansas City have pitcher Clyde Goodwin for $1,000, "providing, however, that there was no cash to be paid down, but an option given the Washington club on the pick of the Kansas City pitchers for $2,500, and if such selection was made Goodwin was to figure in the deal at the price agreed upon." Kansas City tried desperately to get out of the deal when Boston offered them far more for one of their pitchers, and Cantillon finally agreed to rework the deal. By doing so he lost out on the opportunity to have a pitching staff led by Walter Johnson and Smokey Joe Wood (*Washington Post*, June 2, 1908).

One of the masters of this tactic was Branch Rickey. Sportswriter John B. Sheridan observed in 1920: "Rickey did not devise the 'pick of the club' scheme of trading between major and minor league teams. But he worked it to its finest development." As Sheridan explained, Rickey's chief scout Charley Barrett would sign more prospects than the Cardinals could possibly use. He would then offer a minor league club several of the players in exchange for the "pick of the club" at season's end (*Sporting News*, February 5, 1920). In some ways this was the ultimate embodiment of Rickey's "quality out of quantity" philosophy of player development.

Rickey was far from alone, however. The Giants used the scheme to get a Hall of Famer, as Travis Jackson explained: "The New York Giants sent an outfielder named Joe Connolly to Little Rock with the understanding that he could stay there and play center field all season if the Giants could have first pick of the Little Rock players at the end of the year. It turned out I was the first pick and at the end of the '22 season they told me to report to the Giants" (Walter M. Langford, *Legends of Baseball*, 92).

As is seen in the next entry, the "Pick of the Club" scheme overlapped with and often complemented early versions of the farm system.

13.1.5 Farm Clubs and Farm Systems. Most sources credit Branch Rickey with inventing the practice of farming, but this is at best an oversimplification. Rickey was unquestionably the first man to put together what we now call a farm system, in which a player could advance from the lowest rung of the minor leagues to the major leagues while remaining the property of the same organization. But the system of major league clubs using minor league clubs as farm clubs had a lengthy, well-publicized, and controversial history before Rickey's entry into the field.

It could be argued that the use of farm clubs dates all the way back to the very earliest baseball clubs. These clubs were represented in matches by their "first nine," but they also had second and third nines and often junior nines. These extra nines provided reserves when a member of the first nine was injured or unavailable and also helped develop new players.

The League Alliance, formed in 1877 and revived in 1882, was another very rudimentary prototype of the farm club. Harry Wright attempted to form a reserve squad for Boston in 1883, but his idea was considered impractical.

Things changed a year later when the Union Association mounted a challenge to the existing major leagues and the reserve clause. The National League and American Association fought back by forming reserve clubs with the aim of keeping players away from the upstart league. Chicago's A. G. Spalding was one of the first proponents, announcing plans in November 1883 to field an auxiliary or colt team that Cap Anson would train in a "Base

Ball Academy" (*Sporting Life*, November 21, 1883). As one reporter noted, "Harry Wright was ridiculed last season for thinking of such an idea as a reserve team. Now the Boston, Chicago, Cleveland, New York, St. Louis, Allegheny and Cincinnati have followed the example of the old man" (*Brooklyn Eagle*, April 13, 1884).

The reserve teams were characterized as "virtually a training school for professional base-ball players, and is a move that should have been started before" (*Chicago Inter-Ocean*, March 18, 1884). The Union Association lasted only one year, and its demise removed the most obvious reason to sign extra players to contract. When the last teams disbanded, the *Sporting Life* observed, "The reserve plan has served to develop some strong young players, a number of whom are now playing on the regular nines. This was the main object of the reserve nines."

But major league owners had seen the advantages to having additional players available and soon found new ways to resurrect the scheme. In January 1887 the Emporia, Kansas, club offered to keep and pay the salaries of two Cincinnati players for the season, then return them at season's end. While the arrangement fell through, other major league clubs took heed. Detroit president Frederick K. Stearns was paying particularly close attention.

As the regular season opened, word leaked out that Stearns "had been frying a kettle of fish that will open the eyes of [A. G.] Spalding and the other league moguls when the operation is concluded" (*Detroit Free Press*, May 2, 1887). Detroit had three players—Jimmy Manning, Bill Shindle, and George Knowlton—who had been with the team during training camp but had not made the team.

Rather than having to release them, Stearns now had the means to have his cake and eat it too: "Manning, Shindle and Knowlton will be loaned out, not released, to a crack club not in the National League [which turned out to be Kansas City of the Western League], which will pay them the same salaries they now receive. That this is a ten strike must be admitted. Manning, Shindle and Knowlton will not sever their connection with the Detroits, neither will the club have to pay their salaries. If by sickness or accident any of the others of the club should be laid up, the team will not be weakened perceptibly, as a dispatch will bring either or all of the loaned players into the breach as fast as the cars can carry them" (*Detroit Free Press*, May 2, 1887).

Stearns's tactic soon prompted both imitators and controversy. When Cincinnati loaned pitcher Henry Kappel to Nashville, the *Detroit Free Press* reported, "[Manager Charles] Byrne, of the Brooklyns, says that the system of loaning ball players under contract by American Association clubs to clubs in minor leagues is clearly illegal. Cincinnati has done this in the case of Kappell [sic] to Nashville, and Cleveland objects to the action" (*Detroit Free*

Press, May 14, 1887). Vociferous protests were also lodged by the New Orleans club, Southern League president John Morrow, and National League president Nick Young, leading the *Free Press* to add a few days later: "a strong fight is being made against the new scheme of league clubs 'farming' out surplus players to minor association clubs" (*Detroit Free Press*, May 18, 1887). Kappel was speedily recalled by Cincinnati, and Memphis agreed to forfeit the games it had won while he was in the lineup (*Sporting Life*, May 18, 1887). Similar protests met Indianapolis's attempt to loan Joe Quinn to Duluth, and instead Quinn's contract was sold to the Northwest League team (*Indianapolis Sentinel and News*, June 7, 1887).

With that tactic meeting such concerted resistance, the 1888 season instead saw many clubs take the route of purchasing minor league teams and operating them as farm clubs. In contrast to the season before, this practice was conducted openly and created relatively little controversy.

For example, within months of the end of the 1887 campaign, Washington president Walter Hewett revealed that "he is largely interested in the Troy Club, and proposes to make it a training-school or feeder for the Washingtons" (*Washington Post*, December 4, 1887). Ted Sullivan managed Washington in 1888, and the *New York Clipper* noted after the season that Sullivan "organized and managed the Troy team, which was a member of the International Association, while at the same time he acted as a business agent for the Washington Club, who also controlled the Troy Club" (*New York Clipper*, January 12, 1889). *Sporting News* later claimed, "In that year—'88—Sullivan seems to have instituted the first base ball farm in the shape of a minor league team placed in Troy, N.Y., as a member of the International League [sic]. Once a week Sullivan would run over to Troy to see how his farm was getting along and to give some orders to his manager. So it may fairly be said that he was the first manager to run two clubs in one season—a major and a minor" (*Sporting News*, December 30, 1909). While the arrangement attracted little attention, there is no indication it was a secret, with the *Washington Post* remarking at mid-season: "Perhaps few of the Washington baseball public are aware that situated in Troy is an annex to the club here" (*Washington Post*, June 24, 1888).

Researcher David Ball discovered several other major league clubs that operated farm clubs during the 1888 season. New York Giants president John B. Day had previously owned the New York franchises in both the National League and American Association and had taken advantage of this situation to make a number of dubious transactions (see **22.5.2** and **13.2.3**). After the 1887 season Day announced plans to take over the Jersey City club in the Central League and "run it as a reserve for the New-York Club. He thinks that the only way to secure good players is to secure a club in a minor league and develop young men" (*New York Times*, November 5, 1887).

Day reportedly assured Jersey City manager Patrick T. Powers that he would not "take any of the Jersey City players out of the club before the end of the season" (*Chicago Herald*, April 22, 1888). But dual ownership allowed him to sign "a small army" of players during the offseason and then assign them as he saw fit—a precursor to Branch Rickey's "quality out of quantity" philosophy (*Sporting Life*, November 9, 1887). And some contracts were transferred during the season (*New York Times*, July 18, 1888).

St. Louis Brown Stockings owner Chris Von der Ahe operated the St. Louis Whites of the Western Association as a farm club, signing no fewer than twenty-nine players to 1888 contracts by December 1887. Chicago White Stockings president A. G. Spalding appears to have pursued a similar course with another Western Association club, the Chicago Maroons. Although Sam Morton was the nominal president of the Maroons, the club had close connections with the local major league franchise (*Sporting Life*, December 10 and 31, 1887; *Philadelphia Record*, quoted in *Cincinnati Enquirer*, December 29, 1887).

There were hints of several other alliances between major league and minor league clubs that amounted to farming, most notably one involving Philadelphia and Allentown of the Central League (*Philadelphia Record*, quoted in *Cincinnati Enquirer*, December 29, 1887; *Sporting Life*, January 18, 1888). A particularly ominous portent was the grumbling of a *Sporting Life* correspondent from Columbus, Ohio, that Lima had captured the Tristate pennant in large part because of players farmed out by Chicago. In September he intimated: "Lima, for her peculiar, yet fortunate personal relations with Spalding, Anson & Co., has been enabled to receive many inside tips, as well as players, from the Chicago contingency" (*Sporting Life*, September 19, 1888). He went further the following month, complaining that Lima "had a clear advantage over other League cities because of Manager [William] Harrington's intimate relations with Spalding, Anson & Co., of Chicago, who kept him well supplied with good material" (*Sporting Life*, October 31, 1888).

Like so many nineteenth-century minor league clubs, the farm clubs were not financial successes. The St. Louis Whites folded in June 1888, and while the other clubs made it through the season, none seem to have been in the black. The Maroons disbanded at season's end, while the Washington club quietly disposed of its Troy farm club (*Washington Post*, November 14, 1888). Ownership of the Jersey City club in 1888 was reported to have resulted in a $17,500 loss, and although it returned as "an annex to the New York League Club" in 1889, Day apparently sold out in June (*Cincinnati Enquirer*, June 14, 1889; *Sporting Life*, June 19, 1889). Not surprisingly, a consensus emerged that such ventures were too expensive to be maintained.

That perception was one of several factors that led to the multiple experiments with farm clubs in 1888 being followed by six lean years for farming.

A second was the concern voiced by *Sporting Life*'s Columbus correspondent that farming could destroy a minor league's competitive balance. Another important reason was that the attention of the established leagues was focused on the player revolt that led to the creation of the Players' League in 1890. In addition, as is discussed under "Trades" (see **13.2.3**), any exchange of contracts during this period meant releasing the players with the risk of losing them altogether.

By the mid-1890s the latter two problems had been eliminated. The National League was firmly established as the only major league while the rules and practices had changed so that its clubs could move players from minors to majors more easily. As a result the farm issue returned with a vengeance in 1895 when Cincinnati owner John T. Brush began to take advantage of the fact that he also owned the Indianapolis club in the Western League.

The frequent transfers of players between Brush's two clubs prompted criticisms of a system that "permits the big league to pull back farmed-out players whenever their services are needed" (*Sporting Life*, May 18, 1895). A particular concern was that the major leagues reaped benefits from the system that often came at the expense of the minor leagues.

One of the first men to appreciate this was Patrick T. Powers, who had managed the Giants' Jersey City farm club in 1888. Now he was president of the Eastern League and understood the damage that could result from farming. Powers declared, "Each club should stand on its own bottom and each player should be signed regularly and not allowed to be taken away in mid-season just when the man is a drawing card and a favorite, developed at the expense of the local people. . . . No player's services should be accepted by any minor league club without a distinct understanding that the man shall not be recalled before the close of the playing season" (*Sporting Life*, December 7, 1895).

Yet others, such as sportswriter F. E. Godwin, defended farming: "President Brush has been severely criticized for transferring players to and from the Indianapolis Club, but he puts up the money to maintain a club in the Hoosier town, and if he develops a youngster or wants to strengthen his smaller club when he has too many men on his Cincinnati list I see no harm in making the exchange. The idea of having a 'farm' for the development of players is bound to become popular. In the near future I look for a number of magnates to pay for clubs in minor leagues for the benefits that will accrue from the polishing process" (*Sporting Life*, October 12, 1895).

One thing was clear: as long as the practice was legal, it would continue and expand. In mid-season 1895 a Chicago sportswriter observed: "Rockford is our supply depot" (*Sporting Life*, August 24, 1895). By season's end the *Columbus* (Ohio) *Dispatch* was claiming direly that the Western League clubs were all farms now, without individuality or independence (*Columbus*

Dispatch, quoted in *Sporting Life*, December 7, 1895). The offseason brought new reports: "It is understood that Youngstown is to be another Cincinnati farm" (*Sporting Life*, February 22, 1896).

By 1896 the players were beginning to grumble: "Within a few weeks [Bill Hassamaer] was farmed out, recalled and released by Louisville. 'Roaring Bill' is of the opinion that it is not a string which a club has on a player. 'It's a rope, and it's around a fellow's neck,' is his explanation" (*Brooklyn Eagle*, July 18, 1896).

The newspapers had joined the chorus by the following year. A Hartford sportswriter noted, "The local newspapers have begun a sort of a mild war on the teams in the Atlantic League who have 'farmed' players in their ranks, and there is likely to be some trouble over the awarding of the pennant should any of the teams using farmed players win the flag" (*Sporting Life*, July 24, 1897). The *Detroit Free Press* advocated "getting rid of the 'farming' evil as was practiced on behalf of Cincinnati at Indianapolis this year" (*Detroit Free Press*, October 24, 1897). The *Cincinnati Times-Star* complained: "The present arrangement is that the minor leagues are deuces in the deck. Their magnates put out their good money for franchises, develop players who put the clubs on a paying basis and then are compelled to give up their star players for a paltry $500 or less, without any appeal or recourse" (*Cincinnati Times-Star*, quoted in *Sporting Life*, November 6, 1897).

Clubs were also beginning to combine farming with the "Pick of the Club" scheme (described in the preceding entry). The *Cincinnati Times-Star* explained: "According to many reports, a scheme has come up that beats this farming idea all hollow, only in this new practice major league clubs are deprived of the privilege of securing men that they need and who should be accessible to them. The scheme works as follows: A minor league manager who has several players he would like to keep goes to his friend, the major league manager, who does not need the men, and requests him to draft these men or purchase them outright before the drafting season opens—as 'some other manager wants them,' the arrangement between the minor league manager and his friend being that the players are returned to the minor league after the drafting season ends. In this way the minor league manager holds his players and can sell them if he chooses. Of course, he furnishes the money used in 'drafting' or 'buying' the players. Louisville is said to have assisted Milwaukee in this way by 'purchasing' [Robert] Stafford and Lewe [Kid Lewee] for $500. Brooklyn also figured in a like deal by drafting pitcher [Frederick] Barnes of Milwaukee. And it is said that Columbus likewise is saved players by the purchase of [Jack] Crooks, [Frank] Genins and [Peter] Daniels by St. Louis, and [Ike] Fisher, [Billy] Hulen and [Sandow] Mertes by Philadelphia" (*Cincinnati Times-Star*, reprinted in *Sporting Life*, November 6, 1897).

A minor league manager explained the ins and outs: "The secret of Cleveland's purchase of half a dozen players from the Toledo Interstate team last fall is out. Manager [Charles] Strobel tells it himself. He says: 'I sold pitcher [George] Kelb, Meyers [Bert Myers], [Erve] Beck, pitcher John Blue and Captain Bob Gilks to Cleveland. I had an understanding with [Cleveland owners] the Robisons that they would buy these players, put them on the reserve list, so they could not be drafted, and put a price on their releases high enough to prevent any club buying them. Now if none of them is bought at the prices fixed between us all of them but Kelb will be turned back to me by April 10. For this accommodation pitcher Kelb is given to Cleveland outright—not farming—it is really protection. If he suits Cleveland they will buy Beck; if not fast enough I get him back'" (*Sporting Life*, February 5, 1898).

Strobel's account makes it easier to understand why minor league clubs would agree to such arrangements. Hunting for new talent could be costly and time-consuming, and it must have been especially frustrating to know that any good player would soon be lost through the draft. So minor league clubs were naturally tempted by the prospect of a cheap, regular supply of talent.

By 1898 an exasperated Ned Hanlon contended that it would be entirely possible, under the existing rules, for him to farm out stars like Hughey Jennings and Willie Keeler if he desired. He added: "I know of National league players whom other clubs would like to have who will be sent to 'farms' and paid small salaries, simply because the prices put upon their releases are out of all reason. It is simply an outrage—nothing less—and ought to be stopped" (*Sporting Life*, February 5, 1898).

John T. Brush's dual ownership of the Indianapolis and Cincinnati franchises continued to fan the controversy. Sportswriter James Andrew denounced the hypocrisy of claiming that transfers between these two clubs represented legitimate opportunities to advance: "Does any one believe that the Cincinnati Club in drafting all the players of the Indianapolis team which everybody knows it cannot and does not desire to use has had in view even in the slightest degree the welfare of the players or to enable them to advance in their profession?" (*Sporting News*, October 30, 1897).

The *Milwaukee Sentinel* accused Brush of trying to destroy the Western League, claiming, "If legislation is not enacted this year to check the growth of the evils upheld by Brush no one can estimate the damage that will result to base ball" (*Milwaukee Sentinel*, quoted in *Sporting Life*, March 26, 1898). A *Sporting Life* correspondent added, "One of the most flagrant abuses now known in base ball is the 'farming' system, and how it can be successfully checked has agitated the minds of the magnates who are opposed to it, but all legislation leveled at the evil has been successfully side-tracked so far by the autocratic John T. Brush" (*Sporting Life*, March 26, 1898).

Brush defended himself: "As to 'farming' as the transfer of players to a club of an inferior league for development is called, I can't see where it is wrong in theory or practice. If the Cincinnati Club buys a player it acquires an interest in him just as it would if it bought real estate. If the Cincinnati Club is unable to use that player it certainly has the right to dispose of him outright or to send him to another club temporarily until he becomes skillful enough to be used by it. There is no reason why the Cincinnati Club should lose the money it has invested in a player any more than it should sacrifice a real estate investment which did not turn out as well at first as was anticipated. The loan of players by the Cincinnati Club to the Indianapolis Club was beneficial to both parties. It assisted us in the development of our surplus players and built up that city in a base ball sense" (*Sporting News*, May 7, 1898).

But few were buying his version. A *Sporting News* correspondent responded: "From Mr. Brush's standpoint, there is nothing unfair or unsportsmanlike in making minor league teams play against National League talent. That is exactly the condition that has obtained in the Western League every season since Indianapolis became a farm for Cincinnati" (*Sporting News*, June 4, 1898). Another sportswriter pointed out: "Although the rules plainly state that no farmed player shall be recalled . . . before the end of the season, John T. [Brush] goes right ahead and switches players where he can use them to best advantage. Less than two weeks ago, he sent Damman [Billy Dammann] to the Hoosier capital, presumably to help the Indians out during their series with the Blues, for immediately after the completion of the series, he recalled Damman. He then sent Marvin Hawley to the farm club and called it a trade, but has since recalled Hawley" (*Sporting Life*, June 11, 1898).

The unfairness of farming to players was becoming increasingly clear. The *New York Telegram* cited a particularly flagrant example: "The injustice of the farming rule is seen in the case of outfielder [Charles] Frisbee, of the Bostons. Frisbee was turned over to Tom Loftus, of the Grand Rapids team in the Western League, along with $1000, in the deal for backstop Sullivan. This exchange of dollars and one human being for a likely player gave Frisbee a right to file a large and vociferous wail, and he is backed in his grievance by some National League managers, who are desirous of signing so promising a player as the athlete who was relegated to the Grand Rapids farm. In other words, the Boston Club handicaps the future of one good player for the sake of experimenting with another. In the obscurity of a minor league Frisbee may run to seed and his hopes of a future be blasted by the selfishness of grasping magnates. And this is called advancing players in their profession, in the very words of the National Agreement! Out upon such perversion of law and justice" (*New York Telegram*, reprinted in *Sporting*

News, December 2, 1899). Frisbee, who had batted .329 in his rookie season of 1899, would have only thirteen more major league at bats.

In 1900, National League players formed the Players' Protective Association, a modest form of a union. One of this body's goals was putting an end to farming, a practice that it contended was thwarting players from rising in their profession. The American League tried to lure players in 1901 by promising not to farm them. Before the season began, however, there were reports that Detroit was using Montreal as a farm club.

The 1903 National Agreement finally made some effort to limit farming by banning multiple ownership. Robert Burk, however, noted an important loophole: "In its place the pact created an 'optional assignment' procedure in which a major leaguer could be sold to a minor league club, with his former employer retaining the option to repurchase" (Robert Burk, *Never Just a Game*, 164).

The result was that it remained easy for a major league club to collude with a minor league club. The *Chicago Tribune* reported in 1904 that Chicago had made a test case by openly selling George Moriarty to a minor league club with the proviso that they could buy him back before the drafting season for the same price. They asked the National Commission to rule on the case, and it was approved (*Chicago Tribune*, June 26, 1904).

With no check on open arrangements, illicit agreements were rampant. The *Washington Post* explained, "One of the tricks of baseball is for major league clubs to 'buy' stars of the minor organizations before the drafting season opens, and hold the players until the following spring, when they are turned back to their original owners. [Charles] Comiskey last year secured Jakey Atz and others from New Orleans and turned them back without even a trial. He has just 'purchased' Jakey again with some others, and it is suspected that New Orleans is being protected in the same old way" (*Washington Post*, August 25, 1904).

The *Detroit News-Tribune* observed that the National Agreement had helped preserve the integrity of minor league pennant races: "The really raw character of the plan, as exemplified by John T. Brush, the originator, in its operation between the old Cincinnati and Indianapolis teams, has disappeared, and it is very seldom that a player, when once sent to the minors, emerges until the end of the season." But players continued to be denied the opportunity of advancement: "Modern farming is carried on through fake sales of players to a major league team at the close of a season, the players being returned to the little team when the time comes for the beginning of another season. The cases of [Jake] Gettman and [Frank] Laporte, of Buffalo, 'purchased' by Detroit at the close of 1903, were deals of this character exposed for the failure of the players to report even for trials in the spring" (*Detroit News-Tribune*, reprinted in the *Washington Post*, September 18, 1904).

In 1906 the National Commission modified its rules in an effort to eliminate farming: "It is specifically stated in the rule that the club which purchases a player from another club and sells him back to that club without giving him a trial on the field will be considered guilty by that act of purchasing the player merely to cover him up for the benefit of the club which first sold him. Hitherto there has been no definition by which guilt or innocence could be determined. The new provision it is expected will result in a practical abolition of the evil system which has grown to such proportions that few clubs in either major league have not engaged in it more or less. It still will be possible, of course, for clubs to cover up some players by taking them on the spring training trips and making at least a pretense of giving them a trial, but that will be an expensive process" (*Chicago Tribune*, March 4, 1906).

The new rules had teeth in the form of fines of up to $1,000 for offenders, and fines were indeed levied regularly (*Chicago Tribune*, March 28, 1906; April 10, 1906). Nevertheless the fines did little to stem the tide. One sportswriter calculated that "Of the 68 players alleged to have been purchased by the minor leagues last fall, waivers have been asked on all but 18. This is a nice testimonial to the practice of 'covering up'" (*Washington Post*, March 3, 1906).

Washington manager Joe Cantillon was particularly flagrant about subverting the intentions of the draft: "Cantillon has drafted about 20 players from the minor leagues. . . . Of the entire squad, it is not likely that one will ever wear a Washington uniform. Cantillon, however, has holes to plug up in other clubs which have given him material, and he will do it by the draft route" (*Washington Post*, September 1, 1907).

By 1909, *Sporting Life* reported that "the 'farming' evil under the species 'optional agreement' guise has spread into all leagues" (*Sporting Life*, January 2, 1909). The *Chicago Tribune* went further, pronouncing the rules to be "absolutely a dead letter so far as current practice is concerned. There are hundreds of farmed players in the minor leagues today. They are not called that by name and they are not actually loaned to minor league clubs with the understanding they may be recalled on demand. A subterfuge in the form of an 'option' agreement has been sanctioned by the national commission which bears the same relation to farming that a time loan does to a call loan in banking. The players are 'sold' to minor league clubs with a written agreement that they can be repurchased in August at a fixed price and that no other club shall have a right to purchase or draft them if the original loaning club cares to exercise its 'option.' Yet the foundation of organized baseball says specifically, 'All right or claim of a major league club to a player shall cease when such player becomes a member of a minor club.' And the national commission expects respect for itself and the laws it is supposed to enforce!" (*Chicago Tribune*, July 11, 1909).

Sportswriter Joe S. Jackson wrote in 1911 that with the exception of Washington "there seems to be no ownership in the country that is not engaged in a wholesale juggling of players to evade the rules made for the protection of the sport" (*Washington Post*, September 26, 1911).

When Chicago owner Charles Webb Murphy was sanctioned in 1913 for having a secret agreement with the Louisville club, *Sporting News* pointed out the hypocrisy of singling Murphy out: "'Farming' is forbidden by the National Agreement, and is practiced by every club owner in the two big leagues. It has been done so openly by some of the moguls that the example made by Murphy is all the more deplorable" (*Sporting News*, August 28, 1913). A follow-up piece added, ". . . It is likely that 'side agreements' enter into almost every big deal made between a major and a minor league club. It is an indisputable fact that every major league club has minor league affiliations, which enable them to place surplus talent much more advantageously than would otherwise be the case. These affiliations also result in the 'covering up' of valuable players to protect them from the draft by other clubs which might use them" (*Sporting News*, September 4, 1913).

With the farming laws regarded as a "dead letter," major league owners now dropped the restriction on owning minor league clubs. Cleveland became particularly active in this regard. A 1912 article reported that "the Cleveland American League Club is figuring on taking Marion's franchise in the Ohio State League and using this city as a farm" (*Sporting Life*, March 16, 1912). By 1916, Charles Somers of Cleveland owned Waterbury of the Eastern League, New Orleans of the Southern League, and Toledo of the American Association (Robert Burk, *Much More Than a Game*, 35). In 1921 Chicago Cubs owner William Wrigley purchased the Los Angeles Angels of the Pacific Coast League.

It should be clear by this point that the farm system the Cardinals developed in the 1920s and 1930s was not something that Branch Rickey in any meaningful sense "invented." What Rickey did was to tinker with, and then reinvent and expand, an existing idea that had previously been prohibited or deemed too costly.

While other major league clubs had owned minor league clubs, this practice was widely considered to be an almost certain money-loser. This conclusion was founded upon the perception that a minor league club could not produce enough talent suited to the needs of the major league squad to justify the expense. Rickey saw matters otherwise, however, and began to purchase minor league clubs.

Rickey's decision was driven by two important factors. The first was that minor league owners such as Jack Dunn of Baltimore were demanding exorbitant amounts for stars like Jack Bentley and Lefty Grove, and keeping the players if their price wasn't met. This not only drove up the price of talent but also meant that low-budget teams like Rickey's Cardinals would never be able to acquire such players.

This in turn led Rickey to realize that ownership of an entire network of farm clubs could become profitable if, in addition to producing talent for his club, it also yielded excess talent that he could sell to his rivals. Thus Robert Burk has suggested that Branch Rickey was not an inventor but a man with a genius for organizational tinkering: "What set Rickey's approach apart from that of his predecessors was his early grasp of the importance of integrating within the same parent club office the signing of entry-level talent, management of the player promotion process at all levels, and maintenance of a deliberate surplus of young talent to leverage down the major league payroll and make additional profits through sales of surplus players" (Robert Burk, *Much More Than a Game*, 35).

Rickey also recognized that this approach to player development allowed him to make more effective use of his scouts. Previously, major league scouts had been on the lookout for major league–ready talent, but the ownership of multiple minor league clubs allowed the Cardinals to stockpile promising but raw players. Rickey began to evolve his "quality out of quantity" philosophy and instructed chief scout Charley Barrett to sign players who still needed seasoning. As early as 1921, columnist John Sheridan observed that "Barrett's activities are more in the line of finding young players for trading and training purposes than for picking up big league stars" (*Sporting News*, August 4, 1921).

Playing no small part in this scheme was Rickey's self-interest. Beginning with his first Cardinal contract in 1918, Rickey received a share of the club's profits. He would ultimately realize a significant part of his income from the sale of the excess talent produced by the Cardinals' farm system (Murray Polner, *Branch Rickey*, 112).

By the middle of the decade Rickey's efforts were attracting attention that was bolstered by the success of his team. After the Cardinals won the 1926 World Series, sportswriter John B. Sheridan described "the Cardinal system of replacement, that is ownership of a 'vertical trust,' a number of minor league clubs of varying classifications, D, C, B, A, and AA, through which the Cardinal replacements are moved for educational purposes" (John B. Sheridan, *Sporting News*, December 23, 1926).

The success of the Cardinals naturally prompted other clubs to imitate Rickey's methods. On December 15, 1932, major league owners approved the idea of "chain store" baseball in spite of the objections of Commissioner Kenesaw Mountain Landis. Landis would continue to throw wrenches in the works for the remainder of his life by periodically ordering the release of covered-up players. However, even the mighty Landis was not able to undermine a system now firmly in place.

A 1934 *Sporting News* editorial observed that farm systems were not merely expanding but fundamentally changing in nature: "Unless all signs fail, 1934 promises to become known as the 'year of the farms.' Formerly, the fountain head of the system was the major league club. Now a number of the minor league clubs are going in for the farm stuff and the end is not yet in sight" (*Sporting News*, March 15, 1934).

13.1.6   Player Development Plan. For several decades after the permanent establishment of chain-store baseball, minor league owners continued to exercise considerable autonomy. Their freedom to make player personnel decisions allowed them to retain local players who had no hope of making the majors, and these "career minor leaguers" often became fan favorites.

But the future of the minor leagues was jeopardized in the 1950s by a precipitous decline in attendance. As a result, on May 18, 1962, major league baseball adopted the Player Development Plan. The majors increased funding of the minors, in exchange for authority over personnel issues. The plan also abolished Classes B, C, and D and replaced them with the Rookie Leagues. This effectively rendered the minors the developers of talent for the majors that they have been ever since. In the process, the "career minor leaguer" became effectively extinct, yielding his place to younger prospects.

(ii) Trades and Sales

Trades and sales are such an accepted part of baseball today that it is easy to forget how strange they must have once seemed. Just imagine opening the business section of a newspaper and reading that Charles Schwab had sent a money manager to Merrill Lynch for an investment adviser and a bond specialist to be named later. Or that your local hardware store had swapped employees with one of its competitors. The earliest baseball trades understandably struck observers as being equally peculiar. *Sporting Life* observed in 1884, "There is a great deal of nonsensical twaddle uttered by ill-informed base ball reporters about players being bought and sold. If these gentlemen would trouble themselves to examine the rules bearing on the subject they would discover that no player can be transferred, no matter what the consideration, without his own free will and consent. Buying a release from contract is a legitimate transaction and of frequent occurrence in theatrical and business affairs" (*Sporting Life*, August 13, 1884).

13.2.1   Sales. In 1887, John Ward wrote, "The 'buying and selling' of players was unheard of three years ago" (quoted in Bryan Di Salvatore, *A Clever*

Base-Ballist, 195). This was not quite true since, as *Sporting Life* noted in the above passage, buying a release was always a possibility.

The first player sale probably occurred in 1875 when the Athletic Club of Philadelphia purchased the release of Bill Craver and George Bechtel from the cross-town Centennial Club. Francis Richter claimed: "The Centennials played but few games, and their brief existence is only noteworthy for the fact that with them began the sale of players, a custom that has grown to tremendous proportions since. The Centennial Club contained but two first-class players—Craver and Bechtel. The rival Athletic club, of Philadelphia, wanted these two, and two wealthy members of the club paid an official of the Centennial Club $1500 to have the two players released and transferred to the Athletic Club. This was done and shortly after the Centennial Club disbanded. It was a peculiar fact that the first sale of players brought retribution with it, as Craver turned out to be crooked, and Bechtel took [Cap] Anson's place so often that the latter became dissatisfied and later seceded to the Chicago Club" (Francis C. Richter, *Richter's History and Records of Base Ball*, 47).

Henry Chadwick reported after the 1878 season that the "system of releasing players" had led to considerable abuse. He explained that a club could put together a strong lineup, only to have a rival try in mid-season to induce its "players to 'get a release' and then join them, offering tempting baits for secession. As the rule admits of releases and new engagements, of course it does not take long for tempted players to work things to suit them so as to obtain the required release" (*New York Clipper*, January 4, 1879).

There was, however, no viable way to eliminate this possibility. As a result, any time a player went into a slump, there began to be whispers that he was "playing for his release." This state of affairs was harmful both to individual players and to the integrity of the game itself, and it paved the way for open sales of players.

In 1882, John Corkhill was sold for $300 (James A. Williams, quoted in *Sporting Life*, April 25, 1891). By 1884 it was becoming more common for clubs and players to mutually agree to terminate a contract. During that season it was reported that Lew Simmons of the Athletics "gave the Lynn Club $250 for the release of [Henry] Oxley, their catcher," though the deal seems to have fallen through (*New York Clipper*, June 21, 1884). After the 1884 season Tom Deasley learned that New York's National League entry placed more value on his services than did his current employers. So "he paid the St. Louis Club $400 for his release. He then came to [New York], and was at once engaged at a salary of $3,000" (*New York Sun*, April 4, 1886).

Player sales grew after that, in large part because they were much easier to implement than trades. But they remained odious to the players. In his 1887 article "Is the Base Ball Player a Chattel?," John M. Ward reasoned,

". . . When the Chicago club sells [Mike] Kelly for $10,000, it simply makes that sum out of Kelly. . . . Kelly received his salary from Chicago and earned every dollar of it several times over, and yet the Chicago club takes ten thousand dollars for releasing Kelly from a claim for which it never paid a dollar" (John M. Ward, "Is the Base Ball Player a Chattel?," *Lippincott's* 40 [August 1887], 310–319; quoted in *Baseball in Old Chicago*, 50). The 1889 public statement by the players' union, the Brotherhood (see **18.3.1**), similarly denounced the fact that "Players have been bought, sold and exchanged, as though they were sheep, instead of American citizens" ("Brotherhood Manifesto," November 4, 1889; reprinted in Dean Sullivan, ed., *Early Innings*, 188–189).

Their logic was hard to deny, and owners often did give players a part of the purchase price. Deacon White famously said, "No man is going to sell my carcass unless I get half" (quoted in Lee Lowenfish, *The Imperfect Diamond*, 34). Billy Gleason similarly acknowledged in 1894 having been "after a $500 slice of the $2,400 [Ned] Hanlon paid Chris [Von der Ahe] for me, and I am not violating any confidence in assuring you that I got it. When Willie figures in a deal he makes it a point to see that his interests are not neglected" (*St. Louis Post-Dispatch*, September 22, 1894).

13.2.2 Going-out-of-business Sales, Garage Sales, and Shopping Sprees.

By 1883 the reserve clause (see **18.2.1**) had been expanded to the point where owners could essentially retain their entire team. Of course, being able to reserve all these players didn't mean that the club had to sign all of them—or even try to do so. Predictably, some owners began selling off their reserved players to balance their budgets while other owners took advantage of the situation by going on shopping sprees.

Researcher David Ball believes that the Fort Wayne club of the Northwestern League may have initiated this practice by selling most of its reserved players after the 1883 season. The *Cincinnati Enquirer* observed with alarm, "From present appearance it looks as though the managers of the Fort Wayne club had entered the field this season with no other object in view than that of speculating in human beings under the provisions of the reserve rule. . . . Already they have sold three players at figures that will come pretty near paying all the preliminary expenses of the club for next season" (*Cincinnati Enquirer*, reprinted in the *Washington Post*, February 3, 1884). The Fort Wayne club, however, defended its actions by pointing out that the players could have jumped to the Union Association and arguing that it was merely making sure it received something in return (*Fort Wayne Gazette*, January 29, 1884).

David Nemec reported that the Washington entry in the American Association held a fire sale in July 1884 and disbanded shortly thereafter

(David Nemec, *The Beer and Whisky League*, 67). It appears that they succeeded in selling only one player, Frank Fennelly, but the proceeds helped
the club pay the delinquent salaries of other players. Three Ohio clubs—
Columbus, Toledo, and Cleveland—followed this example at season's end by
selling most of their players to Pittsburgh, St. Louis, and Brooklyn, respectively, and giving up their major league franchises.

The 1885 season saw Detroit president Frederick K. Stearns make two
major purchases to upgrade his talent. In June he purchased the players of
Indianapolis's Western Association franchise, which included future Hall of
Famer Sam Thompson. On September 17 he added Buffalo's entire infield,
the so-called Big Four of Dan Brouthers, Hardie Richardson, Jack Rowe,
and Deacon White. The new acquisitions turned a woeful team into a pennant contender in 1886 and a world champion in 1887. But when owners devised a new guarantee system that made it impossible for Detroit to afford
such a payroll, Stearns stepped down. His successors sold off the high-priced
players after the 1888 season and then folded the team.

In the intervening three years, such blockbuster sales had become commonplace, with Chicago selling Mike Kelly and John Clarkson for the
shocking prices of $10,000 apiece and St. Louis auctioning off stars like
Dave Foutz, "Doc" Bushong, and Bob Caruthers.

13.2.3   Trades. Even the idea of a trade was pretty much unheard of until
1883, and it was several more years before it was practical to consummate
one. The most obvious reason for this was that exchanges of human beings
raised the basic human rights issue noted in the rhetorical title of John
Ward's 1887 essay, "Is the Base Ball Player a Chattel?" Trades also brought
into question the principle of the mutuality of a contract, an especially
prickly topic in the 1880s because of the recent implementation of the reserve clause. The result was that in order for two clubs to complete such a
transaction, they first had to agree on the players to be exchanged, then convince all those players to cooperate.

This meant that talk about trades was more common than actual swaps.
The *St. Louis Post-Dispatch* reported in the middle of the 1883 season that
Ted Sullivan, manager of the St. Louis (American Association) club, "has
made a proposition to the Buffalo league club, asking the managers whether
they would release [Jim] Lilly or Schaeffer [George Shafer] for Tom Sullivan" (*St. Louis Post-Dispatch*, June 26, 1883). Even if Buffalo had agreed in
principle to this arrangement, it would have been another matter to orches-
trate it. If the players had in fact been released, there would have been no
way to be certain that another owner would not swoop in and sign them.

For this reason the risk of a slip between the cup and the lip haunted
every prospective transaction. One of the most notorious examples occurred

after the 1884 season, when pitcher Tony Mullane attested in a notarized statement that he would sign with St. Louis if released by Toledo. Instead Mullane inked a contract with Cincinnati and was blacklisted for the 1885 season (Jon David Cash, *Before They Were Cardinals*, 96–97).

While owners were chastened by such incidents, the more determined ones were willing to go to considerable lengths to complete a deal. According to Harold Seymour, "*Sporting Life* reported that in one instance 'wine and women' were used" (Harold Seymour, *Baseball: The Early Years*, 168). A different diversionary approach was employed by the ownership that controlled the New York franchises in both the American Association and the National League. After the 1884 season it was decided to transfer star players Tim Keefe and Dude Esterbrook from the Mets to the Gothams in exchange for two less accomplished players, Frank Hankinson and Ed Begley. Reportedly Jim Mutrie took Keefe and Esterbrook on a cruise during the period they were released to ensure that neither signed with another club (David Nemec, *The Beer and Whisky League*, 92). As noted under "Waivers" (13.3.2), Seymour traced the origins of baseball's waiver rules to this dubious arrangement.

Obviously, owners who wanted to make a deal badly enough were usually able to find a way to surmount the formidable obstacles. The ones that proved easiest to consummate were between a major league club and a minor league club, since such trades offered advancement to the player(s) going to the majors and greater security to those headed to the minors.

Late in the 1885 season Louisville manager Jim Hart acquired highly regarded pitcher Toad Ramsey from Chattanooga, "giving in exchange for him, beside the cash bonus, [John] Connor, the young pitcher he secured from the Buffalos, who is scarcely strong enough for the American, but should do exceedingly well in the Southern League. If Ramsey proportionately pitches for Louisville anything like the ball he pitched for Chattanooga he will prove a treasure for his new club. The bonus paid for the transfer is $750. Chattanooga wanted $1,000 and Manager Hart offered $500. After considerable dickering the difference was split at $750, Hart agreeing, in addition, to give Chattanooga Connor. Ramsey, who has been anxious to get away from Chattanooga, gladly entered into the deal and signed with Louisville for $200 per month" (*Sporting Life*, September 9, 1885).

Researcher David Ball found evidence of a similar deal and a near miss the following summer. He cited a note in *Sporting News* that "it is said" that the Athletics had obtained Macon's star pitcher Cyclone Miller in exchange for cash and their reserve battery of Charles Gessner and Bill Dugan. Late in the 1886 season the Athletics reportedly offered Al Atkinson and cash to St. Joseph for Silver King, though the deal fell through. Ball noted that since minor league teams lacked reserve rights, it was in their best interests to dispose of their best players during the season rather than lose them without compensation. The minor league club also needed to get at least one player in return, since few capable replacements were available. This explains why the pattern of all three deals was a potential star going to the major league club in exchange for cash and a lesser player or players.

The 1886 season saw increasingly common rumors of trades between major league clubs. The *New York Sun* reported, "There is much talk of trading players by several of the Western clubs" (*New York Sun*, July 4, 1886). The most sensational rumor was of a blockbuster deal in which St. Louis would send Fred Dunlap, Jack Glasscock, and Emmett Seery to Boston in exchange for Sam Wise, Tom Poorman, Joe Hornung, and either Charlie Parsons or Billy Nash (*Boston Globe*, June 4, 1886). David Ball has discovered at least a dozen other rumors of trades between major league clubs during the 1886 campaign. It was not, however, until November that the first such trade actually occurred when the Browns sent Hugh Nicol to Cincinnati in return for Jack Boyle and $350.

The complications involved in completing even that trade make it easy to understand why nothing had come of the earlier rumored deals. Cincinnati manager Gus Schmelz explained that he gave St. Louis owner Chris Von der Ahe a document reading, "I hereby agree to pay $350 and Catcher Boyle for the release of Hugh Nicol, conditional on Nicol's signing with the Cincinnati B.B. Club." Von der Ahe gave him a similar document, and both were then presented to league president Wheeler C. Wikoff, who agreed not to approve the two players' releases until they had been signed by their new clubs. Schmelz then instructed Cincinnati president Aaron Stern not to mention the arrangement until he had secured Nicol's signature, before rushing to the player's hometown of Rockford to sign him (Gus Schmelz to Aaron Stern, November 12, 1886, Cincinnati Reds collection, Cincinnati Historical Society, box 2, file 35).

All of these machinations make it easy to see why trades remained uncommon for several more years. They gradually increased in frequency as owners gained the upper hand and inserted clauses in contracts that required players to go wherever their contracts were assigned. David Ball reports that an April 17, 1896, bulletin by National League president Nick Young included the following items: "Released—by Chicago to Cincinnati—Asa Stewart; by Baltimore to Syracuse—George Carey." He believes that this is the earliest official reference to a player's contract being directly transferred from one club to another without the formality of a release.

Even then not all players meekly acquiesced to being shuffled about like pieces of property. As with purchases, many players demanded compensation before agreeing to a trade, and some went further. Brooklyn outfielder Mike Griffin was traded after the 1898 season and found that his new club would not honor his old contract. He successfully sued for damages, but as a result his fine career ended prematurely.

Clark Griffith's career could have met a similar fate. An 1899 article reported: "Both Griffith and [Jimmy] Callahan, of the Chicago Club, are up in arms against proposed trades involving them. Griffith says he will quit the game before he allows himself to be traded to some club for which he does not care to play. Callahan, who has been mentioned as likely to be traded to Boston, says he wants to remain in Chicago if he cannot go to the New York Club. In speaking about the evils of the trading system, Callahan said: 'They have put many a good man out of the business. . . . If we are the attraction which draws the money into the box office, we certainly ought to have something to say about our location on the base ball map. . . . I, for one, do not intend to figure in any trade unless I can better myself by so doing'" (*Sporting News*, December 30, 1899).

As a result of such complications, David Ball reports that it became a fairly common practice during the late 1880s to agree upon a cash equivalent for each player in a trade. Thus if one of the players did not sign with the team he was supposed to go to, the releasing club would pay the money instead. These agreements eroded the bargaining power of a traded player and gradually helped make trades more routine.

Of course players never became entirely reconciled to trades. In 1969 Curt Flood reacted to being traded to the Phillies with words that echoed the title of the essay written by John Ward eighty-two years earlier: "I do not, however, consider myself to be a piece of property to be sold regardless of my desire" (quoted in Charles P. Korr, *The End of Baseball as We Knew It*, 84). Flood lost his subsequent court challenge to the reserve clause, but the support he won from his fellow players helped lead to the ten-and-five rule (see **13.2.7**) and to free agency (see **18.4.5**).

13.2.4 Three-way Trades. Following the 1908 season the Giants traded Roger Bresnahan to St. Louis in a three-team deal. Cincinnati sent George Schlei to New York; St. Louis shipped Ed Karger and Art Fromme to Cincinnati; and St. Louis sent Red Murray and Bugs Raymond to New York (*Sporting News*, December 31, 1908).

13.2.5 Players to Be Named Later. *Sporting Life* reported in 1915, "The Baltimore Club has traded Bill Bailey, the southpaw pitcher, to Chicago for pitcher Dave Black and a pitcher yet to be named" (*Sporting Life*, September 25, 1915).

13.2.6 Throw-ins. There is of course no way to determine a highly subjective category like the first throw-in. Willie Keeler, however, was one of the earliest throw-ins and was likely the first afterthought in a trade to unexpectedly develop into a superstar. He may also have been the first player referred to by this term, as *Sporting Life* claimed in 1895 that Keeler was "the man who was 'thrown in' to fill out" the Brouthers trade, a deal in which Baltimore manager Ned Hanlon secured Keeler and Brouthers in exchange for Bill Shindle and George Treadway (*Sporting Life*, July 13, 1895). According to Burt Solomon, the trade was originally going to be a straight-up swap of Brouthers for Treadway. When Brooklyn asked for Shindle as well, Hanlon requested Keeler. Since Brooklyn intended to release Keeler, they acquiesced (Burt Solomon, *Where They Ain't*, 57–58).

13.2.7 Vetoed Trades. On February 25, 1973, a new Basic Agreement gave the right to veto a trade to players with ten years of major league service and at least the last five with the same team. The "ten and five rule" was often referred to as "the Curt Flood Provision" because it addressed one of the main concerns that prompted Flood's challenge to the reserve clause (Charles P. Korr, *The End of Baseball as We Knew It*, 128). Ten-and-five player Jim Perry of Minnesota was traded to Detroit the following month and consented to the deal (Sporting News, *Baseball: A Doubleheader Collection of Facts, Feats and Firsts*, 454).

Ron Santo became the first player to exercise the ten-and-five rule on December 5, 1973, when he turned down a trade that would have sent him from the Cubs to the Angels. After vetoing the trade, Santo realized that he had put himself in a unique position: "I was concerned. It really didn't hit me until a couple of days later. I realized the Cubs didn't want me and I couldn't possibly play for them again" (quoted by Joe Mooshil, AP wire service story, December 12, 1973). Fortunately for Santo, the Cubs soon arranged a new trade that sent him to the crosstown White Sox.

(iii) Roster Restrictions

13.3.1 Roster Sizes. Roster sizes and efforts to get around them in one way or another affect almost all the basic strategies used by general managers to accumulate and retain talent.

Until 1889 substitutions were allowed only in the case of severe injury. As a result, as noted under "Insertion of Substitutes" (6.2.1), most major league clubs carried only ten or eleven players. Some went with only nine and hired managers or even groundskeepers with the expectation they would serve as emergency substitutes. In the years since, roster sizes have more than doubled, but rarely has an increase come without resistance from some quarters.

This was particularly true in the 1890s when the legalization of substitutes led to rapid increases in roster sizes. For example, in 1892 the *Brooklyn Eagle* contended that the local club's decision to carry seventeen or eighteen players that year was too many (*Brooklyn Eagle*, June 8, 1892). The *Washington Post* argued that on a club that "burdened itself with too many players," a starter was liable to become "disturbed and made nervous by thinking there is another on the team waiting to take his place." It added that a large bench was unnecessary because there was "time enough to look around for a man to fill a position when the one who has it has failed" (*Washington Post*, February 16, 1890).

And *Sporting News* observed in 1900: "The costly experience of the National League clubs in carrying players for whom they can not find a regular position and who are not even needed as substitutes, may lead to a much-needed reform. It is said that there is a movement under way to limit each National League club's right of reservation to 16 players" (*Sporting News*, August 4, 1900).

Such efforts faltered during the challenge of the American League, as teams in both leagues tried to stash extra players on their rosters. Sportswriter J. Ed Grillo noted that this tendency created a great advantage for the richer clubs: "As many as 38 [players] have been carried through a season by some club which could afford it, while one of the weaklings was scouring the country in search of material not as good as that which the strong club was paying to remain idle" (*Washington Post*, December 24, 1909). The result was that once a permanent peace between the two leagues had been reached, they were quick to reinstitute a firm limit on roster sizes.

It took a little longer to settle on the perfect number. Today's size of twenty-five was proposed before the 1909 season and was widely reported as having been adopted (for example, *Chicago Tribune*, February 18, 1909). But implementation of the restriction appears to have been delayed. After the 1909 season many newspapers carried word of a "new" rule limiting rosters to twenty-five players between May 1 and August 20 (*Washington Post*, December 16, 1909; *New York Times*, December 16, 1909; also *Detroit Free Press*, April 10, 1910, "the new 25-man rule, which takes effect in May").

At the same time the prototype of the forty-man roster was created to prevent clubs from bringing enormous aggregations to training camp. In 1910 sportswriter A. J. Flanner explained that a new rule that clubs could only bring thirty-five players to spring training would have significant ramifications: "In recruiting for 1911, the big league manager must consider the quantity and quality of members of his team during the present race, as well as the number and ability, present and prospective, of players on whom he has option, before he can intelligently start to secure minor league stars either by purchase or draft" (*Sporting News*, July 21, 1910).

Minor league roster sizes remained smaller but were beginning to succumb to similar pressures. Early in the 1916 Eastern League campaign the clubs voted to expand rosters from thirteen to fourteen when they realized that "the teams would be unable to get along with only four pitchers during the hot weather when they are playing doubleheaders" (Will Anderson, *Was Baseball Really Invented in Maine?*, 31).

Major league roster sizes were reduced during World War I, but they returned to twenty-five following the war's end and have stayed there ever since, with a few short-lived exceptions. After the 1931 season, rosters were cut from twenty-five to twenty-three because of the depression. In the early 1990s owners briefly cut back to twenty-four-man rosters in another cost-saving measure.

One thing that has never changed is the intimate connection between roster sizes and player development stratagems. In 1915, when the National League restricted roster sizes to twenty-one, John McGraw complained that he was paying scout "Dick Kinsella $5,000 a year to select the pick of the minors and it is pretty tough now that it develops that most of Dick's work has been for the benefit of other teams" (*Sporting News*, February 25, 1915).

13.3.2   Waivers. Major league baseball has had waiver rules since 1885, but they have undergone many alterations over the years as the problems they were intended to address have changed.

The earliest waiver rules were created in an apparent effort to stem the growing threat of clubs selling off their best players to teams in a rival league (see **13.2.2**). Harold Seymour suggested that an infamous deal in which John B. Day essentially transferred star players Tim Keefe and Dude Esterbrook from his American Association franchise to his National League club was the spur (Harold Seymour, *Baseball: The Early Years*, 169). As befits this modest aim, the rules were simple and essentially required that a player had to be offered to every other team in the league for a period of ten days before his contract could be sold to a club outside the league. The early waiver rules involved no payment for a claim and had plenty of loopholes.

In theory, even a trade could not be completed without the players clearing waivers, but in practice owners routinely passed if they knew a trade was being made. For example, researcher David Ball found an 1889 article in the *Washington Post* that explained: "The management of the home team have made arrangements for the exchange of [Jim] Whitney for ["Egyptian"] Healy [of Indianapolis] and the league clubs have been requested to waive claims for both men." To get the process started, Indianapolis sent a telegram to National League president Nick Young that read: "Whenever League clubs waive claim to Whitney and Healy and Washington releases

Whitney Indianapolis will accept his services. At the same time Indianapolis will release Healy" (*Washington Post*, March 24, 1889).

Once farm clubs (see **13.1.5**) became a common way for major league clubs to stockpile players, the waiver rules were modified to try to prevent this practice. As the waiver system and its goals became more complex, the earlier spirit of cooperation disappeared, which made it necessary to clarify or amend the procedures. For example, it was made explicit that a club could revoke its waivers if the player was claimed. A claiming fee was also added to deter frivolous claims. In addition, fairer rules were created for situations when more than one team claimed the same player (originally the player had been allowed to choose).

Despite such amendments, the waiver system proved an imperfect means of preventing farming. For one thing, as is discussed under "Gentlemen's Agreements" (see **13.3.5**), clubs could easily conspire to evade the rules. A related problem was caused by the original club's prerogative to revoke the waivers after a claim. Sportswriter Jack Ryder wrote in 1915, "Usually at this time of the year a raft of requests for waivers is coming in, so that, if obtained, deals for the players may be made with minor league clubs" (*Cincinnati Enquirer*; quoted in *Sporting News*, December 2, 1915). Opposing clubs that put in claims would likely end up only with the players the other team didn't want, so it usually made more sense to pass and let a few capable players slip to the minors. Other abuses of the system were discussed in the entry on farm clubs.

In spite of its many problems, the waiver system was retained and expanded in hopes of remedying a widening range of problems. In the process the waiver rules have greatly increased in complexity. It would now be difficult if not impossible to make a succinct summary of what they accomplish.

It can safely be said, however, that one major goal was improving competitive balance. At the 1921 winter meetings a rule giving the first shot at waived players to the weakest teams was instituted. As is discussed in the next two entries, a similar desire to achieve greater parity motivated restrictions on late-season trades between contenders and also-rans, especially when the players were passing from one league to the other.

13.3.3 Interleague Trading. As noted in the preceding entry, the waiver system was created in 1885 in part to prevent deals between the National League and the American Association. The same principle applied for much of the twentieth century to transactions between the American and National leagues.

The first such trade took place in the summer of 1903, during a brief truce between the warring leagues. *Sporting Life* gave this account of the historic event: "Cincinnati has secured second baseman Tom Daly and outfielder [Cozy] Dolan from the Chicago American League Club in exchange for infielder George Magoon. This is the first inter-league deal as yet consummated" (*Sporting Life*, June 20, 1903).

After a permanent peace had been reached, the two leagues made a concerted and highly effective effort to prevent such trades. The primary reason for this restriction was fear that a tail-ender in one league could sabotage the other league's pennant race by selling their best players to the league leader.

As a result, it came as a great shock to the baseball world when star Yankee pitcher Hank Borowy, despite a 10-5 record, cleared waivers on July 27, 1945, and was sold to the Cubs for a figure close to $100,000. Borowy went on to complete a twenty-win season and lead his new team to the National League pennant.

The transaction raised the hackles and suspicions of many owners. According to sportswriter Warren Brown, however, the explanation was more plebeian: "There were no 'angles' to the deal and no skullduggery as many charged. It was the age-old exemplification of the utter silliness of the waiver rule. Periodically each major league club asks waivers on ballplayers on its reserve list, possibly to establish whether there is any demand for them, possibly just to keep in practice. Most clubs have become committed to the theory that it is useless to refuse to waive on any player who is known to have two arms and two legs, since most of the time the waivers will be withdrawn anyhow. So clubs are apt to be careless in perusing the waiver lists, and even more careless in making an immediate note of someone who must be claimed at once. In the instance of Borowy such American League clubs as said (afterwards) that they could have used Borowy, quite forgot to make a claim for him until it was too late" (Warren Brown, *The Chicago Cubs*, 220).

Red Smith explained in 1952 that teams were continuing to exploit the flaws in the waiver system either by colluding or by loading the waiver wires until someone got through. He elaborated: "Each summer for several years now, the fans have seen the Yankees reach out when the struggle got hot and pluck out of the National League a Johnny Mize or Johnny Hopp or John Sain or Ewell Blackwell. . . . In recent years, National League clubs have contrived to get waivers on players whom the Yankees wanted so the players could be sold to the Yankees at prices far above the waiver figure. On the surface this is entirely legal. [Dan] Topping is telling the truth when he says that the Yankees have not violated the letter of the rule in these deals. He is mistaken when he says there has been no violation of the spirit of the rule" (Red Smith, September 3, 1952, reprinted in *Red Smith on Baseball*).

After the 1952 season the major leagues addressed the issue by requiring two-league waivers on interleague trades after the June 15 trading deadline. An AP report explained that the new rule "will not permit the kind of deals the New York Yankees have been making with National League clubs in recent years. Some even called it a 'Stop the Yankees' move. Last August the Yanks acquired lanky Ewell Blackwell from Cincinnati for $30,000 and 3 players, about 2 months after the trading deadline. They did it under the old waiver rule by which all National League clubs passed up a chance to get Blackwell for the $10,000 waiver price. Once out of the National, he could be sold for whatever the Reds could get. In the future, a player from the league—like Blackwell—would have to be waived out of the National and by all the other American League clubs through the normal waiver channels" (AP: *Washington Post*, December 8, 1952). Of course the rule did not entirely eliminate such deals, but the added restriction did address the widespread perception of unfairness.

After the 1958 season the owners approved the concept of a brief window for interleague trading without any waivers at the end of each season. The first one lasted from November 21 to December 15, 1959, and nine trades involving thirty players were made during that period. The first trade occurred on November 21 and saw the Red Sox send Dick Gernert to the Cubs for Dave Hillman and Jim Marshall. The most significant was probably a trade in which the White Sox sent Johnny Callison to the Phillies in exchange for Gene Freese (Sporting News, *Baseball: A Doubleheader Collection of Facts, Feats and Firsts*, 441).

The first true blockbuster interleague trade did not come until December 9, 1965, when Cincinnati sent Frank Robinson to Baltimore for Milt Pappas, Jack Baldschun, and Dick Simpson.

13.3.4 Trade Deadlines. The other effort to ensure that late-season trades could not undermine pennant races was the creation of a deadline on trades within a league. As has been the case with many rules, the general principle was established before all the details were ironed out.

According to researcher Cliff Blau, the first trade deadline was established in the National League before the 1917 season. The new rule dictated that a sale or trade could not take place after August 20 unless the players had cleared waivers within the league. *Sporting Life* observed that this was "aimed at the practice of strengthening pennant factors at the expense of second division clubs." It cited a number of trades from recent seasons that had prompted the rule and pointed out that the Giants had been involved in every one of the trades (*Sporting Life*, March 24, 1917).

The junior circuit established a similar rule in 1920, with a deadline of July 1. In 1921 both leagues agreed on a trade deadline of August 1.

There is an interesting story behind how today's deadline of June 15 originated. At the end of July 1922 the city of St. Louis was abuzz. The Browns were atop the American League standings while in the senior circuit the Cardinals were hot on the heels of the Giants. Was it possible that that year's World Series would take place entirely in St. Louis?

In a few short days these hopes were dealt two severe blows. The Yankees beat the August 1 trade deadline by acquiring Joe Dugan from the cash-strapped Red Sox, then the Braves shipped star pitcher Hugh McQuillan to the Giants. When the dust settled, that year's World Series featured two New York clubs again while the city of St. Louis fumed.

At Branch Rickey's urging, the city's Chamber of Commerce and Rotary Clubs wrote letters of protest to Commissioner Kenesaw Mountain Landis. Landis couldn't move the World Series to St. Louis, but he did share their concern. The rule was modified that winter so that thereafter a deal could not occur after June 15 unless the players cleared waivers (Frederick Lieb, *The St. Louis Cardinals*, 96; David Pietrusza, *Judge and Jury*, 246–247). The compromise seemed to satisfy all parties, and June 15 has remained a significant date on the baseball calendar ever since.

Nevertheless, with the vagaries of the waiver system it has always been possible to make trades after the deadline, even ones including star players. This has become still easier in recent years. Some of the reasons for this trend are discussed in the next two entries.

13.3.5 Gentlemen's Agreements. Further complicating efforts to understand the waiver rules is the fact that their theory and practice have often been quite different. The earliest waiver rules were intended to prevent players being sold out of the league, so it appears that fellow owners routinely passed when a trade *within* the league was being made.

Such "gentlemen's agreements" continued after the waiver rules were expanded, and frequently subverted the intentions of those rules. Sportswriter Joe S. Jackson explained in 1911, "Magnates are only like other men, and it is possible to induce one to waive on some one he really wants when it is intimated to him that his own requests for waivers, if he has a deal on later, will be blocked just as a comeback" (*Washington Post*, January 11, 1911).

Understandings like these are very difficult to prevent, and they had become so common by 1926 that Edgar Wolfe, a Philadelphia sportswriter who used the penname "Jim Nasium," observed, "For every law that has ever been written there is an 'unwritten law' to nullify it, and the 'unwritten law' that has been worked till the cows come home in baseball is the much-discussed 'gentleman's agreement.' The 'gentleman's agreement' or 'unwritten law' as applied to the waiver rule, if put into words, would read: 'If you waive claim on my players I'll waive claim on yours.' And through the application of this unspoken word, which is an invisible club that each big league team holds over every other big league team, the waiver rule is rendered inoperative and each year big league teams send back to the minor leagues many players who would strengthen a lot of other teams in the big leagues" (*Sporting News*, December 30, 1926).

13.3.6 Waiver Blocking. The fact that most waivers are revocable enables clubs to ask waivers on large numbers of players, only to revoke those that are claimed. Nothing is lost if the waivers are revoked; on the other hand, a player might slip through and allow a trade well after the trade deadline.

A general manager of a contending team looks very foolish if one of his rivals acquires a player when he could have prevented the deal just by making a claim. As a result, sportswriter Mike Berardino noted in 2003, "Waiver blocking became something of a sport unto itself for a while there in recent years."

This, however, is a dangerous game. As Berardino pointed out, the claiming club sometimes gets stuck with the player and his large salary as the result of their claim, if the waiver is not revoked. Examples include Randy Myers, whose enormous contract the 1998 Padres were saddled with when they tried to block a National League rival from acquiring him; and Jose Canseco, who became an inadvertent member of the 2000 Yankees. As a result, general managers must think long and hard before engaging in waiver blocking (Mike Berardino, "Economic Climate Could Snuff Out Waiver Blocking," *Baseball America*, September 1–14, 2003).

13.3.7 Damn Yankees. The Yankees cruised to four straight American League pennants and World Series titles from 1936 to 1939. After the fourth championship, Washington owner Clark Griffith proposed a new rule prohibiting teams from making trades with or selling players to the previous season's pennant winner unless the players cleared waivers. The rule was passed unanimously by the American League but rejected by the National League, so it applied only to the Yankees (John Drebinger, *New York Times*, December 8, 1939).

According to sportswriter John Drebinger, the intention was "preventing a repetition of a deal such as the Yankees engineered last Winter when they obtained [pitcher] Oral Hildebrand" (John Drebinger, *New York Times*, December 8, 1939). Baseball historian Talmage Boston suggested that other clubs feared the Yankees would pursue bigger fish: "With the unlimited Yankees bank account during depression times, and a vast supply of talent in the New York farm system, the other teams foresaw the Bronx Bombers going into the marketplace to get even better by trading for the likes of Hank Greenberg" (Talmage Boston, *1939, Baseball's Pivotal Year*, 128–129).

In 1940 the Yankees were dethroned by Greenberg and Detroit. It was assumed that the rule—which was generally regarded as "an effort to hamstring the New York Yankees"—would be dropped at that point (Irving

Vaughan, *Chicago Tribune*, December 11, 1940). Instead, American League owners voted 5-3 to retain the rule (John Drebinger, *New York Times*, December 11, 1940).

The decision was widely criticized, and at a mid-season meeting American League owners voted to repeal the rule, effective at season's end. A *New York Times* reporter depicted the change of heart as proof that the rule had always been an example of ganging up on the Yankees: "This restriction unquestionably prevented a fifth straight pennant for the Yankees last year. . . . It was not, however, until the ruling hit the Tigers a severe blow this year that this opposition gained the upper hand" (James P. Dawson, "American League Lifts Trading Ban," *New York Times*, July 8, 1941).

(iv) Scouting and Player Development

13.4.1   Scouts. In the early days of baseball the acquisition of new players was handled by the hustlers (see **6.1.3**) who managed clubs. Sometimes club owners became involved, but they did not necessarily have a keen eye for talent.

Actual searches for new talent were understandably superficial or nonexistent. As often as not, new players were signed sight unseen as a result of recommendations or when the players themselves sought out the manager. Some ambitious ballplayers took out newspaper ads, such as the 1866 ad that read: "WANTED—By a base ball pitcher, a 'sit' as a compositor on a weekly paper" (*Kalamazoo Telegraph*, September 5, 1866). While the amateur era prevented him from being more explicit, the pitcher clearly hoped that his ballplaying skills would make his services more attractive.

Ads by players became common in the 1880s when sporting papers proliferated, and continued into the 1950s. In 1978, Earl Williams revived this tradition by taking out an advertisement—"1971 National League Rookie of the Year . . . No Police Record, HAVE BAT—WILL TRAVEL—WILL HUSTLE"— to publicize his availability (*New York Times*, June 12, 1978; Robert Cole, "Ball, Bat and Ad," *Baseball Research Journal* 8 [1979], 77).

Of course there were informal scouting networks. An 1891 article observed that Chicago manager Cap Anson "has agents in all parts of the country who are instructed to keep their eyes open for promising base ball material. Whenever one of these agents thinks he has discovered something in Anson's line he writes to him, and if the answer is favorable, perhaps he sends the 'find' on for a trial" (*Williamsport Sunday Grit*, August 23, 1891).

By this time, however, more organized forms of scouting had begun to emerge. The first prominent scout was T. P. "Ted" Sullivan, who was a ubiquitous figure in the baseball world in the nineteenth and early twentieth centuries and has been unjustly forgotten. Sullivan was born in Ireland around 1850 and raised in Milwaukee. After playing baseball at college, he organized a minor league team in Dubuque in 1879 and began an enduring relationship with one of his players, Charles Comiskey.

During the 1880s, Ted Sullivan became an extremely well-known and celebrated manager of major and minor league clubs. His energy, charisma, and salesmanship became bywords though, like many of the "hustlers" (see **6.1.3**), he was less proficient at following through on what he started. Among his many accomplishments was the creation of one of the first farm teams in 1888 (see **13.1.5**).

By the 1890s, he had turned his skills primarily to the discovery of new talent. Having the field largely to himself, Sullivan worked for any club that would hire him. While he was especially associated with some clubs, he remained independent enough that he was billed as "a broker in base ball players" (*St. Louis Post-Dispatch*, July 20, 1897).

For example, near the end of the 1891 season, *Sporting News* reported that Sullivan had outmaneuvered Jim Mutrie of the Giants to sign two players for St. Louis and remarked: "Ted Sullivan has captured many a good man for the St. Louis Browns. Indeed, he has signed more good men for that club than any other man we know of and in choosing players he very seldom makes a mistake" (*Sporting News*, September 12, 1891). But within a couple of months, the same journal observed: "Ted Sullivan, the base ball scout, is in Chicago in the interests of the Baltimore Club after Jack Pickett and has offered him $3,000 with $400 advance, for next season" (*Sporting News*, November 21, 1891).

During the 1890s it became the conventional wisdom that Ted Sullivan's "abilities as a base ball hustler and judge of a player's merits are well known throughout the country" (*Sporting News*, March 5, 1892). Edgar Wolfe, the Philadelphia sportswriter writing as "Jim Nasium," later aptly noted that Sullivan "put into successful operation the first scouting system and 'discovered' and helped to develop many of the game's greatest stars of other days" (Jim Nasium, "'Ted' Sullivan, Baseball Pioneer," *Sporting Life* [monthly], January 1923).

By the turn of the century the scouting field was becoming increasingly competitive. Sullivan still had the clout and reputation to remain autonomous, as is shown by references to "the many youngsters he has signed this summer for clubs which he represents as scout," and "The veteran Ted Sullivan, who has been scouring the country for three months as player-hunter for the major leagues" (*Washington Post*, September 9, 1904; *Sporting Life*, March 25, 1905).

A few others achieved similar independence. Jimmy Callahan, for example, was reported in 1908 to have been "in the employ of several major league clubs last season as a scout, and he was paid for his work" (*Washington Post*, April 26, 1908). But scouting was becoming a big business, with Garry Herrmann of Cincinnati reportedly spending $100,000 on scouting in the first decade of the twentieth century (unspecified 1911 article by sportswriter Ren Mulford, Jr., reprinted in *Baseball Research Journal* 28 [1999], 89).

In exchange for writing such sizable checks, club owners expected loyalty. By the end of the first decade of the twentieth century, the system of scouts who work exclusively for one club was emerging. Prominent early full-time scouts included Larry Sutton of the Dodgers and Charley Barrett of the Cardinals. As discussed in previous entries (see **13.1.4** and **13.1.5**), Barrett was a pivotal figure in the transition of scouts from hunters of major league–ready talent to searchers for talented but raw players. The tireless pursuit of the "arm behind the barn" remained the essence of the profession for another four decades until it was again revolutionized by the introduction of the amateur draft (see **13.5.3**) in 1965.

13.4.2   Cross-checkers. Cross-checkers are now an integral part of scouting. A cross-checker reviews all the players recommended by regional scouts. This serves both to double-check the original advice and to prioritize the thousands of draft-eligible players.

While the logic of having cross-checkers is obvious, the expense involved means that they did not become commonplace until the amateur draft era. It can be argued that Ted Sullivan was not only the first scout but the first cross-checker as well. In 1905, *Sporting Life* reported that Cliff Blankenship "is on the coast acting as a scout for Cincinnati" (*Sporting Life*, August 19, 1905). A follow-up note a month later observed: "Ted Sullivan is checking the players recommended by Blankenship and has signed pitcher [Carl] Druhot" (*Sporting Life*, September 9, 1905).

In the years that followed, clubs undoubtedly had players double- and even triple-checked, especially when a significant signing bonus was involved. But no systematic approach to cross-checking was used for the simple reason that the players signed by regional scouts represented little or no investment to the clubs.

Branch Rickey of the Cardinals was notorious for signing players to "desk contracts," which he would simply discard if the prospect didn't make good. A player named Don Bollman recalled going to a Cardinals tryout camp during the depression and being thrilled at being signed to a contract. He reported to spring training thinking of himself as "the owner of a baseball contract . . . to me it meant a job, as it did to others. The fact of the matter was, it meant nothing. When I finally arrived at the ball park, I found EIGHTY other guys with the same folded paper, and only *four* positions available" (Don Bollman, *Run for the Roses*, 59). Although Rickey was extreme in his adherence to a "quality out of quantity approach," almost every club found ways to ensure that regional scouts could sign players without a sizable investment by the club.

Baltimore Orioles scouting director Jim McLaughlin introduced a more systematic approach to cross-checking in the mid-1950s (Kevin Kerrane, *Dollar Sign on the Muscle*, 141). The inauguration of the amateur draft in 1964 (see **13.5.3**) meant that every draft pick represented a twofold investment by the club—not merely the bonus to be paid that player, but forgoing the opportunity to sign other players. The use of cross-checkers accordingly became standard.

13.4.3   Central Scouting Bureau. Not long after teams began to employ their own scouts, it became apparent that scouting represented a considerable expense. They began looking for ways to reduce their costs and soon recognized the duplication of labor in having several teams send scouts to look at the same player and pronounce him no good.

They thus began to kick around the idea of having a talent hunter who would file initial reports to more than one club. The one concern was whether such a scout could be trusted to be candid with all the teams.

Fortunately the ideal man was at hand. Cincinnati scout Louis Heilbroner had experiencing in managing, scouting, and front office work and was known for keeping a dope book on every ballplayer in the country. Just as important, he had a reputation for scrupulous honesty and for having been "the first scout in the country to throw off the rubber shoes and mysterious air that formerly marked big league searches for available material."

As a result, on the recommendation of major league presidents Ban Johnson and Tom Lynch, Heilbroner was hired to work as a "special agent for several American and National league clubs. He will furnish dope for these clubs on promising players and will line them up for contracts and in other ways help recruit pennant-winning aggregations" (*Fort Wayne News*, January 30, 1910).

This idea was revived many years later with the advent of the major leagues' Central Scouting Bureau.

13.4.4   Scouting Other Teams' Rosters. Early scouts like Ted Sullivan concentrated on minor leaguers, semipros, and amateurs in hopes of discovering what later became known as "the arm behind the barn." Once it became common for scouts to work exclusively for one organization, a new direction in scouting emerged.

At the onset of 1912 spring training, *Sporting Life*'s Pittsburgh correspondent advised, "Keep a sharp eye on vaporings from Hot Springs and you will see that [Pirates] Chief of Scouts W. Murray [former Phillies manager

William Murray] never basks in the limelight. Murray has a delicate job on hand. He isn't there to criticise players or offer any suggestions to Cap. [Fred] Clarke. He has a distinct and separate duty. Murray's aim is to observe carefully and consistently the workouts of [various clubs'] recruits, paying attention in detail to their quantities and defects. This estimate is to guide Murray and mates in their search campaign for the summer. Colonel Dreyfuss [Pittsburgh owner Barney Dreyfuss] suggested the idea. Every Autumn clubs pick up numerous young players mainly on scout suggestions. They are taken on training pilgrimages and tested. Most every one has more or less talent. They drift back to the minors. Unquestionably some are pretty good. If kept they might become league artists in a season or two. The major portion of this type, however, has been turned back. Next season the same state of affairs is shown.

"Colonel Dreyfuss and business associates have realized that some folly was attached to this method. Was it business acumen to send back this class of youngsters and immediately start scouts out in search of new players, then to pick up boys, pay high prices and go on repeating the process season in and out? Murray will see the tests, observe virtues and defects of players and then give decision as to the likelihood of finding youngsters with more talent than the ones on hand. If he thinks that there is yet hope of digging up boys better balanced, then his decree will banish one or two ball tossers back to the minors and the secret service department will start a quest for the objects devoutly wished for. Sounds like a fine plan, and is to be given a thorough trial by the Pittsburg Club" (_Sporting Life_, March 30, 1912).

In the following week's issue, Cincinnati correspondent Ren Mulford, Jr., added: "Picking stars out of the bushes is not quite as easy a task as it was in the long-ago. During the season there are relatively as many scouts on the trail as you'll find hunters in the Adirondacks during the open season for big game. Scouts are so thick now they are in each other's way. Did you observe that [New York Highlanders scout] Arthur Irwin spent the Spring in friendly visits to the training camps? He was with the Red bunch long enough to get his eyes on most of the material in action. Then he hiked it for other fields. Why the expeditions? Say, just watch Col. Irwin. When the strings are cut on the hopefuls or by any hook or crook some promising youngster is allowed to get away, the chances are that a New York American tag will be quickly affixed. Billy Hamilton, of the Boston Nationals, is another of the scouts who has been looking the Reds over on Southern fields. The idea is not a half-bad one. Many a star-in-embryo has been eclipsed by early managerial action only to break out with more brilliancy in other company" (_Sporting Life_, April 6, 1912).

The new system cannot have entirely caught on, since sportswriter James Crusinberry reported after the 1919 campaign: "When a manager sends a scout out to spy on the training camps of his rivals he's stepping a bit farther than any one ever has before." He explained that Cubs manager Fred Mitchell had assigned newly hired scout Patsy Donovan "to get the 'dope' on dozens and dozens of the live looking youngsters, and then when the rival big league managers ask for waivers, as they always do, the Cubs will know which ones might be worth claiming" (James Crusinberry, "Cubs to Scout for Talent in Enemies' Own Back Yards," *Chicago Tribune*, December 18, 1919).

13.4.5 Advance Scouts. Tony Kubek claimed that advance scouting was originated by Casey Stengel in 1957 (quoted in George Will, *Men at Work*, 16). Bill James correctly responded, ". . . The idea that advance scouting began in 1957 is so misguided as to be comical," and cited many earlier examples of advance scouting (Bill James, *The Bill James Guide to Baseball Managers*, 206).

The practice was most common at the World Series, for the obvious reason that it featured opponents who were unfamiliar with each other's tendencies. Connie Mack sent Athletics pitcher Chief Bender to scout the Cubs before the 1910 World Series (*Sporting Life*, March 25, 1911). Christy Mathewson reported that Mack did likewise the following year, sending "spies" to track "the Giants for weeks previous to the [1911] series" (Christy Mathewson, *Pitching in a Pinch*, 278). In 1913, with the Giants and Athletics again about to meet in the World Series, Mack sent at least three players to watch Rube Marquard pitch a September 26 game (Larry Mansch, *Rube Marquard*, 136).

Bill James cited a number of other examples from the 1920s, '30s, and '40s, the most notable being Mack's sending Howard Ehmke to watch the Cubs in the weeks before Ehmke's surprise start in the 1929 World Series (Bill James, *The Bill James Guide to Baseball Managers*, 206). So it seems clear that the idea of advance scouting has been around for a long time, its use limited only by the usual consideration of whether the benefits outweighed the expenses.

Today there are signs that the traditional advance scout may be a dying breed. Sportswriter Mike Klis observed in 2003 that the "advance-scouting era" appears to be giving way to the "era of advanced technology," in which a videotape package is put together from televised games of a team's next opponent. Klis suggested that the Indians pioneered this practice in 1994, though it appears that they used videotape only to complement their advance scouting. Since then, such clubs as the Cardinals, Tigers, Rockies, Twins, and Padres have at least experimented with eliminating advance scouts altogether (*Baseball America*, August 4–17, 2003).

13.4.6 Tryout Camps. Tryout camps are associated with Branch Rickey, but they also date back to the nineteenth century. For example, an 1891 article about Chicago manager Cap Anson observed: "Frequently Anson will appoint a special day for examining candidates for his team. He is constantly besieged with applications from all parts of the country. He will marshal 30 or 40 of these applicants at the ball grounds and put them through their paces. From his long experience on the ball field he is able to 'size up' a player almost at sight" (*Williamsport Sunday Grit*, August 23, 1891).

13.4.7 Baseball Schools. Baseball schools have had a sporadic history. As early as 1883, A. G. Spalding announced plans to open a "Base Ball Academy" where Cap Anson would serve as lead instructor (*Sporting Life*, November 21, 1883). Spalding's goal appears to have been to keep players from signing with the upstart Union Association, and the school did not last long.

Periodic efforts to start baseball schools occurred in succeeding years. Chicago infielder Fred Pfeffer, for example, ran an instructional camp of some sort (Jonathan Fraser Light, *The Cultural Encyclopedia of Baseball*, 373).

After the 1913 season, former major league Charley Carr brought a new level of planning to the baseball school. Sportswriter Stanley T. Milliken noted: "At last the idea of a regular baseball school has passed from a possibility to a reality. Next Friday Charley Carr will formally open the doors of his baseball university at San Antonio, Tex., for the matriculation of those ambitious youngsters who would enter the big leagues via a route which they hope will entirely eliminate the bush circuit. For several years such a baseball school has been talked over, and many of the leading big club managers have advocated the plan, provided experienced men were put in charge of the project. Carr appears to have entered the field thoroughly equipped, for, according to his prospectus, Owen Bush, Lou Criger, Otto Williams and other well-known baseball players will compose the faculty. The field at Hot Sulphur Wells, San Antonio, will include twenty diamonds, shower, locker rooms, and all other equipment and paraphernalia necessary to teach the novice how to play like Wagner, Collins, and Mathewson" (*Washington Post*, December 29, 1913). The school closed after fewer than eight months (*Washington Post*, August 16, 1914).

Bobby Gilks opened a school in Pensacola, Florida, the following year and tried to benefit from the failure of Carr's enterprise. Gilks "made several important changes in the preamble and methods. His school is not to be for every pupil that sees fit to enroll including amateurs. He will make a specialty of recruit pitchers and catchers of major and big minor league teams, taking pay for their development from the clubs that own them rather than the players themselves" (*Lincoln* [Nebr.] *Daily News*, February 13, 1915).

It was not until the late 1920s that enough parents were willing to pay for instruction for their sons to make the idea a permanent part of baseball. Tubby Walton formed a particularly successful school in 1928, and rivals sprang up during the 1930s (Furman Bisher, *Atlanta Journal*, February 2, 1961).

The best-known baseball school was the academy operated by the Kansas City Royals, which yielded one star in Frank White and another ten-year major leaguer in Ron Washington. Since then, however, clubs have been reluctant to operate such schools, since the amateur draft makes it difficult for them to retain the talent they produce. Clubs do continue to operate academies in Latin American countries, where the amateur draft is not in effect.

13.4.8   Radar Guns. The primary "tool of the trade" for scouts is the radar gun. While accurate handheld radar guns are a recent innovation, the concept of measuring the speed of pitchers is an ancient one.

An 1884 article noted that Longine's chronographs had been used to measure the speed of several major league pitchers. The results were not very meaningful, however, as the reported times that it took for pitches to reach the plate varied from one-fifth of a second to three-fifths of a second (*Sporting Life*, April 23, 1884).

On October 6, 1912, the speeds of Walter Johnson and Nap Rucker were tested at the Remington Arms Plant in Bridgeport, Connecticut. The pitchers' speeds were measured by the time it took for their pitches to reach a steel plate five yards away. Johnson's speed was estimated at 83 miles per hour and Rucker's at 77, but several factors contributed to the low speeds. Most notably, the pitchers had to alter their natural arm motion so that the ball could pass through a two-foot square and be measured (*Syracuse Herald*, October 20, 1912; Eric Enders, "George Napoleon Rucker," Tom Simon, ed., *Deadball Stars of the National League*, 284).

Researcher Dick Thompson discovered an account of an interesting attempt at measurement that occurred in 1939: "The new meter, which gives an immediate reading which engineers said compared with standard laboratory meter accuracy, is built in a trailer. You throw into a hole two feet square. Just inside is a set of photo-electric tubes, and five feet back is another set. The device measures the ball's speed between the two points and flashes it on a scale facing the pitcher" (AP: *Richmond Times-Dispatch*, June 6, 1939).

Several creative but not very precise methods were used to try to measure the speed of Bob Feller's fastball. After that, the practice was pretty much abandoned for a generation.

The handheld radar gun made its way into baseball in an interesting manner. In the fall of 1974, Michigan State University head baseball coach

instruction and riding lessons. Cammeyer also listed baseball as a possible use for the grounds, but it seems to have been little more than an afterthought since he estimated that baseball would represent only 2 percent of the total revenues, from rent charged to baseball clubs.

By the time the Union Grounds opened in May 1862, however, Cammeyer had gained an appreciation of baseball's promise as a revenue sport. The first baseball match was played there on May 15, 1862, in front of three thousand spectators who paid no admission fee. Thereafter fees were collected, and this proved so successful that Cammeyer decided on a share of the gate receipts instead of charging rent to the clubs. Baseball soon became the principal attraction of the Union Grounds, causing competitors to scramble to construct rival diamonds (William J. Ryczek, *When Johnny Came Sliding Home*, 29–31).

Enclosed stadiums were thus inextricably tied to the collection of admission fees, a relationship explored further in **18.1.2**. The principle of economic exclusiveness that fences brought to baseball was soon reframed as a moral issue. The *Brooklyn Eagle* observed in 1864, "Admission to the grounds is only secured on condition of proper conduct, and this is one great advantage of enclosed ball grounds" (*Brooklyn Eagle*, June 29, 1864). While the writer of these words was not identified, it certainly sounds like Henry Chadwick.

Not everyone was persuaded that it was a moral issue, such as the Milwaukee journalist who in 1879 sarcastically described baseball as "a game played by eighteen persons wearing shirts and drawers. They scatter around the field and try to catch a cannon-ball covered with rawhide. The game is to get people to pay 25 cents to come inside the fence" (*Milwaukee Sun*, reprinted in the *Detroit Post and Tribune*, August 2, 1879).

The baseball fence would prove a particular nemesis to young boys, who would try almost anything to get past or see over them (see **15.1.2**). The 1887 World's Series was a movable feast with games all over the country. A day before one game played at Boston's Union Park, a group of boys burned down the left-field fence so they could watch the World's Series (Jerry Lansche, *Glory Fades Away*, 110).

Yet the exclusiveness inherent in enclosed stadiums came to be recognized as conferring special status on those who paid admission. In 1886 Harry Wright said, "The Chicago grounds come nearer to my idea of a base ball inclosure than any other in this country. Surrounded by a high brick wall, which does not mar and disfigure adjoining property like the unsightly board fences, it gives the game a privacy which cannot be had where mobs and crowds hang around for a peep through the knotholes and cracks" (*Brooklyn Eagle*, February 7, 1886).

The walls originally intended to keep things out eventually came to keep in a special sense of belonging and community. And so F. Scott Fitzgerald aptly described baseball as a game "bounded by walls which kept out novelty or danger, change or adventure" (F. Scott Fitzgerald, "Ring Lardner," *New Republic*, October 11, 1933, 254). The related topic of "Spite Fences" is discussed in the chapter on marketing (see **16.2.3**).

14.1.2 Fireproof Stadiums. Nineteenth-century stadiums burned down with disheartening regularity. In 1894 Cincinnati owner John T. Brush took advantage of new engineering trends in making major renovations to League Park. The park reopened with a new grandstand that was a hybrid of iron and wood. But the new grandstand burned down on May 28, 1900, while the old wooden stands survived. The grandstand was again destroyed by fire on May 4, 1901, causing Brush to vow to build a main grandstand of steel and stone. He followed through on this pledge, but the rest of the seating area remained wood (Greg Rhodes and John Snyder, *Redleg Journal*, 110, 137, 139).

In 1905 the Columbus Senators of the American Association tore down the grandstand and replaced it with a double-decked concrete-and-steel grandstand. The bleachers were made from the wood of the old grandstand. The new stadium drew fans in droves and prompted major league owners to consider similar renovations (Marshall D. Wright, *The American Association*, 22).

The first true major league concrete-and-steel ballpark was Philadelphia's Shibe Park, which opened in 1909. It was followed by eight more fireproof stadiums in the next fifteen years.

14.1.3 Night Games. A book could be written about the history of night baseball, and indeed one has: David Pietrusza's *Lights On!* In a nutshell, the idea of playing under the lights intrigued many people long before it became practical from either a technological or financial standpoint. But what makes this such a compelling story is that once the numerous technological and financial obstacles had been overcome, there turned out to be a deep-seated underlying objection to night baseball.

The first preliminary effort took place on September 2, 1880, when teams from two Boston department stores played at Nantasket Beach, Massachusetts, under thirty-six carbon-arc electric lights. Three hundred onlookers watched from the balconies of the nearby Sea Foam House, and differing accounts emerged (Preston D. Orem, *Baseball [1845–1881] from the Newspaper Accounts*, 342). The *Boston Post* claimed that "A clear, pure, bright light was produced, very strong and yet very pleasant to the sight" (quoted in Dan Gutman, *Banana Bats and Ding-Dong Balls*, 102). The *New York Clipper* was less optimistic: "It cannot be said that baseball is likely to be played extensively at night, for the players had to bat and throw with some caution, and the errors due to an imperfect light were innumerable. Fly-balls descending perpendicularly could be caught easily, but when batted a long distance it was easier and safer to get the ball by chasing it after it struck the ground. To the spectators the game proved of little interest, since in general only the players' movements could be discerned, while the course of the ball eluded their sight" (*New York Clipper*, October 2, 1880).

On May 16, 1883, two semipro teams played in Chambersburg, Pennsylvania, by the light of a portable dynamo resting on a flat car. Few details of that game survive, but a much-better-documented night game was played a couple of weeks later, on June 2, in Fort Wayne, Indiana. (Some sources suggest that a second game was also played.)

The *Fort Wayne Daily News* previewed the game, which featured the Methodist-Episcopal College and a local amateur nine: "Apropos of the proposed games of base ball by electric light, it has been suggested that high flies would penetrate a region of outer darkness which the electric light would not reach, and it would be impossible to judge where the balls would come down. 'Why not coat the ball with luminous paint?' suggests a friend" (*Fort Wayne Daily News*, May 28, 1883).

The *Daily News* gave this account on the game in its June 4 issue: "The grounds were illuminated by 17 Jenny [sic] electric lamps suspended, three from the grand stand and the rest from poles placed about the limits of the enclosure. The light was found sufficient to permit of sharp infield play and precise throwing and catching. It was noticed that as the heavens grew darker the apparent illumination of the grounds correspondingly increased. . . . There were no mishaps of any kind save a rather noticeable irregularity of the illumination on two occasions."

Sporting Life added: "The inclosure, which is four hundred by four hundred and fifty feet, was lighted by seventeen of the lamps of the Jenney Electric Light Company, of Fort Wayne. They were suspended as masts, except three that were attached to the front of the grand stand. One of the lights was behind the pitcher, which seemed to light up the diamond splendidly, while the light at the corner made it light enough to see the ball plainly in the center field. The atmosphere was heavy at times, which caused a very noticeable and favorable effect on throwing the light down on the field. All the lights had a powerful reflector behind them. The only thing to mar the exhibition was the light going out entirely twice, caused by defective brushes at the power-house. It was found necessary to change the ball quite often. When a ball became dirty, it could not be seen. With between twenty-five and thirty lights there is no question but what electric light ball playing is an assured success" (*Sporting Life*, June 10, 1883).

The *Fort Wayne Daily Gazette* claimed the game would "make Fort Wayne historic and cause her name to be mentioned wherever civilization extends" (*Fort Wayne Daily Gazette*, June 3, 1883; reprinted in Don Warfield,

The Roaring Redhead, 57). The boast was not entirely unfounded. In 1960 an obituary appeared in *Sporting News* for Sam Wolf, one of the pitchers in the game (*Sporting News*, May 18, 1960).

Experiments with night baseball continued. In 1887 plans were announced to play night ball at St. George Grounds in Staten Island. A Mr. Johnson of the Edison Electric Light Company of New York had concluded that lights placed above the field would not work. After consulting with Thomas Edison himself, however, Johnson planned to "line the *outside* of the diamond, foul lines and extremes of the outfields with electric lights placed *beneath the ground* and projecting, by means of powerful reflectors, the rays upward through covering-plates of corrugated glass" (*Sporting Life*, March 30, 1887).

John T. Brush experimented with installing a lighting system at Indianapolis's Tinker Park in 1888, and initial reports were encouraging. The lights were "located along the centre field fence about thirty yards apart, being between thirty and forty feet high, have a cross-bar at the top like that on a telegraph pole and about the same length. The cross-piece had burners on the upper side, about six inches apart, and when the gas was turned on it makes a solid flame, say about four feet long. The two burners alone make the park perfectly light, and the ball could be seen as well as daytime" (*Sporting Life*, August 29, 1888; quoted in Larry G. Bowman, *Before the World Series*, 145). But a second test on September 6 was less successful, and the idea foundered (*Sporting Life*, September 12, 1888; quoted in Larry G. Bowman, *Before the World Series*, 145).

Galveston and Houston played under the lights on July 22, 1892. Los Angeles and Stockton of the California League played two games under electric lights in July 1893. But *Sporting Life* reported in 1895, "The Chattanooga Club contemplates baseball by electric light. The scheme has been tried many times—always a failure" (*Sporting Life*, July 6, 1895).

Another exhibition game under electric lights was played in San Antonio, Texas, on July 16, 1897. On the evening of May 14, 1902, Scranton and Lancaster played under electric light at Scranton's Athletic Park, "in the presence of one of the biggest crowds that ever saw a game in that city. Arc lights set on twenty foot poles at short intervals made it easily possible for the players to handle and the spectators to follow the ball. Scranton won by a score of 8 to 6. There were only five errors on both sides" (*Sporting Life*, May 24, 1902). An experimental game was played at Athletic Park in Battle Creek, Michigan, on September 4, 1904. The field was illuminated by twenty-five arc lights strung around the field (Marc Okkonen, *Minor League Baseball Towns of Michigan*, 8).

The first serious effort to bring night baseball to the major leagues was initiated in 1908. Cincinnati Reds president August "Garry" Herrmann teamed up with inventor George Cahill and a group of Cincinnati business-men to form the Night Baseball Development Company. On June 18, 1909, their product was demonstrated for the first time when two Elks teams played an experimental game at Cincinnati's Palace of the Fans. Five tem-porary 100-foot towers of arc lights powered by a 250-horsepower dynamo were installed for the game.

Reviews were mixed. The number of strikeouts was inordinately high, and the outfielders' adventures with fly balls caused sportswriter Ren Mul-ford, Jr., to write that "the game was a novelty and at times took on the ele-ments of a diamond comedy." But Reds manager Clark Griffith said he was "surprised at the ease with which the game was played," and Herrmann an-nounced that "Night baseball has come to stay" (all quotes from David Pietrusza, "The Cahill Brothers' Night Baseball Experiments," *Baseball Re-search Journal* 23 [1994], 62–66).

Cahill's next attempt came in Grand Rapids, Michigan, on July 7. After a regular game, Grand Rapids and Zanesville played an exhibition game un-der the lights. Cahill received assistance from the Grand Rapids-Muskegon Power Company in powering his lighting system. Still, the results were dis-appointing, as the *Chicago Tribune* reported that it was "impossible to follow a fly ball" (*Chicago Tribune*, July 9, 1909).

The following season Cahill persuaded Charles Comiskey to let him stage a night game at White Sox Park. On August 27, 1910, two local clubs played under 137,000 watts of candlepower. More than 20,000 fans at-tended the exhibition, and accounts were quite favorable. The *Electrical Review and Western Electrician* reported that "the ball was clearly observed at all times. . . . The Players did not complain of glare from the lamps, some contending that it was not as troublesome as facing the sun" (quoted in David Pietrusza, "The Cahill Brothers' Night Baseball Experiments," *Baseball Research Journal* 23 [1994], 62–66). The *Chicago Tribune* claimed that "The ball could be followed as readily as if thrown under natural light, and the players declared that nothing interfered with their vision." It added that even better results could be expected when the voltage was in-creased and the lamp operators gained experience (*Chicago Tribune*, August 28, 1910). For reasons that are not entirely clear, however, this was Cahill's last effort to light a baseball game.

Toward the end of the 1915 season, Robert B. Ward, one of the owners of the Brooklyn Federal League team, announced plans to install light tow-ers and play a night game (*Sporting Life*, September 11, 1915). Delays brought the regular season to a close before the game could be played, but the lighting system was tested and deemed a success.

But the sudden death of the sixty-three-year-old Ward from heart failure derailed the idea. According to *Sporting Life*, "just before Robert B. Ward died he spent something like $18,000 to install a newly-patented lighting system that he believed would make night base ball practical" (*Sporting Life*, December 25, 1915). Ward's passing not only meant that his pet scheme was abandoned, it also contributed to the demise of the Federal League.

No major league owner picked up Ward's legacy, and no progress toward night baseball was made during the 1920s. One reason for this was the legitimate concern that the frequency with which fly balls were lofted above the lights would make evening baseball forever impracticable. But in a decade that saw streetlamps proliferate, the readiness with which night baseball was abandoned is striking.

George Cahill moved on to sports like boxing and football, and the latter sport's progress was in stark contrast to that of baseball. Football had been a relative latecomer to night action, with the first such professional game having been played in Elmira, New York, in 1902: "The *Elmira Daily Advertiser* did not explain how the field was illuminated, beyond saying that electric lights were used. Tradition has it, though, that huge searchlights were placed at opposite ends of the field, so that the players must have spent most of their time squinting into the glare" (Robert W. Peterson, *Pigskin*, 35).

But by the late 1920s, professional, college, and even high school football stadiums were beginning to install permanent lighting structures. Wellington High in Wellington, Kansas, played under twenty two-thousand-watt lights on September 20, 1929, using a white football (Duane Frazier, "Wellington Celebrates the Evening It Lit Up High School Football," *Wichita Eagle*, September 10, 2004). On November 6, 1929, in Providence, the first National Football League night game was played, with the ball again painted white for visibility.

The decade thus ended with professional baseball lagging behind even high school football, but the impetus for renewed efforts at night baseball was provided by the stock market crash of 1929. Shocked owners of Negro League and minor league clubs realized that this would devastate their core market of the limited number of fans who had the time and disposable cash available to attend afternoon games. A few of these owners had the foresight to immediately reach out to a new clientele of workingmen by offering evening games.

J. L. Wilkinson, owner of the Negro National League's Kansas City Monarchs, took out a $50,000 loan that winter and purchased a portable 100-kilowatt generator with a 250-horsepower, six-cylinder engine. Mounted on the beds of Ford trucks, the lighting system generated nearly 200,000 watts, and the Monarchs hit the road. The portable lighting system was an immediate success, causing the *Kansas City Star* to rave that night baseball "will revolutionize the old game, restoring small town baseball on a paying basis" (reprinted in Larry Lester, "Only the Stars Come Out at Night!: J. L. Wilkinson and His Lighting Machine," *Unions to Royals*, 8–10).

That same offseason, minor league teams in Des Moines, Iowa, and Independence, Kansas, announced plans to install lighting systems. Independence played the historic first regular-season night game against Muskogee on April 30, 1930, and Des Moines followed suit two days later. There were a few glitches, and fans had some trouble picking up the ball, but the players reported that the adjustments were relatively minor (Bob Rives, "Good Night," *National Pastime* 18 [1998], 21–24).

More important, night baseball drew enough fans for these owners to recoup their investments quickly. The success of the two minor league pioneers attracted considerable attention, but even more important was the example of the touring Monarchs, who brought night baseball to the doorsteps of skeptics. While the noisy engine of the Monarchs' generator drew some complaints, the game they were playing was recognizable as baseball. Other minor league owners raced to jump on the bandwagon, and by the end of the year no fewer than thirty-eight minor league teams had lighting systems in place (Larry G. Bowman, "The Monarchs and Night Baseball," *National Pastime* 16 [1996], 80–84).

The success of night baseball in the teeth of the Great Depression was striking and made the major leagues' resistance to the idea all the more conspicuous. And, as G. Edward White pointed out, their reasons sounded increasingly hollow. Giants owner Charles Stoneham, for example, continued to maintain in 1934 that batters would become tentative from playing at night (G. Edward White, *Creating the National Pastime*, Chapter 5 passim, especially 173).

White noted that once the specific concerns about night baseball had been allayed, those with reservations began to describe it as "unnatural." He suggested that such concerns could have hidden an underlying fear—that night baseball would bring more members of the working classes to the ballpark. Washington owner Clark Griffith went so far as to characterize night baseball as "just a step above dog racing" (quoted in Don Warfield, *The Roaring Redhead*, 59). The message seemed to be that night play might be very well for football, but baseball wanted to attract a more affluent class of fans.

On December 11, 1934, Cincinnati president Larry MacPhail brought the issue to the National League's winter meeting. According to MacPhail, Commissioner Kenesaw Mountain Landis told him before the meeting: "Not in my lifetime or yours will you ever see a baseball game played at night in the majors." But MacPhail's three-hour presentation was so convincing that he got the necessary votes to allow any team to schedule a maximum of seven night games per season (Don Warfield, *The Roaring Redhead*, 57–58).

MacPhail's Reds were the only club to take advantage of the opportunity in 1935. General Electric installed 632 lights in Crosley Field, and the first night game took place against the Philadelphia Phillies on May 24, 1935. More than twenty thousand fans turned out, including George Cahill, the inventor who had tried to interest major league owners in night baseball a quarter-century earlier. Franklin Delano Roosevelt threw the switch from the White House to turn on the lights for the historic game.

Two long fly balls were dropped (and scored as base hits), but otherwise things ran smoothly. But the success of the venture did little to dispel the widespread reluctance of the owners. The American League denied requests by Cleveland owner Alva Bradley to stage evening games, then banned night baseball entirely. No other major league team duplicated the experiment until MacPhail was hired by the Brooklyn Dodgers in 1938.

Eventually the continuing financial struggles of major league clubs forced them to reconsider. In 1939 the American League reversed its position and three clubs added lights, with the circuit's first night game taking place at Shibe Park in Philadelphia on May 16, 1939. More than 55,000 fans thronged to a June 27 game in Cleveland. By 1941 twelve of the sixteen major league franchises had staged at least one night game. But even when these experiments proved a financial success, evening baseball continued to be looked upon as a novelty that would lose its appeal if overused.

The turning point was President Franklin Roosevelt's famous "green light" letter of January 15, 1942. Major league owners had asked the president's advice as to whether baseball should continue in spite of the war. Roosevelt advised them to go ahead because the game was good for the country's morale and added, "incidentally, I hope that night games can be extended because it gives an opportunity to the day shift to see a game occasionally." As a result, the allotment of seven night games per team was doubled to fourteen, and the attendance at these games was so large that unlimited night baseball was approved in July 1944.

By 1948 every major league club except the Chicago Cubs had lights, and night baseball was well on its way. The first night World Series game took place in Pittsburgh on October 13, 1971, between the Pirates and Orioles, and it would soon become common for World Series games to be played under the lights. Even the Cubs finally began playing a limited schedule of evening encounters in 1988.

In many ways the history of night baseball parallels the emergence of competitiveness (see **1.29**) eighty years earlier. Opposition to the idea was much stronger than the reasons being given for that resistance, suggesting underlying concerns about class issues. Resistance was swept away by the

but by the twentieth century these too were increasingly being covered by ground rules.

14.2.3 Tailoring a Park to a Team or Player. The often odd configurations of early ballparks occasionally made it possible for a home team to gain a substantial advantage by manipulating the ground rules. The most notable example occurred in Chicago in 1884: "At the old Lake-Front grounds there was a rule that the batter was to take only two bases on a hit over the right field fence. Then Chicago found it had the advantage in left-handed batters, who could put the ball over the right field fence pretty near when they pleased, and this rule was abolished, the men getting a home run for every such hit" (*Chicago Tribune*, April 1, 1894). Four White Stockings players hit over twenty home runs that season, and the next year the league ordered that such hits be counted as doubles.

Early groundskeepers had their hands full just making a field playable, without worrying about trying to help the home team. But by the 1890s the groundskeeper's art and the tools of the trade had progressed to the point that clubs began thinking of ways to give themselves a home-field advantage.

The battling Baltimore Orioles of the mid-1890s were most associated with this tactic. Groundskeeper Thomas J. Murphy worked closely with the players on what park factors to include. Hugh Fullerton described the results: "The most unfair grounds ever constructed were those of Baltimore. . . . The team that won three championships there was composed of small, fast men, bunters and clever base runners. The ground was sloping toward right field, where [Willie] Keeler played, and right field always was ragged and full of weeds, rough spots, hollows, and hills. Besides, the base lines were filled in with a cementlike substance, which was wetted down and tamped hard. The edges of the base lines were banked up like billiard cushions to keep bunts from rolling foul. The pitcher's box was a foot higher than the plate. The runways were down hill to first base, down hill to second, up a steep grade to third, and down hill to home. In right field Keeler had a lot of runways, like rabbit paths, that no one except himself knew, and he knew the angles of a throw when the ball rolled down the hill, out into foul ground, and into the deep gulley [sic] against the stand. . . . The grounds, adapted perfectly to the home team's style of play, did more to win pennants than anything else" (*Chicago Tribune*, August 5, 1906).

In 1895 Charles Comiskey found another way to tailor his ballpark to suit his players: "Comiskey has seven left-handed hitters in his St. Paul team, and, realizing the advantage it would be to them, he has adjusted his diamond so that the right foul line crosses the fence just a little beyond first base, nearly twenty-five feet nearer even than the close fence at the grounds back of the West. In order to make this arrangement some strange work had to be done in the rest of the field, the third base being almost within a traveling distance of the front of the bleacher, and the left foul line running almost parallel with the long fence. One-half of the grand stand, too, has to face the sun in order to accommodate Charley's eccentric batsmen" (*Sporting Life*, May 4, 1895).

Similar ploys have been attempted by many twentieth-century clubs. Perhaps the most notable example came when the Pirates acquired Hank Greenberg in 1947 and immediately reduced the distance to the left-field fence by thirty feet. The new area beyond the fence became known as Greenberg Gardens. Sportswriter Larry Marthey cited a number of earlier examples involving such sluggers as Al Simmons and Ted Williams (Larry Marthey, "Park Tampering Is Old Custom," *Detroit News*, April 7, 1959, T-15).

Frank Lane took the practice to another level in 1949 by moving the fences at Comiskey Park in or out when specific opponents were in town. A rule had to be passed to prevent such shenanigans (Michael Gershman, *Diamonds*, 94–95). Kansas City Athletics owner Charles O. Finley had a similar battle with Commissioner Ford Frick in the mid-1960s over his "Pennant Porch."

The computer age brought a new twist in the 1980s. Dan Evans was hired to operate the White Sox' computerized tracking system in 1982. He noticed that the club had hit far more balls to the Comiskey Park warning track than had their opponents. In response the club shortened the distances to the fences in 1983 and saw positive results (Alan Schwarz, *The Numbers Game*, 143). Even in this instance, however, it was only the tool that was new. In 1937 Brooklyn manager Burleigh Grimes announced his intention to "count the number of drives his boys bounce off the [right field screen in Ebbets Field] in comparison to the enemies' totals," then decide how many bases such hits be allowed by the ground rule (Richard McCann, NEA wire service: *Frederick* [Md.] *Post*, May 13, 1937).

Perhaps the most unique home-field advantage in baseball history was one inadvertently gained by the American League's Philadelphia Athletics in 1902. John I. Rogers, owner of the Philadelphia Phillies, had Pennsylvania Supreme Court injunctions against a number of top American League players for breaking their contracts with him. As a result, when their teams visited Philadelphia, such stars as Nap Lajoie, Ed Delahanty, and Elmer Flick did not accompany them. This helped the Athletics compile a 56-17 home record and win the American League pennant.

Chapter 11, part two, has several examples of dubious ways in which a groundskeeper gave his team an advantage against a specific rival.

14.2.4 Dragging the Infield. According to baseball historian William B. Mead, Cincinnati Reds manager Luke Sewell introduced the practice of having the grounds crew drag the infield in mid-game. This took place during Sewell's tenure as manager of the Reds, from 1949 to 1952. Mead stated that this was done both to keep the infield surface smooth and to increase concession sales (William B. Mead, *Even the Browns*, 68).

But Pacific Coast League player Chuck Stevens told Andy McCue in 1997 that the Hollywood Stars started the practice at about the same time. From 1949 to 1951 the Stars had a quick-working pitcher named Jack Salveson. According to Stevens, concessionaire Danny Goodman came up with the idea of dragging the infield so that he would have more time to sell refreshments when Salveson was pitching (May 17, 1997 interview, cited in Andy McCue, "The King of Coolie Hats," *National Pastime* 19 [1999], 24–27).

Whichever one came first, the custom soon caught on. Jonathan Fraser Light noted that an April 24, 1968, game between the Astros and Mets ended in the twenty-fourth inning on a bad-hop grounder. As a result of this play, Mets general manager Johnny Murphy successfully pushed for a rule that the infield be dragged every five innings during an extra-inning game (Jonathan Fraser Light, *The Cultural Encyclopedia of Baseball*, 308).

14.2.5 Tarpaulins. Abner Powell is often credited with inventing the tarpaulin, based upon his 1943 claim to have done so while running the New Orleans club (Val J. Flanagan, "Rain-Check Evolved to Check Flood of Fence-Climbers, Says Originator, Now 83," *Sporting News*, April 8, 1943). While Powell did not specify a year, he did not become involved with the New Orleans club until 1887, and the tarpaulin was in use several years earlier.

Henry Chadwick commended St. Louis "ground-keeper" August Solari for having "introduced an improvement which might be copied to advantage. It is the placing of tarpaulins over the four base positions to protect them from wet weather" (reprinted in the *St. Louis Post-Dispatch*, March 15, 1884). The fact that Solari had been the owner of one of the first important St. Louis baseball fields may have contributed to his farsighted approach.

Within two weeks the pitcher's box was also being covered with a tarpaulin (*Sporting Life*, March 26, 1884). By May the tarpaulin was being hailed as a great success and an additional one had been added to cover the base paths (*St. Louis Post-Dispatch*, May 5, 1884; *Cincinnati Enquirer*, May 12, 1884, discovered by David Ball and cited in Frederick Ivor-Campbell, "When Was the First? [Part 4]," *Nineteenth Century Notes* 95:3, 4, Summer/Fall 1995, 12).

An 1893 note made clear that by then it had also become routine for the area around home plate to be covered: "After every game the pitcher's and batter's boxes [in Pittsburgh] are covered over with large tarpaulins, in case it should rain before the next game, and to keep the ground from dew" (*Sporting News*, December 9, 1893). In spite of this rapid expansion of the number of areas being protected, it was not until the twentieth century that clubs began to cover their entire infields with a single tarpaulin.

In 1906 it was reported that "Protection for the diamond during rain varies at different parks. Some clubowners protect only the pitcher's slab or the home plate, others cover the bases as well, and one clubowner, [George] Tebeau of Louisville, is said to have a circus tent with which he covers the whole infield when it rains" (*Chicago Tribune*, September 30, 1906).

Others wondered if there wasn't a more efficient way to cover the infield. Washington inventor Lee Lamat announced plans in 1907 to "build a truck on very wide wheels, which will be placed in the center of the diamond. The canvas is rolled up on it and will be run out in all directions covering the entire infield by means of small trucks, which carry the canvas to the extremes of the infield. In this way the infield can be covered and protected from the rain in less than ten minutes, and it can be cleared and ready for play in about the same time" (*Washington Post*, June 15, 1907).

Sporting Life reported at the start of the 1908 season: "Pittsburg, always in the lead, will spring a novelty at the base ball grounds this season. The Pittsburg Base Ball Club proposes to solve the 'wet grounds' problem. A contract was signed yesterday by [owner Barney] Dreyfuss with the Pittsburg Waterproof Company for a tarpaulin to cover the entire playing field at the ball park. The tarpaulin will contain 1,800 yards of brown paraffined duck and will cost $2,000. It will be 120 × 120 feet square. The center of the tarpaulin will be attached to a truck 10 × 15 feet. The truck will be three feet high and the wheels will have a tire six inches wide. The tarpaulin and transportation truck were designed by the Pittsburg Waterproof Company, which will make application for a patent. Before and after a game, particularly in threatening weather, the truck will be run out and the playing ground covered with the tarpaulin. Should there be a shower within half an hour of the time for beginning the game, or should there be a heavy rain at night, the tarpaulin will protect the playing field, and there should be no more deferred games on account of wet grounds, unless the rain should fall during the progress of a game. It is calculated that the cover can be spread in 15 or 20 minutes and removed within the same length of time. When not in use it will be folded on top of the truck and the latter trundled to a remote part of the field" (*Sporting Life*, May 2, 1908). The "canvas tent" was unveiled for the first time on May 6 (*Chicago Tribune*, May 7, 1908).

Other clubs were quick to adopt Barney Dreyfuss's idea. Within two weeks of the Pirates' announcement, Chicago owner Charles Webb Murphy followed suit (*Sporting Life*, May 16, 1908). By 1912 most other clubs had adopted the technique, as sportswriter Joe S. Jackson explained: "These cov-

line of the pitcher's box. The back line thus essentially assumed the role of today's pitching rubber and effectively prevented pitchers from stepping beyond the front line.

In 1893 the pitcher's box was finally eliminated entirely and replaced with a single plate with which the pitcher's foot had to remain in contact until the ball left his hand. No doubt it was with a mind to the previous experience with pitchers' footing that this was made of rubber, and became known as the rubber. Although it has been made of rubber ever since, the same quaint urge that keeps "knocked out of the box" current has spawned terms like "slabman," "on the slab," and "slab artist."

14.3.9 Mounds. The pitcher's mound originated sometime in the late 1880s or early 1890s, but there are surprisingly few claimants for the distinction of having created the first mound. John Thorn and John Holway suggested that John Ward may have pioneered the mound in 1893, but Ward biographer Bryan Di Salvatore disputed this (John Thorn and John Holway, *The Pitcher*, 149; Bryan Di Salvatore, *A Cunning Base-Ballist*, 433).

In fact the baseball mound does not appear to have been invented by anyone at all, but instead to have had humbler origins. Researcher Tom Shieber explained, "A common theory is that soon after the allowance of overhand pitching, it became apparent that a downward slope over the range of the pitcher's stride increased the speed of a pitched ball. Groundskeepers, in an effort to aid the pitcher's footing after a rain storm, would often add dirt to the pitcher's box area, but soon dirt was requested with or without rain" (Tom Shieber, "The Evolution of the Baseball Diamond," in *Total Baseball IV*, 120).

This hypothesis that the earliest mounds were intended for drainage is supported by references such as this one: "When the Trenton team reached the Hartford ground yesterday they found five men with sponges hard at work on the diamond, and [pitcher Mike] Tiernan was mounted on a pile of sawdust" (*Trenton Times*, April 28, 1885). Researcher Clifford Blau discovered a letter written before the 1888 season noting that only at the St. Louis grounds did the pitcher's box have a distinct elevation above the batter's box (*Sporting Life*, February 22, 1888).

This letter writer believed that St. Louis pitcher Bob Caruthers had gained an advantage from the raised pitching area and would not be as effective now that he had been sold to Brooklyn. Aside from this claim, however, most references to mounds in this period imply that they were perceived as drainage devices rather than as potential competitive advantages. There are two plausible explanations for this. One is that few realized that such an elevation would benefit the pitcher. Another is that some crafty souls did recognize the potential benefit but sought to keep this knowledge to themselves. Since such coyness can never be ruled out, it is impossible to determine precisely when mounds changed from being utilitarian anti-flooding devices to deliberately crafted pitchers' aids. Nonetheless it is worth trying to narrow it down.

A roundup of the usual suspects must begin with the Orioles' innovative duo of manager Ned Hanlon and groundskeeper Thomas J. Murphy. Hugh Fullerton later reported that during the Orioles' heyday in the mid-1890s, "The pitcher's box was a foot higher than the plate" (*Chicago Tribune*, August 5, 1906).

Ned Hanlon moved on to manage Brooklyn in 1899 and brought the pitcher's mound with him. The *Boston Globe* reported at the beginning of the season: "Manager 'Buck' Ewing, of the New York Club, thinks that Brooklyn will have the best of it this season, as Hanlon has raised his pitcher's box nearly one foot, making it difficult for the visiting players. The home players are able to overcome the handicap by practice. Ewing thinks that all diamonds should be made level. 'Hanlon has no more right to raise his pitchers' box a foot than New York has a right to dig a trench one foot deep from the home plate to the pitcher's box at the Polo Grounds,' says 'Buck'" (reprinted in *Sporting Life*, April 7, 1899).

By this time others were using similar techniques. David Ball discovered a claim by Dick Harley in 1897 that New York manager Bill Joyce had "worked the old racket at the Polo Grounds. . . . Scrappy [Joyce] has built up the pitcher's box, and the result is a handicap to the visiting pitchers and the visiting batsmen." Harley believed that this gave an advantage to tall New York pitchers like Jouett Meekin and Amos Rusie while handicapping visiting pitchers who were unaccustomed to the raised pitcher's area. "I do not know whether there is any rule against this trick of palming off a 'phony' pitcher's box on a visiting club, but there ought to be. I am told that Scrappy worked the same trick when he was in Washington. It's an old one, and the inventor of it was Mike Kelly. Mike introduced the trick when Larry Cochrane [sic] pitched for Uncle Anson's Chicago Whites, back in the eighties" (*Washington Post*, August 29, 1897). This last claim must be taken with skepticism, since Harley was far too young to have firsthand knowledge of these events, and Corcoran and Kelly were already dead.

By the turn of the century, mounds were becoming a common sight. In 1900 a *Sporting Life* correspondent reported, "One of the secrets of the success of the Cleveland Club at home came to light last night [August 25]. Some time ago 'The News' had a story regarding the effective pitching in the League this season, and gave as the reason the fact that in the different parks the pitcher's box was raised from one to two feet, thus enabling the pitchers to throw down hill, and get not only more speed, but better control as well. This is the case in every city except Cleveland.

"Here the batters' box has been raised nearly twelve inches above the pitchers' slab, and the boxmen are forced to throw up-hill. The Cleveland pitchers, working at home half the time, have thoroughly mastered the difference in the two positions, and can, by reason of the fact that they work oftener at home than on any other one field, have much greater command of the ball and know exactly how to work the variations in their delivery. The question of relative positions of the plate and pitcher's box with the other parts of the diamond is one which just now is of much interest, and will be discussed at the annual meetings this fall" (*Sporting Life*, September 8, 1900).

In 1903 a rule was instituted that mounds could not exceed fifteen inches. While this rule was primarily designed so that home teams could not force visiting pitchers to adapt to life on a hillock, the idea that mounds benefited pitchers was gaining currency. Before the season a *Sporting Life* correspondent observed, "Last year every ground in the Eastern League had a raised pitcher's box, and it increased the power of the slabmen" (*Sporting Life*, March 21, 1903). A follow-up piece reported: "The Washington Club has protested all games played in Boston on account of an illegal pitcher's box, the allegation being that the box is higher than fifteen inches" (*Sporting Life*, May 16, 1903).

Adoption of a maximum mound height did not prevent clubs from tinkering with its height to suit the preferences of its pitchers and to inconvenience the opposing pitcher. Brooklyn manager Ned Hanlon responded to the new rule by altering the pitcher's area whenever Christy Mathewson was scheduled to pitch there. According to Mathewson, "Every time he thought I was going to pitch there, he would have the diamond doctored for me in the morning. The groundkeeper sank the pitcher's box down so that it was below the level of all the bases instead of slightly elevated as it should be" (Christy Mathewson, *Pitching in a Pinch*, 288). As is discussed under "Mound Building" (11.2.3), such tactics continued until 1950.

In addition, acceptance of the notion that pitchers benefited from a mound was still far from universal. In particular, *Sporting Life* editor Francis Richter attributed the decline in hitting to his pet peeve, the foul strike. But players had begun to recognize a relationship, and when *Sporting News* polled players after the 1904 season on how to increase offense, Jack Holland of Spokane suggested putting hitters above pitchers (*Sporting News*, December 17, 1904).

14.3.10 Pitcher's Paths. Old-time ball fields usually featured a pitcher's path or alley leading from the plate to the mound, a characteristic that has been revived at Arizona's Bank One Ballpark and Detroit's Comerica Park. The origins of the path are somewhat obscure, but researcher Tom Shieber has unearthed what is almost certainly the explanation. He noted that early baseball clubs often played on cricket grounds, where the two wickets were connected by a dirt path to ensure more reliable bounces. He speculates that early baseball clubs found that the path led to fewer passed balls and made it customary. Shieber cites a description that appeared in the *New York Clipper* in July 1860.

Shieber's theory accounts for how these dirt strips originated, but it doesn't explain why the alleys were retained long after catchers were stationed directly behind the plate. I think the explanation is simple: since it is very difficult to maintain grass in well-trodden areas, the alleys represented the groundskeepers' best effort to keep foot traffic off the grass. They probably had a hard time convincing the players to adhere to this, but at least the groundskeeper and his assistants could do so.

This hypothesis also explains why the alleys gradually disappeared without much notice being taken. Once the sizes and budgets of grounds crews increased and ventilation and irrigation improved, there was less need to keep traffic off the grass. Eventually pitcher's paths began to be eliminated altogether.

(iv) The Amenities

14.4.1 On-deck Circles. It appears that the on-deck circle was created with the same basic aim as the coach's box (see **7.1.1**). The *Boston Globe* reported in 1886 that in a Detroit–St. Louis game, Fred Dunlap of St. Louis objected to Detroit's Dan Brouthers standing close to the plate while Hardy Richardson batted (*Boston Globe*, June 17, 1886).

Waite Hoyt said that by the time he debuted in the American League in 1919, "two or three batters were allowed to stand up, waiting for their turns to bat. There wasn't any batting circle then and they stood where they wanted to." An opponent took advantage of this in Hoyt's first game to call him "every dirty name he could think of" (quoted in Eugene Murdock, *Baseball Between the Wars*, 32). The on-deck circle appears to have debuted soon afterward, but I have not been able to pinpoint the details.

14.4.2 Hitting Backgrounds. Greg Rhodes and John Snyder claimed that a hitter's background was first introduced when Cincinnati's League Park was redesigned in 1894. Batters had been complaining that advertisements in center field were obscuring their vision. As a result, park superintendent John Schwab created a deep green backdrop in center field (Greg Rhodes and John Snyder, *Redleg Journal*, 111; Rhodes and Snyder listed this as John Schwab's son Matty, but he did not succeed his father as the club's groundskeeper until 1903).

When Brooklyn's Washington Park opened in 1898 it was immediately apparent that it had been designed by architects "not versed in the practical ins and outs of base ball. They extended the center-field bleachers across the field from left to right, thus balking the vision of the batsman and backstop. When the Dodgers leave for their Western trip President Ebbetts [Charles Ebbets] will employ a gang of carpenters to lop off 200 feet of bleacher room in center, thus giving the batsmen and wind paddists [catchers] a clear view of the perspective in the deep center garden. The lopped-off seats will be transferred to right field" (*Sporting News*, May 21, 1898).

Christy Mathewson noted in 1912 that clubs were becoming increasingly aware of the importance of hitting backgrounds: "Frequently, backgrounds are tampered with if the home club is notably weak at the bat. The best background for a batter is a dull, solid green. Many clubs have painted backgrounds in several contrasting, broken colors so that the sunlight, shining on them, blinds the batter. The Chicago White Sox are said to have done this, and for many years the figures showed that the batting of both the Chicago players and the visitors at their park was very light. The White Sox's hitting was weak anywhere, so that the poor background was an advantage to them" (Christy Mathewson, *Pitching in a Pinch*, 296).

Johnny Evers and Hugh Fullerton observed in 1910 that many pitchers would "shift from side to side in the slab to make the ball come to the batter on a line with some blinding sign." However, because there were more batters than pitchers on every team, they were able to "insist upon good solid green backgrounds to increase hitting, and overrule the pitchers, who prefer glaring yellow, or white, or a motley of colors" (John J. Evers and Hugh S. Fullerton, *Touching Second*, 117).

The mood began to shift when several serious beanings were attributed to batters' inability to pick up pitches. Players' Fraternity head David Fultz lobbied on the issue, and in 1914 the National Commission passed a rule that every park in the majors and high minors had to have a blank green wall in center field (Robert F. Burk, *Never Just a Game*, 194, 197).

This rule was not always adhered to closely. Luke Sewell recalled that when he came up in the early 1920s, "they had advertising signs out on the wall in center field and the pitchers would throw out of those signs, making it a little hard to see. Connie Mack had a scoreboard out there that his left-handers would pitch out of" (quoted in Walter M. Langford, *Legends of Baseball*, 132).

14.4.3 Foul Poles. Henry Chadwick advised in 1860: "The foul ball posts are placed on a line with the home and first base, and home and third, and should be at least 100 feet from the bases. As these posts are intended solely to assist the umpire in his decisions in reference to foul balls, they should be high enough from the ground and painted so as to be distinctly seen from the umpire's position" (*Beadle's Dime Base-Ball Player*, 18).

14.4.4   Screen on the Foul Pole. On July 15, 1939, in a game at the Polo Grounds between the Reds and Giants, Harry Craft of Cincinnati hit a ball down the left-field line. The ball went into the stands near the foul line, which was marked only by a white pole. Home plate umpire Lee Ballanfant called it a home run, prompting heated protests from the Giants. Giants shortstop Bill Jurges ended up exchanging punches with umpire George Magerkurth, and both were suspended for ten games. The Giants' loss was magnified the next day when Jurges's replacement, Lou Chiozza, broke his leg. As a result, National League president Ford Frick mandated screens being added to the foul poles to make the call easier for the umpire (for Ballanfant's version of the incident, see Larry R. Gerlach, *The Men in Blue*, 41).

14.4.5   Backstops. Some form of backstop was in use by 1867, when a Detroit newspaper complained that "The 'stop' bound behind the catcher was too close to this player" (*Detroit Advertiser and Tribune*, September 20, 1867). Most early backstops appear to have been utilitarian affairs which offered limited protection to the spectators while often obstructing their view.

By the end of the 1870s these were beginning to be replaced by screens. The *Detroit Post and Tribune* reported in 1879 that at Detroit's new Recreation Park, "It is intended to put up a wire screen behind the catcher instead of the unsightly boards generally used" (*Detroit Post and Tribune*, April 28, 1879). Cleveland installed a similar screen: "A wire screen has been placed in front of the grand stand at Cleveland to protect its occupants from foul flies, etc." (*Chicago Tribune*, May 11, 1879). David Nemec included in his *Great Encyclopedia of 19th Century Major League Baseball* a photo of Providence's Messer Park in 1879 that appears to include a protective screen (David Nemec, *Great Encyclopedia of 19th Century Major League Baseball*, 125).

The early screens were not terribly popular. Researcher Frank Vaccaro found that a wire screen was installed at Milwaukee's Wright Street grounds on June 25, 1884. Upon its debut, the local paper commented, "The wire screen recently erected in front of the grand stand protects spectators from ugly fouls, and does not interfere in the least with the view of the field" (*Milwaukee Daily Journal*, June 27, 1884). But it was removed only one week later in response to the complaints of spectators (*Milwaukee Daily Journal*, July 3, 1884).

14.4.6   Benches. In the early days of baseball, benches and chairs were not required, and players often had to sprawl on the ground or sit with the spec-

give him a trial. But after Ted's gun delivered a few curves with a muzzle velocity of 1000 feet a second around the ears of the batters, they said 'Nay, Paulin!' and refused to face machine pitching" (*St. Louis Post-Dispatch*, August 19, 1910).

In 1890 the *Pittsburgh Commercial Gazette* reported on another attempt made by two players on the local team: "Fred Carroll and Billy Kuehne have invented a very curious yet simple means for training the eye to judge swiftly pitched curved balls. The machine, or whatever it may be called, has been erected in the extensive back yard of an Allegheny residence and the boys expect to do business with it daily. At the upper end of the yard the machine is set up. It is a spring securely fastened to a piece of heavy timber. On the top of the spring is a cup-like arrangement in which the regulation base ball snugly fits. This is pulled down and fastened to an ingeniously made catch, or series of catches rather, for it can be set at any curve or angle to suit the operator. The spring is on a line with a home plate at the lower end of the yard. One of the players manipulates the machine, while the others take turns with the bat. A ball is placed in the cup, and the operator fastens the spring down to any catch he chooses, the combination of curves and straight balls being almost innumerable, while at the same time it is an utter impossibility for the batsman to anticipate how it is going to come. When ready the operator releases the catch and the ball is thrown with the force of a bullet. It requires a mighty quick eye to get on to it, and furnishes not only excellent practice but a great deal of amusement. The balls go over the plate much swifter than it is possible for the strongest pitcher in the country to send them, and by becoming proficient in sizing them up a batsman will have no difficulty in hitting the most skilled twirler, as the hardest pitched ball would look slow and easy in comparison with those thrown by the spring. The inventors will probably apply for a patent" (*Pittsburgh Commercial Gazette*, reprinted in *Columbus* [Ohio] *Press*, March 15, 1890).

More publicity was received by a device that was invented by Princeton mathematics professor Charles H. Hinton. Hinton referred to his creation as an "automatic pitcher," but it so closely resembled a gun that it soon became known as a pitching gun. The *Boston Globe* reported in 1896, "Professor Hinton of Princeton has, it is said, invented a machine that will pitch balls automatically, and that will curve them also. The apparatus will deliver a ball every twenty seconds, but the time between balls can be changed. The speed of the balls can be regulated as well as the curves. The balls always go directly over the plate. It is said that the Princeton tigers [sic] will use this for batting practice next year" (*Boston Globe*, April 16, 1896).

Professor Hinton's invention did make it off the drawing board. A demonstration of his machine was given in a Princeton gymnasium on December 15, 1896: "The gun, which is a breech-loading cannon, 24 inches in length and placed upon a two-wheeled carriage, was put at one end of the gymnasium. At the other end was a net, at which the professor pitched several balls from his cannon. All were successful and the curves could be seen as distinctly as if sent from the hand of one of Princeton's 'varsity twirlers" (*Nevada State Journal* [Reno], December 26, 1896). In light of the successful exhibition, the school's baseball club made plans to use it for winter practice (*Newark Daily Advocate*, December 16, 1896; Lee Allen, *The Hot Stove League*, 96).

Hinton gave a more extensive display of the machine at Princeton the following June 10 in front of a large crowd that included Mrs. Grover Cleveland. The machine pitched for both sides in an exhibition game between two Princeton social clubs, allowing four hits and one walk in three innings. This description was given of the machine's workings: "The gun is discharged by the batsman who, when ready for the ball to be delivered, steps upon an electrical intercepting plate which is connected by wires with the trigger of the cannon. The speed with which the ball is thrown is regulated by compressed air, and pronglike projectors from the cannon's mouth impart a rotary motion to the sphere when it is discharged, producing a curve in any direction according as the position of the projecting prongs is changed" (reprinted in *Delphos* [Ohio] *Daily Herald*, June 11, 1897).

Hinton's machine had fixed the problem that had doomed Kennedy's: "During the first inning, the batsmen were timid about standing near the plate and the big curves caused them to jump back. But, as the big gun continued to throw strikes, they plucked up courage, stood closer to the plate, and succeeded occasionally in making safe hits." The machine did, however, have one serious drawback: "the long time required for reloading" between pitches (reprinted in *Hawaiian Gazette*, July 13, 1897).

As a result, it was eventually concluded that the gun was "impractical for regular use." Hinton moved on to the University of Minnesota, where he continued to work on the project (*North Adams* [Mass.] *Transcript*, June 13, 1898).

The professor unveiled a retooled version of the gun in Memphis on August 13, 1900. The exhibition impressed onlookers and Hinton was hopeful that his invention would "take the place of pitchers in the preliminary spring batting practice" (*Cincinnati Enquirer*, reprinted in Dan Gutman, *Banana Bats and Ding-Dong Balls*, 45). But this goal was thwarted by the length of time it took to reload the machine, and Hinton died in 1904 without perfecting his gun (Dan Gutman, *Banana Bats and Ding-Dong Balls*, 46).

The goal of a pitching machine didn't die with Hinton, but nor did it make much progress in the years that followed. The Senators were batting against a "pitching cannon" in preparation for the 1903 season (Mike Sowell, *July 2, 1903*, 191). George Cahill, pioneer of baseball lighting systems, was reported in 1908 to have invented a pitching machine that employed compressed air (David Pietrusza, "The Cahill Brothers' Night Baseball Experiments," *Baseball Research Journal* 23 [1994], 62–66). Yet no advances appear to have been made toward solving the critical problem of excessive reloading time.

This long list of unsuccessful efforts caused sports columnist Eddie Wray to sniff in a 1910 column: "Every known gun has either recruited the hospital list or frightened out of the prospective slugger every vestige of desire to increase his batting efficiency. The pitching gun is a beautiful theory. It is also a dead one" (*St. Louis Post-Dispatch*, March 1, 1910). But then, only a few months later, Wray reported, "An Annapolis professor is said to have invented a pitching gun which will do all that [Ted] Kennedy claimed for his" (*St. Louis Post-Dispatch*, August 19, 1910).

In a 1938 issue, *Sporting News* had a photo of a new pitching gun being used in St. Louis. Unfortunately it had the same limitation that had long plagued such efforts: it was capable of throwing only four balls per minute (*Sporting News*, September 8, 1938).

The prototype of today's pitching machines, which utilize spinning wheels to propel the baseball, was patented in 1956 by a Detroit policeman named Eliot Wilson. The patent was then purchased by a man named John Paulson, who created Jugs, Inc., in the early 1970s to sell the device (Dan Gutman, *Banana Bats and Ding-Dong Balls*, 53).

14.4.12   Bullpens. Baseball's earliest "bullpens" were not places for pitchers to warm up but rather discount seating areas. A local paper reported in 1877, "The bull-pen at the Cincinnati Grounds, with its 'three-for-a-quarter' crowd, has lost its usefulness. The bleaching-boards just north of the north pavilion now hold the cheap crowd which comes in at the end of the first inning on a discount" (*Cincinnati Enquirer*, May 9, 1877). On April 4, 1879, the National League's Providence Grays introduced a "bull pen" in center field, which fans could enter after the fifth inning by paying a reduced fifteen-cent admission fee (James Charlton, ed., *The Baseball Chronology*, 38).

Bullpen was also the name of an early ball game. The *Oxford English Dictionary* notes that it appeared as early as 1857 and meant "A schoolboys' ball game, played by two groups, one group outlining the sides of a square enclosure, called the 'bull-pen,' within which are the opposing players."

The enclosure we now call a bullpen began much later because relief pitchers were highly uncommon in early baseball. The reasons that led to its emergence were described in 1890: "The attention of club officials has been called to the dangerous practice of pitchers exercising in front of the grand stand. Time and again has the ball passed into the stand and hit spectators, who are at the mercy of the ball. As they seldom see it until there is no time for avoiding it. Pitchers can practice just as well in front of the club house where their graceful movements can be admired without any dangerous results from wild pitching. It is to be hoped that the abominable practice will be stopped" (*New York Clipper*, May 3, 1890).

It was a couple more decades before relief pitchers became common enough to make permanent bullpens necessary. Their name primarily reflects the fact that the area was an enclosure, but it may also have been influenced by the Bull Durham signs that were prominent in ballparks from 1911 to 1913 (see **18.6.3**). Supporters of this theory note that the earliest known reference dates to 1913: "Ira Thomas is the skipper of the [Athletics'] pitchers. He corrects the faults of the youthful trajectory hurlers and takes them to the 'bullpen' in the afternoon and keeps them warmed up" (*Washington Post*, August 17, 1913).

14.4.13 Bullpen Phones. Bullpen phones seem to have made their way into baseball with a minimum of publicity. The earliest allusion to one that I could find was a 1930 reference to a bullpen phone at Yankee Stadium (*Sheboygan* [Wis.] *Press*, July 25, 1930).

Eddie Collins reported that Fred Lake devised a forerunner to the bullpen phone during his stint as Red Sox manager, which lasted from 1908 to 1909. According to Collins, "Lake devised a scheme whereby he could keep in touch with his warm-up battery out back by the clubhouse, and at the same time not leave the playing field. He rigged up an electric battery, with the bell in the clubhouse and a push button on the bench. One ring meant 'warm up,' two rings 'work hard,' and three rings 'come in to pitch.'" Unfortunately the electric battery failed one day, and struggling pitcher Frank Arellanes was forced to remain in the game and endure a drubbing (*Washington Post*, February 5, 1911).

14.4.14 Pennants and Bunting Flying. As noted under "Trophies" (see **22.3.1**), pennants were being awarded as early as 1858, though the one referred to in that entry does not appear to have been flown at a ballpark. James Terry noted that Brooklyn's Union Grounds were decorated with bunting and the whip pennant signifying the national championship when the Eckfords of Brooklyn defended the title against the Mutuals of New York in 1862 (*Brooklyn Eagle*, August 25, 1862; James L. Terry, *Long Before the Dodgers*, 38).

The pennants were expensive and quite elaborate. The entry fees in the first major league, the National Association, went to the purchase of a pennant. After the 1884 season the Providence Grays proudly flew a pennant made "of white silk with black letters and trimmings, and a beautiful piece of work it was of the whip variety and about 30 feet long" (William Perrin,

But being close to the action proved to be a mixed blessing. In a game at the Irvington grounds, a fight among the spectators spilled over into the press area and the reporters were toppled (*The Ball Player's Chronicle*, August 8, 1867). Henry Chadwick reported that during an 1867 game between the Mutuals and Athletics: "[Athletics pitcher Dick] McBride then exercised himself in the foul ball line for twenty minutes, the scorers' stand apparently being his objective point. By one shot he demoralized friend [William] Meeser, who sat next to us, and by another nearly knocked [David] McAuslan out of time, Gill, of the *Clipper*, changing his base during the flying of the shells from McBride's battery. After having considerable fun to himself, Dick hit a hot fair grounder to third" (*The Ball Player's Chronicle*, August 22, 1867).

Nor was this the last time that reporters had reason to suspect that balls were being deliberately directed at their sanctuary. The issue resurfaced when Athletic Park, home of the Washington entry in the American Association, opened in 1884. The reporters' stand was so close to the field that "general interest is about evenly divided between the game and luckless reporters. [Catcher John] Humphries seems to take a fiendish delight in allowing balls to go by him" (*Washington Post*, April 13, 1884).

Reporters understandably began to agitate for seating assignments that offered more protection while still allowing them a good view of the action. Henry Chadwick reported approvingly in 1870 that the Olympic Club of Washington had established new grounds that included "a fine pagoda over the back stop, secluded from the crowd, for the scorers and reporters of the press" (*New York Clipper*, February 19, 1870).

The issue was addressed at the Philadelphia grounds by building in 1871 "a reporters' stand . . . sufficiently elevated to be out of the reach of strong foul balls that may chance their way" (quoted in Michael Gershman, *Diamonds*, 19). Others followed suit.

The general establishment of separate areas for the press was not without controversy. For one thing, reporters often had vastly different ideas of suitable accommodations. At Detroit's grand baseball tournament of 1867 they were housed in a huge box constructed around the trunk of a large elm. A Chicago reporter grumbled that "the most splendid arrangements are made for everybody except the reporters of the press" (*Chicago Tribune*, August 16, 1867). A scribe from Rochester, New York, however, went out of his way to praise the special arrangements provided for the press, which he said gave them a splendid view of the whole field (*Rochester Evening Express*, August 21, 1867; quoted in Priscilla Astifan, "Baseball in the Nineteenth Century Part Two," *Rochester History* LXII, No. 2 [Spring 2000], 18).

Another common complaint was voiced by a *London* (Ontario) *Free Press* reporter in 1877: "so long as the Directors of the Club allow the Press Stand to be used as a 'free and easy' resort, to the annoyance and discomfort of the Press representatives, the latter cannot be expected to do the work assigned them. (This is hint no. 1.)" (*London Free Press*, May 10, 1877). It would be far from the last such hint.

By the 1880s, requests for enclosed facilities were becoming common. At some ballparks they were accommodated, though it is often difficult to determine whether a "box" was a genuine enclosure or merely a roped-off area. An account of 1885 renovations to Philadelphia's Recreation Park mentioned that "the reporter's pavilion has been boxed in" (*Sporting Life*, July 15, 1885).

Unfortunately, as the facilities for reporters became more appealing, the problem of outsiders trying to take the seats increased. The *Washington Post* noted in 1884 that reporters' names now appeared on the desk in front of their chairs (*Washington Post*, April 6, 1884). Such hints seem to have done little to reduce the problem. A Boston reporter complained in 1886, "The press enclosure at the Boston grounds is made for the use of the directors of the club, the members of the press and such others as the directors and reporters invite to occupy seats there. Many people do not seem to understand this fact, and crowd into the enclosure, to the great discomfort of those for whose special convenience it is set apart" (*Boston Globe*, May 31, 1886).

This problem was naturally most prevalent whenever the enclosure was most needed, such as on rainy days or when a big crowd was on hand. It was especially conspicuous at postseason matches, where both issues often arose. The 1897 Temple Cup prompted bitter complaints about the inadequate facilities for the press at Boston's South End Grounds. The Boston club sold to the public all the seats in the "miserable unscreened press stand," which "offers opportunities to practice lively dodging of foul tips and wild pitches." Sportswriters had to pay for admission and were consigned to "the slanting roof of the stand, accompanied by the telegraph operators, where they perched among the rafters and trusted a kindly Providence to keep the wires clear" (reprinted in Ernest J. Lanigan, *The Baseball Cyclopedia*, 103).

A continued lack of adequate facilities for reporters led to the foundation of the Baseball Writers Association of America in 1908, whose primary initial demand was permanent press boxes at all ballparks (see **23.1.4**).

14.5.4 Covered Seating. Early baseball matches were sometimes played in structures such as racetracks that already had covered seating. It was not long after the emergence of ballparks designed for baseball that similar accommodations began to be added. In 1864 the Capitoline Grounds in Brooklyn erected "covered seats for lady spectators" (*Brooklyn Eagle*, June 1, 1864).

14.5.5 Reserved Seats (with exact seating specified). The 1880s saw a number of experiments with reserved seating. When Detroit got its first major league team in 1881, it was decided that "Every holder of a season ticket [to Recreation Park] will have an opportunity to draw for a choice of seats, and that seat will be reserved for them throughout the season. No other seats will be reserved, but will be open to whoever wishes to pay fifteen cents therefor. When a seat is reserved its number and section will be placed upon the season ticket, so that no mistakes can occur" (*Detroit Free Press*, April 23, 1881).

In 1885 new seats were added to Philadelphia's Recreation Park that were "numbered and reserved for the use of ladies and gentlemen" (*Sporting Life*, July 15, 1885). But such innovations were not always popular. The *New York Sun* reported the following season that "The reserved-seat plan at the Polo Grounds has been done away with, and hereafter the early comers will get the best seats" (*New York Sun*, September 5, 1886).

14.5.6 Cheap Seats. Cincinnati sportswriter O. P. Caylor observed in 1877, "The bull-pen at the Cincinnati Grounds, with its 'three-for-a-quarter' crowd, has lost its usefulness. The bleaching-boards just north of the north pavilion now hold the cheap crowd which comes in at the end of the first inning on a discount" (*Cincinnati Enquirer*, May 7, 1877).

14.5.7 Standing Room Accommodations. Standing room tickets were being sold by at least 1886, when the *Detroit Free Press* reported: "After the seats have been all sold a sign 'standing room only,' will be put up" (*Detroit Free Press*, August 17, 1886).

14.5.8 Folding Chairs. In 1884, the *Washington Post* reported that "Folding opera chairs are being placed in the grand stands of several clubs" (*Washington Post*, March 16, 1884). The experiment obviously was successful as Brooklyn owner Charles Byrne announced before the 1887 season, "Both the old and new grand stands will be fitted up with the Andrews folding chair, which will be found to be a great improvement over the chairs formerly in use, being much more comfortable and convenient and doing entirely away with the dragging of chairs over the floor" (*Brooklyn Eagle*, March 23, 1887).

14.5.9 Seat Cushions. Lee Allen reported in a 1968 column, "Cushions were first rented by grandstand customers at the park in Cincinnati on June 25, 1879" (*Sporting News*, April 20, 1968; reprinted in *Cooperstown Corner*).

14.5.10 Dugout-level Seating. Dodger Stadium has the most famous example of dugout-level seating for fans. Bob Timmermann points out that a press release on the Dodgers website states that the seats came about because "The dugout boxes, which afforded a ground-level view of the game, was an idea that [owner Walter] O'Malley borrowed from Japanese ballparks he saw during the Dodgers' goodwill tour of the country following the 1956 season."

But neither the Dodgers nor the Japanese can claim preeminence. In 1903 *Sporting Life* recorded, "The boxes at the Jersey City grounds are under the grand stands, and the occupants sit below the field level, the ground coming up to their waist, an innovation which makes the play seem prettier" (*Sporting Life*, June 20, 1903).

14.5.11   Upper Deck. *Sporting Life* described improvements to Philadelphia's Recreation Park in its July 15, 1885, issue, one of which was that "immediately adjoining the grand stand double-deck pavilions have been built."

14.5.12   Music. Music was, from time to time, played at early ballparks as part of special events. For example, in an 1867 match between clubs from Wauseon, Ohio, and Morenci, Michigan, both towns brought brass bands along to entertain the onlookers (*Adrian Daily Times and Expositor*, August 26, 1867). The city of Philadelphia was represented in the National Association by two franchises from 1873 to 1875, and games between the rivals were accompanied by a brass band from each club (Tim Murnane, *Boston Globe*, January 31, 1915). The *Washington Post* observed in 1913, "James A. Hart, former president of the Chicago league ball club, always advocated adding music to the games as a regular feature. His idea never proved popular with his associates, and was not adopted. When music does become a regular thing at ball parks it will be another instance in which Mr. Hart proved himself several years ahead of the game" (*Washington Post*, August 3, 1913). But the cost of hiring that many people prevented music from being a regular feature.

The situation didn't change until public address systems made it possible to amplify music. On April 26, 1941, the Chicago Cubs unveiled an organist named Roy Nelson, who entertained the crowd with "a varied program of classic and soulful compositions" (*Sporting News*, May 1, 1941). Other clubs soon chimed in.

14.5.13   Public Address Systems. As noted earlier, umpires were expected to address crowds during the nineteenth century. Increasing crowd sizes made this impractical, and megaphones began to be used around the turn of the century. The Giants introduced the first electronic public address system on August 25, 1929: "One of the most interesting features at the Polo Grounds yesterday was the operation of the Giants' newly installed amplifying set, which not only broadcasts the batteries and substitution of players but which enables the umpire to call out each ball and strike so all may hear. This he does by standing on two plates behind the catcher and talking into a microphone attached inside his mask. To [umpire] Charlie Rigler fell the lot of introducing the innovation to the fans and even the players had to admit that Charlie had an excellent voice, though as usual they did not always agree with his decisions" (*New York Times*, August 26, 1929). But public address systems do not appear to have become commonplace until the 1940s. The practice of announcing the lineups before games may have originated at Yankee Stadium on Opening Day of the 1943 season, when the *New York Times* recorded: "Introducing a custom, the entire batting order of the teams was announced before the game" (James P. Dawson, *New York Times*, April 23, 1943).

14.5.14 Scoreboards. The limited size of early baseball crowds ensured that the scoreboard was also a gradual development. Early spectators could sit close enough to the scorer's table that there was no need for an enlarged tote board. As crowd sizes grew, the need for a board that was distinct from the scorer's table slowly became evident. For instance, at a game in Columbus, Ohio, in 1875, mention was made of the "bulletin-board near the scorers' table" (*New York Clipper*, July 17, 1875).

The result was that the evolution of scoreboards into more elaborate affairs occurred not at ballparks but outside of newspaper offices. The practice seems to have originated out of necessity. As historian George B. Kirsch noted, by the late 1860s, large crowds often "hovered around the doors" of newspaper and telegraph offices awaiting the results of baseball matches (George B. Kirsch, *The Creation of American Team Sports*, 203–204).

The throngs became such a nuisance that action was necessary. E. H. Tobias's chronicle of the history of baseball in St. Louis recorded that the 1875 season saw the emergence of the prototype of the sports bar: "Massey's billiard hall, corner of Fourth and Olive streets . . . became the gratifying point for base ball news, arrangements having been made with the Western Union Telegraph Co. for a report of each half inning, which, on receipt, was displayed on a black board, thereby rendering the place the most popular resort in the city. It was a new departure that took from the start and every one asked: 'Why hadn't it been done before?' Soon afterward the newspaper offices adopted the same method to the great delight of all classes, ages and sex" (E. H. Tobias, *Sporting News*, February 8, 1896). An important game that season was followed eagerly throughout the city: "All the newspaper offices and a number of prominent saloons exposed bulletins, upon which was represented the result of each inning as telegraphed from the baseball park" (*New York Clipper*, May 22, 1875).

Bulletin boards in saloons and in front of newspaper offices soon became a popular feature in many other towns. The boards attracted enormous crowds and prompted business for the saloons and for Western Union while not interfering with the business of the newspaper and telegraph offices (Gerard S. Petrone, *When Baseball Was Young*, 59). They also created new enthusiasts for the game of baseball while deepening the allegiance of existing fans—and yet, as we shall see in the entry on "Telegraphs" (see **16.3.2**), not everyone saw it that way.

14.5.15   Out-of-town Scoreboards. In 1880 the *Chicago Tribune* remarked: "Some improvements have been made at White Stocking Park during the absence of the Chicago team. A large bulletin-board has been erected upon which will be painted in large figures, legible to all the spectators, giving [sic] the results of innings both here and in the League games played elsewhere" (*Chicago Tribune*, June 20, 1880). The feature caught on, and its popularity was shown in 1894 when telephones began to be used at the Cincinnati ballpark to keep the board up to date (*Sporting Life*, April 14, 1894).

14.5.16   Electronic Scoreboards. As is common with technological innovations, the electronic scoreboard emerged in fits and starts as America lurched into the electronic age. Nevertheless many of the key elements of today's multi-media extravaganzas were in place earlier than might be expected.

The *New York Sun* reported in 1888: "A new feature was introduced on the Boston grounds on Friday in the shape of a base ball register. A board partition was erected on the centre field fence, a little to one side of the flag pole. By means of electric wires which run from the board along the fence to a position in the pavilion an operator sitting in the latter, by touching a knob registered on the board the decisions of the umpire as to balls and strikes, giving the number of each, and also whether a batter or runner was out, or when the ball hit was a foul. This will prove an advantage to those people who in case of unusual noise cannot hear the umpire's decision" (*New York Sun*, May 27, 1888).

The first electronically operated scoreboard was introduced at the grounds of the St. Louis American League franchise in 1902: "The St. Louis grounds are adorned by a score board that will be of considerable value when the electronic apparatus that goes with it is put in working order. There is a place on the board on which is posted the number of the inning, as well as the half, and there is also one usual arrangement for display of score by inning, all of this being attended to in the ordinary manner. The new features are three large dials, one to indicate the number of men that are out, another the number of strikes on a batsman, and a third the number of called balls on the batsman. The figures for these three dials are to be controlled by the club's official scorer, sitting in the press box, keys connected with electrical apparatus being under his hand. The board will be of especial value when there are big crowds, many of the spectators being so far from the umpire that they cannot well hear what he says. The apparatus is already in place, but is waiting a stronger battery than the first one provided" (*Detroit Free Press*, May 1, 1902).

A product called the Rodier Electric Baseball Game Reproducer was introduced in 1909. Because it was frequently referred to as the electric scoreboard, it is often described as baseball's first electronic scoreboard. But, as is discussed in the entry for "Broadcasts of Baseball" (see **16.3.3**), it was designed for use outside of ballparks.

14.5.17 Messages on Scoreboards. The *New York Times* informed Yankee fans before the 1959 season that an "electronic marvel" would be ready to greet them on Opening Day. The article explained that the club's new scoreboard would include a "changeable message area of seven lines, eight letters to the line, at the bottom of the center tower. Here unusual plays, rulings and pertinent information can be flashed on a moment's notice" (*New York Times*, February 12, 1959). Two months later the *Times*'s coverage of Opening Day included a photo of the "miracle board" bearing the words "THIS IS TURLEYS FIRST OPENING GAME START AS A YANKEE" (*New York Times*, April 13, 1959). It obviously took more than a miracle to produce an apostrophe.

14.5.18 Exploding Scoreboards. The exploding scoreboard was introduced in 1960 by master showman Bill Veeck, who spent $800,000 to be able to generate high-tech pyrotechnics after every White Sox home run. The scoreboard had its first opportunity to explode on May 1, 1960, following an Al Smith homer: "As the ball landed in the 415-foot center field bull pen, the board lighted up like a giant pinball machine and rocket type aerial bombs shot skyward from ten launching towers across the top of the board" (UPI: *Holland* [Mich.] *Evening Sentinel*, May 2, 1960).

Fans loved the scoreboard, but not everyone felt that way. During a May 22 game the scoreboard went haywire and stayed on for a full minute after a Minnie Minoso home run, prompting reporters to dub it "Veeck's Folly." A week later Cleveland Indians outfielder Jimmy Piersall fired a baseball at the scoreboard and called it "baseball's biggest joke."

14.5.19 Computer-generated Scoreboards. Charley Finley's "Fun Board," installed in Oakland in 1969, provided fans with a variety of messages, cartoons, and automatically computed statistics. Its manufacturer claimed that the Fun Board was the first computer-controlled scoreboard used in any sports stadium (UPI: [Reno] *Nevada State Journal*, April 2, 1969). Sports-writer Ron Bergman explained, "The Astrodome scoreboards in Houston, for instance, operate by projecting films behind them onto photo-electric cells. The Finley Fun Board, however, is totally activated by pressing a button on the computer operated from a booth at press box level" (Ron Bergman, "Computer Calls Shots for Finley Fun Board," *Sporting News*, May 24, 1969).

14.5.20   Replays on Scoreboards. In 1976 the Yankees and Red Sox became the first clubs to have instant replay on their scoreboards. Things went smoothly until a game at Yankee Stadium on August 8, 1976, when a controversial call went against the home side. After the game the Yankees were fined $1,000 by the American League for using the replay board to "produce fan reaction against the umpires." League president Lee MacPhail alleged that the Yankees had shown a replay of the play, then put the names of the umpires on the board, and that a fan had responded to this provocation by throwing a bottle at one of the umpires.

The Yankees' version was rather different. They maintained that the bottle had been thrown before the replay was shown and that the umpire's names had appeared a full inning afterward. A spokesman for George Steinbrenner was defiant: "The board cost us $3 million and we see no reason, with this great innovation, why fans at the ball game should see any less than the fans at home" (*New York Times*, August 11, 1976). The umpires responded by requesting a unilateral ban on scoreboard replays (*Sporting News*, August 28, 1976). They didn't entirely get their way but were assured that close plays would not be shown.

14.5.21   Color Replays on Scoreboards. Color replays were first seen at a major league game at the 1980 All-Star Game in Los Angeles when the new Diamond Vision scoreboard was unveiled.

14.5.22   Parking Facilities. The first baseball fans to fork out extra for parking were the patrons who paid an additional twenty cents to bring their carriages into Brooklyn's Capitoline Grounds in 1864 (James L. Terry, *Long Before the Dodgers*, 45). Other ballparks followed suit; the entry on "Season Tickets" (see **15.1.1**) mentions that the Forest Citys of Cleveland offered a season ticket plan in 1871 that included carriages. Fans in Boston were informed: "Persons visiting the grounds in carriages will hereafter be required to take positions assigned them by the police, to avoid obstructing the view of spectators" (*Boston Globe*, May 23, 1872). But it seems safe to assume that spectators at these parks didn't encounter the traffic jams that became common in the twentieth century.

The automobile revolution soon gave rise to parking issues. The new bleachers installed at Boston's Huntington Avenue Baseball Grounds in 1904 were designed to accommodate "automobiles and pleasure carriages" (Jacob Morse, *Sporting Life*, May 21, 1904). When Philadelphia's Shibe Park opened in 1909 it featured "a two-hundred-car public garage equipped with a complete service department" as well as an auxiliary garage for the vehicles of management and ballplayers (Bruce Kuklick, *To Every Thing a Season*, 28). The crosstown Phillies took notice and revamped their own stadium at season's end: "The main reason for the rebuilding of the left field bleachers is to make room beneath for a garage. The Fifteenth Street side of the grounds on the outside has always been crowded and many persons have been kept away from games in the past because they did not care to risk their machines in the street. Under the new plans every machine can be taken care of and will be safe in the garage" (*Sporting News*, December 9, 1909).

Once automobiles became affordable for middle-class Americans, parking became an enormous part of the ballpark experience. Sportswriter John B. Sheridan observed in 1922 that, "The man who drives his car to the baseball park takes on a free-for-all fight" for the few parking spots on the street (*Sporting News*, February 9, 1922).

14.5.23   Drive-in Ballparks. Horseless carriages were allowed to flank the outfield fences at many early ballparks. According to Al Reach, it was a common sight for baseball diamonds to be "two-thirds surrounded by carriages and wagons" (*Sporting Life*, March 13, 1909). In a legendary eighteen-inning 1882 National League game, a potential game-ending home run was averted when Detroit outfielder Lon Knight retrieved the ball from between the spokes of a carriage and relayed it home to nab Providence batter George Wright at home plate.

Researcher David McDonald reported that between 1912 and 1915 the Ottawa Senators of the Canadian League allowed motorists to drive their cars into Lansdowne Park. Their vehicles were parked down the outfield lines and were supposed to be at least forty feet from fair territory, but the rule was rarely enforced. There were sometimes enough cars to necessitate special ground rules, such as a game on Queen Victoria's Day in 1913 that drew fifty-two cars—about 10 percent of the number of automobiles in the entire city (David McDonald, "The Senators' Diamond Dynasty," *Ottawa Citizen*, March 25, 2003).

The Albuquerque Sports Stadium, which opened in 1969, featured a bluff behind the outfield wall where fans could park and watch the game. Dukes general manager Jim Blaney said that fans who parked in the section "bring campers, school buses, anything. Whenever something happens, they honk horns instead of clapping" (quoted in David Pietrusza, *Minor Miracles*,

69). The Dukes left town after the 2000 season; by the time baseball returned to the stadium in 2003, the drive-in area had been eliminated.

14.5.24 Amusement Rides. After the 1885 season the Metropolitans were sold to the owner of a Staten Island amusement park, and for the next two seasons the ball club was used as little more than another attraction. On May 23, 1897, Brown Stockings owner Chris Von der Ahe opened a "shoot the chutes" waterslide at St. Louis's Sportsman's Park to try to attract—or distract—customers who were not interested in watching his last-place team.

14.5.25 Day Care. In 1903, the Columbus entry in the American Association announced plans to add a nursery (*Sporting Life*, April 18, 1903).

Chapter 15

FANS

THERE IS a very long tradition of fans who take the game too seriously. As early as 1872 a Cleveland newspaper bemoaned, "It pains us to announce the fact that another promising young man, the pride and joy of his parents, has succumbed to that fell destroyer—base ball. Ever since the spring weather opened he has been troubled with the premonitory symptoms of the disease, and a boot poultice applied daily by his father produced no effect save to develop the complaint, while of late he has been comparatively useless to his employers, and spent his time in reading ten cent works on the 'National Game,' and hanging around the boarding places of the members of the Forest City club" (*Cleveland Leader*, May 3, 1872). Four years later a concerned father wrote to the *Rochester* (N.Y.) *Evening Express* to complain that his son's "foolish infatuation" with baseball was being fed by the paper's lengthy accounts, with the result that he was "scarcely fit for anything else" (*Rochester Evening Express*, May 26, 1876; quoted in Priscilla Astifan, "Rochester's Last Two Seasons of Amateur Baseball: Baseball in the Nineteenth Century, Part Four," *Rochester History* LXIII, No. 2 [Spring 2001], 8).

In the 1880s two terms emerged to describe devoted baseball followers, neither of which initially had positive connotations. The word "crank" was popularized at the 1881 trial of Charles Guiteau, the assassin of President James Garfield, where it was used to describe a person who becomes deranged by an obsession.

The term "fan" emerged at about the same time and was no more flattering. While usually claimed to be a shortened version of "fanatic," there is strong evidence that it may in fact derive from a perceived similarity to the type of fan that blows wind but produces no substance. This likeness was so striking to one reporter that he observed in 1889: "The 'fan' has a mouth and a tongue. In fact that is about all there is to him. The other members are so small that they are lost in the shuffle. The 'fan' uses his mouth and tongue whenever there is no occasion to use them. People would rather not listen to him but he is irrepressible and will talk whether one likes it or not. . . . The 'fan' always jumps at conclusions; he never stops to investigate. If he was to do a little investigation he would not be a 'fan'" (*Sporting News*, November 2, 1889).

Although it was easy—then as now—to poke fun at the obsessive nature of baseball aficionados, their allegiance was the foundation of the game's development into a profitable and successful enterprise.

(i) Getting Them in the Door

15.1.1 Season Tickets. The sale of season tickets began as soon as clubs started to schedule an extensive number of games. In 1870 the White Stockings had "150 honorary members, who pay ten dollars a year each and get a season ticket" (*Titusville* [Pa.] *Morning Herald*, November 18, 1870). The *New Dickson Baseball Dictionary* cited an 1870 example of the term. The following season the Forest Citys of Cleveland announced these plans: "Season tickets are provided in two classes. The first is sold for $10 and admits the possessor with a lady and carriage to all games played this season. . . . The other class of season tickets will be sold for $6 each, and admit the bearer alone to all games played this season" (*Cleveland Leader*, May 9, 1871).

15.1.2 Knothole Gangs. The first organized Knothole Gang was established in St. Louis in 1917 by businessman W. E. Bilheimer. The idea was used to help sell stock in the team, with each fifty-dollar purchase of stock entitling the investor to one kid's ticket in the Knot Hole section (Frederick G. Lieb, *The St. Louis Cardinals*, 61). According to Branch Rickey, the section was filled with as many as ten thousand boys and five thousand girls for a single game (Branch Rickey, *Branch Rickey's Little Blue Book*, 75).

The idea was based upon a much older tradition. As early as 1868 spectators were staking out "the prominent 'peek-holes' in the fence" (*New York Clipper*, September 12, 1868; quoted in George B. Kirsch, *The Creation of American Team Sports*, 195).

It was usually children who peered through the knotholes. A reporter observed in 1869: "The gamins in possession of knot holes in the fence and of precarious positions on top of the fence were as numerous as on any previous occasion" (*New York Herald*, June 18, 1869). In 1886 the *New York Times* wrote of a huge crowd: "the hundreds of knotholes in the fence that surround the large grounds were plugged up by youthful eyes whose owners' pockets could not stand the strain that would necessarily have been imposed upon them had they passed through the gates" (*New York Times,* June 1, 1886). In 1890 the directors of the New Haven club concluded that "it does not pay to have all the knots driven out of the fence to give the boys a chance to see games, and they have decided to issue tickets to boys under 12 years for 15 cents" (*Boston Globe,* March 9, 1890).

Owners could hardly blame such youngsters for trying to watch the games, but adults were another matter. An 1883 account reported: "Large as the audience has been at many of the games at League Park, a much larger audience has regularly witnessed the contests from positions outside the enclosure. It appears that knives and even hatchets have been mercilessly used in the cracks of the pine fence, and hundreds of peep holes have been made by grown men oftener than by boys, persons who believe a day is well spent in standing without the fence and 'getting a quarters worth the best of them base ball fellows'" (*Fort Wayne Daily News,* June 2, 1883). In 1886 Harry Wright said, "The Chicago grounds come nearer to my idea of a base ball inclosure than any other in this country. Surrounded by a high brick wall, which does not mar and disfigure adjoining property like the unsightly board fences, it gives the game a privacy which cannot be had where mobs and crowds hang around for a peep through the knotholes and cracks" (*Brooklyn Eagle,* February 7, 1886).

15.1.3 Rain Checks. The origins of the rain check have been complicated by confusion over a couple of issues. The first is the distinction between the concept of a rain check and the means of distributing them. The second is that, as with Ladies' Day (see **16.1.7**), the concept was experimented with many times before owners accepted that it made good business sense.

As a result, while it is often reported that rain checks were first used in baseball in the late 1880s, they are actually much older than that. The National League voted to end the practice on March 8, 1881, so obviously they were being used before then (James Charlton, ed., *The Baseball Chronology,* 44). The issue remained a contentious one, with the *St. Louis Post-Dispatch* reporting in 1883: "The crowd insisted that they should get back either money or rain-checks, but President [Chris] Von der Ahe refused to do either" (*St. Louis Post-Dispatch,* June 21, 1883).

Abner Powell is usually credited with inventing the rain check in the late 1880s, but he made no such claim. What Powell actually took credit for was inventing the *detachable* rain check. A 1943 article by a sportswriter who had interviewed Powell made clear that the practice itself was already in vogue: "all ball clubs used a hard rectangular cardboard ticket, which was sold over and over again, day after day. Ticket buyers would turn them in to the gatekeeper, who deposited the pasteboards in a box. . . . If rain halted a game before the fifth inning, the spectators would line up at the gate to receive a ticket for the next day as they passed out of the park" (Val J. Flanagan, "Rain-Check Evolved to Check Flood of Fence-Climbers, Says Originator, Now 83," *Sporting News*, April 8, 1943).

The spectators were handed the same tickets they had turned in at the gate. But Powell found that the number of tickets refunded would usually exceed the original sale. He attributed this to boys who had scaled walls, slipped through the drainage ditch, or sneaked in the service entrance. Accordingly, he devised detachable tickets, so that rain checks could be issued only to actual ticket purchasers. The article does not specify a year, but Lee Allen indicated that this took place in 1888 (Lee Allen, *The Hot Stove League*, 95).

It seems to have taken many more years before the practice of issuing rain checks became firmly established in the major leagues. In 1906 *Sporting Life* reported, "The Brooklyn Club will start off with the new ticket system which it put into effect late last year. Every purchaser of a ticket will receive a postponed game check" (*Sporting Life*, April 21, 1906).

(ii) Root, Root, Root for the Home Team

15.2.1 Partisanship. Consistent with the game's gentlemanly origins, early baseball fans were censured if they showed partisanship. Henry Chadwick was a leader in this regard, but many newspapers followed his example. For instance, the *Philadelphia Mercury* complained in 1867 that "the behavior of some of the friends of the Harvard [club] was not calculated to exalt them in the estimation of disinterested spectators. Their friendship for the Harvards led them into extremes. . . . If Harvard College inculcates or encourages such conduct, and lets loose upon the world such narrow-minded, selfish and ungentlemanly specimens of unfinished humanity, the fanaticism ascribed to be popular in this vicinity is not likely to decline or die out with the rising generation" (*Philadelphia Mercury*; reprinted in *The Ball Player's Chronicle*, July 4, 1867).

When the Red Stockings of Cincinnati completed a big 1870 win over the Athletics of Philadelphia, "cheers went up as enthusiastic as ever distinguished favorable election returns" (*Rocky Mountain* [Denver] *News*, June 24, 1870). And the *Detroit Evening News* observed in 1875, "In large cities the spectators of a base ball match applaud good play without reference to the club. But in the rural villages, when the local club is being worsted, they observe an ominous silence when the visiting nine makes good hits or catches, and when the match is over the whole population gets together and groans at the umpire" (*Detroit Evening News*, June 19, 1875).

Historian Allen Guttmann noted that Walter Camp tried to convince football spectators to adopt a similar nonpartisanship. But, Guttmann contended, "This historically unprecedented code of sportsmanship was an anomaly. The history of sports spectatorship shows nothing quite like it prior to the Victorian era" (Allen Guttmann, *Sports Spectators*, 88–89).

15.2.2 Tipping the Cap. The custom of players tipping their caps to the fans goes back to the nineteenth century. The *Brooklyn Eagle* reported in 1893 that outfielder Mike Griffin "had to doff his hat repeatedly to the applauding spectators as he came in" after making a great catch (*Brooklyn Eagle*, May 7, 1893). The *Washington Post* noted in 1904, "[Joe] Cassidy had to dip his skypiece in response to the applause after he speared Donohue's [Red Donahue's] grass disturber" (*Washington Post*, August 28, 1904).

15.2.3 Fan Clubs. Boston's Royal Rooters became famous at the turn of the century and attracted many imitators. But an earlier such organization was reported in 1890: "A society of base ball cranks has been formed in Evansville, Ind. A suitable decoration will be worn by the members" (*Columbus* [Ohio] *Press*, February 14, 1890).

15.2.4 Booing. Instances of spectators hissing can be documented as early as 1867 (see **8.2.1** "Verbal Abuse"; also, George B. Kirsch, *The Creation of American Team Sports*, 186). Predictably, Henry Chadwick was outspoken in his opposition, writing in an account of a heatedly contested June 1, 1867, match in Medford, Massachusetts, between Lowell and the Harvard nine: "sharp, short huzzas and hisses follow[ed] the plays and decisions made, the former being excusable, but the latter a disgrace" (Henry Chadwick, *The American Game of Base Ball*, 87).

Hissing had become common enough by the 1870s that the 1876 National League Constitution instructed that "any person hissing or hooting at [the umpire] . . . must be promptly ejected from the grounds." This doesn't seem to have helped much, as an 1884 account noted: "The season is but two-thirds over, and yet it has been marked by cowardly personal assaults on umpires in the field, scenes of disgraceful rows by club 'heelers' hissing and insulting remarks by partisans in grand stand assemblages" (*Brooklyn Eagle*, August 17, 1884).

Umpires were the most frequent targets of this abuse, but players also increasingly came to be on the receiving end. As described in several earlier entries (see **2.2.1** "Bunts," **2.2.2** "Fair-fouls," **5.5.1** "Running into Fielders," and **6.4.1** "Intentional Walks"), players were usually hissed not for inept play but for tactics that were deemed unmanly or unsporting. Yet there were exceptions, as Chadwick noted with dismay later in the account of the match at Medford: "The yells of derision, when errors were committed, were only equalled by the jeers of juvenile roughs in New York on similar occasions, and were entirely out of place as emanating from an educated crowd" (Henry Chadwick, *The American Game of Base Ball*, 87).

15.2.5 Organized Rooting. As discussed in the chapter on coaches, coaches of the 1880s functioned as combination noisemakers and cheerleaders, with only occasional interruptions to direct base runners. By the twentieth century, fans were beginning to follow their lead, but their efforts weren't always appreciated. *Sporting Life* reported in 1904: "A blow has been struck in Denver at the time-honored privilege of the rooter to howl himself hoarse if the exigencies of the situation demanded it. An order has been issued by the owner of the team that 'rooting' must stop, and policeman are now stationed in front of the various stands to enforce the rule. The fans are indignant, and threaten to stay away from the game unless the order is rescinded" (*Sporting Life*, May 28, 1904).

Four years later the *Philadelphia Record* remarked, "So Ban Johnson is to put a stop to the disgraceful organized 'rooting' by baseball fanatics which marked the close finish in the American League pennant race last season. Decent patrons of the game will be thankful and all fair-minded individuals will laud Johnson on the stand he has taken, for some of the carryings-on last year were very unsportsmanlike. This organized 'rooting' for the purpose of rattling the players of the opposing team was started last year in Chicago by the followers of the White Sox, and was taken up at Detroit and also in this city. All sorts of noise-making devices were called into use to help along the work of disconcerting the players of the visiting team, and the sounds produced were simply hideous to all save the frenzied base ball 'fans,' who felt that they were helping to win the game. A man who pays to see a base ball match is entitled to shout his lungs out, if he chooses, hooting the players of either team or cheering any play that excites his admiration. But there is no reason why anyone should be allowed to go to a game armed with a megaphone for the express purpose of hurling epithets at the players of either team, or why a number of individuals, all armed with megaphones, should be permitted for day after day to make remarks to the players of the opposing team that angers or disconcerts them so that they cannot play their best ball" (*Philadelphia Record*, reprinted in *Sporting Life*, April 11, 1908).

15.2.6 Curtain Calls. Writer Bruce Shlain credited Mark "The Bird" Fidrych with being responsible for the first curtain call in 1976 (Bruce Shlain, *Oddballs*, 151). While Fidrych may have helped to revive this tradition, he certainly didn't originate it.

For example, during Detroit's first major league game in 1881, the *Detroit Free Press* reported that Charley Bennett hit a home run that "was loudly applauded, and the crowd would not desist until he bowed in acknowledgment" (*Detroit Free Press*, May 3, 1881). In 1884 *Sporting Life* noted that in Cuba "a home run raises the vast assemblage to its feet as one man and one woman, and the play has to be stopped until the 'home skipper' has passed in front of the grand stand and received not only the congratulations of the beautiful ladies, but many golden tokens of appreciation" (*Sporting Life*, June 10, 1884).

15.2.7   Brooms. The use of brooms to commemorate a sweeping victory or a series sweep is much older than today's fans might expect. It appears that brooms were initially used by visiting spectators in hopes that their association with witchcraft would bring bad luck to the home team. Their popularity was probably also aided by the fact that they helped identify a small group of spectators who were rooting for the visiting team. In any event, they played a major role in the fun in nineteenth-century baseball grandstands.

After the Atlantic Club of Brooklyn beat the Unions of Morrisania in 1868 to recapture the championship, this account appeared in the *Brooklyn Eagle*: "In procession came three carriages, and in front of the first one was elevated a broom, the pine handle of which was ornamented with gay colored ribbons; the occupants of the carriages appeared to be enjoying a happy state of feeling. Inquiry was made, and the well-informed were heard to say that it was the Atlantic Club returning from Morrisania, after playing with the Union Club, and that the broom carried in front meant that having whipped the champions, it could now sweep everything out of its way" (*Brooklyn Eagle*, October 7, 1868).

When Boston won a big game at Hartford in 1875, the team was accorded a reception at the Boston train station by a large throng that included fifty men with brooms who led a parade through the streets (*Boston Herald*, reprinted in *St. Louis Globe-Democrat*, May 24, 1875). In 1880, after the White Stockings of Chicago reeled off a historic twenty-one straight victories, club president William Hulbert presented the players with "gold 'broom' badges, emblematic of their ability to sweep everything before them" (*New York Clipper*, July 31, 1880).

This mode of celebration gained additional momentum in 1886. In early May a sizable assemblage of New York partisans accompanied their team to Philadelphia for a series: "Upwards of 9000 persons witnessed the game, including a couple of hundred New Yorkers. The latter brought with them a bunch of new brooms which they tacked to the posts of the grand stand, in which they occupied seats. They meekly but gracefully presented the brooms to the Philadelphia players at the conclusion of the game" (*Boston Globe*, May 4, 1886). A few days later, Columbia students celebrated a win over Harvard with "a pair of crossed brooms" (*Boston Globe*, May 9, 1886).

The ritual reached new heights when the second-place and defending champion Chicago White Stockings visited surprise league leaders Detroit for a crucial three-game series in late June. Detroit's Wolverines entered the series with a perfect 18-0 record on their home grounds, and Chicago partisans were willing to try anything to break the skein. As a result, a mascot and nearly two hundred well-wishers equipped with brooms, whistles, duck calls, wooden clappers, and other noisemakers accompanied the Chicago club to Detroit on a special train. Upon disembarking, the throng caused quite a commotion in downtown Detroit by holding aloft large brooms with the inscription "Record breakers" as they were led to their hotel by Chicago stars "Cap" Anson and Mike Kelly (*Boston Globe*, June 20, 1886).

At the first game of the series the next day, the visitors' hex seemed to work as Detroit's star catcher Charley Bennett was injured in the eighth inning, and a passed ball by his replacement allowed the White Stockings to score the winning run. But Chicago's luck turned the next day with Anson sitting out because he had gone fishing and caught a fish that showed him its teeth before it died. He considered this to be such a harbinger of bad luck that he believed it useless for him to play (*Chicago Tribune*, June 22 and 23, 1886). Detroit won the second and third games, leading many of the Chicago supporters to abandon their brooms or meekly surrender them to their hosts.

The next month a crowd of Detroiters accompanied the Wolverines to Chicago sporting miniature brooms on their lapel pins. They proved even less successful, as Chicago swept the three-game series en route to regaining the championship.

While these discouraging results put a damper on the use of brooms, the practice did not entirely vanish. In 1904 Boston's Royal Rooters brought brooms with them to New York for the season's pivotal series. And so when today's fans celebrate a sweep of a series by waving brooms they are merely reviving a very old tradition, which is steeped in the superstitions of the nineteenth century.

15.2.8 Radios at the Ballpark. The Reverend Percy Kendall brought a thirty-inch, seventeen-pound "portable" radio to Cleveland Indians games as early as 1937 (G. Edward White, *Creating the National Pastime*, 221). But the practice naturally did not become prevalent until radios had become significantly smaller. Red Smith, in a 1948 column, mentioned that during that year's furious American League pennant race between the Red Sox and Indians, fans at Fenway were listening to Cleveland's game against Detroit (Red Smith, October 4, 1948, reprinted in *Red Smith on Baseball*).

By 1955 Smith was reporting with dismay that there were sections in Chicago's Wrigley Field and Philadelphia's Connie Mack Stadium where the radio broadcast of the day's game was piped through the amplifiers: "There the customer who has paid for the privilege of watching with his own eyes sits helpless while a disembodied huckster plucks at his sleeve, bludgeons him with advice, burdens him with statistical trivialities, embarrasses him with autobiographical revelations, hectors him to buy beer or cigarettes" (Red Smith, August 22, 1955, reprinted in *Red Smith on Baseball*).

15.2.9 Helping (or Hindering) Players. The blocked-ball rules of early baseball (see **12.6**), though intended to take the fans out of play, sometimes had the opposite effect. The importance of the early umpire's cry of foul gave spectators another way to interfere. As early as 1857 spectators were yelling "foul" on fair hits to trick the opposing club (*Porter's Spirit of the Times*, September 5, 1857; cited in George B. Kirsch, *The Creation of American Team Sports*, 192–193).

Tim McCarver noted that a much more recent spectator found a similar way to involve himself in the game. McCarver described a 1997 game at Cincinnati's Cinergy Field in which a Reds fan waited until Mets catcher Todd Hundley set up and then yelled his location to the batter. According to McCarver, "Hundley had to figure out how to cross up the fan, and his manager, Bobby Valentine, had to resort to shouting gibberish to drown him out" (Tim McCarver with Danny Peary, *Tim McCarver's Baseball for Brain Surgeons and Other Fans*, 69).

(iii) You Can't Beat Fun at the Old Ballpark

For some fans, if the home team doesn't win it's a crying shame, but others are just out to have a little fun.

15.3.1 Beer at the Ballpark. At least some National Association clubs sold alcohol in the stands. But National League founder William Hulbert was opposed to the sale of alcohol, and Cincinnati's expulsion after the 1880 season was at least in part the result of beer sales.

After the American Association was founded a year later, the sale of alcohol at its parks became one of its best-known features. It is said that tavern owner Chris Von der Ahe bought the St. Louis Brown Stockings to assure that he would have the lucrative beer concession.

The last major league team not to sell beer at the ballpark was the expansion Toronto Blue Jays, because the province of Ontario refused to allow the team a liquor license. Many believed this was the result of a promise that Ontario premier William Davis had made to his mother. When she died, the club received permission to sell beer in 1982.

15.3.2 Food. A three-course meal featuring a pasta dish was served at Brooklyn's Union Grounds in 1862 (David Pietrusza, Lloyd Johnson, and Bob Carroll, eds., *Total Baseball Catalog*, 28).

15.3.3 Peanuts. The *Youngstown Vindicator* reported in 1898, "the man who held the refreshment privileges last year, will have charge again this season. As usual, no intoxicants will be sold and mild peanuts, red, white and yellow pop, etc., will be dispensed" (*Youngstown Vindicator*, April 7, 1898).

15.3.4 Hot Dogs. With its large German population, St. Louis featured a popular "Weiner wurst" stand in the 1880s (*Cleveland Leader and Herald*, March 20, 1886). It is more difficult to be certain of who first thought of packing sausages in buns, but legendary concessions operator Harry M. Stevens claimed to have originated the practice at the Polo Grounds in April 1901. Stevens credited his son Frank with having convinced him that fans would welcome a change from ham and cheese sandwiches (Frederick G. Lieb, "A Man Who Has Made Millions from By-Products of Sport," *Sportlife*, December 1925, 94).

15.3.5 Sushi. Researcher Bob Timmermann noted that sushi undoubtedly made its baseball park debut at a stadium in Japan. It was introduced to the United States at Jack Murphy Stadium in San Diego on Opening Day of the 1989 season. The *Los Angeles Times* gave this account of its reception: "'This sushi stuff is ridiculous,' said San Diego Police Officer Rick Schnell. 'They ought to be selling hot dogs and hamburgers. They've never done those that good to begin with. Sushi makes us the wimp capital of baseball—at least until October, when we'll beat everybody. But in October, when the World Series comes here, selling sushi will be embarrassing. We'll have to be extra good just to cover up the scorn'" (*Los Angeles Times*, April 4, 1989). Other fans seem to have been more accepting of the innovation. The Angels added sushi the following year, and the Dodgers a few years later.

15.3.6 Seventh-inning Stretch. The seventh-inning stretch is often erroneously said to have originated in the early twentieth century when President William Howard Taft arose from his seat in the middle of the seventh and fans respectfully did likewise. In fact, stretches were in use as early as the 1860s, though it took many years for the seventh inning to become standard.

After a June 1869 game the *New York Herald* reported, "At the close of the long second inning, the laughable stand up and stretch was indulged in all around the field" (quoted in Jonathan Fraser Light, *The Cultural Encyclopedia of Baseball*, 662). That same year Harry Wright wrote: "The spectators all arise between halves of the seventh, extend their legs and arms, and sometimes walk about. In so doing they enjoy the relief afforded by relaxation from a long posture on the hard benches" (quoted in Greg Rhodes and John Erardi, *The First Boys of Summer*, 70).

An entrepreneurial San Franciscan named W. J. Hatton helped arrange the Red Stockings' 1869 visit to California. To increase revenue, a ten-minute intermission took place after the sixth inning. A Cincinnati reporter called this practice "a dodge to advertise and have the crowd patronize the bar" (*Cincinnati Commercial*; quoted in Greg Rhodes and John Erardi, *The First Boys of Summer*, 70).

And Jonathan Fraser Light cited this description in *Sporting News* of a game between the New York Giants of the National League and Brooklyn of the American Association in the 1889 World's Series: "As the seventh opened somebody cried, 'Stretch for Luck!' And instantly the vast throng on the grand stand rose gradually and then settled down, just as long grass bends to the breath of the zephyr" (Jonathan Fraser Light, *The Cultural Encyclopedia of Baseball*, 246).

15.3.7 The Wave. One might think that at least the wave is a recent addition to baseball. But there is compelling evidence to the contrary.

Tom Shieber reports that a Hall of Fame volunteer discovered a clipping giving this account of an October 15, 1866, match between the Atlantic and Athletic clubs that took place at the Capitoline Grounds in Brooklyn: "Quite an amusing scene was here enacted. One individual, cramped by sitting two or three hours on the low temporary bench at the left of the field, stood up, stretched his body, arms and neck to their fullest tension, and appeared to feel quite refreshed; his next neighbor imitated his example, and one after another almost every one in the crowd stood up, straightened himself and then resumed his seat. The effect was ludicrous to the extreme, and after the straightening process had been indulged in all around the arena the portion of the crowd on the left commenced waving their handkerchiefs to the crowd on the right, and these returned the salute, so that at one time there were at least a thousand cambrics shaking around the field. This episode seemed to put the crowd in extra good humor, and from time to time the process was repeated."

Dean A. Sullivan discovered this 1889 account of a forfeited game between St. Louis and Brooklyn: "The bleacheries were black with people and on the pathways surrounding these seats the people were jammed together in one immovable mass, and the only time they could gather themselves together was when the excitement got the best of them and everybody was forced to throw up their hands and were compelled to sway about like a WAVE on the ocean from the irresistible and frenzied throng" (*Brooklyn Eagle*, September 8, 1889; reprinted in Dean A. Sullivan, ed., *Early Innings*,

183). The description of that fall's World's Series that was cited in the previous entry is clearly the same idea. Gerard S. Petrone reported that Detroit fans were also using a version of the wave in 1900 (Gerard S. Petrone, *When Baseball Was Young*, 173).

15.3.8 Fireworks. Chris Von der Ahe initiated the use of fireworks at the ballpark shortly after purchasing the Brown Stockings in 1882 (J. Thomas Hetrick, *Chris Von der Ahe and the St. Louis Browns*, 11). A few years later he announced plans to use pyrotechnics for an entirely different purpose. Before the 1886 season the *Boston Globe* reported, "Chris Van [sic] der Ahe has a new scheme. He intends to fire off a bomb that can be heard all over St. Louis five minutes before the beginning of each game. His object is to notify people on bad days if there is to be a game" (*Boston Globe*, January 18, 1886). It seems unlikely that this harebrained scheme was ever tried; if it were, Von der Ahe would presumably have quickly learned that there were a lot of St. Louis residents who preferred not to receive such notifications. That same year the Metropolitans were moved to Staten Island in order to pair baseball with "other attractions, such as electric and pyrotechnical displays" (*Sporting News*, May 17, 1886).

15.3.9 Hit/Error Posted on Scoreboard. John B. Foster reported in 1923 that there had been a proposal at the recent American League meetings to post whether a play was scored as a hit or an error on league scoreboards. The proposal was defeated for a surprising reason. Foster explained that there was a significant amount of wagering in the stands on the result of individual plays, and the owners feared that posting scoring decisions would only encourage this practice (*Sporting News*, March 8, 1923).

The scheme does not appear to have reemerged until 1928, when the *New York Times* mentioned: "An innovation at the Polo Grounds is a system of signaling the official scorer's decision on closer plays. A little arm is thrown up on top of the score board, between 'strikes' and 'balls' and shows an 'H' for a hit and an 'E' for an error" (*New York Times*, April 14, 1928).

(iv) Souvenirs

Whether any object is worth keeping or not is in the eye of the beholder, a reality driven home to many youngsters when their prized baseball card collections were thrown out by unappreciative parents. In early baseball matches the losing club presented the winners with a baseball, and these were often regarded as trophies. For example, the Atlantics of Brooklyn preserved more than two hundred such souvenir balls in a glass case (photo in James L. Terry, *Long Before the Dodgers*, 77). But, as is explained in the chapter on marketing (see **16.2.7** "Keeping Balls in the Stands"), it was many years before spectators had the opportunity to keep foul balls.

Early baseball enthusiasts nevertheless accumulated a variety of keepsakes. Obvious candidates such as programs and baseball cards are discussed in the entries that follow, but they were far from the only souvenirs. Newspaper clippings were a popular one, as is shown by an 1886 reference to "the base ball cranks of Boston, such as General Dixwell, who keeps four different base ball scrapbooks, one for each Boston morning paper, and spends all the time he has when not witnessing ball games, in figuring out averages" (*Boston Globe*, May 17, 1886).

In general, collectibles were fairly rare among early baseball fans, and some of the items that were preserved are surprising. Seymour Church, for example, accumulated a large gallery of baseball-related art (*Sporting Life*, November 18, 1905).

15.4.1 Throwing Balls Back onto the Field. The practice recently popularized by Chicago Cubs fans of throwing opposition home run balls back onto the field is new to a certain extent, since it does not appear that fans had ever before done this to show their allegiance to the home team.

But there is nothing new about fans throwing balls back on the field. As noted in the introduction to this section, fans in early baseball were not allowed to keep foul balls, and regularly threw them back onto the field. Even when this began to change, some spectators followed the old practice; Shirley Povich noted in 1931 that fans at Griffith Stadium were given a "crescendo of razz" if they committed a "breach of etiquette" by tossing a ball back onto the field (*Washington Post*, July 6, 1931). During World War II it became customary for fans to throw foul balls back onto the field so they could be donated to military posts (William Mead, *Even the Browns*, 2).

15.4.2 Scorecards/Souvenir Programs. Scorecards had begun to appear by 1866 and are first known to have been sold at a match that year between the Atlantics of Brooklyn and the Athletics of Philadelphia (Dan Gutman, in *Banana Bats and Ding-Dong Balls*, 108, said the game occurred on October 11, 1866; in the special pictorial issue of the *National Pastime* in 1984, John Thorn gave the date as October 1, 1866; the two clubs actually played on the 15th and 22nd of that month). Researcher Mark Rucker tracked down a copy of "Parker's Improved Score Cards," used at a game played in Hoboken, New Jersey, on October 29, 1866 (Frederick Ivor-Campbell, "When Was the First? [Continued]," *Nineteenth Century Notes* 95:1 [Winter 1995], 2). The word "Improved" implies that they had been used still earlier.

An important step toward turning scorecards into keepsakes occurred in 1871 when Mort Rogers of Boston began selling scorecards with photographs. Another new touch was added in 1879 when it became popular to attach handles so that they could be used as fans (*Detroit Post and Tribune*, August 2, 1879).

By the 1880s scorecards were coming to be viewed as an essential part of the ballpark experience. An 1881 rule requiring managers to submit their lineups by 9 a.m. was intended to ensure that that game's scorecards were accurate (*New York Clipper*, January 8, 1881). *Sporting Life* observed in 1884, "one requires a score card at a ball game quite as much as a programme at a theatre. It is wanted for constant reference to identify players, positions, striking order, & c., even if you do not keep the score" (*Sporting Life*, April 23, 1884).

They were also becoming increasingly elaborate. The St. Louis Browns commemorated Ladies' Day in 1883 "by the presentation to every lady attending of a handsome souvenir score card" (*St. Louis Post-Dispatch*, May 23, 1883). Two days later the paper reported: "The 500 souvenir programmes . . . were given away early in the day."

A sure sign they were becoming more popular is the emergence of competition. An 1886 article observed, "Boston management refuses to give out the batteries because somebody is printing and selling a rival score card. In spite of this precaution the outside score-card people get it as right as the inside. In ten games the official score card has been right but two. The public wants to know who the pitchers are to be, and the management loses money by not announcing them" (*Boston Globe*, June 6, 1886).

The demand and the competition inspired some clubs to produce still fancier scorecards, as this 1890 article demonstrates: "The official score book of the Brooklyn Club, of the National League, is not only a novelty in its way, but is neat and handsome. The book contains thirty-two pages, over which are distributed beautifully engraved likenesses, with biographical sketches, of every member of the team. The two middle pages are devoted to the scoring of the game. The frontispiece is the design of Secretary Charley Ebbets, of the Brooklyn Club. The bat contains the name 'Brooklyn.' The homeplate beneath has the words 'at home with,' and then twenty-four balls, arranged in the form of a diamond, has the games to be played at home, and in chronological order. Upon each corner is a base with various inscriptions thereon. Nothing like this score book has ever been published before" (*New York Clipper*, May 3, 1890).

15.4.3 Baseball Cards. Baseball and photographs began to—ahem—develop at about the same time, and there was a natural desire to combine them. As documented in Mark Rucker's beautiful book *Base Ball Cartes*, one of the earliest manifestations occurred in the 1860s with the carte de visite. As Rucker explained, a carte de visite was a paper photoprint of approximately two-and-a-half by four inches that was glued to a card mount. The carte de visite originated in France in the 1850s and was popular in the United States in the 1860s and 1870s.

These cartes gradually evolved into trade cards, with the photographs of ballplayers being used to promote businesses or commercial products. Cigarette manufacturers began to mass-produce them in the 1880s (David Pietrusza, Lloyd Johnson, and Bob Carroll, eds., *Total Baseball Catalog*, 118).

The first card to depict a bat-and-ball game may predate the Knickerbockers. Researchers Henry Thomas and Frank Ceresi reported that a card depicting a pitcher tossing a ball to a batsman was discovered in a Maine attic a few years ago. While the exact date and provenance of the card cannot be established, there is evidence that it may date to the 1830s and be part of a series of illustrated children's educational cards (http://www.fcassociates.com/ntearlybb.htm).

15.4.4 Tickets. Lee Allen pointed out that the greatest obstacle to tickets becoming souvenirs was a practical one: "In the earliest days spectators turned in oblong tickets, which the takers deposited in boxes and used again and again for subsequent contests" (Lee Allen, *The Hot Stove League*, 95).

At least one person must have hung on to a ticket from an 1866 game, since sportswriter William Rankin reported in 1909, "I have one of the original tickets used on the old Capitoline Grounds, Brooklyn, in 1866. The size of the ticket—which is red,—and the inscription on it, are as follows:

Capitoline Grounds

25 CENTS

Weed & Decker, Proprietors" (*Sporting News*, October 7, 1909).

The twentieth century has seen interest in this form of souvenir manifest itself in particularly excessive forms. For example, sportswriter Jerry Crasnick observed: "There were 15,758 people in the Wrigley Field stands on May 6, 1998, when Cubs righthander Kerry Wood struck out 20 Astros in his fifth major league start. A day later, 150 would-be capitalists called the Cubs' box office looking for unsold tickets from the game as collector's items" (Jerry Crasnick, *Baseball America*, October 27–November 9, 2003).

15.4.5 Autographs. According to Lee Allen, the first recorded autograph request was received by the Cincinnati Reds on May 10, 1890, from a woman who was working on a quilt and wanted to reproduce the players' signatures (Lee Allen, *The Hot Stove League*, 147).

At first pass it would seem unlikely that an 1890 autograph request could be a first. A fascination with autographs that was initially considered a "fad" swept the country in 1883 (*Washington Post*, April 8, 1883). The fad proved to have staying power, and between 1890 and 1910 "a flood of magazine articles defined the 'art' of autograph collecting" (Frank W. Hoffmann and William G. Bailey, *Sports and Recreation Fads*, 19–21).

Rather than targeting athletes, however, early autograph seekers generally sought out intellectuals. Serious hobbyists wrote letters to prominent writers, politicians, scientists, and ministers in hopes of receiving a signed letter in reply. These requests placed considerable demands on the time of recipients, and collectors gradually realized that their chance of success was better if they asked only for a signature.

The fact that ballplayers were not the targets of early autograph collectors reflects the low social status of athletes at the beginning of the twentieth century. Turn-of-the-century outfielder Davy Jones, for example, had to break up with his high school sweetheart: "baseball wasn't a very respectable occupation back then . . . after I became a professional ballplayer her parents refused to let me see her any more. Wouldn't let her have anything more to do with me. In those days a lot of people looked upon ballplayers as bums, too lazy to work for a living" (Lawrence S. Ritter, *The Glory of Their Times*, 38).

The status of baseball players rose rapidly in the first few decades of the twentieth century. In 1925 Ty Cobb observed, "There was a time—twenty years ago—when first-class hotels would not take ball clubs as guests. Now the most refined hotels in the country seek baseball patronage. That is certainly an indication of progress" (Ty Cobb, *Memoirs of Twenty Years in Baseball*, 6). (An indirect beneficiary of this progress was Davy Jones, who ran into his high school sweetheart after both were widowed and finally married her.)

This coincided with autograph seekers beginning to seek signatures instead of highly crafted letters, with the result that it became more and more common to target athletes and movie stars. By 1937 requests to ballplayers for autographs had become common enough that Pepper Martin began using a rubber stamp for autographs.

15.4.6 Stamps. The first U.S. postage stamp with a baseball theme was issued in 1939 to honor the centenary of the now discredited story of Abner Doubleday's invention of the game. Several foreign countries had earlier featured baseball on stamps, beginning with the Philippines in 1934 (Robert Obojski, *Baseball Memorabilia*, 89).

15.4.7   Bobbleheads, etc. Researcher Andy McCue reported that longtime Los Angeles Dodgers concessionaire Danny Goodman claimed to have introduced bobblehead dolls and plastic bats, both in 1958, as well as souvenir hats, pennants, and other souvenirs (Andy McCue, "The King of Coolie Hats," *National Pastime* 19 [1999], 24–27).

15.4.8   Fantasy Camps. Randy Hundley staged the first fantasy camp for adults in Scottsdale, Arizona, in January 1983. Sixty-three men paid $2,195 each to work out with members of the 1969 Cubs (Roy Blount, Jr., "We All Had a Ball," in John Thorn, ed., *The Armchair Book of Baseball*, 67–82).

Chapter 16

MARKETING
AND PROMOTIONS

"What is the use in doing anything to help baseball? Ain't we done everything we could do to kill it? And look at it!" (Pirates owner Barney Dreyfuss, quoted in *Sporting News*, February 9, 1922).

"I don't care what you say about me or my ball club, just so you say something" (onetime Cubs owner Charles Webb Murphy, a former journalist, quoted in *Sporting News*, December 15, 1921).

A CHAPTER on marketing was not in the original plans for this book. The idea gradually forced itself upon me as entry after entry showed that many of baseball's best marketing techniques were not created by design. In fact a long line of the innovations that have helped increase the audience for the game first had to overcome stubborn resistance from ownership.

In most cases the owners have contended that the benefits of exposure were outweighed by the costs of what they viewed as giving away their product. Eventually they have given in and reluctantly embraced new media and concepts that have brought baseball to a wider audience and thereby paved the way for the wealth that the game enjoys today.

An irritated Ted Sullivan once observed that baseball owners were "wise in everything, excepting the art of making the public believe that the time has come to give up the half-a-dollars . . . they do everything on earth excepting to make arrangements for the pleasing of the public. I cannot understand it. I fail to remember any particular occasion when any considerable crowd of people went out to a ball park to look at a magnate" (*Sporting Life*, January 5, 1901).

The point is not simply to bash the owners. There are two basic ways to promote a product: by making it scarce and hoping to increase its perceived value, or by giving it away. Needless to say, the two are in direct conflict, meaning that promotional efforts always tiptoe a delicate line between exposure and overexposure.

In many cases, as we shall see, the owners had understandable reservations that would have concerned any good businessperson. But by putting these items together in a chapter, a clear and intriguing pattern emerges in which efforts that were initially deemed to be "giving the product away" have consistently been the ones that produced long-term growth.

That pattern is, I believe, worthy of consideration by the people who currently market baseball. They might particularly want to think about it when they reflect upon the shortsighted policy of allowing World Series games to start at times that assure they will conclude after the bedtimes of the next generation of fans.

The first section of this chapter considers planned promotional events, such as days and giveaway items. The second section examines the unplanned promotional concepts that have often overcome the protests of owners to outstrip promotions that were carefully conceived. The third section looks at mass media, as the inception of each new medium has led to an impassioned dispute about whether it will attract new fans or cause existing ones to stay at home.

(i) Planned Days and Events

16.1.1 Schedules. The practice of giving away pocket schedules was in vogue by the 1870s, with the *Chicago Tribune* observing in 1879: "Clayton and Co., of 83 Madison Street, have issued for gratuitous distribution neat cards giving the dates and places of all League games for the season. They are convenient and popular" (*Chicago Tribune*, April 6, 1879).

16.1.2 Advertising Campaigns. Nineteenth-century baseball clubs naturally thought about ways to advertise games, but their efforts remained modest. According to Harold Seymour, most settled for notices in the local papers and such methods as "streetcar billing, sign boards at street corners, handbills, window hangers, posters, and boys parading the streets with banners" (Harold Seymour, *Baseball: The Early Years*, 196).

By the mid-1880s clubs were at least thinking about new ways to attract spectators. As noted under "Fireworks" (see **15.3.8**), Chris Von der Ahe announced before the 1886 season that he would "fire off a bomb that can be heard all over St. Louis five minutes before the beginning of each game" (*Boston Globe*, January 18, 1886). There is no evidence that his scheme was tried, but he did display a golden ball with the words "Game Today" or a flag reading "No Game Today" from the Golden Lion Saloon (Harold Seymour, *Baseball: The Early Years*, 196).

Another club devised a much more ambitious approach. The *Cleveland Leader and Herald* explained: "Detroit believes that advertising is profitable. The base ball games in that city this season will be billed like a circus. Secretary [Bob] Leadley is sending out advertising matter for the opening games in Detroit to all the cities and villages throughout the State, and excursion trains will be run to many of the games" (*Cleveland Leader and Herald*, April 26, 1886).

Most nineteenth-century clubs, however, relied upon less expensive forms of marketing. Until around 1910, major league teams commonly dressed at their hotel so that the players could serve as moving billboards as they walked to the ballpark (Gerard S. Petrone, *When Baseball Was Young*, 17). This practice continued in the minor leagues; a 1917 article observed: "Under a ruling adopted at the [Western League's] meeting visiting teams must 'parade the streets to the parks in uniforms,' for the purpose, it was said, of advertising" (*Sporting Life*, January 27, 1917).

Philip K. Wrigley brought a new sophistication to baseball marketing shortly after he inherited the Chicago Cubs from his father in 1932. J. G. Taylor Spink reported in 1935 that the maverick Wrigley was launching an actual advertising campaign, "somewhat to the amazement of his fellow magnates." Wrigley's bold idea was a series of advertisements in Chicago papers over the winter designed to bolster attendance that summer. No doubt the bleak economic situation contributed to his willingness to try new ways of drawing fans to the ballpark.

Wrigley's assistant, Charles F. Drake, explained that "the theme of the campaign is sunshine, recreation and pleasure. Mr. Wrigley is applying merchandising methods to baseball. It is his belief that, in the past, too much stress has been laid upon the team through newspaper publicity and not enough attention given to selling baseball as a great outdoor game, offering many healthful benefits and hours of pleasure to the fans. It is perhaps unusual to launch a campaign of this character in the winter, with no immediate prospects of a return at the gates. But Mr. Wrigley has found in his chewing gum business that constant repetition of advertising builds in the public's consciousness a desire for a product, so he is applying the same principle to advertising the Cubs."

In addition, Wrigley had hired a young man whose job was "to circulate through the park, learn the wishes of the fans, and try in every way possible to obtain ideas that will make Wrigley Field more enjoyable." He could hardly have found someone better suited for the position: the young man he hired was none other than Bill Veeck (*Sporting News*, January 17, 1935).

16.1.3   Public Relations Director. In 1905 the Giants assigned Charles Webb Murphy to head "the club's Bureau of Publicity." Murphy "started off at a rapid pace, and he promises to keep the scribes loaded up with stories. Murphy's engagement is another illustration of the changes that follow when competition becomes keen" (*Sporting Life*, February 18, 1905). But his tenure was brief because later that year Murphy purchased the Cubs, who became the Giants' bitter rivals.

It appears to have been another twenty-five years before the position reemerged. Gene Karst was a reporter for the *St. Louis Globe-Democrat* in 1930 and was frustrated by the poor quality of the publicity material provided by major league teams. Much of the copy was written by the traveling secretary, and Karst found that he had to entirely rewrite it to make it usable.

That gave Karst an idea, and that winter he wrote to Branch Rickey, of the St. Louis Cardinals, who hired him to publicize the club (Bill Borst, *Baseball Through a Knothole*, 60–61). Karst summarized his responsibilities: "I offered radio stations and metropolitan and rural newspapers within a 300-mile area baseball material featuring the Cardinals. This resulted in our getting great quantities of space in numerous sports pages and lots of free time on the radio. The game was not so commercialized in those days. Players cooperated, making public appearances on the air and at community-sponsored luncheons and dinners, for free" (Gene Karst, "Ready for the New Asterisk War?," *Baseball Research Journal* 26 [1997], 66–67). All the free exposure thus garnered helped broaden and expand the club's fan base.

16.1.4   Days. A common feature of early baseball was the benefit game, which was staged to raise proceeds for a needy player or someone else associated with the game. It was also customary to admit women free because of their beneficial influence on the male patrons (see **16.1.7** "Ladies' Day"). But today's practice of having fan-oriented days, either to attract a certain type of spectator or to give a free item to fans, does not seem to have appeared until the 1880s. Lee Allen reported that the Phillies held a bootblack day during spring training in 1883, admitting bootblacks, newsboys, and other urchins free (Lee Allen, *Sporting News*, April 20, 1968, reprinted in *Cooperstown Corner*).

Jonathan Fraser Light reported that a number of clubs held days in 1915 in response to the rival Federal League. These included Boosters Day, Flag Day, Newsboy Day, and Schoolchildren's Day (Jonathan Fraser Light, *The Cultural Encyclopedia of Baseball*, 593).

It was not until the 1930s that baseball clubs began to make extensive use of marketing techniques to lure fans to the ballpark. One such entrepreneur was Al Eckert of Springfield, Missouri, whose initiatives prompted *Sporting News* to report in 1933 that "special nights of all sorts have been found highly successful by [Al] Eckert. At these 'special nights' he has staged pajama parades, horse shows, given away electric refrigerators, cash, free tickets, honored various ball players, and managers, used the city's famous Boy Scout band for concerts before the games, and countless other little tricks to pep up attendance" (*Sporting News*, January 19, 1933).

Not everyone welcomed this innovation. A *Sporting News* editorial in 1935 noted that such events boosted attendance but warned that they also had "a tendency to cheapen the game if indulged in too often. Such days may keep the ordinary fan at home waiting for a bargain day. He asks himself why he should pay the regular price for admission when his attendance can be postponed until a 'community day.' He gets the idea that baseball is available with the purchase of a tube of shaving cream or a loaf of bread, or that a quarter will do the same duty at the park gate as will a half-dollar or dollar." The editorial concluded that the "community day" was a good idea on rare occasions, "but harmful if it becomes a common practice" (*Sporting News*, July 18, 1935).

16.1.5   Fan Appreciation Days. *Sporting News* reported in 1933 that Larry MacPhail, then president of the Columbus team, had "inaugurated a system of 'appreciation days,' on which thousands of unemployed fans were permitted to witness the games free of charge" (*Sporting News*, February 23, 1933).

16.1.6   Bat Days. The idea of giving a free item to fans may have occurred to some early club owners, but they no doubt concluded that the expenses would outweigh the benefits. In particular, giving away a valuable item like a bat would have seemed madness.

Accordingly, it was not until 1952 and under unusual circumstances that Bat Day became part of baseball. Bill Veeck was running the St. Louis Browns "when a guy who dealt in bankrupt firms came around with a shipload of homeless bats. I foisted him off on Rudie Schaffer, and Rudie worked out a deal in which we paid eleven cents for every finished bat, and the guy threw in all the unfinished ones for free. This gave us some indication why the firm had gone bankrupt, since the wood alone was worth more than we were paying. Rudie came back and suggested that we give them away on Father's Day" (Bill Veeck with Ed Linn, *The Hustler's Handbook*, 16).

The giveaway proved very popular, and similar events were successfully tried in other cities. This helped change the idea of a promotional day from one on which certain types of fans got in free to one in which the fans got free stuff.

16.1.7 Ladies' Days. In an important sense there is no such thing as a first Ladies' Day, since the practice of admitting female spectators without charge began almost as soon as admissions were charged at baseball games. This course was initiated in Brooklyn in 1865: "Hereafter ladies will be admitted free of charge, to all matches on the Capitoline grounds. No tickets of admission will be required" (*Brooklyn Eagle*, September 4, 1865). At one of the first games with paid admission in Michigan, a state championship game on June 8, 1866, between the host Detroit Base Ball Club and the Washington Base Ball Club of Bay City, men were charged ten cents while women were admitted free. Similarly, admission was first charged in St. Louis for a game on July 10, 1867, with men paying twenty-five cents and ladies being admitted gratis (E. H. Tobias, *Sporting News*, November 16, 1895).

The practice remained common for many years to come. Ladies were admitted free when the Red Stockings played at Pittsfield, Massachusetts, on June 3, 1870 (Greg Rhodes and John Erardi, *The First Boys of Summer*, 103). It was reported that the customary free list would be suspended for a much-anticipated 1875 game in Detroit, with the "exception of ladies, who are always free" (*Detroit Evening News*, August 28, 1875). A typical 1876 ad in a Rochester, New York, newspaper read: "ADMISSION TWENTY FIVE CENTS, LADIES FREE" (*Rochester Democrat and Chronicle*, September 1, 1876; reprinted in Priscilla Astifan, "Rochester's Last Two Seasons of Amateur Baseball: Baseball in the Nineteenth Century, Part Four," *Rochester History* LXIII, No. 2 [Spring 2001], 8). In 1878 the *Washington Post* reported that "admission is fixed at the low figure of ten cents, with no charge for ladies" (*Washington Post*, April 25, 1878). There is documentation of countless other instances.

Special arrangements were often made for women attending early baseball games. At an 1857 match it was reported that "A tent for the female friends of the players had been prepared" (*New York Clipper*, July 18, 1857). Separate seating accommodations for women was also a common practice.

This was not simply a case of generosity or chivalry on the part of owners, since it was generally accepted that the presence of women increased male attendance and ensured better behavior from the men. As Henry Chadwick explained, "The presence of an assemblage of ladies pacifies the moral atmosphere of a base ball gathering, repressing, as it does, all outbursts of intemperate language which the excitement of a contest so frequently induces" (*The Ball Player's Chronicle*, June 13, 1867).

The attentions directed at female spectators sometimes had unexpected results. One newspaper account chided Frank Norton for having "one bad fault, and that is endeavoring to make fancy catches when the ladies are on the ground. Those look pretty but are not safe" (William Rankin scrapbook, April 17, 1869). And a University of Michigan student managed to get picked off first base while trying to catch the eye of a "pretty Detroit lady in the gallery" (*Detroit Post*, September 30, 1867).

It has often been reported that Ladies' Day originated in the 1880s and was either invented by Abner Powell or popularized by handsome pitcher Tony Mullane. It is true that it became more popular to advertise Ladies' Day as an attraction in the 1880s. But the billing of Ladies' Day as a special event suggests not that this was a new idea but just the opposite—that it had become the norm to charge women for admission.

In succeeding years Ladies' Day went in and out of fashion as owners vacillated on whether they could afford to admit women for free, which led to considerable confusion. Curt Smith, for example, credited the invention of Ladies' Day to William Wrigley, who bought a controlling interest in the Cubs in 1918 (Curt Smith, *Voices of the Game*, 14). Incredibly, *Baseball Magazine* ran an article on Ladies' Day in 1939, asking players' opinions on the idea, which apparently was again being considered new. Jim Bagby, Jr., called Ladies' Day "a truly wonderful institution" and added, "I wonder why they didn't think of it a long time ago" (Harold Winerip, "Opinions on Ladies' Day," *Baseball Magazine*, July 1939; reprinted in Sidney Offit, ed., *The Best of Baseball*, 132–136). Ummmm, they did!

16.1.8 Name-the-team Contest. In the nineteenth century the formal name of a club was usually along the lines of the "Washington Base Ball Club." Many clubs did have nicknames and some of these were long-standing, but others were prone to change without much warning if their popularity waned.

The first name-the-team contest seems to have taken place in 1905, when *Sporting Life* informed its readers: "The new owners of the Washingtons are tired of the nickname 'Senators,' and want somebody to suggest something better. President [Thomas C.] Noyes has offered a season ticket to the person sending in the best nickname for the club" (*Sporting Life*, February 11, 1905). The *Washington Post* reported a month later that 2,305 suggestions had been received, some of which "contained a great deal of originality. One man asks that the club be called the 'Ball-bearers,' because they are so easily worked. Another thinks the 'Weather Prophets' would be a good name, presumably because they are so unreliable. Others want the club called the 'Worms,' because they will turn. Some names in the batch that will probably be considered are Atoners, Waifs and Improvers" (*Washington Post*, March 12, 1905). Eventually the name "Nationals" was selected because this was the name of successful Washington clubs of old.

Ironically the "new" name did not capture the public imagination, and newspapers soon began to refer to the team as the Senators. Nonetheless Nationals remained the club's official nickname until 1956. Another strange coincidence occurred when baseball returned to Washington a century after this contest and once again settled upon the name of Nationals.

16.1.9 Talking to Fans. Perhaps the ultimate example that the people who run baseball have not always promoted their product very well was a rule instituted by the National League in 1932 that uniformed personnel could not talk to fans. On April 27, Cardinals manager Gabby Street broke the rule in a game in Cincinnati when an uncle whom he had not seen in twenty years hailed him. Street stopped to talk to his long-lost relative and was fined five dollars for doing so (*Sporting News*, May 5, 1932). The bizarre rule was rescinded on May 19 of the same year.

(ii) Promotional Concepts and Themes

16.2.1 The National Pastime. Arguably baseball's first and most effective marketing technique was the positioning of baseball as America's national game. This will be discussed in more detail in Chapter 25.

16.2.2 Code of Conduct. Owners have long recognized that squeaky-clean behavior by the players would be beneficial for the game. Getting them to act so is another matter. The *St. Louis Post-Dispatch*, for example, wrote in 1889, "Such language as 'say, yer rotten, yer stinkin',' as Tebeau yelled frequently at Latham yesterday is rather coarse to be used in the presence of ladies and should not be tolerated on the ball field" (*St. Louis Post-Dispatch*, April 27, 1889). But how do you prevent players from hollering "yer rotten, yer stinkin'"?

Clubs of course have always been free to implement and enforce their own team rules, and many have tried to require a high standard of personal conduct. Philadelphia owner John I. Rogers, for example, claimed in 1898 that all his players had signed temperance pledges (*St. Louis Post-Dispatch*, April 10, 1898). But this could obviously lead to double standards for star players.

In 1898 the National League adopted a much more comprehensive player behavior code which had been devised by Cincinnati owner John T. Brush. The Brush Resolution was intended to eliminate cursing and other conduct that was being blamed for declining attendance, but the penalties that it authorized proved too harsh. No one was willing to report violations, and the scheme died a quiet death.

A still more unrealistic approach was to involve law enforcement, such as when catcher John J. Dillon of Albany was arrested for using profane language during a game at Binghamton on June 12, 1905 (*Sporting Life*, July 1, 1905). Such efforts were obviously doomed, and though the standard players' contract continued to forbid certain activities, the owners gradually came to accept that some forms of morality cannot be legislated.

When the All-American Girls Baseball League was formed in 1943, it made a similar effort. The league instituted a strict contract filled with behavioral restrictions based upon the Actors' Equity agreement. Players were forbidden, among other things, from smoking, drinking hard liquor, or appearing "unkempt" in public. Any social engagement had to be approved in advance by the club's chaperone.

Nor were the clauses restricted to "don'ts." In the early years of the league, players were required to attend a charm school at which they were taught etiquette for social occasions, beauty tips, and how to "avoid noisy, rough and raucous talk and actions." One player later remembered how hard it was "to walk in high heels with a book on your head when you had a charley horse" (Lois Browne, *Girls of Summer*, 38–39, 43–45).

16.2.3   Spite Fences. In 2002 the Chicago Cubs draped their wire fences behind the bleachers to prevent the long-standing practice of watching the game from the rooftops of the apartments overlooking Wrigley Field. This was only the latest—and indeed was one of the most civil—skirmishes in a perennial battle. Indeed, it is not too strong to say that no sooner did baseball begin to be played in enclosed stadiums (see **14.1.1**) than people started trying to find sneaky ways to get inside the walls or watch the game by some other means.

This was particularly common in the early days of professional baseball. In 1876 Boston installed a barbed wire fence around the South End Grounds and reported that it significantly reduced the number of gate-crashers (Michael Gershman, *Diamonds*, 29). That alone did not prove enough, and three years later the club announced plans to make the fence around the grounds "20 feet higher, much to the grief and disgust of the people on adjacent streets who have been in the habit of letting seats on their roofs at reduced rates" (*New York Clipper*, September 13, 1879).

Similar conflicts were occurring in other cities. Hartford president Morgan Bulkeley erected an addition to his outfield fence that year to stem the practice of parking carriages outside the grounds and charging people to sit on top of them (David Arcidiacono, *Grace, Grit and Growling*, 61). A different tack was taken in Rochester, New York, where the club persuaded the city fire marshal and wooden building commissioner to declare rooftop throngs unsafe (Priscilla Astifan, "Baseball in the Nineteenth Century Part V: 1877—Rochester's First Year of Professional Baseball," *Rochester History* LXIV, No. 4 [Fall 2002], 5).

The *Washington Post* complained in 1878, "unless the lovers of this game relinquish choice positions outside the fence and plunk down their money and come within, the plans of the club for a brilliant series of games will be seriously crippled" (*Washington Post*, April 22, 1878). The *Brooklyn Eagle* observed that same year: "The Centennial Ground is not the most attractive place for spectators. If the covered seats happen to be full—and they only seat about 200 on each stand—and the people have to stand around to watch the game, they immediately become the target of abuse from the fence peepers, who claim the right to drive every man standing inside the enclosure who is in the way of their view out of their view" (*Brooklyn Eagle*, August 22, 1878).

The following year Henry Chadwick urged the Jersey City management "to put up some barrier cutting off the free view of the play on the field obtained from the trestle-work 'grand-stand' outside the inclosure back of the catcher's position" (*New York Clipper*, June 28, 1879).

This was clearly about more than just saving money, since some spectators were so anxious to get a free view of the action that they disregarded personal safety. The *Washington Post* observed in 1884, "The building inspector has warned the owners of the building near the National grounds not to allow so many people on the roof of the building. An accident is liable to occur there any game" (*Washington Post*, July 6, 1884). Twice during the 1875 season, spectators in Columbus, Ohio, were injured when the roof of a shack near the park collapsed under the weight of too many people (*New York Clipper*, July 24, 1875).

A paper in Columbus, Ohio, reported in 1883: "The owner of the lot on the west side of Recreation Park not being satisfied with a scaffold, has erected a regular tier of seats over looking the grounds. He will probably make quite a 'spec' tomorrow on this little enterprise, although he is reported as being opposed to Sunday games. As a piece of 'gall' and littleness this takes the premium" (*Columbus* [Ohio] *Sunday Morning News*, July 8, 1883).

But in fact, if such a premium had been offered, there would have been stiff competition. An 1886 account noted, "The directors of the Bridgeport Club have decided to tar the telegraph poles and the trees that surround their grounds so as to keep people from climbing them to watch the game" (*Detroit Free Press*, April 7, 1886). At a game in Boston on July 19, 1884, the spectators who climbed poles to witness the game got an even more unpleasant surprise. Someone painted the poles during the game, so the freeloaders had to ruin their clothes in order to get down (*Sporting Life*, July 30, 1884).

In 1886 the National League's Detroit Wolverines unsuccessfully sued a man who had been selling seats overlooking Recreation Park. After losing the case, the club built a fifty-foot fence to settle the matter. The *Detroit Free Press* reported, "The struggle of the tower stand-builders and the fence-builders is still going on at Recreation Park, with the odds in favor of the latter. An enterprising firm is erecting an advertising fence that will shut out the view from outside stands, and the sharks that have lived off the base ball club will have to go to work again" (*Detroit Free Press*, June 4, 1886).

That same season, Boston was involved in a conflict with an entrepreneur named Sullivan who erected a tall tower overlooking right field and began selling admission to it. Boston management erected a screen to block their view, so Mr. Sullivan added another story to his structure, prompting another addition to the screen (*Boston Globe*, May 31 and June 1, 1886).

Sullivan eventually outlasted the ball club, and Sullivan's Tower became one of the Hub's landmarks (*Boston Globe*, July 29, 1888; August 4, 1892; April 19, 1896). The tower inspired one regular to write a poem that included stanzas such as this one: "Packed like sardines in a box / One tier above another / We all look down for miles around / (Enough to make 'em shudder); / Some pays a dollar to see the fun, / But Me and Din McQuade, / We pays a dime to see the nine/ From Sullivan's palisade" (*Boston Globe*, July 10, 1889).

In the 1890s club owners began to use canvases. An 1894 account reported: "The [Norfolk] management have constructed a great scheme to down the 'dead heads' who line the roofs of houses surrounding the ball grounds. They have rigged up poles and run up canvas on them" (*Sporting Life*, May 5, 1894). Other ballpark owners followed suit, but such canvas contraptions weren't always foolproof. In 1893 the Renovo, Pennsylvania, "grounds were enclosed by a seven foot canvas. The canvas did not keep away the 'dead beats,' as the coal wharf and other elevated places were thronged by men and boys who wished to witness the sport without cost and without price. It appears the problem of making the non-players pay has not been solved by the canvas" (*Williamsport Sunday Grit*, May 21, 1893).

The multi-tiered stadiums built in the early twentieth century gradually made the issue less common. But the problem continued to plague semipro and barnstorming clubs. Guy Green, who managed a famous touring club of Indians in the first decade of the twentieth century, wrote with dismay about the "deadheads" who sought to watch without paying. He observed that "The number of people who will put forth five dollars' worth of effort in order to see a twenty-five cent ball game without paying the admission price, is surprising" (Guy W. Green, *Fun and Frolic with an Indian Ball Team*, 37–40). Small-town papers like the *Belle Plaine* (Minnesota) *Herald* regularly complained about spectators who "selected the best places to witness the game and then didn't even have a nickel when the hat was passed around" (Tom Melchior, *Belle Plaine Baseball, 1884–1960*, 47; also 50, 53, 69, etc.).

From time to time new moves and countermoves were introduced. In Adrian, Michigan, in 1910 the home team moved the location of the scoreboard in order to block the view of employees of the Lamb Fence Factory, who had been watching the games with a powerful telescope (Marc Okkonen, *Minor League Baseball Towns of Michigan*, 4).

The most celebrated case of the twentieth century took place at Philadelphia's Shibe Park, home of the Athletics. Soon after the park opened in 1909, residents on North Twentieth Street, across from the ballpark, began charging admission to watch games from their homes and rooftops. By the late 1920s the practice had grown to the point that thousands of spectators were watching from the rooftop stands, and the club felt compelled to act.

The Athletics first attempted to address the problem by using their political contacts to enforce building codes and fire regulations. Then they attempted to compromise by asking tenants to agree not to undersell them nor to sell the rooftop seats unless a game was sold out. When neither course was successful, the ball club took a more direct approach. Before the 1935 season the club built a thirty-eight-foot corrugated metal addition to the twelve-foot right-field fence.

The addition was constructed to end the practice of deadheading, but it may have ultimately done the club more harm than good. Bruce Kuklick noted that what became known as the "spite fence" engendered fan bitterness against the club that lasted for years and even generations (Bruce Kuklick, *To Every Thing a Season*, 73–76).

16.2.4 Doubleheaders. More than one game was sometimes played on a day in the early days of baseball, but this practice had largely ended before the advent of professional baseball. There were two good reasons for this. First, owners saw no reason to give away twice as much of their product for the regular price. Second, the absence of lights meant that play would have to begin very early to be certain of completing two games.

The Resolutes and Boston did play a planned doubleheader on July 4, 1873, with separate admissions being charged (William J. Ryczek, *Blackguards and Red Stockings*, 116). Twinbills were occasionally staged in the ensuing years, usually out of necessity when a canceled game had to be rescheduled.

As Charlie Bevis has reported, the 1880s saw separate-admission doubleheaders become common on holidays. Initially there were only two such holidays during the season—Decoration Day (now Memorial Day) and Independence Day. But in 1888 Labor Day began to be recognized by several states, and it became a national holiday in 1894. All three holidays provided a special opportunity for working-class fans to attend games, which ensured enough demand for a morning game and an afternoon game (Charlie Bevis, "Holiday Doubleheaders," *Baseball Research Journal* 33 [2004], 60–63).

By the turn of the century, holiday twinbills were routinely drawing enormous crowds. Cincinnati business manager Frank Bancroft tried to capitalize by introducing the idea of playing two games for a single admission price on nonholidays. He also coined a new term for them, as was explained in an 1898 article: "Bancroft is responsible for 'double header' being used to designate 2 games for 1 price of admission. Bannie advertised his double attraction as a 'double header,' and it was not long until every club in the league was using the term" (*Cincinnati Enquirer*, July 24, 1898).

The practice was met with considerable resistance. Sportswriter H. G. Merrill, for example, argued that the practice cheapened the game: "I sincerely trust that both the big leagues will refrain from indulging in doubleheaders, or 'bargain days' to the extent that was the case last season" (*Sporting News*, July 30, 1904).

Despite such naysayers, doubleheaders became a fan favorite. Researcher Charlie Bevis reported that during World War I the separate-admission twinbill began to go out of favor, and the 1920s saw the single-admission doubleheader become a mainstay on Sundays and holidays (Charlie Bevis, "Holiday Doubleheaders," *Baseball Research Journal* 33 [2004], 60–63).

16.2.5 Pennant Races. A pennant race is one of the most surefire ways to raise the level of interest in baseball, though it is impossible to guarantee one. Indeed, the paradoxical reality is that it is easier for a league's owners to do things to ruin the pennant race of a rival league than to ensure that they have one themselves. It is sometimes claimed, for example, that the American League made a deliberate effort in its early years to sign players from every National League team except Pittsburgh, thereby ensuring that the Pirates would run away with the pennant. While it seems unlikely that there really was a plan by the American League, that situation did in fact prevail and the National League's dull pennant races helped the American League gain fans.

16.2.6 World Series. The World Series has proved to be a crucial marketing tool for baseball, creating the suspense and anticipation that enliven the dog days of the long season. Like so many of the game's most effective marketing devices, its importance was discovered accidentally.

As noted in the chapter on competition, baseball postseason championships date back to the early 1880s. These were, however, generally viewed by those inside baseball as being a way of making a little extra money. There was an understandable sentiment that the season-long accomplishment of amassing the best record was a more significant achievement than the results of a short series.

This was particularly the case in the early 1880s when the American Association was perceived as being inferior to the National League. As the decade wore on, the strengths of the two leagues became more balanced, and interest in the series showed a corresponding rise. When the two leagues merged after the 1891 season, the newly formed big league experimented with a couple of different formats for recapturing fan interest. These showed some promise at first, but anticipation about a series between clubs that had been competing all year soon waned. The lack of interest reflected the fact that the players regarded the regular season as the true championship and the Temple Cup as merely a way to make some quick cash.

The American League's emergence as a rival major league in 1901 and the peace treaty between the leagues two years later created a potential windfall. Not only was there natural curiosity about which champion club was better, but the interest was further fueled by the well-documented animosity between the two leagues. Baseball cashed in on the situation with a World Series in 1903 that was a financial success, and yet many within baseball viewed the event as little more than an exhibition.

The 1904 season saw renewed enmity between the two leagues that piqued interest in a postseason series. Instead, as the New York Giants moved toward clinching the 1904 National League pennant, club owner John T. Brush announced that his team would not face the American League champions. He explained that the champion of the National League should not have "to submit its championship honors to a contest with a victorious club of a minor league" (quoted in Benton Stark, *The Year They Called Off the World Series*, 160).

This reasoning was obviously disingenuous, since the American League's representatives had triumphed in the 1903 series. It is equally clear that Brush's decision was greatly influenced by the seething resentment that he and Giants manager John McGraw held for key American League figures, most notably circuit president Ban Johnson.

Nonetheless it must be emphasized that Brush's position is far more reasonable than it appears today. He and McGraw were voicing the sentiment of many by viewing the regular season as the true championship and believing that postseason games could only detract from that accomplishment. Whether this was their true motive or merely a justification, the principle they cited is a legitimate one. McGraw had especially good reason to have felt this way, since he had played in all four Temple Cups in the early 1890s (see **22.2.2** "Intramural Playoffs") and learned how a postseason playoff can undermine the regular season. Moreover, the fact that the Giants were sacrificing the opportunity to make a substantial amount of money suggests that principle played at least some role in their decision.

Whatever their motivation, Brush and McGraw seem to have been genuinely surprised by the extent of the backlash that ensued. The *New York World* typified the response, asking what right Brush had "to deprive the baseball public of an opportunity to see what would undoubtedly be the most interesting baseball series ever played? He gets his money from the sport-loving public of this city and should consider their wishes" (quoted in Benton Stark, *The Year They Called Off the World Series*, 163). The *Chicago Tribune* was even more direct, calling Brush "a businessman, and not in any sense of the word a sportsman" (quoted in Benton Stark, *The Year They Called Off the World Series*, 165). Note the fascinating turn of events: instead of being credited for forsaking a mercenary series, Brush is being accused of denying the public of something they demanded.

Fans joined in the outcry, with one writing: "Public opinion says play! and few there are who have dared to face public opinion and attend its overthrow!" (letter to *New York Herald* by C. Allyn Stephens; quoted in Benton Stark, *The Year They Called Off the World Series*, 164). John Brush stuck to his guns, and the World Series was not played that year. Nonetheless he clearly realized that he had misgauged public sentiment and, as a result, forsaken both a lucrative opportunity and a splendid marketing tool for baseball. That offseason he helped negotiate the Brush Rules, which established the World Series as an annual showcase for baseball.

16.2.7 Keeping Balls in the Stands. Early baseball matches concluded with the ritual of the losers presenting a baseball to the winning side. Some clubs would proudly display the balls thus earned in a special trophy case (see **22.3.1** "Trophies"). While few of today's fans are aware of this long-extinct custom, the mad scrambles for foul balls suggest that fans continue to sense that there is a special status associated with taking a ball home from the game.

In early baseball there was no question of fans keeping balls that went into the stands. As noted in the entry on new baseballs (**1.26**), the rules referred to the ball in the singular until 1876. The rules also specified that the game be stopped for up to five minutes so that players could search for a lost ball. As late as the 1880s, legendary manager Harry Wright was keeping a log of every ball owned by his team and its condition.

Nor were balls that were hit out of the grounds abandoned. Small children gathered outside ballparks during games, hoping to retrieve a foul ball and receive the customary reward of free admittance. As the *Chicago News* observed in 1884, "foul balls were invented in the interest of the small boy, and one is admitted every time the ball goes over the fence" (*Chicago News*, reprinted in the *Winnipeg Times*, May 23, 1884). But adherence to the custom was not universal; researcher David McDonald found that a Toronto paper reported in 1887: "Fifteen balls were knocked over the left field fence at Buffalo Monday and were stolen by bad boys" (*Toronto World*, June 1, 1887).

In response, clubs became more systematic in their ball-retrieval methods. Washington hired a fleet-footed groundskeeper named Charlie in 1892 to chase down balls. By 1899 the club had hired a fleet of young boys to fetch baseballs (Gerard S. Petrone, *When Baseball Was Young*, 58).

By the turn of the century it was becoming increasingly common for fans to try to retain foul balls. The *Detroit Free Press*, for example, recorded in 1902, "Baseballs that go into the stands at St. Louis are hopelessly lost, the man who first gets his hands on the flying sphere clinging to it" (*Detroit Free Press*, May 2, 1902).

But baseball management was not willing to surrender the point without a fight, sometimes literally. It is said that when a spectator at a game in New York refused to return a foul ball, John McGraw responded by stealing the man's hat. At least a couple of fans—one in Washington in 1901 and another in New York in 1903—were arrested for trying to keep foul balls (*Washington Post*, May 1, 1901; *New York Sun*, April 22, 1903). By 1904 the New York Giants were talking about broader measures: "A crusade against the holding out of balls hit into the bleachers is being introduced on the Polo Grounds. The practice has grown here at both grounds, and of late the pitchers have been forced to use a great many new balls in the course of a game. Secretary [Fred] Knowles says that hereafter anyone who keeps a ball batted or thrown into a stand will be arrested" (*Sporting Life*, August 27, 1904).

The contentious issue quickly spread to other cities. In Chicago, sportswriter W. A. Phelon reported, "[Club president] James A. Hart turned policeman the other day and his work in administering the law aroused great excitement in the stand. In these strenuous days of the big strike, policemen do not go to ball parks any more, while in former times it was impossible to bat a foul without hitting a copper. Hence the balls hit into the seats are not coming back as they used to and Mr. Hart determined to make an example of somebody. Finally, seeing a well-dressed man in a box hide a ball under his hat Mr. Hart went after him, pulled him out of his box, and after a short but brilliant battle, had him arrested. Harry Pulliam and Willie Shettsline watched the fray with great enthusiasm, and offered many valuable suggestions as to the best way of catching, holding and whacking the prisoner. The man—who turned out to be a prominent citizen named Scott—retaliated by getting out warrants charging Mr. Hart with fifty-seven different varieties of offenses" (*Sporting Life*, July 1, 1905). The man in question was actually a man named Samuel Stott, who was a member of the Board of Trade (*Chicago Tribune*, June 22, 1905).

The mayhem continued to spread to other cities. Francis Richter reported after a 1905 game in Philadelphia, "At least fifty balls were stolen during Saturday's game. Nearly every ball batted into the crowd was pocketed" (*Sporting Life*, July 15, 1905). *Sporting Life* noted the following year that "sometimes balls knocked into the crowd mysteriously disappear" (*Sporting Life*, March 31, 1906). In 1908 the *New York Tribune* reported: "Brooklynites seem to prize highly balls which go into the bleachers. During the preliminary practice [John] McGraw grew tired of seeing balls knocked into the stands never to return. He finally sent a policeman after them and they were thrown back. [Christy] Mathewson picked out a man whom he charged with stealing a ball and the culprit was arrested" (*New York Tribune*, April 21, 1908; reprinted in G. H. Fleming, *The Unforgettable Season*, 46).

As is suggested by this acrimony, the issue was not merely a symbolic one. For one thing, balls that were pocketed represented a sizable expense for club management. The *Ottawa Citizen* reported in 1913: "Prosecutions will follow if the deliberate appropriation of baseballs continues at Lansdowne Park. Yesterday no fewer than four which went into the grandstand were pocketed by souvenir-hunting fans or youngsters. The balls cost about $1.50 each, and the supply is one of the biggest items of expenditure which the Ottawa club has to foot. Chief Ross has instructed the men to keep a sharp lookout on the thieves" (*Ottawa Citizen*, August 19, 1913).

There were also other considerations. As it became harder to rely upon children to retrieve balls hit out of the park, more clubs began to station grown men behind the stands to throw back foul balls (*Boston Globe*; reprinted in *Sporting Life*, September 30, 1905). This undoubtedly began as a cost-saving measure, but before long it was recognized that this lent itself to strategic possibilities.

Brooklyn manager Wilbert Robinson began to notice in 1915 that the speed of ball retrieval in Boston seemed to vary according to which club was batting. Balls were returned much more rapidly when the visiting club was batting, thus giving the home club more opportunities to hit newer, livelier balls. Accordingly, "Claiming that Jack Coombs had been deprived of a win in Boston by fans keeping balls, [Robinson] urged Dodger fans to be selective, just as they were in Beantown. The locals there, he claimed, kept only balls that had been battered and scuffed when the local team was at bat. This forced the umpires to put a clean ball into the game to the advantage of Boston's batters. Robbie urged Brooklyn's fans to do the same. 'Throw back the scuffed balls if our team is in the field,' he counseled, 'and give our pitchers an edge.' To Ebbets' chagrin, Brooklyn fans were impartial in their greed. They kept every ball they could get their hands on and battled ushers and park police to keep them" (Jack Kavanagh and Norman Macht, *Uncle Robbie*, 79).

Since fans were no more willing to concede the point than were the denizens of baseball front offices, the conflict raged on. In addition, the nature of baseball meant there would be plenty of foul balls to spark such confrontations. As a result, ushers, policemen, and stadium officials continued to battle fans for stray balls, engendering no end of ill will.

The first man to wave the white flag was Cubs owner Charles Weeghman, who announced that the team's fans would be allowed to keep balls hit in the stands beginning on April 29, 1916. It is often assumed that Weeghman's concession was the turning point for the issue, but other owners were reluctant to follow his cue. The Phillies, for instance, requested compensation for eight baseballs hit into the stands during pregame batting practice at Weeghman Park and retained by the fans (*Chicago Tribune*, July 15, 1916).

It accordingly seems more accurate to view Weeghman's decision as the first of several important factors that led to the change. The second one was initiated during World War I when owners donated used balls to servicemen. As Billy Evans explained in 1920, this generosity had unintended consequences:

"The baseball fan for some reason believes any ball he grabs becomes his property. Such a custom was largely developed during the war days. At that time if a ball was fouled off and secured by one of the spectators he tossed it to one of the men in the service—provided an attendant approached to get the ball. If no attendant was in the vicinity the fan often appropriated the ball for himself. Otherwise he looked around for a fellow in the garb of the army or navy and tossed it to him. A patriotic spirit kept the attendant from seeking the ball from a man in the service.

"Now that the war is over, the custom of tossing the ball around the stand continues. If some one gets a ball, and an attaché of the park spots him, and approaches to get it, he tosses it back or forward a few rows. This practice continues until the attendant gives up in disgust" (*Sporting News*, December 30, 1920).

Another contributing factor was the concerted effort being made to replace used balls with fresh ones. While major league owners still wished to retain used balls, they now only wanted to do so for use in practice. This made the position of those charged with trying to retrieve balls even more difficult. How do you tell a fan who has caught a prize that it needs to be returned so it can be dropped in a ball bag for use in practice?

The trend toward replacing balls is often attributed to the fatal beaning of Ray Chapman in 1920. In fact it had begun more than a decade earlier and had accelerated when fans responded positively to the home run feats of Babe Ruth. But Chapman's tragic death certainly placed renewed emphasis on replacing sodden baseballs, since he had apparently been unable to pick up the discolored ball that killed him.

The final factor was a May 16, 1921, incident in which a fan named Reuben Berman caught a foul ball at the Polo Grounds. When asked to return it, Berman instead followed the practice described by Evans and tossed it to another spectator. He was interrogated by security officers and ejected from the ballpark after being refunded the price of his ticket. Berman sued for $2,000 in damages and won his case, though he was awarded only $100 (Peter Segroie, "Reuben's Ruling Helps You 'Have a Ball,'" *Baseball Research Journal* 20 [1991], 85; David Mandell, "Reuben Berman's Foul Ball," *National Pastime* 25 [2005], 106–107).

The decision in the Berman case applied only to New York, and even there it is far from clear that it would have survived appeal. The recent court case involving two fans who claimed to have ownership of Barry Bonds' seventy-third home run revealed that there is little legal precedence for the voluntary relinquishment of valuable property. So the club could certainly have taken its chances on appeal.

But developments of the preceding five years had changed the climate dramatically. Clubs were beginning to recognize that winning such legal battles would cost the club more in ill will than it would save in used balls. Thus the Giants gave in to the inevitable and decided not to appeal.

The issue continued to flare up in other ballparks. Within months of the Berman case, Pittsburgh police arrested three fans for keeping foul balls at Pirates games. The fans threatened legal action and caused Pittsburgh Director of Public Safety Robert Alderdice to instruct Pittsburgh policemen to stop such arrests (*New York Times*, July 10, 1921). Park officials, however, could still take action.

The next year an eleven-year-old Philadelphia boy named Robert Cotter was arrested and spent a night in jail for keeping a foul ball. He was released by a judge who commented, "Such an act on the part of a boy is merely proof that he is following his most natural impulses. It is a thing I would do myself" (Tim Wiles, "The Joy of Foul Balls," *National Pastime* 25 [2005], 104).

A similar incident was reported in the *Washington Post* the following year: "Refusal to return a foul ball which had been knocked into the grandstand at American League park during yesterday's game between Detroit and Washington caused the arrest of William E. Drury, of Leonardtown, Md., on the charge of petty larceny. According to the report made at the Eighth precinct, where Drury was booked and later released on $5 collateral, Drury caught the ball as it entered the stand and refused to surrender it when requested to do so. He was taken from the park to the Eighth precinct by the police" ("Keeps Foul Ball; Held for Theft," *Washington Post*, August 19, 1924; cited in Reed Browning, *Baseball's Greatest Season, 1924*, 170).

Such publicity was enough to convince most clubs, but there were still a few holdouts. One was the Chicago Cubs, who were no longer owned by Charles Weeghman. On June 24, 1930, Hack Wilson of the Cubs fouled a pitch into the seats, where it was retrieved by a seventeen-year-old fan named Arthur Porto. Porto was confronted by a Wrigley Field usher who told him that he could not keep the ball. When a tussle ensued, the young fan and two friends were charged with disorderly conduct. In court the next day, the judge ruled that the boy had a right to the ball, and the charges were dismissed (*New York Times*, June 26, 1930).

That was essentially the owners' last stand. In 1937 a spectator at Yankee Stadium tried to remove a ball that was lodged in the screen behind home plate and was roughed up by ushers. The fan sued the Yankees and won $7,500. During World War II it became customary to donate used balls to soldiers, but after the war the owners finally conceded the issue, and foul balls became souvenirs.

While it may seem in retrospect that the owners' relinquishment of balls hit into the stands was inevitable, that wasn't the case. As shown, the issue was a long and contentious one. In addition, in many other sports, such as basketball, tennis, soccer, and volleyball, fans still routinely return balls that leave the playing area.

16.2.8 All-Star Games. The first major league All-Star Game was announced on May 18, 1933, and took place at Chicago's Comiskey Park on July 6, 1933. The event was the brainchild of *Chicago Tribune* sports editor Arch Ward and was played as part of the World's Fair.

Of course the idea of an All-Star Game was not new, dating all the way back to an 1858 game at the Fashion Race Course, when the best players from Brooklyn and New York had thrilled baseball's first paying spectators (see "Admission Fees," **18.1.2**, for more details). Nor was there anything new about Arch Ward's idea. In 1908 a fan named Arthur H. Koehne wrote to *Sporting Life* to inquire, "In the event of a Field Day, which, in my estimation, appeals to every fan, why not play an inter-league game after the field contests have been decided, provided the sixteen major league teams gather, as no doubt they can when the Eastern teams go west and vice versa. A battery could be chosen from one team and for the remaining seven positions one man could be selected from the other seven teams. A formidable team from each league could then take the field and play a game which every fan in the country would be interested in beyond the question of a doubt" (*Sporting Life*, April 11, 1908).

Baseball Magazine had also lobbied for such an event for many years. Ward's colleague at the *Tribune*, George Strickler, noted that such an event "had been talked about for years. It was thought to be impossible. But Arch had sufficient persuasion and was enough of a politician to put it over" (quoted in Jerome Holtzman, *No Cheering in the Press Box*, 157–158).

According to Strickler, Ward had to use all of the *Tribune's* clout to make the game a reality: "the National League almost killed it. Arch had to put pressure on the Boston Braves and Judge Fuchs. Arch called Fuchs and said, 'Look, we're going to announce this the day after tomorrow, and either we're going to announce there is a game, or that we almost had one and didn't because of you. Now can you and the National League stand that kind of publicity?'" (quoted in Jerome Holtzman, *No Cheering in the Press Box*, 158).

The first All-Star Game was thus apparently played under coercion and was intended to be a one-time-only event. But the game proved both a popular and aesthetic success. It began with the teams entertaining the fans by playing hand-over-hand on a bat to decide which team would bat first. A Babe Ruth home run provided a fitting climax to an American League victory. Perhaps most important, nearly fifty thousand fans turned out for the game and half a million cast votes to select the participants.

The senior circuit requested a chance to host a return match the following year, and its success caused the All-Star Game to become an annual event and a great showcase for baseball. The Negro Leagues began their own long-running All-Star series one month later, also at Comiskey Park. The success of the concept also prompted Arch Ward to follow it up the next year by inaugurating football's College All-Star Game, which pitted the best college seniors against the NFL champions.

(iii) Mass Media

The fundamental dilemma of marketing is when giving away one's product stimulates interest and when it amounts to no more than giving away for free what one wanted to sell. For baseball owners this issue has always been crystallized by the birth of new communications media that have made it possible for fans to follow the games without going to the ballpark. Not without cause, owners have been apprehensive about the effects of new media on attendance. Will the new medium fire the faithful up about the home club and get them to attend more games? Or will they become complacent and replace the ballpark experience with the vicarious one? These same basic questions have accompanied the birth of each new medium of mass communication.

16.3.1 **Newspaper Coverage.** Newspapers don't seem like a very powerful medium to us today, but they were an extraordinarily potent one in mid-nineteenth-century America. On one hand, they had long been established as the country's most important and effective means of mass communication. Yet rather than becoming stodgy, as usually happens to long-established media, newspapers had been infused with a new sense of immediacy by the introduction of the penny paper in the 1830s. This development changed the basic dynamic of the medium by creating a new feeling of interactivity. As Paul Starr observed, newspapers suddenly "anticipated the modern structure of media enterprise" by selling "their readers to advertisers as much as they sold copies to readers" (Paul Starr, *The Creation of the Media*, 131–135).

As a result, when baseball entered the picture the hold of newspapers on the public imagination was profound. Moreover, baseball's great boom from 1865 to 1867 came at a time when the newspapers needed that game to fill the news void that had resulted from the end of the Civil War. Baseball would likewise come to rely deeply on the newspapers, yet the game's relationship with this medium remained uneasy, a development that would prefigure similar discomfort with the more rapid media that later emerged.

Early baseball reporters generally had a very close relationship with the clubs they covered. More than a few, such as William Cauldwell (see **23.1.3** "Baseball Reporters"), were members of the clubs on which they reported. Today that would be viewed as a breach of journalistic ethics, but in the 1860s that whole concept was still in the developmental stage.

By the late 1860s, distance was developing between players and reporters. Part of the problem was that players usually enjoyed coverage only when their club was doing well. But the development of an adversarial relationship often manifested itself in much more tangible forms.

At least one player prefigured Steve Carlton's policy of not speaking to reporters. When early star Jack Burdock died in 1931, his obituary noted: "Several years ago Burdock was asked by Joe Vila, New York sports writer, to say something about his career, but he replied: 'I never talked to a reporter when I was playing ball, and it is too late to begin now'" (*Sporting News*, December 10, 1931).

The *New York Clipper* reported in 1864, "[Charles Bomeisler] threatened us with personal chastisement if we ever put his name in the papers again" (*New York Clipper*, August 13, 1864). As described in the entry for "Press Boxes" (**14.5.3**), Henry Chadwick seems to have suspected that Dick McBride was deliberately aiming to hit reporters with foul balls during an 1867 game. In 1870 Bob Ferguson "threatened to knock every tooth out of the head" of a *New York Herald* reporter who had questioned his competency as captain of the Atlantics of Brooklyn (*New York Herald*; reprinted in Preston D. Orem, *Baseball [1845–1881] from the Newspaper Accounts*, 105).

An 1895 article reported that at least one player had followed through on his threats: "[E. T.] Purcell, the new catcher of the [Norfolk, Virginia] team, thinks the newspapers have only the right to praise and not condemn a player's work. So when Mr. Tanner, of the 'Pilot' staff, 'wrote him up' not to his liking, the said Purcell proceeded to punch Mr. Tanner's head" (*Sporting Life*, May 18, 1895).

Threats of violence were not always one-sided. Early in the 1885 season, Louisville catcher Dan Sullivan was arrested for assault on *Louisville Commercial* reporter William G. Osborne (*St. Louis Post-Dispatch*, May 30, 1885). David Nemec noted that the reporter "swore revenge and had a big family in the Louisville area to help him carry out the threat. Fearing for his life if he went back to 'the dark and bloody ground of Kentucky,' Sullivan gladly accepted a transfer to St. Louis" (David Nemec, *The Beer and Whisky League*, 102).

It was rare, but not unheard of, for such antagonism to go beyond spontaneous outbursts and wind up in court. In 1883 *Harrisburg Sunday Telegram* editor John Moore described Thomas Burns of the local minor league club as a ruffian, and Burns responded by suing for libel (*Sporting Life*, September 24, 1883). In 1878 George Campbell of Syracuse umpired a game between clubs representing Rochester and Buffalo. The *Buffalo Express* accused him of dishonesty, and Campbell sued the paper. He agreed to drop the case two years later when the newspaper printed an apology (*New York Clipper*, May 8, 1880; October 16, 1880). There is at least one more recent instance of this sort. In 1954 *Durham Morning Herald* sports editor Jack Horner wrote a column entitled "Incompetent Umpires Always End Up in Rhubarbs." The subject of the piece, Carolina League umpire Harry "Ike" Reeder, was not rehired the following season. Reeder then sued Horner and his paper and received a substantial settlement (Jim L. Sumner, *Separating the Men from the Boys*, 135).

Some reporters were made to feel unwelcome in slightly subtler ways. Chicago captain Jimmy Wood informed a *Chicago Tribune* reporter in 1875 that "there are thousands of people who buy the papers simply for the reports of the games, and who would not otherwise think of looking at a newspaper" (*Chicago Tribune*, June 18, 1875). Even some baseball clubs went out of their way to inconvenience reporters. In 1877 the National League made an effort to make reporters pay for admission to the ballpark.

While the friction manifested itself in a variety of ways, the underlying conflict remained the same. The newspapers, having advertised the games, felt obliged to report on the games regardless of the result. The players, in contrast, wanted coverage only of their triumphs.

The result of such incidents was to seriously damage a valuable—*and thus far free*—means of publicity. Historian George B. Kirsch reported that "by the late 1860s many [newspapers] had begun to charge a fee for announcements of club meetings and elections of officers. Some, like the *Philadelphia*

Press, refused to cover ball games unless the clubs advertised in their columns" (George B. Kirsch, *The Creation of American Team Sports*, 203).

Other newspapers responded with sarcasm, such as the Michigan newspaper that reported after an 1875 game: "We made inquiries as to the result and received this intelligence: Aughhellwedontwantanypuffonthat" (*Jonesville Weekly Independent*, May 13, 1875). In a similar vein a Grand Rapids, Michigan, newspaper wrote sardonically in 1879: "The Hastings base ball club played a game yesterday. A Grand Rapids nine was present, but it is understood that they took no part in the game, as they refuse to say anything about the score when approached on the subject" (*Grand Rapids Daily Leader*, August 31, 1879). Many papers did the game even more harm by simply dropping their coverage.

The task of journalists who continued to report on baseball was not easy. A Chicago newspaper noted in 1870, "It became customary last season to publish the scores of games played between the less known clubs of this city—clubs with barbaric, comic, stupid or overridiculous names, and whose scorers did write most villainously, and spelt at random. . . . A report of one of these games would be left at the office, stating that the Young Americas had beaten the Hopefuls by a gigantic score. The next day the Captain of the Hopefuls, aged 4 to 9, after climbing our 80 stairs with great difficulty, would appear panting, and claim that his organization had the great score, and the others, the small one. He would frequently argue for half an hour as to the vital importance of a correction, and would denounce the unscrupulous mendacity of the Young Americas. Repressing a strong inclination to give him five cents to buy marbles with, we promised to correct, and he went downstairs exultant" (*Chicago Times*, November 27, 1870; quoted in Robert Pruter, "Youth Baseball in Chicago, 1868–1890: Not Always Sandlot Ball," *Journal of Sport History*, Spring 1999).

Too few baseball players seem to have realized the consequences of such shortsighted attitudes. One exception appears to have been A. G. Spalding. Anticipating by nearly a century the maxim that "the only bad publicity is no publicity," Spalding claimed in his autobiography that attacks on him by a Chicago journalist were helping his club's attendance. Consequently, when they began to subside, he began sending the reporter additional material (Albert Spalding, *America's National Game*, 527–528; Peter Levine, in *A. G. Spalding and the Rise of Baseball*, 44–45, discussed this claim without reaching a firm conclusion on it).

The twentieth century saw the issue continue to percolate. Sportswriters of the first half of the century were often grouped into either the "gee whiz" or the "aw nuts" school. The "gee whiz" writers, such as Grantland Rice, accepted the public's adulation of athletes and did nothing to challenge that mind-set. The "aw nuts" school, exemplified by such writers as Westbrook

Pegler, Ring Lardner, and W. O. McGeehan, took a more cynical, world-weary approach. They sought to demythologize ballplayers, though never to debunk them.

By the second half of the century the "gee whiz" school had lost favor. A new group of sportswriters sprung up who were known as the chipmunks. This new breed saw no reason to write as if they were "grateful to be covering the great New York Yankees" (David Halberstam, *October 1964*, 175–176). Instead they asked tough questions of the players and were willing to debunk when necessary. They were so anxious not to be hero worshipers that, in the view of sportswriter Jimmy Cannon, "they only discuss what they've written. They don't watch the game. They hate baseball. They hate the players" (quoted in Jerome Holtzman, *No Cheering in the Press Box*, 280).

By this time most clubs accepted the basic premise that newspaper coverage was good for business whether it was positive or negative. As a result, even reporters such as the chipmunks who raised the hackles of players and management were viewed as necessary evils.

But a reservoir of antipathy to printed criticisms surfaced when active players began to write books that offered a candid view of the game. When Reds pitcher Jim Brosnan published *The Long Season* in 1960, the club tried to silence him by invoking a clause in the uniform players' contract that forbade players from saying or writing anything without his team's permission.

Bill Veeck noted that that approach demonstrated an extremely short-sighted viewpoint: "Brosnan should have been a gift from heaven. Here is a character no one could possibly make up, a big-league ballplayer who writes a best-selling book. Here you have a character who writes better than most of the writers and knows what he is writing about. If I had him I'd not only permit him to go around making speeches blasting me and baseball, I'd pay him to do it. I'd challenge him to a public debate (wouldn't it be a shame if we swindled some free TV time?) and I'd pen angry broadsides to answer his angry broadsides. (Wouldn't it be a shame if customers came into the park to boo or cheer him—or me—in person?)" (Bill Veeck with Ed Linn, *The Hustler's Handbook*, 132).

Veeck obviously believed in the maxim that there is no such thing as bad publicity, but few in baseball shared this view. When Jim Bouton's *Ball Four*—written with "chipmunk" Leonard Shecter—hit the best-seller list a decade after Brosnan's book, baseball again reacted with outrage and dismay.

16.3.2 Telegraphs. American newspapers, telegraphs, and railroads all came of age during the 1850s and 1860s and made the country seem a much smaller place. The parallel development of baseball was closely tied to each.

Telegraphs began to be used to transmit baseball results back to newspaper offices almost as soon as the technology allowed. The development prompted a reporter for the *Doylestown* (Pennsylvania) *Democrat* to marvel in 1867: "We scarce supposed in our hours of buoyant boyhood . . . that the telegraph, then unknown, would, by woven wire, hasten to inform distant parts of our Union by sunrise next morning how Jim's side had come out first best, but that Joe's side made excellent playing" (*Doylestown Democrat*, quoted in *The Ball Player's Chronicle*, August 8, 1867). Soon results were being relayed not just at the end of a match but often inning by inning. The Red Stockings of Cincinnati relayed home the results of an 1869 game in Troy after each inning, and several cities repeated the experiment in 1870 (Greg Rhodes and John Erardi, *The First Boys of Summer*, 86).

As noted in the entry on "Scoreboards" (14.5.14), by 1875 saloons were contracting with Western Union to receive updated reports on baseball games. Many newspapers were posting the telegraphed results on large bulletin boards, which led club owners to become concerned about the potential erosion of their fan base.

When the practice caught on in Hartford, the *Hartford Courant* noted that this was a cheap form of advertisement (*Hartford Courant*, May 30, 1876; quoted in David Arcidiacono, *Grace, Grit and Growling*, 60). Club president Morgan Bulkeley didn't see it that way and made several efforts to curtail the practice, even trying to prevent the telegraph company from buying a ticket. Bulkeley gave up only when it became clear that he was creating ill will (David Arcidiacono, *Grace, Grit and Growling*, 60–61).

Club managements elsewhere were also casting a wary eye toward such practices: "The manager of the Cincinnati Club has refused to allow the score of games played in the pork-packing city to be telegraphed to the poolrooms by innings, hoping thereby to secure the attendance at the games of those who generally learn of the play on the outside. The press of that city informs him that it 'won't work'" (*Boston Globe*, May 19, 1877).

This didn't stop clubs from trying. A report soon surfaced from Troy that "An amusing controversy is going on between the Troy Club and the Atlantic and Pacific Telegraph Company. The company having refused a request to frank all messages on club affairs, their operator was refused admission to the ground and accordingly climbed a convenient pole and tapped the wire. The manager was so pleased with the operator's exploit that a seat is to be rigged on the pole. To prevent a successful issue of this device, the Troy directors have ordered a large canvas to obstruct the operator's view" (*New York Clipper*, July 24, 1880).

By this time telephones were being used as well. An 1880 article observed, "Down at Worcester the telephone exchange advertises to furnish the score of all the League games played at the home grounds by innings to the subscribers at the rate of twenty-five cents per game. Rather a novel idea" (*Washington Post*, May 16, 1880).

The controversy was still raging in 1886 when the *St. Louis Post-Dispatch* observed, "The system adopted by [local owners] Messrs. [Henry] Lucas and [Chris] Von der Ahe of withholding the score of the games played at their parks from the bulletins down town has been tried and found wanting. The policy will not gain the good will of the public for either manager. Of course the cranks will continue to go to the parks whether the score is bulletined or not, but it is a question whether it is not better to have their good will as well as their good money" (*St. Louis Post-Dispatch*, April 10, 1886).

That same year Boston sold exclusive rights to telegraphing scores from their ballpark to the Baltimore and Ohio Company, and denied the previous year's company, the Western Union Telegraph Company, access to their grounds. Western Union responded by constructing a perch for their operator, a man named Tobin, on a telegraph pole overlooking the park. The Baltimore and Ohio erected a screen to block his view, but someone poked holes in it. When it was repaired, Western Union put up a new pole, prompting another rejoinder (*Boston Globe*, May 31 and June 1, 1886).

By this time, however, a resolution was at hand, and it came in a form that would become a recurring element in the introduction of new media. Western Union began to pay clubs for broadcast rights around 1886, and the company expanded the practice in the 1890s (Jonathan Fraser Light, *The Cultural Encyclopedia of Baseball*, 223–224).

Naturally the issue did not entirely vanish. It resurfaced in 1898 when it was reported that "Some of the League's clubs are trying to bar out the Western Union's 'ticker' wires from their grounds, because they believe that if such a move is made the gate receipts will be increased." Yet clubs were beginning to take a more farsighted view of the matter: "The New York club, however, has refused to entertain the proposition, for it is believed that the 'ticker' helps to boom base ball" (*New York Sun*, reprinted in *Sporting Life*, January 8, 1898).

When necessary, compromises were reached. An article in *Sporting Life* in 1906 noted that the Southern League had renewed an exclusive contract with Western Union for telegraphing within the ballpark "with the condition that no tickers are to be used and no information furnished to matinees at home when the club is at home. When the club is abroad and a matinee is given in the home town, no results on tickers are to be allowed" (*Sporting Life*, March 31, 1906).

As we shall see in succeeding entries, these controversies and their resolution would prefigure later ones involving threats and perceived threats from new media.

16.3.3 Broadcasts of Baseball. The visual appeal of tracking the results of games on blackboards and bulletin boards is limited, which led to some noteworthy efforts to embellish the telegraphed results of the ball games.

In 1884, under the name Messrs. Morgan & Co., three telegraph operators from Nashville, Tennessee—J. U. Rust, E. W. Morgan, and A. H. Stewart—hit upon an innovative way of turning the dots and dashes into a form of performance art. Their dramatization of a game that the local club was playing in Chattanooga proved so popular that they began to expand it.

The next year the Augusta, Georgia, correspondent to *Sporting Life* reported: "We have a blackboard at the Opera House and a diamond on it, with holes punched for each base, with flags showing how each base runner gets his base, with the batting order of each nine. The whole game is sent by telegraph, showing how each player plays. They charge ten cents for each day. We have gotten the games played by our nine in Atlanta, Chattanooga, Memphis and Nashville and will get Columbus and Macon" (*Sporting Life*, May 27, 1885).

A few weeks later his Nashville counterpart added, "We have been able to keep up with every item of each game played by our home team while on our trip, by the introduction on the stage of our Masonic Theatre of a black board picturing the diamond position of players, batteries, etc., with telegraphic reports of complete details of the game, viz., strikes, balls, etc., etc. It is novel and almost as interesting as being on the grounds where the game is progressing, several hundred miles away. It is managed by Messrs. Morgan and Rust, two enterprising telegraphers" (*Sporting Life*, July 8, 1885).

The idea seemed nearly ready to be launched in major league cities. The *Boston Globe* reported, "Ormond H. Butler, ex-umpire and ex-manager, sees millions in a new idea. He is negotiating for a down-town theatre or hall in Chicago to report games by telegraph. The stage is to be set in the form of a miniature ball field, on which every movement of the game will be shown" (*Boston Globe*, August 10, 1885).

By the following spring, additional dramatic elements had been added to the performance: "Several hundred people were present again today at the opera house to witness the game between Atlanta and Charleston. A novel feature of the report was the actual running of the bases by uniformed boys, who obeyed the telegraph instrument in their moves around the diamond" (*Atlanta Constitution*, April 17, 1886).

The show was next taken to major league cities, where it was warmly received. The *Chicago Tribune* gave a detailed account: "A small but deeply interested crowd of spectators assembled in Central Music Hall yesterday afternoon to witness the game between the Chicago and St. Louis teams by means of the new system introduced by a couple of enterprising young men of Nashville, Tenn., and which last week created no little enthusiasm at Cincinnati in demonstrating the play of the Cincinnati and St. Louis teams at St. Louis.

"Upon the stage was a canvas screen, twenty feet square, and upon it was painted a very realistic view of a ball-field, with the diamond in the centre and the fence, hills, and blue sky beyond. In the centre of the pitcher's and catcher's box, at the home-plate, and at each of the three bases slots had been cut, through which an assistant behind the picture inserted 12 × 4 inch cards bearing the names of the players as they took their positions. A telegraph operator was seated at one corner of the scene, the wire from the instrument before him connecting with one in the grand stand at St. Louis. At fifteen minutes to 4 o'clock the operator announced the batting orders of both teams with [John] Gaffney as umpire. At 4 o'clock the instrument ticked out 'Game,' and a minute after 'Play ball.' Instantly the name of [Emmett] Seery appeared at home plate, and those of [John] Clarkson and ['Silver'] Flint as the Whites' battery. 'One strike,' called the operator, then 'one ball,' 'two, three, four, five, six balls,' and the name of Seery disappeared from the home plate and reappeared at first base, while that of Glasscock showed up at the home plate. 'One strike, two strikes,' called the operator, and the crowd applauded Clarkson. 'Three strikes, and Glasscock knocks the ball to ['Cap'] Anson, who throws to Clarkson at first. Glasscock out, and Seery to second on the play,' called the operator and the crowd applauded and seemed delighted with the novelty of witnessing a game 300 miles distant. [Fred] Dunlap then made a two-bagger through centre, and Seery came home. [Alex] McKinnon hit the ball, and got to second on a bad throw, but was cut off at the home plate from centre, while [Jerry] Denny was left on first.

"Next the Chicagos came to bat, [Abner] Dalrymple reaching first on called balls, and in this and the succeeding half inning each play was promptly telegraphed and promptly announced. To those who knew the players personally, the exhibition was wonderfully realistic, and the many little points in play brought out made it more so. In the third, for instance, Glasscock hit foul and instantly the operator announced, 'Foul ball over the grand-stand. A new ball.' Again in the third [George] Gore was caught while trying to steal second and the operator announced, 'Gore kicking hard, but Anson laughing at him.' In the fifth came the announcement: 'Fine stop by [Tom] Dolan. Hurt his finger. All the players around him. [Charlie] Sweeney very wild. They are now pulling Dolan's finger in place. Game.' And the play went on as before. It was a close game up to the eighth inning, when unfortunately the wire got out of gear somewhere along the line, and a wait of nearly ten minutes occurred. Then the rest of the game was rapidly announced, and the score stood 7 to 3 in favor of the White Stockings. The exhibition, it is thought, will be very popular in Chicago while the home team is absent in the East. Today's game between the Chicago and St. Louis teams will be called at Central Music Hall promptly at 4 o'clock" (*Chicago Tribune*, May 4, 1886).

The unique performance arrived in Detroit on July 8, 1886. Six hundred spectators turned out at the Detroit Opera House to watch an enactment of the home team's game at Chicago. The audience got into the spirit of things, bursting into applause when Detroit did well, and hissing whenever the name of Chicago captain "Cap" Anson was announced.

Morgan and Rust seem to have abandoned the project, but others took it up and added new touches. The *New York Sun* reported in 1890: "On and after April 25, it will be possible to witness two league base ball games, played miles apart, at the same time, in Webster hall, 119 East Eleventh street. The hall will be connected by telegraph wires with every league ball ground in the United States. Reporters will telegraph every play which will be immediately reproduced on one of the improved base ball bulletins in Webster hall. Each of the bulletin boards will be fifteen feet square. The background is white, and the lettering which refers to both of the clubs playing is in black" (*New York Sun*, reprinted in *Columbus* [Ohio] *Post*, April 24, 1890). In 1895 the *Washington Post* noted: "Manager Eugene Kernan will inaugurate a new system of illustrating baseball games in detail from the stage of the Lyceum this summer, while the Senators are out of the city" (*Washington Post*, April 14, 1895).

By this time technological upgrades were breathing new life into the presentations. An 1895 account from Philadelphia explained: "The new system of electrical reproduction of ball games known as the Crowden system, invented by Mr. Samuel H. Crowden, of Richmond, was produced at the Walnut Street Theatre last week and voted a great success. . . .

"The feature is the exact reproduction of every move and play of the participants in the game. The field is laid out in an exact representation of the regular diamond. Every player is in his position and constantly in motion, giving the appearance of being living. Each player is equipped with a ball and a bat and when he makes a catch or throws the ball it can be seen in his hands, or when batting, the bat, which is connected by his legs, works automatically and comes into a position for striking.

"After a man has made a catch or a batter has hit the ball the ball is thrown to the base or player and the batsman drops his bat and runs. Slides to bases, running for fouls, caught napping, and the pitcher and catcher in convention are all equally and minutely displayed. The most important feature is that when a ball is hit the audience can see where it goes, by whom it is fielded, and where it is thrown. Every game played away from home will be exactly reproduced at the Walnut Street Theatre by this system, and anyone failing to witness it will miss the greatest thing in this way ever exhibited" (*Sporting Life*, July 6, 1895).

The reliance on new technology enabled these depictions to appeal to a class of fans who were not at home in opera houses but were beginning to discover the appeal of the new genre of motion pictures. *Sporting Life* observed in 1900: "During the playing season, while the Pittsburg team is on the road, the games are reproduced in miniature at the Academy. Betting on the game and on fouls is in full blast, foul balls being recorded by the flashing of a red light. It is said that frequently the telegraph operators miss the foul balls, or at times there is a lull in the games, and to keep interest alive a few extra fouls are added to make the betting more keen" (*Sporting Life*, November 3, 1900).

Large crowds watched the two spectacular pennant races of 1908 from afar on lighted electric diamonds (David W. Anderson, *More Than Merkle*, 157, 171). The 1909 campaign saw the introduction of the Rodier Electric Board Game Reproducer, which kept a running tally of outs, innings, and score and used electric lights to simulate the action. The Rodier machine was unveiled on July 16, 1909 in Washington, D.C., and more than two thousand fans stood in the street and "watched" a game that was being played in Detroit (Gerard S. Petrone, *When Baseball Was Young*, 59–60). Excitement about the new board was so great that during the 1909 World Series between Pittsburgh and Detroit, the device was installed at Washington's Columbia Theater and fans paid twenty-five cents to watch the progress of the Series "be vividly reproduced" in the comfort of theater seating (*Washington Post*, October 5, 1909).

The novelty of paying admission to theaters for such reproductions wore off, presumably a victim of competition from the far more captivating images that could be viewed at nickelodeons. But monitoring the results of important ballgames on electric telegraph boards remained a popular custom for another decade. Thousands gathered annually in New York's Times Square to monitor the results of the World Series in the era's closest equivalent to "real time." The practice began to dwindle in 1921, the year radio broadcasts were initiated (Dan Gutman, *Banana Bats and Ding-Dong Balls*, 116–117).

16.3.4   Radio Broadcasts. In *Middle Innings*, Dean Sullivan reprinted an article published during the 1920 World Series that described what might have been a radio broadcast. The article recounted a "wireless party" hosted by the *Cleveland Press* during the fifth game of the World Series. It explains that hundreds of wireless men within a 750-mile radius were able to receive and "listen" to play-by-play reports sent by U.S. Naval Station electrician A. A. Penland. The article always placed the word "listen" in quotation marks, leaving doubt as to the nature of the broadcast ("Wireless Fans Fan at Press Series Party," *Cleveland Press*, October 12, 1920; reprinted in Dean Sullivan, ed., *Middle Innings*).

What is generally considered to be the first radio broadcast of a major league game took place on August 5, 1921, when Harold Arlin announced a game between Pittsburgh and Philadelphia for KDKA in Pittsburgh. Arlin said later that the broadcast of baseball was viewed by the station as "sort of a one-shot project" (Curt Smith, *Voices of the Game*, 7).

That perception reflected the fact that, once again, baseball had gotten in at the outset of a new medium to which its fortunes would become closely tied. KDKA is credited with initiating the heyday of radio's popularity with its November 2, 1920, broadcast of the result of the presidential election. At that point there were only a handful of radio stations in the whole country; it took a full year for a significant number to emerge and a radio craze to ensue (Paul Starr, *The Creation of the Media*, 330–331).

By that time the enduring link between radio and the national pastime had begun. Listeners of at least three stations were able to hear some coverage of the 1921 World Series. KDKA listeners heard Grantland Rice give periodic updates of the action. Meanwhile Tommy Cowan did studio recreations of the entire Series based upon reports from the ballpark that were broadcast on WJZ in Newark and WBZ in Springfield, Massachusetts (Curt Smith, *Voices of the Game*, 8).

At the following season's World Series, radio announcers "sent play by play a talked off story of the big games" (*Sporting News*, October 12, 1922). The 1923 World Series was the first to be broadcast nationally, with Graham McNamee providing the play-by-play.

Beginning in 1924 the Cubs became the first team to allow regular radio broadcasts of their games. For some years afterward there was a schizophrenic attitude toward the new medium, with baseball's confusion mirroring that of American society as a whole. As Paul Starr has noted, radio had an amalgam of the characteristics of the media that preceded it, making it difficult to know how to treat it.

Was radio part of the press and worthy of the First Amendment privileges accorded newspapers? Was it merely a form of entertainment like the movies? Or was it a common carrier like the telephone or telegraph that ought to provide equal access to all? And what would be the respective roles of private enterprise and government? Which governmental department should set policies for radio broadcasts—the Navy, the Post Office, Commerce, or a new one? While the resolution of these issues may seem inevitable in retrospect, Starr observed that "before 1927 it was far from obvious what the outcome would be" and that other countries took very different courses from the one pursued in the United States (Paul Starr, *The Creation of the Media*, 329–330).

The dilemma was especially immediate in the case of baseball since radio stations did not have to pay for broadcast rights, which made baseball a very appealing programming option. But most major league clubs were reluctant or unwilling to allow radio broadcasts, fearful they would hurt attendance. This concern was apparently belied by the fact that Cubs attendance was booming, but most owners saw no reason to take the chance that this trend would continue. Their anxiety was undoubtedly increased when radio was blamed for a sharp decline in the sale of sheet music and records (Paul Starr, *The Creation of the Media*, 339).

The first major league team to allow play-by-play broadcast of all their games was the Cincinnati Reds in 1929, with announcer Harry Hartman calling the games for WFBE in Cincinnati. But that same year saw the backlash against radio broadcasts begin to gain momentum, especially in the minor leagues. Club officials in San Francisco did a study and concluded that attendance dropped by 12 percent when games were broadcast. The Southern League took action and banned radio altogether (*Sporting News*, May 16, 1929).

Baseball owners continued to have a skittish attitude toward radio during the 1920s and 1930s. Any dip in attendance during the period led to talk of prohibiting radio broadcasts and often to actual bans. After the 1932 season, with the country in the throes of the Great Depression, these concerns were particularly widespread. With many expecting major league owners to announce a ban on radio broadcasts at their winter meetings, Cincinnati Reds broadcaster Harry Hartman made the case that "radio is the best advertiser that baseball could want."

In a 1932 article, Hartman argued that ticket prices "would strain any man's pocket book these days. Citing this situation of the man who can't afford this, it is better to at least keep his interest in the game alive, and radio will do that. If he is given a broadcast account of the game, he will remain sport conscious, and let me say here, that the desire in any rabid, dyed-in-the-wool baseball fan is much too strong to be satisfied with just the mere broadcasting of a game. He must go out there to his park and see it for himself. Take radio away from the man who can't afford the price of attending games regularly and you take away a customer who would occasionally attend the game if he has the money." Hartman further contended that radio broadcasts were essential to bringing the game to new fans and to shut-ins and the handicapped (*Sporting News*, November 17, 1932).

By then, however, the commercial tenor of American radio was becoming established, which brought a solution to the thorny issue. Rights to broadcast the World Series were sold for the first time in 1934 to the Ford Motor Company for four years at $100,000 per year. The problem was not resolved overnight, as the three New York clubs maintained a non-radio pact until 1939. But once big-money sponsorships entered the picture, it was inevitable that baseball would overcome its resistance to radio broadcasts.

16.3.5 Television. The first televised baseball game may have occurred in Japan. Researcher Bob Timmermann brought my attention to the fact that the Japanese were experimenting with prototypes of television by the early 1930s. One of the sites was Waseda University in Tokyo, and on February 17, 1931, an attempt was made there to televise a baseball game. If the game was indeed visible, it was seen only in a laboratory.

The first U.S. telecast of a baseball game was of a collegiate game between Princeton and Columbia on May 17, 1939. The game was shown on W2XBS, an experimental NBC station in New York City. NBC program manager Thomas H. Hutchinson said presciently, "outdoor sports will furnish much of the most interesting material we could televise." Announcer Bill Stern was assigned "to identify players and interpret the play," and it turned out that that was exactly what he had to do (_New York Times_, May 18, 1939).

The _Times_ reported the next day that "Those who watched the game at Radio City agreed that the commentator 'saved the day,' otherwise there would be no way to follow the play or to tell where the ball went except to see the players run in its direction. The announcer revealed whether it was a foul ball or hit" (_New York Times_, May 19, 1939).

The single camera that was used proved incapable of keeping up with the action. At the start of the game the position of the sun caused the entire screen to be "blurred, with the reproduced faces dark. But as the game progressed the sun moved around out of the camera's 'eye' and the diamond became clear and the skyline of apartment buildings sharply defined in the background."

Unfortunately the greater ease of viewing the apartment buildings did not make it much easier to follow play: "Seldom were more than three players visible on the screen at one time, and until the picture was clarified after the fourth inning the outfielders were 'forgotten men.' The ball was seldom seen, except on bunts and infield plays comparatively close to the camera, stationed between third base and home plate" (_New York Times_, May 19, 1939). Stern later admitted, "We actually prayed that all the batters would strike out because that was the one thing that the camera could record."

Despite the inauspicious debut, at least one commentator recognized the potential of the new medium. _New York Times_ columnist Orrin E. Dunlap, Jr., observed, "It's no easy trick to put a baseball acreage and its scattered action on a 9 by 12 inch screen." He explained that the newness of the technology and the expense of cameras meant that it was too soon "to 'paint' electronically such a panoramic view," but he expressed confidence that "the future will bring the complete picture." Dunlap predicted that baseball telecasts would eventually blend the angles of multiple cameras trained on home plate, the infield, the outfield, and even one atop the grandstand for a bird's-eye view and another with "a roving assignment" of the dugout and bleachers (Orrin E. Dunlap, Jr., "Batter Up!," _New York Times_, May 21, 1939).

The first telecast of major league baseball was a Reds-Dodgers game on August 26, 1939. The game was broadcast by Red Barber and again appeared on W2XBS. In return for allowing the game to be televised, Larry MacPhail asked only that NBC install a set in the Dodgers' press box. The *New York Times* reported that "considerable progress" had been made since the Columbia-Princeton game (*New York Times*, August 27, 1939). Two cameras were used in this game, both on the third base line, but one by the visitors' dugout and the other behind the right-handed batters' box. In addition, a truck was set up outside the ballpark.

Seeing the ball remained a major problem for viewers. Sportswriter Harold Parrott reported, "The players were clearly distinguishable, but it was not possible to pick out the ball." Another account was slightly more optimistic: "At times, despite the great speed of play, the baseball was visible in the television image, particularly when Pitchers Luke Hamlin and 'Bucky' Walters resorted to slower delivery, or when the batter drove out a hit directly away from the iconoscope camera" (both quoted in Lawrence S. Katz, *Baseball in 1939*, 115).

16.3.6 Sale of Television Rights. The Yankees sold telecast rights for $75,000 in 1946 (Jonathan Fraser Light, *The Cultural Encyclopedia of Baseball*, 725). It was a decision that would have far-reaching repercussions.

Baseball was noticeably less cautious in its approach to television broadcasts than had been the case with radio. There are several apparent reasons for this tendency. One is that the fears about radio hurting attendance had proved largely unfounded. Another is that some of baseball's efforts to restrict broadcasts fell afoul of antitrust laws and had to be dropped (Dean Sullivan, ed., *Late Innings*, 42–45).

Perhaps the biggest reason was that baseball began to accept television money at a time when the technology of the medium was still quite primitive. By the 1940s the ball itself had become visible to viewers, but not much else was.

A perfect indication of how rudimentary telecasts of this era were comes from a humorous 1951 piece by columnist Weare Holbrook, who devised a set of Unofficial Rules and Regulations of TV Baseball. Holbrook observed that the players all appeared to be wearing uniforms of "a pale gray, shaggy material which occasionally sprouts feathers" and could only be "distinguished by the numerals on their backs—with the exception of numbers three, five, six and eight, which can't be distinguished at all." This difficulty was compounded by the fact that only one to three players were visible at a time, who: "may be (a) pitcher, batter, and catcher, or (b) base runner and infielder, or (c) outfielder. This count does not include fractional players. A double play, for example, may include the base runner, the second baseman, and the legs of the shortstop; and a pop fly may include an outfielder and the truncated torso of the third baseman."

At least the ball was now "a white fuzzy object about the size and shape of a half-dissolved aspirin tablet." Batters swung at it with a bat that seemed to "be constructed of some flexible, rubbery substance which enables it to grow longer when held horizontally, and thicker when held vertically" (Weare Holbrook, "TV Scrambles a Ball Game," syndicated column, *Washington Post*, August 5, 1951).

Such features meant that when owners first began to sell telecast rights in 1946, they did not anticipate that television would become much of a substitute for attending a game. Baseball came to rely on television revenues, and when the technology began to advance dramatically it was difficult to go back. As a result, money has been a driving force in the relationship between baseball and television to an even greater extent than was the case between baseball and radio.

There was, of course, some resistance. For example, Branch Rickey protested in the early 1950s: "Radio created a desire to see something. Television is giving it to them. Once a television set has broken them of the ballpark habit, a great many fans will never reacquire it. And if television makes new baseball customers, as some are claiming, why don't Broadway productions televise their shows? The only way you can see a Broadway production is to buy a ticket—and I cannot concede that baseball has, under the oft-used heading of the 'public interest,' any obligation to give away continuously at only a fraction of its real worth the only thing it has to sell" (*Newsweek* interview, quoted in Robert W. Peterson, *Pigskin*, 200).

But money rather than arguments would carry the day. Within a year of the first sale of baseball television broadcasting rights, those revenues played a key role in the funding of the first major league pension fund. While a pension fund is certainly unobjectionable, other consequences of baseball's reliance on television money raise much more serious concerns.

Leonard Koppett, for instance, wrote in 1964 that "The trouble with television is that it exists. . . . A baseball game on television remains a television show: it may make some baseball addicts, but it certainly makes more television addicts. Thus, one more distinguishing feature of baseball is removed and it becomes 'just another entertainment'" (Leonard Koppett, "The Ex-National Sports Looks to Its Image," *New York Times*, December 20, 1964).

Such developments as the broadcast of World Series games at hours far too late for youngsters to watch cause understandable concern that baseball is allowing itself to become "just another entertainment."

16.3.7 Real-time Broadcasts. The most recent dispute over whether broadcasts promote or give the product away is the still ongoing controversy over real-time broadcasts and webcasts. In 1996 the NBA sued Motorola and STATS, Inc., on the grounds that a real-time data service being offered by those companies was an unlicensed broadcast. The defendants ultimately won the case by successfully arguing that the essence of their product was gathering and transmitting facts (Alan Schwarz, *The Numbers Game*, 188–192). The issue, however, has not gone away, and the increasing sophistication of webcasts has brought it back to the fore.

In spite of the precedent of the Motorola and STATS, Inc., case, the position of major league baseball continues to be that "pitch-by-pitch is an exhibition of a baseball game" (Bob Bowman, chief executive of Major League Baseball Advanced Media, quoted in Alan Schwarz, "Real-time Broadcasts Lead to Copyright Questions," *Baseball America*, September 15–28, 2003). As a result, Alan Schwarz predicted that "when a site starts streaming the trajectory of the ball, and has lifelike, animated men throwing it to first, you can bet a clarification of 'news' will be in order" (Alan Schwarz, "Real-time Broadcasts Lead to Copyright Questions," *Baseball America*, September 15–28, 2003).

Chapter 17

STATISTICS

BASEBALL EMERGED as a prominent part of the American experience in the mid-nineteenth century, at about the same time that statistics were also becoming a staple of American life. Historian of science Thomas Kuhn characterized the mid-century as the scene of a second scientific revolution that revolved around quantification (Thomas S. Kuhn, "The Function of Measurement in Modern Physical Science," *Isis*, Vol. 52, Issue 2 [1961], 161–193; quoted in Jay Bennett and Aryn Martin, "The Numbers Game: What Fans Should Know About the Stats They Love," Eric Bronson, ed., *Baseball and Philosophy*, 234).

As baseball sought to appeal to adults instead of children, it made use of this emphasis on measurement and quantification. Early baseball statistics were based largely on those of cricket, but it would not take long for that to change. By the 1870s, as we shall see, the game was well on its way to amassing the formidable and often baffling array of statistics that it now features.

All these numbers were an effective way of demonstrating that what had once been a child's game could now be taken seriously. Before long, another discernible theme to all the measurements emerged: baseball as a democratic institution. Slowly but surely, baseball statistics came to embody the notion that every player's contributions counted and were being measured. As sportswriter Jim Murray later quipped, "A king may be a king because his father was, but a ballplayer is a major leaguer only so long as his average shows he is" (quoted in Jonathan Fraser Light, *The Cultural Encyclopedia of Baseball*, 626).

This reality caused Grantland Rice to observe, "I have often wondered how the populace at large would feel if the daily records of every one were exposed to public inspection—the politicians, bankers, lawyers, doctors, union labor and industrial leaders, writers, radio artists, grocers, butchers, clerks and all others who make up the motley mass of humanity. . . . The ball player has no such soft break. The box score soon proves whether he is a Williams, DiMaggio, Feller, Marion or a Class B product headed for the bush again" (Grantland Rice, *New York Sun*, April 16, 1946).

A final theme that recurs throughout this chapter is that baseball statistics have been very conservative entities, often intended not so much to measure the accomplishments that win games but to encourage acts that embody desirable moral traits. There was widespread sentiment in the nineteenth century that pitchers had usurped too great a role and that walks and strikeouts were bad baseball. Beliefs such as these were reflected in early baseball statistics, which is why, for example, batting average has always been one of the game's magic numbers while on-base percentage didn't emerge for another century. The latter statistic is a better measurement of the value of a player's contribution, but the former is a better embodiment of an accepted nineteenth-century principle that "bases on called balls [is] something no good batsman likes to do" (*Brooklyn Eagle*, May 9, 1871).

More than with the topic of any other chapter in this book, the history of baseball statistics is a work in progress, in need of continual rewriting and reexamination. Bill James is most responsible for this process because of his persistence in empirically testing assumptions about baseball statistics that had long been taken for granted. His approaches and ideas have inspired an entire generation of analysts, many of whom have made their way into baseball front offices. While I follow the results closely, especially James's ongoing work and that of the *Baseball Prospectus* team, I have primarily confined myself in this chapter to tracing the origins of traditional measures. More recent approaches and statistics are too new to evaluate fairly, too technical to summarize aptly, and simply too abundant to do justice to them in this work. Fortunately Michael Lewis's *Moneyball* and Alan Schwarz's *The Numbers Game* have begun the process of telling that story in the depth it deserves. Still more fortunately, most of the pioneers are still active in the field and are more than capable of telling their own stories.

17.1 Box Scores. The earliest known box score appeared in the *New York Herald* on October 25, 1845, after a game between the New York Base Ball Club and a club from Brooklyn. The box score (which is reproduced in Melvin L. Adelman's "The First Baseball Game, the First Newspaper References to Baseball, and the New York Club: A Note on the Early History of Baseball," *Journal of Sport History*, Vol. 7, No. 3 [Winter 1980], 134) includes only the names of the eight players on each side, along with the number of runs scored and outs made by each.

A 1925 article by a writer named H. H. Westlake contended that the box score was invented by Henry Chadwick in 1859. Westlake reprinted a box score that appeared in the *New York Clipper* in 1859. He acknowledged that there were earlier box scores but pointed out that the 1859 box score was expanded to include five categories: runs, hits, putouts, assists, and errors.

Westlake did not explain why these categories are essential to a box score. Instead he brought out all the rhetorical whistles and bells to state as a "fact" that "the real simon-pure discoverer and inventor of the now invaluable box score was none other than Henry Chadwick, now passed to the great beyond and remembered as the famed 'Father of Baseball'" (H. H. Westlake, "The First Box Score Ever Published," *Baseball Magazine*, March 1925; reprinted in Sidney Offit, ed., *The Best of Baseball*, 68–73).

This article was highly influential, and *Baseball Magazine* received more requests to reprint it than any other article in its fifty-year history (Sidney Offit, ed., *The Best of Baseball*, 68). As a result, Chadwick is generally credited with being the inventor of the box score. But the facts seem to suggest that, at most, Chadwick deserves credit for adding a few categories to it.

Chadwick's 1859 creation was not the end of the expansion of the box score. On August 7, 1860, the *Detroit Free Press* published an astonishingly detailed box score of the first defeat ever suffered by the Detroit Base Ball Club. It began with a basic table listing hands left (outs) and runs for each batter. A second table broke down the outs created by each batter into five different categories. A third table delineated the number and type of outs recorded by each fielder. The fourth and final table enumerated each inning's totals of pitches thrown by the pitcher, foul balls hit, and passed balls (reprinted in Peter Morris, *Baseball Fever*, 59).

As if this weren't enough, additional notes pointed out details for which there was not sufficient room, including the one batter who had the misfortune to strike out. In short, it had almost everything that today's most demanding baseball fan could ask for—with one glaring exception that will be discussed in entry **17.3**.

17.2   Line Scores. A line score would have been a printer's nightmare in the very early days of baseball, when nine innings was not standard (see **1.6**) and dozens of innings might have to be played to reach a conclusion. Accordingly, it was not until 1855 that line scores began to emerge, and they became common after nine innings became the norm in 1857.

17.3   Base Hits. As noted in the entry on "Box Scores" (**17.1**), one statistic was almost always missing from early box scores—base hits!

This omission seems shocking at first, but on reflection it becomes more understandable. Much of baseball's scoring system was borrowed from cricket, where a hit almost always meant at least one run. As a result, cricket scorekeepers understandably kept track only of runs. The early developers of baseball scorekeeping saw no reason to keep track of base hits in a sport where runs determined the victor.

Henry Chadwick gradually came to feel that this was a mistake. He wrote in the 1864 *Beadle's Guide*, "Many a dashing general player, who carries off a great deal of eclat in prominent matches, has all 'the gilt taken off the gingerbread,' as the saying is, by these matter-of-fact figures, given at the close of the season; and we are frequently surprised to find that the modest but efficient worker, who has played earnestly and steadily through the season, apparently unnoticed, has come in, at the close of the race, the real victor."

After reflecting on this for a few years, Chadwick decided on an appropriate course. He initiated the recording of base hits in *The Ball Player's Chronicle*, and stressed before the 1868 season that "there is but one true criterion of skill at the bat, and that is the number of *times* bases are made on clean hits" (Henry Chadwick, *The American Game of Base Ball*, 64, 68). At a game between the Eckfords of Brooklyn and the Mutuals of New York on August 14, 1868, he went further by offering a bat to the player who made the most safe hits. Nearly half a century later, Jimmy Wood claimed with pride that he had earned the prize by making four hits, and "that bat, suitably engraved, is my most treasured possession today" (James Wood as told to Frank G. Menke, "Baseball in By-Gone Days," syndicated column, *Marion* [Ohio] *Star*, August 15, 1916).

Henry Chadwick conducted an intensive publicity campaign for the new statistic. He repeatedly pointed out that run-scoring depended on teammates while there could "be no mistake as to the feat of a batsman making his first base by a good hit or by an error of a fielder. This therefore becomes the only criterion of batting, and therefore in judging a batsman's skill we should first look to his score of the number of times he makes his first base on a good hit or by an error of a fielder" (*National Chronicle*, January 9, 1869). Before long he was proclaiming, "the fraternity in general now recognize that style of batting which secures the first base by 'clean' hits the greatest number of times as the only true criterion of skillful and scientific play at the bat" (*Brooklyn Eagle*, March 25, 1872). Chadwick had a tendency to present his own views as being those of "the fraternity in general," but in this case base hits did indeed become a standard baseball measure.

Contemporary statistical analysts point out that a shortcoming of statistics like hits and batting average is that they make no distinction between a single and a home run. That was not an oversight on Chadwick's part. While he initially advocated tracking both the number of base hits and the total bases from those hits, he always believed that the former was more important (Henry Chadwick, *The American Game of Base Ball*, 62–68). As the years went by, he became increasingly critical of using total bases and even tried to convince his readers that in most cases a single was preferable to a home run. He explained that the object of the batter is "to secure [a run] with the least fatigue. If the batsman hits the ball over the heads of the outfielders he gets his run at once, but at what cost? Why at the expense of running one hundred and twenty yards at his utmost speed, the result being that he arrives home out of breath, and entirely unfit for further play without rest" (*New York Clipper*, April 12, 1873).

Ironically, it appears that Chadwick eventually came to feel that by popularizing hits he had helped to create a monster. In 1880 he complained, "Until a system of averages is adopted which will do justice to the class of batsmen who sacrifice their individual record in order to play for the side, the season's averages, as now made out, will continue to be erroneous data" (*New York Clipper*, December 11, 1880). Five years later, he added: "What with the scoring rules of the League and American associations which not only give such prominence to batsmen who make 'two and three baggers' and 'home runs,' and the system of publishing the batsmen's average every month, every encouragement is given to players to play ball not for the side, but for their individual records." The man who had once presented averages as the only way to ensure the accurate measurement of every player's contributions now complained that averages neglected clutch hitting (*Brooklyn Eagle*, August 4, 1885).

17.4 Batting Averages. The idea of attempting to measure the frequency with which a batter made a base hit is almost as old as the base hit. Henry Chadwick published a table of hits divided by games played in his *National Chronicle* on January 16, 1869. Two of the publications for which Chadwick wrote, *Beadle's Dime Base-Ball Player* and the *New York Clipper*, were soon publishing averages that were computed by using games played rather than at bats as the denominator.

This method was less precise than a batting average, but there were two good reasons for the choice. First, the average reflected the influence of cricket, where batters generally got to hit until they were retired, so that opportunities were equal. Second, counting the number of at bats represented considerable extra work and didn't seem worth the bother.

As these averages began to be taken more seriously, their inequities became more apparent. Marshall Wright reported that the season-ending statistics of two 1870 clubs, the White Stockings of Chicago and the Stars of Brooklyn, included hits, at bats, and the percentage thereof (Marshall Wright, *The National Association of Base Ball Players, 1857–1870*, 287). Most, however, were slower to adapt.

When the National Association was formed in 1871, league secretary Nick Young continued to divide hits by games played. H. A. Dobson of the *New York Clipper* wrote a letter to Young to point out two problems with this method: "In the first place, it is wrong from the fact that members of the same nine do not have the same or equal chance to run up a good score. In the second place it is wrong when comparing averages of players of different nines" (*New York Clipper*, March 11, 1871).

Dobson proposed a fairer method of compiling the new league's averages: "According to a man's chances, so should his record be. Every time he goes to bat he either has an out, a run, or is left on his base. If he does not go out he makes his base, either by his own merit or by an error of some fielder. Now his merit column is found in 'times first base on clean hits,' and his average is found by dividing his total 'times first base on clean hits' by his total number of times he went to the bat. Then what is true of one player is true of all, no matter what the striking order" (*New York Clipper*, March 11, 1871).

It appears that Young ignored Dobson's plea. As late as 1875 the *Brooklyn Eagle* was still presenting "batting averages" that were calculated by dividing hits by games played (*Brooklyn Eagle*, February 4 and March 29, 1875). Accordingly, John Thorn and Pete Palmer have concluded that batting average was "first introduced in its current form" in 1874 (John Thorn and Pete Palmer, *The Hidden Game of Baseball*, 17). It was the *Boston Globe* that did the legwork and was able to inform its readers: "Prior to the departure for England, the batting average of the Boston Club was made out, by which George Wright takes the lead, having made 54 base hits in 139 times at bat in 27 games, or a percentage of .388; Spalding was second, with 75 first base hits in 198 times at bat in 38 games, a percentage of .378" (*Boston Globe*, August 10, 1874).

The *Globe*'s enterprise may have been precipitated by the reporter's greatest bugaboo: the slow news day. In the middle of the 1874 season, the Boston and Philadelphia clubs made a month-long tour of England in an effort to increase overseas interest in America's national pastime. This initial offering of the current version of batting average may simply have reflected a reporter's desperate effort to give his readers some news about a team that was an ocean away. At any rate, when the home club was again stateside, the *Globe* seems to have returned to more standard forms of coverage.

In 1875 college averages were computed by using at bats, but these involved far fewer games. It was not until 1876 that anyone was again willing to undertake the spadework necessary to compute major league batting averages based upon at bats.

At the end of that season the *Chicago Tribune* presented a complete table of games played, at bats, hits, and batting averages, and commented: "It has been a matter of no little difficulty to obtain the record of times at bat with sufficient accuracy to base a table on it, but by dint of much corresponding the necessary figures have been obtained, and a table is made on the correct basis. It is the first time that anything of the kind has been attempted in the United States, and it would be fair for such other papers as prefer to use these figures to making out lists of their own (for which many of them may very likely not have the data) to remember where they found them" (*Chicago Tribune*, October 23, 1876).

Henry Chadwick commended *Tribune* reporter Lewis Meacham for averages "very promptly made out on the bases of times at the bat" (*New York Clipper*, November 11, 1876). Otherwise the *Tribune*'s plaintive cry for some credit for all its hard work seems to have fallen upon deaf ears, as the figures were widely reprinted without attribution. The following year the *Tribune* indulged in some justifiable boasting for having published batting averages based on at bats on the day after the last game of the season (*Chicago Tribune*, October 7, 1877). In 1878 the National League began to use at bats to calculate their official batting averages, and the public soon came to expect and even demand a new standard of speed and accuracy in their averages (John H. Gruber, "Order of Batting," *Sporting News*, February 10, 1916).

As noted in the preceding entry, Henry Chadwick eventually had a change of heart about base hits and batting average. In 1902 he commented, "A batsman's effectiveness is shown by the number of base hits he makes which forward runners, not by the figures of his base hit percentage" (*Spalding's Official Base Ball Guide*, 1902, 70).

17.5 Earned Run Averages. It is not surprising that the concept of the "earned" run, with its strong moral undertones, was championed and likely invented by Henry Chadwick. As Jules Tygiel has observed, the term "earned" originally reflected the batter's perspective rather than the pitcher's. Accordingly, earned runs were designed to isolate runs garnered by safe hits from those resulting from "skillful base running and the fielding errors such running involves" (*Spalding's Official Base Ball Guide*, *1894*, quoted in Jules Tygiel, *Past Time*, 25).

By the 1870s the role of pitchers—so long a subject of controversy (see Chapter 3, especially the introduction)—was being grudgingly accepted as a permanent part of the game. Henry Chadwick wrote with his usual conviction in 1879 that "the only correct basis of a pitcher's skill is that of earned runs" (*New York Clipper*, November 29, 1879). In 1888 the National League and American Association began officially to track the statistic.

But using a hitter's statistic as a yardstick for pitchers was not ideal. The inconsistency of giving a pitcher a free ride for walks and stolen bases did not escape notice. A *Sporting Life* correspondent grumbled that "many pitchers save their records by deliberately giving bases on balls, knowing that earned runs cannot be secured, and thus they save their records" (*Sporting Life*, October 24, 1891). The additional complication of scorekeeping inconsistencies from park to park meant that the statistic was not the most accurate measure of a pitcher's performance.

Even Henry Chadwick, rarely one to reverse his course, became a harsh critic of the statistic he had once championed: "The absurd system of scoring earned runs which governs the code of scoring rules and which mixes up runs earned off the *fielding* as well as the pitching, entirely precludes the use of such earned runs as the basis of estimate. We have therefore ranked the pitchers of 1889 in the order of best percentage of victories" (*Spalding's Official Base Ball Guide, 1890*, 45–46).

Earned runs accordingly fell into disrepute. *Sporting News* explained in 1910: "There is no such thing now, officially, as an earned run. When earned runs were recognized, their specifications changed frequently. There were times when reaching first on four balls, a steal of second and a home run would have meant two earned runs. In 1897, however, the last year they were recognized, an earned run was only credited when scored by the aid of base hits alone" (*Sporting News*, September 1, 1910).

The next few years, however, saw increasing sentiment to rework the statistic. In 1912 the *Washington Post* reported: "There is a move to bring back this feature of the box score, and it is probable that if it is revived a run starting with a base on balls will be counted as one earned, there being no legitimate reason why the pitcher should be favored" (*Washington Post*, May 12, 1912).

That was precisely what happened in the National League that season, with league secretary John Heydler advising "official scorers this year to include bases on balls in earned runs, but not to include stolen bases" (*Chicago Tribune*, June 16, 1912). At season's end, Heydler decided to rank pitchers on this basis in the official statistics (I. E. Sanborn, "Rates Pitchers by New Method," *Chicago Tribune*, December 9, 1912).

Most observers recognized that the resulting statistic was fairer to pitchers on weaker teams, and it was adopted for 1913 by the American League and many minor leagues, with a few modifications. The *Washington Post* explained, "This year the two major leagues have cut away from this archaic system" of ranking pitchers by their won-lost records. It noted approvingly that pitchers would henceforth be ranked "according to their efficiency. The new rating will be based on a modification of the old 'earned run,' the difference being that the modern 'earned run' will include all tallies for which a pitcher is responsible, either by being hit safely or by giving base on balls or wild pitches. Stolen bases also will figure in 'earned runs' on the theory that a considerable percentage of steals are due to the pitcher's inability to hold the runners to their bases, thereby making it practically impossible for catchers to throw them out" (*Washington Post*, June 22, 1913).

The paper went still further a couple of months later, noting how preferable this revised calculation of earned run average was to "the absurd system, left over from the dark ages of baseball, of rating pitchers by the number of games their teams won or lost for them" (*Washington Post*, August 31, 1913). And yet, more than ninety years later, pitchers continue to be given an inordinate amount of credit for the "number of games their teams won or lost for them."

17.6   Won-Lost Percentages. The *Chicago Tribune* observed in 1877, "the *St. Louis Republican* offers a column of 'percentage of games won to games played,' and adds that it is 'something never before published.' The truth is that Little Walker, of the *Chicago Times*, invented, applied and kept up that system through 1870" (*Chicago Tribune*, October 3, 1877). It is not clear whether this comment refers to the records of teams or pitchers, but at least it shows that the concept of using percentages to measure records dates back to very early baseball.

17.7   Runs Batted In. According to Ernest Lanigan, an unspecified Buffalo paper introduced RBIs in 1879 (Ernest J. Lanigan, *The Baseball Cyclopedia*, 56). The following year the new yardstick was picked up by the *Chicago Tribune*. After explaining the method of computing runs batted in, the *Tribune* informed readers: "These figures may, we think, be taken on the whole as a fair criterion of the value a batsman is to his team; for surely the man who hits safely when men are on bases, or who hits so hard as to compel fielding errors on the other side, is of far more value to his club than the man who earns a base for himself twice as often, and makes a weak hit or fouls or strikes out when the bases are loaded."

The *Tribune* noted that Chicago first baseman Cap Anson led the team in the category and claimed that he "undoubtedly leads the league." It further added: "If the record had been kept since the organization of the League it would unquestionably be found that no man ever played ball who batted home so many runs as Anson has done. He seems to have in a wonderful degree the genius of hitting at the right time—an accomplishment which all batsmen will do well to cultivate to the best of their ability" (*Chicago Tribune*, July 11, 1880).

Perhaps the *Tribune* thought that having a local player on top in the category would lead to its ready acceptance. If so, they were mistaken. According to Preston D. Orem, "Readers were unimpressed. Objections were that the men who led off, [Abner] Dalrymple and [George] Gore, did not have the same opportunities to knock in runs" (Preston D. Orem, *Baseball [1845–1881] from the Newspaper Accounts*, 336).

Henry Chadwick, however, liked the statistic and continued to champion it. In 1891 the National League instructed official scorers to keep track of runs batted in. But according to Ernest Lanigan, the scorers disliked the statistic and it was soon dropped. Lanigan reported that it was popularized again by the *New York Press* when he became its sports editor in 1907. The RBI finally became an official statistic in 1920.

17.8   Runs Batted In Opportunities. The same basic problem with runs batted in that was pointed out by *Tribune* readers in 1880 has been a recurring theme of recent sabermetricians. Their mutual complaint is that the statistic is misleading because it takes no account of the number of opportunities. John Thorn and Pete Palmer reported that runs batted in opportunities were an official statistic for the first three weeks of the 1918 American League season. It proved to be too much work and was dropped (John Thorn and Pete Palmer, *The Hidden Game of Baseball*, 25). Elias Sports Bureau began to track the statistic again in 1975, but it has attracted little attention (Dennis Bingham and Thomas R. Heitz, "Rules and Scoring," *Total Baseball IV*, 2549).

17.9   Strikeouts. Tallies of strikeouts were rare in early baseball, for several reasons. First, as John Thorn and Pete Palmer noted, Henry Chadwick "saw them as a sign of poor batting rather than good pitching," and convinced many others to view them that way (John Thorn and Pete Palmer, *The Hidden Game of Baseball*, 25). Chadwick rarely passed up an opportunity to counsel: "Great speed with an inaccurate delivery may yield outs on strikes, but that is no criterion of a pitcher's skill, though many entertain that erroneous idea" (*New York Clipper*, November 4, 1876).

Second, strikeouts were viewed as making for dull baseball, increasing the sense that they should not be encouraged in any way. As the *Grand Rapids Democrat* observed, "Those who attend the games enjoy a good fielding game much better than one won by the crooked and deceiving balls thrown by a pitcher, which causes the umpire to call 'three strikes, and out'" (*Grand Rapids* [Mich.] *Daily Democrat*, August 16, 1883). Finally, since an out is an out, there is no obvious reason to track strikeouts any more than, say, foul outs.

Nonetheless the advent of overhand pitching in the early 1880s led to dramatically higher strikeout totals and greater attention being paid to the statistic. In 1887 pitchers' strikeouts began to be tabulated. Batters' strikeouts began to be reported by former major leaguer Clarence Dow of the *Boston Globe* in 1891 but did not become an official National League statistic until 1909. Bill James noted, however, that the New England League, a minor league, tallied batter's strikeouts in 1890, nearly two decades before the major leagues began to do so (Bill James, *The New Bill James Historical Baseball Abstract*, 64).

17.10   Walks. Even more than strikeouts, walks were viewed as failures rather than successes in early baseball. The schizophrenic treatment they received reflects the fact that their origins (see **1.10** "Balls and Strikes") led them to be regarded as, at best, a necessary evil. Henry Chadwick classed them with wild pitches and passed balls as "battery errors." In 1876 they were grouped with outs (John Thorn and Pete Palmer, *The Hidden Game of Baseball*, 36). Nick Young informed scorers before the 1877 season that "Bases on balls should be charged as an error against the pitcher" (*Chicago Tribune*, April 26, 1877).

A controversial one-year experiment in 1887 saw walks counted as hits. This attracted widespread opposition, and walks were the subject of many derisive references. At the end of the campaign the *New York Times* wrote, "It is true that patience and good judgment on [the batter's] part may help to earn a base under such circumstances, but it is mainly due to the pitcher's error, and the phrase 'phantom hits' shows the popular estimation of such additions to batting records" (*New York Times*, October 9, 1887). Others referred to them as nominal hits or bloodless hits.

Bases on balls by batters were tabulated by Clarence Dow of the *Boston Globe* in 1891 and occasionally tracked by the National League in subsequent years. They finally became an official National League statistic in 1910, and the American League adopted them three years later.

17.11   Total Bases Run. Total bases run was a statistic kept during the 1880 season, which credited players for each base advanced. The statistic was proposed before the season by Harry Wright, a former cricket player: "Harry Wright suggests that the score-sheet shall be changed so as to place to the credit of each player the total number of bases run during the game, with the exception where he reaches first base as the result of the putting out of another player" (*New York Clipper*, February 21, 1880).

It took only one season to make it abundantly clear that a figure that was a basic unit in cricket was essentially meaningless in baseball. Not only was it a lot of work to compile, it measured neither team success—since the team derived no benefit from advancing a runner to third—nor individual accomplishment. Pete Palmer and John Thorn understandably called it a "wonderfully silly figure which signified nothing about either an individual's ability in isolation or his value to his team" (John Thorn and Pete Palmer, *The Hidden Game of Baseball*, 19). Nonetheless it seems worth remembering because it is indicative of the great difficulty of adapting statistics from the apparently similar game of cricket to baseball. Oh, and since

Abner Dalrymple was crowned as the only champion, it means that at least one Abner D. had a significant baseball accomplishment.

17.12 Catcher's ERA. Craig Wright, a pioneer of sabermetrics who helped popularize the catcher's ERA, credited the Japanese with introducing this measurement to him: "In 1982 I read a very interesting article contrasting the attitudes found in Japanese baseball and in American baseball. The central point was that in Japan they emphasize the idea that a team is more than the sum of its parts. Players are evaluated not just on their individual accomplishments, but also by their impact on their teammates and, ultimately, the team itself. The strongest example of this principle is their attitude toward catchers. When a pitcher is struggling in a game, the Japanese manager will sometimes change the whole battery, or perhaps leave the pitcher in and change catchers. And in their statistical records, many teams keep track of the number of runs allowed per nine innings caught for each of their catchers—a catcher ERA, or CERA" (Craig Wright and Tom House, *The Diamond Appraised*, 22).

17.13 Fielding Percentages. The basic concept of the fielding percentage, in which the number of chances successfully handled by a fielder is divided by his total opportunities, was in place by the 1870s, and the term came into use a few years later. Indeed, John Thorn and Pete Palmer note that there were six standard fielding categories in 1876 and the same number a century later (John Thorn and Pete Palmer, *The Hidden Game of Baseball*, 19). That stands in stark contrast to the proliferation of statistics used to measure the performance of pitchers and hitters.

17.14 Range Factor. Bill James is rightly credited with giving attention to range factor as the best measure of defensive prowess. In doing so he was not creating a new measure so much as reviving a very old one.

John Thorn and Pete Palmer noted that journalist Al Wright devised a statistic called "fielding average" in 1875 that was calculated by dividing putouts plus assists by games played: "Does Wright's 'fielding average' look familiar? You may have recognized it as Bill James's Range Factor! Everything old is new again" (John Thorn and Pete Palmer, *The Hidden Game of Baseball*, 19).

The idea has continued to resurface periodically. Sportswriter Thomas S. Rice argued in 1922, "To our mind the element of fielding averages which tells the most, and as a rule, is the only element of real weight, is the number of assists, especially in the case of infielders. You can't get assists unless you go after the ball or have the brains to station yourself where the ball is likely to go. The percentage of assists per game for an infielder will come pretty near to demonstrating his effectiveness and his general help-fulness. Further, as the more desperate the chances at which the player stabs the greater will be his number of errors, as a rule, errors for a man who excells in assists are a sort of tribute to the winning spirit" (*Sporting News*, January 13, 1922).

Forty-five years later, Lee Allen observed, "fielding cannot be mea-sured to the same fine degree that batting is. Fielding percentage is almost meaningless, and lifetime fielding is almost never published. . . . There is one way in which fielding ability can be demonstrated to some extent, and that is to rate players by the chances they accept per game" (*Sporting News*, July 15, 1967).

17.15   Sacrifice Hits. The idea that a batter deserves credit for giving him-self up to advance a runner seemed to originate in the late 1870s as a lin-guistic idea, with the invention of the commendatory term "sacrifice hit." The earliest use of the term that I have found appeared in the *Detroit Post and Tribune* on April 20, 1878.

The following year the *New York Clipper* claimed that Ross Barnes "was among the first to practically introduce the now well-known 'sacrifice hits,' which were written up in baseball books of 1869–70" (*New York Clipper*, May 3, 1879). I believe this statement confuses two different concepts. The bunt (see **2.2.1**) had begun to emerge by the late 1860s, but the term "sacrifice hit" does not appear to have been in use that early.

Additionally, the idea of expending an out to advance another runner is more clearly the product of a later era. In the 1860s, when the bunt origi-nated, the offensive side was so dominant that it would have been foolish to deliberately give up an out. Thus a player who bunted was doing so with the intention of getting a base hit. During the 1870s, however, run scoring dropped so precipitously that a sacrifice hit became a much more reasonable strategy. Since the bunt was out of favor by then, I assume that the "sacrifice hits" referred to above were grounders or fly balls (such as the "right field base hit" discussed in the next entry) that advanced a base runner.

It was not until bunts returned to prominence that batters were given any statistical credit for a "sacrifice hit." In 1889 the statistic began to be of-ficially compiled, but batters were still charged with a time at bat. It took about five more years before the batter's "sacrifice" was recognized by not charging him with an at bat.

17.16   Sacrifice Flies. The sacrifice fly has an extraordinarily schizophrenic history which reflects controversy over whether it should be regarded as a deliberate and successful attempt to drive in a runner or an unsuccessful bid for a hit. John H. Gruber stated that, before scoring rules began to be standardized in 1880, a few scorers advocated the "right field base hit," in which a batter would be credited with a hit for deliberately hitting a fly ball that advanced a runner (John H. Gruber, "Base Hits," *Sporting News*, April 6, 1916). Sacrifice flies were included with sacrifice hits in 1889, but five years later the scoring practice was changed so that a sacrifice could only be credited on a bunt. The sacrifice fly was introduced as an official statistic in 1908, but the rule was repealed or modified several times before finally coming back for good in 1954.

17.17   Saves. Wouldn't it be great to invent a statistic to prove that you were right about something and everyone else was wrong? And then have everyone else not only accept your premise but make it one of the game's fundamental measures? According to sportswriter Deron Snyder, that's exactly what happened to Chicago scribe Jerome Holtzman.

Snyder explained that Holtzman invented the save because he believed that Cubs relief pitchers Don Elston and Bill Henry had had better years than Pirates reliever Elroy Face in 1959. Nobody took his argument seriously because the Cubs relievers had no statistics as glitzy as Face's 18-1 won-lost record. So Holtzman invented the save to prove his point (Deron Snyder, "A Stat Worth Saving," *USA Today Baseball Weekly*, July 21–27, 1999).

As with the sacrifice hit, acceptance of this statistic was eased by the fact that it measured a concept that was already part of the language of baseball. Negro National League founder Rube Foster wrote in 1907 that when a young pitcher is used in relief, "it is natural that he should want to save the game, and so is likely to forget to get into the pitching gradually" (Jerry Malloy, ed., *Sol White's History of Colored Base Ball*, 99). Johnny Evers and Hugh Fullerton observed in 1910, "Three times in the late season [Fielder Jones] summoned [Ed] Walsh to pitch just one ball, and two of the games he saved" (John J. Evers and Hugh S. Fullerton, *Touching Second*, 256).

Sportswriter I. E. "Sy" Sanborn described a 1911 game in which Mordecai Brown "had to rush to the rescue" of starter "King" Cole in the sixth inning. Manager Frank Chance gave Brown fifty dollars from his own pocket as a reward for the "feat of life saving" and told his other pitchers that "hereafter when any one of them was all through pitching in six innings and Brown had to be called to the rescue, Brownie would get $50 for the rescue and the said $50 would be taken out of the short winded pitcher's salary." A note in an adjacent column added, "Manager Chance's decision to reward Life Saver Brown hereafter at the expense of the short winded pitchers on his staff will meet with the approval of the players and public in general" (*Chicago Tribune*, May 21, 1911).

Thus, as with many other statistics, the save originated as a linguistic means of expressing a principle that was deemed important—in this case, that pitchers should finish what they start. The acceptance of this term paved the way for an actual measurement to be devised and become popular.

17.18   Stolen Bases. Stolen bases were a big part of nineteenth-century baseball but were not tracked at all until 1886. Even then official scorers had such different ideas of what constituted a stolen base that the *Providence Journal* concluded that the new rule was "not observed with sufficient uniformity to be of any benefit" (*Providence Journal,* quoted in *Cleveland Leader and Herald,* May 16, 1886). Reaching a consensus on the matter proved very difficult, with the unfortunate result that the statistic was not valid for comparison purposes until 1898. Even more regrettable is that many have used this dispute as an excuse to disregard all nineteenth-century statistics.

17.19   Caught Stealing. Ernest Lanigan says that totals for caught stealing began to be tracked in 1912 at the request of catcher Charles Schmidt (Ernest J. Lanigan, *The Baseball Cyclopedia,* 56). Schmidt presumably was primarily interested in this statistic from the catcher's perspective, but Lanigan compiled it both ways. His totals for caught stealing by both catchers and base runners appeared in December of 1913 in both *Sporting Life* and *Sporting News.*

17.20   On-base Percentages. On-base percentage, which measures how frequently a batter reaches base by hit, walk, or being hit by a pitch, was one of the formulas used by statistician Allan Roth in the early 1950s at the behest of Branch Rickey (Branch Rickey, "Goodby to Some Old Baseball Ideas," *Life,* August 2, 1954, 78–87; cited in Alan Schwarz, *The Numbers Game,* 58–59). Pete Palmer was the first to isolate on-base percentage, and he added it to the American League averages book in 1979. It finally become an official statistic in 1984 (John Thorn and Pete Palmer, *The Hidden Game of Baseball,* 25).

17.21   Slugging Averages. Henry Chadwick published a table of total bases divided by games played in his *National Chronicle* column of February 13, 1869. But Chadwick was not fond of extra-base hits, and the statistic was not permanently adopted until 1923 (John Thorn and Pete Palmer, *The Hidden Game of Baseball,* 21).

17.22   Quality Starts. Author Glenn Guzzo reported that around 1985 *Philadelphia Inquirer* sportswriter John Lowe introduced the quality start, which is defined as any start in which the pitcher lasts at least six innings and allows no more than three earned runs. Lowe saw two primary benefits to the statistic: (1) it was an accurate reflection of what managers expected of their starting pitchers, and (2) fans could easily calculate the statistic by glancing at a box score.

17.23   GWRBI. The game-winning RBI was added to the roll of official statistics in 1980 and dropped nine years later.

17.24   Individual Statistics Emphasized. There have long been divergent viewpoints as to whether keeping track of individual statistics encourages or discourages team play. As noted in the entry on base hits (17.3), Henry Chadwick initially depicted them as a way of ensuring that each player did his part, but later had doubts.

Individual statistics were being widely disseminated by the 1870s, and it did not take long before awareness of them began to have an effect on the game. The term "record player" became common in the 1880s to refer to a player who would not jeopardize his own numbers to try to help the team. This was most conspicuous with fielders, who could usually avoid being charged with an error by not quite getting to a hard-hit ball. Pitchers similarly were accused of deliberately walking dangerous batters, since bases on balls did not count toward earned runs. An 1891 article observed, "The record playing fielder is frowned upon alike by player and public, but the record playing pitcher has in many instances been getting away with it in good style and drawing big incomes" (*Sporting Life*, October 24, 1891).

Batting statistics were less prone to manipulation, but they certainly did attract the attention of players. In 1885 George "Orator" Shafer complained to his team owner that the official scorer was short-changing him (*St. Louis Post-Dispatch*, July 9, 1885). A 1900 article observed that hitters kept close tabs on their batting averages and that, "According to several ex-Indianapolis players, [George Hogriever] sends his base hit record home to his wife every night and has her figure out his percentage at the end of every week" (*Sporting Life*, November 17, 1900).

17.25   Career Milestones Emphasized. When the countdown to Carl Yastrzemski's three thousandth hit in 1979 became a media circus, Red Smith wrote: "When Cap Anson reached 3,000 hits in 1897, there was no congratulatory phone call from President McKinley, who was preoccupied getting a protective tariff through Congress. When Ty Cobb made it in 1921, news accounts of the game mentioned his achievement in the 12th or 14th paragraph. When Sam Rice retired in 1934 with 2,987 hits, it didn't occur to him that maybe he should stick around for 13 more" (Red Smith, September 14, 1979, reprinted in *Red Smith on Baseball*).

I presume that Smith's point is that earlier generations made less of a fuss about career milestones. This is a valid point, but it is important to emphasize that it reflects in large part the unavailability of reliable counts. In addition, there are problems with many of his assertions.

When Cap Anson reached the three-thousand-hit mark, it can be safely assumed that no one had an accurate total. Indeed, Anson's total has been changed several times since then. If his National Association hits are included, he would actually have reached three thousand in 1894.

According to Marc Okkonen, when Cobb reached three thousand hits on August 19, 1921, there was no coverage at all in the local newspapers (Marc Okkonen, *The Ty Cobb Scrapbook*, 157). Again, it is possible that journalists had a slightly different count. Walter Miller, a teammate of Tris Speaker, recalled that when Tris Speaker got his three thousandth hit, "I don't remember a person saying a darn word about it" (Eugene Murdock, *Baseball Between the Wars*, 247). Once more, it is hard to be sure whether this meant that no one thought it significant or that no one had an accurate count. The latter seems more likely, since when Babe Ruth hit his five hundredth home run in 1929, he "dispatched a courier in quest of the priceless ball" and exchanged it with the passerby who had retrieved it for twenty dollars and two autographed baseballs (*New York Times*, August 12, 1929).

We can be surer in the case of Sam Rice, who later recalled, "At that time not much attention was paid to records. The truth of the matter is I did not even know how many hits I had. A couple of years after I quit, Clark Griffith told me about it, and asked me if I'd care to have a comeback with the Senators and pick up those thirteen hits. But I was out of shape, and didn't want to go through all that would have been necessary to make the effort. Nowadays, with radio and television announcers spouting records every time a player comes to bat, I would have known about my hits and probably would have stayed to make 3,000 of them" (Lee Allen, *Kings of the Diamond*; quoted in Jonathan Fraser Light, *The Cultural Encyclopedia of Baseball*, 736).

Rice's contention that radio and television announcers were responsible for the heightened awareness of career milestones is an intriguing one, but it is difficult to prove or disprove. What is indisputable is that the three-thousand-hit barrier assumed a new prominence as baseball was making the transition to new forms of media coverage. In 1942 Paul Waner became the first major leaguer in seventeen years to reach the milestone and was conscious enough of the event that he asked the official scorer not to credit him with a questionable hit. By the time Stan Musial became the next player to join the three-thousand-hit club in 1958, its significance was assumed.

It is also worth noting that there is no particularly good reason for the inordinate publicity given to the three-thousand-hit plateau in recent years. Baseball has so many statistical categories that not all of them can receive the same attention. Sportswriters have simply chosen to emphasize three thousand hits, five hundred home runs, and three hundred pitcher wins while downplaying equally impressive accomplishments, such as one thousand stolen bases, two thousand runs scored, or two thousand RBIs.

Thus the lack of attention to the milestones cited by Red Smith is a complicated phenomenon that cannot be entirely attributed to a lack of interest in statistical accomplishments. Instead a particular milestone comes to be viewed as important based on a number of factors, such as context, attainability, and assorted imponderables.

Due to the vagaries of early record-keeping, it is hard to be sure what was the first milestone to attract widespread attention. The most likely candidate is Cy Young's five hundredth win, which *Sporting Life* hailed as "a unique feat requiring 21 years of continuous effort, which has no parallel in baseball annals, and may never be repeated by any pitcher now before the public, with the possible exception of the illustrious Mathewson" (*Sporting Life*, July 30, 1910; reprinted in Reed Browning, *Cy Young*, 188).

17.26   Streaks. Tracking the length of any particular streak does not require an enormous amount of work. Determining where a streak ranks in comparison with every other player in the history of the game is an extremely daunting task. Thus, as with career milestones, the emphasis on streaks in recent years has been made meaningful by a great deal of hard work by baseball record-keepers.

That does not of course mean that it is only a recent phenomenon for streaks to capture the public's imagination. Around 1910 performance streaks began to attract attention, but there was no accurate tally of the record for such streaks. Rube Marquard's nineteen straight victories in 1912, for example, attracted enormous attention, but there was no consensus as to whose record he was pursuing (Larry Mansch, *Rube Marquard*, 106; Francis C. Richter, *Richter's History and Records of Base Ball*, 247). Walter Johnson was closing in on the record for consecutive scoreless innings in 1913 when it was disclosed that he was actually chasing Jack Coombs and not "Doc" White, as had been supposed (Dick Jemison, "Jack Coombs, Not Doc White, Scoreless Innings Champion," *Atlanta Constitution*, May 14, 1913; George L. Moreland, *Balldom*, 218–219). In 1914 George L. Moreland reported that the longest hitting streak was twenty-five games by Otis Clymer. Later research discovered some much longer streaks, including a forty-four-gamer by Wee Willie Keeler (George L. Moreland, *Balldom*, 271).

Even earlier than that, there had been fascination with consecutive-games-played streaks. This seems to have begun in the 1890s when several catchers, most notably minor leaguer Henry Cote and National Leaguer Deacon McGuire, attracted considerable attention for their hardiness by long skeins of playing in every game (George L. Moreland, *Balldom*, 208).

This interest gradually transferred to players at other positions. In 1909 it was reported that James "Lil" Sager of Evansville had played in 506 consecutive games, which was claimed to be the longest such streak "since the introduction of the national game" (*Sporting News*, July 29, 1909). Sager's streak was finally snapped on May 6, 1911, after 895 games in which he had not missed an inning (*Sporting Life*, June 17, 1911).

Someone soon concluded that the major league record for consecutive games played was 525. During the 1919 season, Fred Luderus of the Phillies had a streak of more than 400 games, but it looked like it would end when he was replaced in the starting lineup. Statistician Al Munro Elias pleaded with the Philadelphia manager to get Luderus in the game, and he was eventually used as a pinch hitter. Luderus ran his streak to 533 games and was hailed for breaking the record (Joe Dittmar, "Fred Luderus," Tom Simon, ed., *Deadball Stars of the National League*, 206). But Luderus lost his record to a long-retired player when "baseball historians dug into the musty archives of the sport to find that George Pinckney, shortstop of the Brooklyn club of 1885–90, had taken part in 578 games without a break" (*Atlanta Constitution*, June 16, 1920).

Thereafter the interest in streaks was assured. During spring training of 1923 a great deal of attention was paid to the fact that Everett Scott had played in more than one thousand consecutive games. One writer crowed that "The odds against beating Scott's record in the future are anything you choose to name" (*Sporting News*, March 22, 1923). A few months later a youngster named Lou Gehrig made his major league debut.

17.27 Record Bureaus. Erratic record-keeping persisted well into the twentieth century, but, as shown by the burgeoning interest in streaks, it was not the result of a lack of interest. A *Sporting News* editorial in 1910 observed that "Scores of fans over the country daily already ask questions pertaining to base ball records no one can answer with assurance for the simple reason that in the past no authentic record has been made of the hundreds of things in base ball calling for emulation."

It accordingly suggested: "The next important evolution of base ball should be a bureau of records, the possibilities of which are as alluring as they are broad. Established under the auspices of the National Commission . . . its first duty should be to receive the official scores direct from official scorers throughout all organized base ball. . . . Such a system would not only relieve the various league presidents and secretaries of laborious routine labor, but would insure the preservation of base ball records in full—which is at present left to private enterprise and is therefore on a more or less haphazard basis. The second prominent advantage to accrue from such a bureau would be the preservation of acknowledged specific records, without which base ball has already been too long" (*Sporting News*, August 18, 1910). Unfortunately, nothing came of this suggestion.

17.28 Single-season Records. As with career totals, seasonal records often got little attention in early years due to the difficulty of keeping track of them. Seasonal totals were not official until tallied at season's end, making it very difficult to honor record breakers. Alan Schwarz cited a 1910 article that observed, "By striking out ten of the White Sox yesterday Walter Johnson established a new strikeout record—it will take the official count to decide whether he has fanned 307 or 308 to date" (*Washington Evening Star*, September 29, 1910; quoted in Alan Schwarz, *The Numbers Game*, 39).

An extreme example happened when Owen Wilson hit thirty-six triples in 1912, a record that still stands. It was not until the following spring that Ernest Lanigan pointed out that Wilson had established a record. The reason it had taken so long to figure this out was that a typographical error had led to Napoleon Lajoie being listed with forty-three triples in 1903 instead of thirteen (the figure has since been corrected to eleven). Lanigan noted that the same typo had also deprived Joe Jackson of credit for having established a new American League record for triples (*Sporting News*, March 13, 1913).

17.29 Detailed Breakdowns. The Dodgers' 1954 yearbook included "a section entitled individual batting breakdowns. It gives each Dodger regular's games played, at bats, hits, home runs, runs batted in and percentage at home and on the road, in day and night games, for each month of the season, before and after the All-Star game, at home against each club, on the road against each club, against right-handed and left-handed pitching, with nobody on base (NOB), with runners on base (ROB) and as a pinch-hitter. . . . There are similar gory details about pitching, fielding, opposing players, life-time records, all-time Dodger marks and so on" (INS wire service: *Syracuse Herald Journal*, April 18, 1954).

17.30 Asterisks. When Roger Maris hit sixty-one home runs in 1961, the asterisk suddenly became the most notorious symbol in baseball. As has frequently been pointed out, Commissioner Ford Frick did not actually specify that an asterisk be used to denote that Maris's feat had occurred during a season eight games longer than the one played by Babe Ruth (Ford Frick, *Games, Asterisks and People*, 154–155). But in any event there was nothing new about having an asterisk in a baseball record book. Gene Karst explains that he wrote to *Who's Who in Baseball* editor F. C. Lane in the early 1930s to suggest that league leaders be denoted with an asterisk. Lane began to do so in the 1933 edition (Gene Karst, "Ready for the New Asterisk War?," *Baseball Research Journal* 26 [1997], 66–67).

17.31   Tape-measure Home Runs. The idea of estimating the length of home runs surfaced in baseball's early days. In 1865, the *Brooklyn Eagle* reported that Lip Pike's brother Boaz "struck the longest ball yet batted on the field, not less, perhaps, than 600 feet straight ahead" (*Brooklyn Eagle*, July 11, 1865). As with many baseball statistics, it was some years before the need was felt for more precise measurement. Moreover the accomplishment was highly dependent upon the elasticity of the ball being used.

As a result, far more attention was given to the measurement of long throws. Throwing contests were common in early baseball, and records were kept with great care. When Ed Crane apparently broke John Hatfield's long-standing record in 1884 with a throw of 135 yards, 1 foot, and ½ inch, the exact distance was verified by a team of civil engineers (*Cincinnati Enquirer*, October 14, 1884). Nonetheless the throw was not generally accepted (George L. Moreland, *Balldom*, 265).

By the 1880s the concept of measuring long home runs began to come into vogue. Lee Allen reported that a fungo hit by C. R. Partridge of Dartmouth College in 1880 was measured at 354 feet, 10 inches (*Sporting News*, April 20, 1968; reprinted in *Cooperstown Corner*). It was topped two years later: "Oscar Walker yesterday at the suggestion of several friends ascertained the exact place where his long hit on Sunday landed. The measurement was carefully made and the tape line told a story of 427 feet, or 142 yards 1 foot, which will do to start a record of long hits against" (*St. Louis Post-Dispatch*, April 11, 1882).

17.32   Simulation Games. The national pastime has long inspired efforts to recreate its pleasures in the form of parlor games. As statistics have become a larger part of the baseball experience, their role in these endeavors has seen a corresponding increase.

"Parlor Base-Ball" was invented by Francis Sebring, a pitcher for the Empire Base Ball Club in the mid-1860s. John Thorn reported that the game was depicted in the December 8, 1866, issue of *Leslie's* magazine and advertised in sporting papers the next year. The game used springs to propel a coin from the pitcher to the batter and then out into the field (David Pietrusza, Lloyd Johnson, and Bob Carroll, eds., *Total Baseball Catalog*, 322). Sebring's version of Parlor Base-Ball seems to have resembled a primitive form of pinball (Dan Gutman, *Banana Bats and Ding-Dong Balls*, 125).

In 1885 pitcher Jacob Aydelott moved closer to simulation when he patented a game that, strangely, was also called "Parlor Base Ball." Aydelott's game involved drawing from a deck of 125 cards that represented specific events (*Sporting Life*, February 25, 1885).

The use of dice to ensure statistical sampling appears to have been introduced in 1887 when two Philadelphia men named McGill and Delany "issued an illustrated card, which forms the diamond field of a new 'game of base ball,' played by means of the chances of dice, each throw constituting a different point of play. Two dice and nine counters, with the board in question, form the materials of the new game and it is played by from 2 persons to 18. It is an excellent parlor game, especially for boys familiar with the points of play in base ball" (*Brooklyn Eagle*, January 9, 1887).

The following year saw the McLoughlin Brothers of New York City unveil a game known simply as the "Game of Base Ball." The game used two dice and appears to have been quite simple, with each sum corresponding to a particular event (David Pietrusza, Lloyd Johnson, and Bob Carroll, eds., *Total Baseball Catalog*, 320).

The first commercially marketed game to try to replicate actual player performance was Clifford Van Beek's "The National Pastime," which he started working on in 1923, patented in 1925, and began to distribute in 1931. It was followed by the more widely marketed Ethan Allen's "All-Star Baseball" in 1941. Van Beek's game used cards while Allen's used a spinner and individualized game pieces for each batter. The new features meant that hitters would produce results that resembled their real-life records, but there was no such allowance for pitchers. These games might be viewed as yet another reflection of the mind-set that pitchers had usurped a role in baseball to which they were not entitled. (Perhaps it is no coincidence that Allen was a major league outfielder.)

It was another generation before simulation games took the next step and incorporated the performance of pitchers and fielders. Richard Seitz introduced "APBA" in 1951, and Hal Richman followed with "Strat-O-Matic," a game he developed during the 1950s and began to mass-market in 1961. Although based upon different principles, both games yielded a degree of statistical realism previously unknown. APBA and Strat-O-Matic attracted loyal bands of followers and dominated the market until the computer revolution, which brought a bevy of new, still more statistically sophisticated games.

17.33   Rotisserie Leagues. So-called rotisserie baseball has brought fascination with baseball statistics to an implausibly wide audience. Daniel Okrent sketched out the basic rules for rotisserie baseball on November 17, 1979, on a flight to Austin, Texas. He presented them to a group of friends at a restaurant called The Pit, but they were uninterested. Two weeks later he explained them to another group of friends at La Rotisserie Francaise in New York, and the game was born.

While the specifics of rotisserie baseball were new, others had previously arrived at similar concepts. Frank W. Hoffmann and William G. Bailey reported that a man named Joe Morgan of Middletown, Ohio, began running a similar league in 1964 and wrote a book about it in 1975 (Frank W. Hoffmann and William G. Bailey, *Sports and Recreation Fads*, 121–123). The writer Jack Kerouac also created a game that operated along the same general lines. And my editor, Ivan Dee, was a founder of the Chicago Baseball League, which started in 1978 and continues to this day. Even Okrent had been inspired by a game designed by Bob Sklar, one of his professors at the University of Michigan.

Chapter 18

MONEY

<hr>

"Just why the nines are called amateurs is a hard question to answer, as all the resident professionals in both cities will play with the clubs."—*St. Louis Post-Dispatch*, May 29, 1886

"Johnny Leber . . . will not report. He says he can make more money playing 'amateur' ball in Cleveland."—*Sporting Life*, April 14, 1917

THE PARADOX embodied in these epigraphs reflects a deep ambivalence that has always characterized the relationship between baseball and money. That relationship has attracted increasing attention in recent years, for the obvious reason that baseball players have become extraordinarily well paid, but there is nothing new about it, as the following entries will demonstrate.

(i) The Transition from Amateurism to Professionalism

During the 1860s and early 1870s, despite vociferous protests from many quarters, baseball was transformed from an amateur activity to one in which money played a pivotal role. The basis of professionalism varied from club to club, with cooperatives and stock corporations the most common forms. The stock corporations made it possible for nonplayers to profit from baseball for the first time, and some did. But the precarious financial situation of the clubs meant that for the most part professionalism enriched only the ballplayers themselves, and most of them were struggling to make enough to live on.

18.1.1 Organization. Although the Knickerbocker Club was opposed to professionalism, the club's members sowed the seeds for professional baseball. At a meeting on December 6, 1856, they passed a resolution calling for a convention of the various clubs playing baseball. The meeting was held at Smith's Hall, 426 Broome Street, New York City, on January 22, 1857, and was attended by sixteen clubs, all of them from the New York City area. It led directly to the founding of the National Association of Base Ball Players (NABBP) and to the adoption of a code of standardized playing rules.

While baseball clubs had previously collected membership fees, this meeting may have marked the first exchange of money between clubs. A man named W. W. Armfield, representing the Eagle Club, moved that each club remit two dollars to cover incidental expenses. The motion passed, prompting treasurer E. H. Brown of the Harlem Club to inform the assemblage, "I don't take Spanish quarters." Brown then collected two dollars from each club, and baseball began a long and relentless march toward professionalism (*Spirit of the Times*, January 31, 1857; reprinted in Dean Sullivan, ed., *Early Innings*, 22–24).

Although the NABBP maintained a rule against professionalism until the 1869 season, it became increasingly evident that it lacked the ability to enforce the rule. Moreover baseball's new level of organization soon ensured that the influence of money would be felt.

18.1.2 Admission Fees. A fifty-cent admission charge—a significant amount of money for the time—was collected for a series of 1858 games between all-star squads of players from Brooklyn and New York City. The games were played at the Fashion Race Course, in what is now Corona, with the proceeds going to a fund for widows and orphans (James L. Terry, *Long Before the Dodgers*, 23).

Some fifteen hundred people attended the first game on July 20, in spite of the cost and the inaccessibility of the grounds. The game was umpired by E. H. Brown of the Metropolitans—presumably the same man who had declined to take Spanish quarters at the previous year's meeting.

Because early parks were not enclosed, it was several years before admission fees became common. The first enclosed stadium to host baseball regularly was Brooklyn's Union Grounds in 1862. Many spectators initially balked at the prospect of paying admission to watch a baseball game, but most of them "gradually became used to the idea" (James Wood as told to Frank G. Menke, "Baseball in By-Gone Days," Part 3, syndicated column, *Indiana* [Pa.] *Evening Gazette*, August 17, 1916).

One of the things that helped ease the transition to collecting admission fees were exhibition "benefit" games, which were staged to raise money for a worthy cause. For example, a ten-cent admission was charged at an 1862 game between the Atlantics and Eckfords of Brooklyn to raise funds for the Sanitary Commission (*Brooklyn Eagle*, November 5 and 7, 1862; the former article said that the game took place in July, but Marshall Wright's *The National Association of Base Ball Players, 1857–1870*, listed those clubs as playing on August 11, August 18, and September 18. The first article is a letter alleging that the funds were misappropriated, but this charge was refuted in the second article).

Often, however, benefit games were thinly veiled methods of getting around the NABBP's rules and paying the players, as this 1861 account suggests: "a complimentary arrangement for the benefit of Messrs. Pearce and Creighton, of the Atlantic and Excelsior clubs, took place on Thursday, Nov. 7th . . . from the comparatively slim attendance of spectators, we should judge that these benefit matches do not find favor in the ball playing community, free contests being the order of the day among them" (*New York Clipper*, November 16, 1861). James L. Terry noted that benefit games were also held for Harry Wright in 1863 and Joe Start in 1864 (James L. Terry, *Long Before the Dodgers*, 30–31).

When a worthy cause was involved, such games gradually gained acceptance. The 1864 announcement that benefit games would be played for soldiers in Brooklyn was warmly received: "Such a class of matches, while they would commend themselves to the patronage of every admirer of the game, if only for the charitable objects in view, would be entirely devoid of the objectionable features of the championship contests, which experience has taught us to be prolific of ill feelings between rival organizations, and productive of scenes at ball matches likely to bring discredit upon the same" (*Brooklyn Eagle*, June 1, 1864). Philadelphia's new ball grounds at Twenty-fifth and Jefferson Streets were inaugurated on May 25, 1864, with a benefit game for the Sanitary Fair that raised five hundred dollars (*New York Clipper*, November 6, 1880).

The new Philadelphia grounds were unenclosed, which presented a daunting problem for anyone hoping to collect an admission fee. This didn't stop Athletics president Colonel Thomas Fitzgerald from trying to do so at a match later that year: "At the various entrances . . . the Colonel posted his doorkeepers. It may be asked (as this was a kind of historic occasion) who these doorkeepers were. But those who know the Colonel do not need to be told. The doorkeepers were the Colonel's sons—not all of them, but those who were, at the time being, the smaller of the series. The receipts of the afternoon were $14. This was not a heavy return, considering especially that the crowd was greater than had ever up to that time attended a match in that city. But the entrance charge was considered more or less as a joke by nearly everybody" (*New York Clipper*, November 1, 1879). Experiments like this made it clear that an enclosed stadium was a prerequisite for collecting admission fees and, as was noted in the entry on "Spite Fences" (**16.2.3**), even that was far from foolproof.

18.1.3 Professional Players. The identity of the first professional player will always be clouded by the rules of the National Association of Base Ball Players, which meant that he received the money under the table and therefore had good reason not to advertise the fact. When Al Reach died, it was reported that he had been the first player to be regularly paid, receiving twenty-five dollars a week before 1860. But Reach's playing career doesn't seem to have begun in earnest until 1861, and the amount cited probably refers to what Reach received for joining the Athletics in 1865.

A much more likely candidate is Jim Creighton, who was almost certainly receiving under-the-table payments for several years before his premature death in 1862. In 1873 the *Brooklyn Eagle* referred to "the noted Excelsiors, who in 1859 practically inaugurated the professional system by their engagement of Creighton, the first pitcher to introduce the disguised underhand throw of the ball to the bat" (*Brooklyn Eagle*, July 16, 1873). If Creighton wasn't the first, he was certainly one of the earliest.

18.1.4 Professional Player to Change Cities. As with the first professional, Al Reach's name is frequently cited. A. H. Spink indicated that "Reach had been playing with the Eckfords of Brooklyn, when Philadelphia enthusiasts, who wanted to get a great team together for the Athletics of that city, offered him a salary which he accepted and it was the first ever paid a professional player. Subsequently [Patsy] Dockney and [Lip] Pike of the Atlantics of Brooklyn were also offered salaries to join the same team" (A. H. Spink, *The National Game*, 190).

The problem with this assertion is that, even if Reach did receive a salary to move to Philadelphia, he likely wasn't the first. Spink claimed that this happened in 1864, while Melvin Adelman gave the year as 1863 (Melvin Adelman, *A Sporting Time*, 151). In fact Reach didn't begin to play with the Athletics until 1865. Two seasons earlier, pitcher Tom Pratt of the Athletics had joined the Atlantics in mid-season and led them to an undefeated season in 1864.

In 1891 an old player wrote to the *Philadelphia Times*: "I distinctly remember, after the Rebellion, the start of the professional business. William [sic] Pratt was taken over to Brooklyn to play with the Atlantics, under salary. The Mutual Club, of New York, was the great rival of the champions across the river, and Pratt's pitching ability was needed by the Brooklyn club. Dick McBride about the same time was put into the City Treasurer's office, with a $1200 salary and nothing to do. There were no contracts in those days, but the Athletics, just the same, captured Al Reach from the Eckford, of Brooklyn, and set him up in a cigar store on the south side of Chestnut street, above Fourth. Then followed [Patsy] Dockney, from New York, who used to play ball every afternoon and fight and drink every night. He was a tough of the toughs. Next came Lip Pike and Fergy Malone, and so on until the nine was composed of players for cash, although an attempt was made to keep it from the public" (*Philadelphia Times*, reprinted in *Sporting Life*, October 24, 1891).

While the nature of the question makes it impossible to prove, it seems most likely that Tom Pratt was the first player to be lured from one city to another by money. Incidentally, the importing of paid professionals bore an intriguing relationship to the Civil War. The *Brooklyn Eagle* reported on August 25, 1863, that Pratt had been discharged from his regiment and joined the Atlantics.

18.1.5   Players Lured West by Money. Detroit may not seem like the West today, but in the 1860s that was how it was considered. For the 1865 season, Henry S. Burroughs of the Eurekas of Newark moved to Detroit and became the captain of the Detroit Base Ball Club. Burroughs also served as a "professor" of gymnastics at the Detroit Gymnasium, where he did offer instruction. But the newspapers of other cities stated that he received some inducements to move to Detroit, and there is evidence to support this claim (see Peter Morris, *Baseball Fever*, 91).

18.1.6   Revolving. By the early 1860s, baseball clubs were actively recruiting the best players of other nines, and those who accepted such offers were known as "revolvers." It may surprise many to learn that the source of this practice was cricket.

As early as 1857, American cricketers were complaining about "the unfair custom of cricketers, who belonged to different clubs, for the purpose of playing in matches" (*Porter's Spirit of the Times*, May 9, 1857; quoted in George B. Kirsch, *The Creation of American Team Sports*, 30). In 1861 the *New York Clipper* observed: "the 'revolver' system not only deprives the contest played in that way of all interest, as a test of strength and skill between the two clubs, but as it is a system of taking unfair advantages over opponents, it in all cases leads to ill feelings on both sides" (*New York Clipper*, July 13, 1861). Once again, the sport being described was not baseball but cricket.

In 1867 Henry Chadwick remarked: "One of the greatest drawbacks to the adoption of the English game of cricket in this country is to be found in the custom in vogue in England, and introduced by English cricketers here, of strengthening themselves in contests by accessions from strong clubs, half a dozen players of an eleven in a strong club being found among the contesting elevens of half a dozen other clubs" (*The Ball Player's Chronicle*, June 20, 1867).

And while baseball may have borrowed revolving from cricket, the practice is much older than either sport. Astylos of Kroton won two sprints apiece in the ancient Olympiads of 488, 484, and 480 B.C. In the latter two he announced himself as being from Syracuse to win favor from the king of Syracuse. The citizens of Kroton responded by pulling down his statue and converting his house into a prison. A century later Sotades of Crete won the same long-distance race in two successive Olympiads. In the second he accepted a bribe from the Ephesians and proclaimed himself to be from Ephesos, which led to his being exiled from Crete (Pausanias, ca. A.D. 170, quoted in Stephen G. Miller, *Arete*, 183–184).

18.1.7 Player Banned for Accepting Money. According to A. H. Spink, James E. Roder was expelled from the Empire Club of New York in 1865 for accepting money to play (Alfred H. Spink, *The National Game*, 5). While it seems unlikely that this was simply made up, neither have I found any support for this statement. The NABBP's rule against professionalism was essentially unenforceable, so it would have been up to an individual club to take such action.

18.1.8 All-professional Clubs. All questions involving early professionals are made problematic by the National Association of Base Ball Players' ban on professionalism, since players could not be candid about receiving payments. The question of the first all-professional club is even thornier, because it is still harder to determine how many players on a club were being paid.

Additionally, many early clubs played on a co-op basis, by which players would recoup their expenses by sharing gate receipts. Sometimes such clubs were described as professionals, other times as amateurs. It is therefore likely that all the members of some clubs were receiving payments by the early 1860s, though they may have been meager amounts.

A still more common practice was to recruit players with the promise of a well-paying do-nothing job. One of the most prominent examples was the famous National Club of Washington, many of whose stars were lured to the capital from New York by offers of positions in the Treasury Department. As Ted Sullivan later remarked coyly, "They were nearly all clerks in the Government Departments at Washington, but I cannot gainsay that they did not get their jobs in Uncle Sam's service for being the possessors of par excellent baseball skill" (*Washington Post*, February 11, 1906).

By the mid-1860s salaries were common enough that there may have been some all-salaried clubs. A. H. Spink claimed the Forest City Club of Rockford, Illinois, formed on August 10, 1865, was the first club to pay regular salaries to its players. Spink was rather ambiguous about when they started receiving salaries, but he seemed to mean that it occurred in 1865 (A. H. Spink, *The National Game*, 5). In an 1895 interview, Joe Start said of the early Atlantics: "We didn't get any salaries, I remember very well, for

three or four years . . . [they were introduced] about 1866, as near as I remember" (*Sporting Life*, November 16, 1895).

In 1869 the NABBP finally changed its policy and let clubs designate
themselves as either amateur or professional. The Red Stockings of Cincinnati were one of the clubs that chose the latter course by openly announcing
that its players would receive salaries. It is difficult to overestimate the importance of the club's demonstration that season that professional baseball
did not have to be sordid. But the oft-repeated statement that the Red
Stockings were the first all-professional club is simply untrue.

Even the contention that they were the first all-salaried nine is open to
dispute, as at least one other club announced plans to pay a salary to each of
its players. Before the season began, the *National Chronicle* reported: "The
[Mutual] Club will adopt a new system this coming year in dealing with their
professional members. A stated sum per season is to be given each professional, in lieu of the gate money dividend heretofore awarded" (*National
Chronicle*, February 20, 1869). The following week it added, "The Mutuals
have organized for the campaign in tip-top style, and are in a flourishing
condition. They have $15,000 in their club treasury, have twelve picked pro-
fessional players from which to select their nine, each of whom will not only
receive a regular salary to be paid whether games are played or not. . . . Premiums will be paid to those who excel in the special departments of the game
as shown by regular statistics at the close of the season" (*National Chronicle*,
February 27, 1869).

A number of other clubs chose open professionalism in 1869, but as far
as is known all of them adopted the cooperative method. The 1870 season
saw eighteen clubs play as professionals, with five of them joining the Mutuals and Red Stockings in paying salaries (*New York Times*, April 7, 1870;
reprinted in William J. Ryczek, *When Johnny Came Sliding Home*, 263). The
National Association included a number of cooperative clubs, but most of
them were unsuccessful and salaries have been a standard feature of major
league baseball since the advent of the National League in 1876.

(ii) Owners Grab the Reins

With the advent of the National League in 1876, the control of clubs by outside parties seeking to make a profit became a permanent part of baseball.
The owners, or magnates as they were usually called in the nineteenth century, instituted the new features that will be discussed in this section.

In the owners' view, these provisions were necessary to reinvent baseball
as a stable business. The players, however, soon began to suspect that the
owners' primary consideration was actually their own profits.

18.2.1   Reserve Clause. Before the adoption of the reserve clause in 1879, players had essentially been free agents at the end of their contracts. That didn't stop clubs from trying to hang on to their players. The rules of the National Association of Base Ball Players dictated that clubs had to honor each other's expulsions. When Lipman Pike resigned from the Irvington Club in 1867 in order to play for another club, the Irvingtons voted instead to expel him. As William J. Ryczek points out, if other clubs had honored this vote, it would have amounted to an early version of the reserve clause (William J. Ryczek, *When Johnny Came Sliding Home*, 145).

Within a few years of the organization of the National League in 1876, the circuit had begun to compile a blacklist (see **18.2.2**) which it used for similar purposes. Before then, however, the league's owners were also laying the groundwork for a more comprehensive restriction on players' leverage. At their annual meeting following the 1877 season, all six owners pledged not to begin discussing 1879 contracts with players until September 1, 1878.

Two years later they went much further. At a meeting in Buffalo on September 29, 1879, the six returning National League clubs agreed to recognize each other's rights to retain the rights to five players. The new rule is often reported to have been the brainchild of Boston owner Arthur H. Soden (see, for example, Francis C. Richter, *Richter's History and Records of Base Ball*, 280). According to researcher David Ball, however, the evidence is far from clear-cut. A year later the *New York Clipper* referred to Soden as the man who "originated" the rule that was initially known as the five-men rule (*New York Clipper*, October 16, 1880). Yet only a few years later the *Chicago Herald* declared: "The fact is Mr. [William] Hulbert was the author of the reserve rule, and at the recent league meeting in Buffalo the fact was unanimously conceded" (*Chicago Herald*, March 7, 1884). So it seems more likely that the rule was a joint effort rather than the idea of any one owner.

The enactment of the reserve rule was not officially announced, but it seems to have been an open secret. Henry Chadwick commented perceptively, "The plan said to be adopted by the League to prevent competition between the several clubs for the others' players is open to criticism, as by it a League club could force a player who had been with it the past season to either play at a reduced salary or play with no League club the coming year" (*New York Clipper*, October 18, 1879).

The scheme spawned more immediate controversy when Chicago signed Troy's Fred Goldsmith two days later. The Troy club naturally objected that this was "a violation of the arrangement entered into at the recent Buffalo meeting, and will protest against the action of the Chicagos in the matter" (*New York Clipper*, October 11, 1879). A couple of months later, Buffalo complained that Cincinnati had signed one of its reserved players, John

Clapp (*New York Clipper*, December 6, 1879). The reserve clause thus began on a fittingly contentious note.

The new rule essentially ended the career of one of the greatest players of the era. George Wright had led Providence to the National League pennant in 1879 but wanted no part of the new rule: "There appears to be no prospect of settling the difference between George Wright and the Providence management. Being still held by the 'five men' rule, Wright cannot sign elsewhere, although he would like to go to Boston" (*Chicago Tribune*, January 18, 1880).

Wright turned down the club's offer and told a reporter that the "so-called 'five-man agreement' was outrageous, with no particle of justice in it" (quoted in the *New York Clipper*, September 4, 1880). He refused to report to Providence and played in one game for Boston on May 29. Providence protested his appearance, and he then sat out the remainder of the 1880 season. Providence relinquished the pennant to Chicago while Wright turned his attention to business.

A motion was made to repeal the rule at the next year's meeting, but it survived and was strengthened in subsequent years (*New York Clipper*, October 16, 1880). The number of players who could be reserved was steadily increased, and from 1883 onward it encompassed enough players that owners could essentially retain their entire team. The rule was incorporated into a standard clause in player contracts that asserted the club's right to retain the player if it so desired. Moreover the owners considered the clause to be perpetually renewable—that unilaterally renewing it one year gave them the right to do so again the next year.

After winning fifty-nine games in 1884, Charley Radbourn observed, "The only difference between the league and slavery is that the managers can't lick you. They have you down so fine that you have no say in the matter at all. I sign a contract with a club, and they can hold me forever, if they see fit, or so long as I want to play ball" (quoted in the *Williamsport Sunday Grit*, October 19, 1884).

The noose was tied still more tightly by the various contracts known as the National Agreements (see **18.2.3**). These accords ensured that leagues would respect each other's reserves. Even a superstar like Radbourn thus had only the most limited of options: "I can jump a contract with the league and join the association, but I can never get back into the league. If I was offered $1,000 a year more by another club I couldn't go, unless I got a release; and there is a combination among the managers to not make any such offer as it might be possible to buy yourself off" (*Williamsport Sunday Grit*, October 19, 1884).

The reserve clause seemed rather obviously to lack "mutuality," a fundamental principle of contract law. Owners did their best to avoid legal challenges because it was widely believed that "baseball men have always known

. . . that their contracts will not stand a test. There is no mutuality, the club having the right to reserve from year to year, and to release at any time, while the player cannot change his employment of his own accord" (*Washington Post*, June 4, 1910). In the 1912 National Agreement, owners tried to address the concern by specifying that 75 percent of a player's salary was for that year's service and the balance was for the right of reservation.

Somehow the owners managed to forestall or deflect legal challenges to the reserve clause for nearly a hundred years. Courts often seemed to be swayed less by legal principles than by the owners' claims that baseball could not survive without the reserve clause. As the *New York Clipper* snidely put it, "they say it is the reserve rule that has elevated baseball and made it what it is. No doubt. Turkey for the clubs and buzzard for the players" (*New York Clipper*, May 3, 1890).

The reserve clause stood until pitchers Andy Messersmith and Dave Mc-Nally did not sign contracts for the 1975 season and then brought a grievance to a three-man arbitration panel. Curiously, like baseball's early umpiring system (see **1.13** "Judgment Calls"), it consisted of two highly partisan representatives—Marvin Miller of the players' union and owners' negotiator John Gaherin—and a neutral third party, Peter Seitz. Seitz, in casting the deciding vote, wrote that the owners' position was "incompatible with the doctrine or policy of freedom in the economic and political society in which we live," and declared both players free agents. After two unsuccessful appeals of the ruling, the owners negotiated the issue with the players' union and a limited form of free agency was incorporated into the 1976 Basic Agreement.

18.2.2 Blacklists. The muscle behind the reserve clause was supplied when the National League adopted a blacklist to ensure that no other team negotiated with a player who had refused to sign with the team that had reserved him. The first blacklist was established on September 29, 1881, and the first players included were Sadie Houck, Lip Pike, Lou Dickerson, Mike Dorgan, Bill Crowley, John Fox, Lew Brown, Edward Nolan, Emil Gross, and Ed Caskin. There were no specific criteria for inclusion, so players could be added for arbitrary reasons.

After the National Agreement (see **18.2.3**) had been expanded to include most professional leagues, a blacklisted player was left with few if any options for making a living in baseball. The blacklist thus proved a powerful device that the owners could hold over the heads of players. The unpopularity of the blacklists was one of the reasons for the founding of the Players' League in 1890.

The Players' League folded after one season, and the owners thereafter ceased to publicize the blacklist. But while it received less publicity, the list continued to be an effective method of discipline. Many "outlaw leagues" thrived in the early twentieth century, but players who joined them knew that they might not be able to return to organized baseball.

The teens and twenties saw a significant number of players banned from organized baseball for life. Most were players such as the Black Sox who had been involved in gambling, but others, such as Ray Fisher, were blacklisted at the whims of capricious owners.

The blacklist returned to prominence in 1946 with the challenge of the Mexican League. Jumpers were threatened with bans from organized baseball for up to five years, which helped dissuade many potential defectors.

18.2.3 National Agreement. The first National Agreement, often referred to as the Tri-Partite Agreement, was signed by the National League, the American Association, and one minor league, the Northwestern League, on February 17, 1883. The three circuits agreed to respect one another's contracts and blacklists, expand the reserve clause, and define territorial rights. Subsequent National Agreements followed, expanding the number of leagues involved and forming the basis of organized baseball. The leagues that signed the National Agreement became collectively known as organized baseball, while nonsignatory leagues were referred to as outlaws.

18.2.4 Territorial Rights. Territorial rights, by which a league grants each club an exclusive franchise for its city and the immediate vicinity, have played an important role in the history of professional baseball in general and the National League in particular.

The high expense of travel was probably the most important obstacle faced by the early clubs that made tentative steps toward professionalism. It was therefore a windfall to have a strong rival in close proximity—indeed a virtual necessity for survival. That was changing by the late 1860s as cheap railroad travel began to make professional baseball viable. Clubs no longer necessarily appreciated having a rival nearby since this cut into the attendance of both clubs.

The National Association, which operated from 1871 to 1875, allowed any club to join by paying the small membership fee. As a result, more than one club could, and often did, share the same town. On one hand, this was convenient for visiting clubs and could create rivalries. On the other, one of the clubs would usually overshadow the others. By the end of the National Association's existence, most felt that the benefits of such an arrangement were outweighed by the disadvantages.

When the National League succeeded the National Association in 1876, it restricted membership to large cities but initially had no policy on territorial rights. Chicago lawyer A. G. Mills wrote a newspaper article criticizing the new league for not granting a guarantee of exclusivity to each franchise. Chicago owner William Hulbert read the article and asked Mills to help him formulate such a plan. When Hulbert became league president, he hired Mills as an adviser, and Mills succeeded Hulbert upon the latter's death in 1882 (James Mallinson, "Abraham Gilbert (A. G.) Mills," in Frederick Ivor-Campbell, Robert L. Tiemann, and Mark Rucker, eds., _Baseball's First Stars_, 114).

The National League's initial plan gave clubs a modest five-mile territorial right. This apparently arbitrary choice took on importance when Albany sought to join the league in 1879 and the Troy club did not want so close a rival. The actual distance between the city centers was about eight miles, but the Troy city engineer used the closest city limits and gave a sworn statement that the two cities were four and three-quarter miles apart (_Chicago Tribune_, April 27, 1879).

A year later the Troy owners decided it would be advantageous to have such a rivalry. Accordingly, the critical distance specified by the league's constitution was modified to four miles. But Albany chose not to enter the National League.

Territorial rights have remained a foundation of the National League since, so much so that they are often taken for granted. While a number of cities have been and continue to be simultaneously represented in the American and National leagues, only the Brooklyn Dodgers and New York Giants have ever competed in the same league and municipal region.

In spite of the storied rivalry between those clubs and the recent success of interleague play, there seems to be no thought of repeating that endeavor. Indeed, there has recently been talk of whether Baltimore's franchise has been damaged by the relocation of the Montreal Expos to Washington, D.C. That is an interesting development, considering that Washington had an American League club at the time that Baltimore moved from St. Louis.

The expansion of territorial rights to include minor league clubs has again made this a hot-button issue in recent years. Minor league owner Joe Buzas was fined more than $2 million for violating the rights of the Salt Lake City Trappers of the Pioneer League by moving his Triple A Portland, Oregon, franchise to Salt Lake City in 1994. In 1999 the Yankees and Mets waived their territorial rights, enabling the New York–Penn League to place franchises in Staten Island and Brooklyn.

(iii) Players Seek a Bigger Share

Once baseball was established as a profitable industry, players began to raise concerns about the practices of owners. As we shall see in these entries, it

took many years before the players were able to organize themselves effectively and thereby create the adversarial system that is the basis of today's
collective bargaining arrangement.

18.3.1   Unions. Players' unions have a long but intermittent history and
have generally sprung up in response to the introduction of new tactics by
owners, such as the reserve clause or salary caps.

Ballplayer-turned-sportswriter Tim Murnane claimed that an early attempt at unionization was made by several Boston players, among them
A. G. Spalding: "About 1872 or 1873, in the old gymnasium on Elliott
street, with George Wright, Ross Barnes, Harry Schaffer and Jim White, Albert and his fellow-players went so far as to draw up an agreement for the
players' signatures." Murnane indicated that "The objects of that proposed
brotherhood were commendable, and, like most organizations of the kind, it
was intended as a hold back to the men who were running the business at a
pressure too high for the equal benefit of all" (*Chicago Tribune*, January 19,
1890; *Chicago Tribune*, January 12, 1890; *Sporting Life*, October 5, 1887).

In 1883 the *Cleveland Leader* reported, "In order to get square with the
eleven men agreement [i.e., the reserve clause] entered into by the professional associations, the players are agitating a project for organizing a protective association, which every professional player will join" (*Cleveland
Leader*, March 30, 1883).

These plans apparently foundered, causing a reporter to comment the
next year: "Baseball players appear to be driven like a flock of sheep. There
is nothing like a protective organization among them, and until they band
together for mutual protection and benefit, they must expect to get the
worst of it" (*Washington Post*, March 16, 1884).

One year later, journalist and minor league manager Billy Voltz attempted with little success to form a protective association. Instead John
Montgomery Ward and several New York teammates secretly formed baseball's first such organization, the Brotherhood of Professional Base Ball
Players, in October 1885 (Robert F. Burk, in *Never Just a Game*, p. 96, placed
the date of the Brotherhood's formation on October 22, 1885, five days after the owners had made their plans for a salary cap public. Bryan Di Salvatore, however, stated in *A Clever Base-Ballist*, p. 176, that the meeting took
place three days before the owners' announcement).

As Bryan Di Salvatore has noted, the Brotherhood tried to avoid the appearance of being a union. Its constitution was "vague, formal, and high-
minded," with an emphasis on such unthreatening principles as aiding "a
brother in distress" and promoting "a high standard of professional conduct" and "the interests of the game of base ball" (Bryan Di Salvatore,
A Clever Base-Ballist, 175–177). During the 1886 season players from other

teams were covertly recruited, until its membership included 90 percent of National League players (Bryan Di Salvatore, *A Clever Base-Ballist*, 178). The Brotherhood went public on November 11, 1886.

The defining moment of the Brotherhood was the formation of the Players' League, which competed with the two existing major leagues in 1890. This would also prove to be the union's swan song, as the upstart league folded after one year. The National League took full advantage of the players' defeat. After merging with the American Association and thereby reducing the players' leverage, it slashed salaries and moved the game dangerously close to becoming a trust (see **22.5.3**).

By 1898 the players were sufficiently fed up to again consider organizing. The *St. Louis Post-Dispatch* reported that the players were meeting to form a union that would demand higher salaries, pay for spring training, and the abolition of the compulsory farming system (*St. Louis Post-Dispatch*, April 6, 1898). Clark Griffith kept the idea alive in 1899, and it gained additional impetus after the season when the elimination of four National League clubs threw many players out of work (*Washington Post*, April 3, 1900).

As the opening of the 1900 season approached, American Federation of Labor president Samuel Gompers explained why he believed the time was right for a movement that could succeed where the Players' League had failed: "The Brotherhood was practically a fight of capital against capital; the present movement has simply in mind the formation of an organization of a self-protecting and benevolent character." Gompers indicated that he was willing for a union of baseball players to operate under the AFL's auspices but expressed a preference that they go it alone: "Personally I would like to see the players organize, with officers from their own ranks, and I know there are some bright, level heads among them" (quoted in the *Washington Post*, April 3, 1900).

On June 9, 1900, the Players' Protective Association was organized in New York. The association decided not to join the AFL, and veteran player Chief Zimmer was elected as president. The Protective Association pursued an aggressive agenda of reform, with one hundred players gathering in New York on July 29 to demand an end to the unpopular practice of farming (see **13.1.5**) and a share of the purchase price when sold. Rumor also had the association reaching out to minor leaguers so that "before the season closes there will not be a ball player in the country unassociated with the organization" (*Washington Post*, June 28, 1900).

The association initially won some important concessions from the owners, but its claim to moral high ground was weakened that offseason when players began to jump their contracts to join the American League. With the players no longer unified, the association faltered, and by 1903 it was dead (Francis C. Richter, *Richter's History and Records of Base Ball*,

161–165). Its demise prompted the *Washington Post* to remark, "The apathy of the players in allowing their union to blow up would indicate they have little fear of a deep cut in salaries. Fancy stipends may be chopped some, but the normal pay will not shrink, the wise ones say" (*Washington Post*, August 9, 1903). That mind-set remained in ascendance for another decade.

The Players' Fraternity was formed during the 1912 season and made permanent on October 20. Headed by lawyer and former major leaguer Dave Fultz, the fraternity made some initial progress but failed to establish a working relationship with the owners (Francis C. Richter, *Richter's History and Records of Base Ball*, 165–172). The fraternity was one of the casualties of the demise of the Federal League; three more decades would pass before there was another serious attempt to unionize.

On April 17, 1946, labor relations lawyer Robert Murphy formed the American Baseball Guild and began trying to convince major league players to join. Ralph Kiner later recalled that Murphy cannily "was careful not to call it [the Guild] a 'union'; he always had a euphemism" (quoted in Charles P. Korr, *The End of Baseball as We Knew It*, 16). Even so, the idea created considerable anxiety. Jack Norworth, author of "Take Me Out to the Ball Game," was quoted in *Sporting News* as saying that if the Guild were successful, it might inspire him to write a new song in which "ticket line" would rhyme with "picket line" (*Sporting News*, June 5, 1946).

The idea made major league owners even more anxious, and they swiftly announced plans to offer several concessions to the players. These included a minimum salary, spring training expenses (which is still known as "Murphy money"), and the first pension fund for players. This conciliated a sufficient number of players, and the Guild did not win the necessary votes. Murphy abandoned his efforts, but not before telling a reporter, "The players have been offered an apple, but they could have had an orchard" (quoted in Lee Lowenfish, *The Imperfect Diamond*, 151).

On August 21, 1953, player reps Ralph Kiner and Allie Reynolds hired labor leader John Norman Lewis to give them legal advice during negotiations with the owners. Lewis's goals were limited and his accomplishments still more modest, but his hiring established the Players Association as a permanent entity. Lewis was succeeded in 1959 by the equally innocuous Judge Robert Cannon, who continued to focus on gaining improvements to the players' pension fund while stressing that he "was not there to fight ownership" and had no desire to "jeopardize the fine relationship existing between the players and club owners" (quoted in Charles P. Korr, *The End of Baseball as We Knew It*, 27, 23).

Under Cannon's leadership, the Players Association remained, in the words of longtime director Frank Scott, a "House Union" (quoted in Charles P. Korr, *The End of Baseball as We Knew It*, 2). Charles P. Korr noted that during these years, "Even the word 'union' did not come easily to the vocabulary of the players; 'association' and 'players' group' were the preferred terms" (quoted in Charles P. Korr, *The End of Baseball as We Knew It*, 1).

In 1966, when Marvin Miller replaced Cannon, the Players Association quickly assumed the traditional functions of a union. Although some player reps continued to be uncomfortable with "the word 'union,'" Miller distanced the organization from such euphemisms (Bob Barton, quoted in Charles P. Korr, *The End of Baseball as We Knew It*, 108). He declared in 1972, "I don't know why there is confusion about this, but the Major League Baseball Players Association is a union in structure, in purpose, in its functioning, it is a union under the law, and it has all the rights, duties, and obligations of any other bona fide union" (quoted in Charles P. Korr, *The End of Baseball as We Knew It*, 66).

18.3.2 Player Strikes. Baseball has been blighted by a series of strikes and lockouts over the past thirty years. While shutting down the entire game is a new development, the threat of such disruptions by individual teams has a much longer history than most fans realize.

According to Jimmy Wood, labor unrest was part of baseball as early as 1865. Owners of ball fields had been keeping all the admission fees in exchange for allowing players to play and practice rent-free. But when players became aware of the profits that could be made, they demanded: "Give us part of the gate receipts or we won't play!"

There were eventually allotted 25 percent of the gate receipts, but soon they decided that wasn't enough. They next demanded 35 percent—"again threatening a strike"—and got it. Within two years "the players, by use of threats of quitting the diamond, had forced the club owners [sic] to pay them 75 per cent of the gross receipts of each game, that sum being divided equally among the players" (James Wood, as told to Frank G. Menke, "Baseball in By-Gone Days," Part 3, syndicated column, *Indiana* [Pa.] *Evening Gazette*, August 17, 1916).

Once leagues were developed, club owners signed players to contracts that minimized their leverage. It was not, however, long before the threat of strikes again surfaced. On August 31, 1878, the Milwaukee Cream Citys threatened not to take the field for a National League game against Indianapolis (Donald Dewey and Nicholas Acocella, *The Ball Clubs*, 305). On May 2, 1889, the St. Louis Browns nearly went on strike after owner Chris Von der Ahe suspended "Yank" Robinson. The team finally agreed to play their next series but lost three straight to lowly Kansas City by lopsided margins, prompting suspicions that they had deliberately thrown the games.

Later that same season, Louisville was in the midst of a major league record twenty-six-game losing streak when team owner Mordecai Davidson threatened to fine his players if they lost their next game. Since Davidson was behind in paying the team their salaries, the players were understandably outraged, and only six of them showed up for the team's game on June 15. The team used three local recruits and was beaten 4-2. The regulars returned the next day.

Both disputes were fueled by a contentious relationship between players and owners which led to the formation of the Players' League in 1890. With three major leagues, everyone lost money in 1890. The Philadelphia franchise in the American Association was especially hard-hit and fell far behind in paying its players. By the end of the season most of the players had abandoned the club, and it relied more and more on picking up local amateurs.

When Cleveland star Addie Joss died suddenly in 1911, American League president Ban Johnson initially refused to cancel Cleveland's scheduled game with Detroit on April 17, the day of the funeral. But with Cleveland on the verge of revolt and Detroit rumored to be likely to join them, Johnson backed down and canceled the game.

The following year the Tigers did hold a one-day strike on May 18, 1912, in protest of Johnson's suspension of Ty Cobb. Detroit manager Hugh Jennings penciled two coaches and seven sandlot players into the lineup and was beaten 24-2. The regular Tigers returned the next day at Cobb's urging.

Another crisis occurred in 1914 when pitcher Clarence Kraft was ordered by the National Commission to report to Nashville in the Southern League. Kraft understandably balked when he learned that he would receive $150 less a month in Nashville than he had been earning for Newark of the International League. Players' Fraternity leader David Fultz saw the case as the epitome of the need for reform. After a number of threats, he prepared "a letter which is generally termed in baseball circles an ultimatum from the fraternity to organized baseball" (*Washington Post*, July 21, 1914). A strike was averted when Charles Ebbets purchased Kraft's contract and assigned him to Newark with back pay.

Midway through the 1918 World Series, the players on both sides threatened to strike over the paltry shares they were to receive. The start of the fifth game had to be delayed when the players refused to take the field. The owners refused to budge, however, and were successful in convincing the players that they would appear greedy if they went on strike while the country was at war.

On July 10, 1943, Brooklyn's players threatened to strike after Leo Durocher suspended Bobo Newsom; only the last-minute intervention of Branch Rickey enabled the Dodgers to field a team. Brooklyn took out their frustrations on the Pirates instead, with ten-run outbursts in both the first and fourth innings.

A few weeks later, on July 28, 1943, the Phillies nearly struck to protest the firing of manager Bucky Harris. On June 7, 1946, the Pirates voted 20 to 16 to walk out for that day's game—but a two-thirds vote was necessary to strike, so the game went on.

Strike action at the minor league level has been less common due to the comparative ease of replacing the players. One exception occurred in 1950 when the Waterbury team of the Colonial League fired all its players on July 14 after they refused to board the team bus because of several issues, including the safety of the vehicle. The issue became moot when the Colonial League disbanded the next day.

The first collective strike took place in 1972 when the major league season was delayed by a strike that wiped out 36 games. Since then labor disputes have plagued major league baseball. The 1981 major league season was interrupted by a two-month strike that led to the cancellation of 706 games. Another strike began on August 6, 1985, but was settled after one day.

A lockout interrupted spring training in 1990 and delayed the start of the season by a week. In 1994 the last two months of the season and the World Series were canceled due to baseball's longest and most harmful strike. The 1995 season was also shortened by eighteen games because the previous season's strike was not resolved until the eve of the season.

18.3.3   Player Reps. With the threat of Robert Murphy's Guild looming, baseball owners invited player representatives to attend several of their meetings in 1946 and 1947. Commissioner Ford Frick maintained that the invitation was not a preemptive move; he claimed that he had been planning to do so since 1936, "but inertia got hold of me" (William Marshall, *Baseball's Pivotal Era, 1945–1951*, 74–75). Each league was represented by three players—Johnny Murphy, Mel Harder, and Joe Kuhel from the American League, and Dixie Walker, Marty Marion, and Billy Herman from the National League. Murphy and Walker acted as spokesmen for their respective leagues and were the only players invited to most of the meetings. As is noted in the next entry, they were accorded significant concessions on such issues as pensions. The success of Murphy and Walker at gaining ground on these fronts was made easier by their willingness to accept the reserve clause, which both men defended as being "essential for the players' protection as well as the owners'" (AP: *Washington Post*, January 21, 1948).

18.3.4   Pension Fund. There is no better symbol of the deep enmity between players and owners than the problems that have plagued the seemingly innocuous issue of pensions. Umpires actually had a pension plan several years before players did (Herbert Simons, "Life of an Ump," *Baseball Magazine*, April 1942; reprinted in Sidney Offit, ed., *The Best of Baseball*, 156–162).

With Robert Murphy attempting to form a players' guild, major league owners finally agreed to a pension plan for players on July 8, 1946. The details were ironed out by a committee that included player representatives Johnny Murphy of the Yankees and Dixie Walker of the Dodgers, and were approved by the owners on February 1, 1947. The plan guaranteed any player with five years' service an income of at least fifty dollars a month beginning at age fifty. The moneys were drawn from contributions by both players and owners, along with All-Star Game revenues and World Series broadcast revenues (John Drebinger, "Pension Program for Players Voted by Major Leagues," *New York Times*, February 2, 1947). The plan went into effect on April 1, 1947, and the first pension recipient was the widow of Ernie Bonham, who died in 1949 while still an active player.

Lee Lowenfish noted that "Because the pension was established by the owners as a sop to forestall player unionization, it would regularly become an area of great controversy every five years when it came up for renewal" (Lee Lowenfish, *The Imperfect Diamond*, 149). That was not an overstatement.

By the early 1950s owners were refusing to give the players an accounting of the pension fund. In fact there was no pension fund. More recent requirements that pension money be held in trust did not yet apply, so pension revenues and payments were being made from the commissioner's central fund (Charles W. Bevis, "A Home Run by Any Measure," *Baseball Research Journal* 21 [1992], 67).

Ongoing concerns about the pension led the players to hire their first paid representative, John Norman Lewis, in 1953. Pensions still topped their agenda in 1966 when Marvin Miller was hired to head the Players Association. A near-strike in 1969 and baseball's first in-season strike in 1972 both revolved around pension issues. In 1994 the already contentious negotiations were further damaged when the owners withheld a scheduled payment to the players' pension fund (Charles P. Korr, *The End of Baseball as We Knew It*, 75–76, 103–115, 259).

18.3.5 Player Agents. Player agents as we now know them did not exist in the nineteenth century, though there were some attempts along that line. Researcher Bryan Di Salvatore found an ad in the *New York Clipper* of February 16, 1884, for a Baseball Employment Bureau operated by S. G. Morton of Chicago, secretary of the Northwestern League. Clubs paid ten dollars or players five dollars to use Morton's services. Di Salvatore also found a note in the *New York Clipper* of November 6, 1886, describing an agency started in Philadelphia by O. P. Caylor. This note indicated that there had been a similar agency in Philadelphia sixteen years earlier but that its unidentified founders "speedily found that there existed no field for such an agency" (cited in Frederick Ivor-Campbell, "When Was the First? [Part 4]," *Nineteenth Century Notes* 95:3, 4 [Summer/Fall 1995], 10–11).

Minor league executive Jesse Frysinger set up a player agency in Chester, Pennsylvania, in 1901 to capitalize on his extensive connections: "it is safe to say there are few clubs or players within a radius of 300 miles he doesn't know personally. Last season he secured positions for several hundred players and aided over 50 clubs to get good men" (*Chester Times*, reprinted in *Sporting News*, May 11, 1901). In 1905 sportswriter Tim Murnane recorded the formation of another such agency: "The International Base Ball Bureau of Syracuse, N.Y., with George Geer and Jay Faatz as managers, is now open for business. The idea is to furnish jobs for ball players and umpires taking as a fee one half of the first month's salary" (*Sporting News*, January 7, 1905).

Player agents in their current form seem to have first entered the game in the 1920s. A *Sporting News* correspondent reported in 1922: "Officials of clubs in the Coast League say it's hard to find a good looking prospect these days who isn't being 'managed' by somebody. If the ball player is asked to sign a contract his answer is that his 'manager' will have to be consulted about the terms. . . . Sometimes a busher demands a bonus as high as $1,000 or $1,500 before he signs, and the manager-agent also gets a cut out of that" (*Sporting News*, February 9, 1922).

Another *Sporting News* correspondent noted five years later, "Branch Rickey, acting as field agent for Sam Breadon, discovered that [Tommy Thevenow] had an adviser, manager, or something. Great horrors, multiplied! When this intelligence was transmitted to Breadon, the even-mannered chief executive of the Cardinals fairly exploded. With each spoken word rolled clouds of blue smoke. Private managers. They're the bane of Sam's life.

"It will be recalled that Rogers Hornsby had a manager, or two, to advise him in his late lamented affair with the Cardinals, so it takes no stretch of the imagination to appraise the feelings of the club president—Rickey's too, for that matter—when Tommy bobbed up with his 'adviser.'

"Forthwith came an ultimatum from Breadon. Tommy was advised to rid himself of 'his friend' before he could expect further consideration from the club in re his contract. Therein, the Cardinals are holding out, with no telling when the matter will be adjusted if both sides hold their ground.

"'I am sick and tired of this "third party" business when it comes to dealing with ball players,' said Breadon. 'I offered Thevenow a more substantial salary than ordinarily is given a second year man. But it's not a question of salary now, but a question of 'third party' advice that is holding the player back" (*Sporting News*, March 10, 1927).

Owners continued to fight the use of agents tooth and nail. Players won the right to hire representatives in 1946, but only for financial planning rather than negotiating. In the 1960s pitcher Earl Wilson brought agent Bob Woolf with him to help negotiate his contract, but Woolf was asked to leave by Tigers general manager Jim Campbell. Woolf sat out in the car, and Wilson periodically asked for bathroom breaks so he could get advice (John Helyar, *Lords of the Realm*, 94).

Only in the 1970 Basic Agreement were agents granted the right to take an active role in contract negotiations.

18.3.6   Basic Agreement. The first Basic Agreement between the players and owners was signed on February 19, 1968. As Charles P. Korr has noted, the very idea of a collective-bargaining agreement "ran counter to the norms of professional sports" (Charles P. Korr, *The End of Baseball as We Knew It*, 69). Thus members of management such as Braves general manager Paul Richards viewed the development as "the end of baseball, as we knew it." The assessment proved so apt that it became the title of Korr's outstanding history of the Players Association (quoted in *Atlanta Journal*, December 1, 1967; reprinted in Charles P. Korr, *The End of Baseball as We Knew It*, 1). Most of baseball's labor wars in the years since have concerned the renewal of the Basic Agreement.

(iv) Negotiations

Players and owners have sought to strengthen their bargaining positions in a number of creative ways, but as a rule the same few basic factors have always been most important.

18.4.1   Rival Major Leagues. Challenges to the National League date back to its beginning in 1876. Some of these stimulated competition and brought new life to the game while others created a warlike atmosphere that damaged and impoverished both sides. The consequences have been less equivocal for players, invariably providing them with leverage that has led to material improvements in their lot.

The rival leagues that have earned official recognition as "major" are the American Association (1882–1891), the Union Association (1884), the Players' League (1890), the American League (1901–present), and the Federal League (1914–1915).

It is important to understand, however, that the decision to categorize a rival league as "major" is not always cut and dried. There are those who contend that some of the above leagues were not of sufficient quality to warrant major league status. On the other hand, there have been numerous other threats to the recognized major leagues that were taken very seriously at the time, whether or not they ever played a game.

In 1894 Fred Pfeffer, Billy Barnie, and Al Buckenberger were behind an abortive effort to revive the American Association (David Q. Voigt, *The League That Failed*, 212–213). The effort was detected by the National League, whose board blacklisted all three men and wrote sanctimoniously: "To-day the future of base ball is confronted by a new condition, a condition which in every particular is as harmful and in many respects far more dangerous than open dishonesty or flagrant dissipation. That is, treachery within the lines. To-day, and for months past, we have had men identified with professional base ball who for years have been the beneficiaries of the game, have received liberal compensation for the work they have done, earned their livelihood entirely and absolutely from the opportunities afforded them by clubs and organizations operating under the national agreement, and we find and now know that these men, during this time, have persistently been identifying themselves with schemes and combinations the sole purposes of which are to weaken and perhaps destroy the splendid fabric of our national game" (*Spalding's Official Base Ball Guide, 1895*, 5). The blacklist was lifted, but the initiative had been crushed.

A more protracted effort to revive the American Association occurred in 1900. Such prominent baseball men as Cap Anson, Al Spink, and John McGraw were involved in the venture, but the league never got off the ground. It did, however, pave the way for the success of the American League (Adrian C. Anson, *A Ball Player's Career*, 329–336).

The American and National leagues were at peace by 1905, but it was not long before other leagues were challenging them for supremacy. According to Francis Richter, there was an abortive scheme to merge the Eastern League and American Association into a third major league in 1907 (Francis C. Richter, *Richter's History and Records of Base Ball*, 156).

In 1910 a promoter named Dan Fletcher began work on a novel rival league that he called the All-Star League, but which was generally referred to as the Option League. Fletcher had little money of his own but nonetheless was the front man for a very ambitious scheme (*Frederick* [Md.] *News*, November 2, 1910). He began signing major leaguers to optional contracts, which guaranteed them a $10,000 bonus to sign a subsequent contract with a league *if Fletcher was able to organize one*. If the league did not materialize, they received nothing (*Nebraska State* [Lincoln] *Journal*, October 23, 1910).

Exactly how many major leaguers Fletcher signed up is a matter of debate. Fletcher himself claimed to have the signatures of eighty star players, and sportswriter William A. Phelon estimated that he signed "some

70 well-known players" (William A. Phelon, "Shall We Have a Third Big League?," *Baseball Magazine*, March 1912, 10). Others believed the figure to be lower, but even detractors of the scheme acknowledged that "a great many players did sign these conditional contracts" (Francis C. Richter, *Richter's History and Records of Base Ball*, 157).

By December it was clear that the league would not be able to make a go of it (*Wisconsin Daily Northwestern*, December 10, 1910). Nonetheless the effort "demonstrated that the big baseball asset is easily acquired" and that "players are simply crazy for something to break loose," which doubtless encouraged other rival leagues (*Indianapolis Star*, November 13, 1910). Fletcher's league had another intriguing legacy. His league acquired a plot of land in Chicago that was bordered by Sheffield, Addison, Seminary, and Waveland, and began grading it (*Washington Post*, December 30, 1910). The Federal League subsequently acquired the land and built the stadium that is now called Wrigley Field.

Sportswriter W. A. Phelon believed that while Fletcher showed the potential for a rival big league, he also damaged the cause: "Fletcher spoiled the players. One and all of them, they are now as suspicious of new league promoters as a tomcat is suspicious of three bulldogs." To characterize the response of star players to talk of new leagues, Phelon used a phrase that would be featured in a much more recent movie: "No more Fletcher stuff in mine. Show me the money, right here in my hand, and I'll talk to you" (William A. Phelon, "Shall We Have a Third Big League?," *Baseball Magazine*, March 1912, 11).

As a result of this suspicion, the next few seasons saw a number of efforts that were modest in scope and produced still less impressive results. In 1912 John T. Powers of Chicago outlined plans for a Columbian Baseball League, which was to be centered in the Midwest with franchises in Kansas City, Chicago, St. Louis, Louisville, Indianapolis, Detroit, Cleveland, and Milwaukee. Cap Anson was reportedly also a principal in the endeavor, but interest proved tepid and the circuit never played a game (*New York Times*, January 14, 1912; February 13, 1912; *Chicago Tribune*, March 6, 1912; Francis C. Richter, *Richter's History and Records of Base Ball*, 158).

The United States League got a little further in challenging the majors that same year. The league was the brainchild of William Abbott Witman, Sr., of Reading, Pennsylvania, and fielded clubs in Chicago, Cleveland, Cincinnati, Pittsburgh, New York, Reading, Richmond, and Washington.

The effort was plagued from the start by indecision as to whether it was challenging the existing major leagues. Witman made brave talk about the antitrust activities of the existing major leagues and about omitting the reserve clause from contracts (*Atlanta Constitution*, December 22, 1911). Yet at the same time he emphasized that his league would respect the contracts of organized baseball and had no intention of starting a war (*Atlanta Constitution*, December 22, 1911; *Washington Post*, January 30, 1912).

The result was the perception of the new league as "meek" (*Los Angeles Times*, March 10, 1912). Worse, it meant that the league was made up of castoffs from organized baseball. A few well-known names such as Jack O'Connor and Deacon Phillippe signed on as managers, but the only noted player to sign was Bugs Raymond, a notorious drinker. The league began play on May 1 but was on shaky financial footing from the start and folded after five weeks (Francis C. Richter, *Richter's History and Records of Base Ball*, 158).

Witman revived the United States League for the 1913 season, limiting his scope this time to the East Coast by awarding franchises to Baltimore, Brooklyn, Lynchburg, Newark, New York, Philadelphia, Reading, and Washington. The league commenced play on May 10 but folded only three days later, leaving many players stranded (*Chicago Tribune*, May 15, 1913; Francis C. Richter, *Richter's History and Records of Base Ball*, 158–159).

The apparently fruitless efforts of 1912 and 1913 did yield one highly significant outcome. In 1913 John T. Powers formed another independent league along the same lines as the Columbian and United States leagues. The new Federal League operated for one season as an independent minor league and was not perceived as a threat by organized baseball. After one year it reinvented itself as a rival major league and became the most serious challenger of the twentieth century.

The collapse of the Federal League after two seasons, and the United States' entry into World War I, left the field free of challengers for several years. By the 1920s it had become clear that there was a large group of players of major league caliber who were being denied access based solely on their skin color. At least one promoter, Andy Lawson, considered a rival major league that would be based on these talented players. When Lawson announced plans for his Continental League in 1921, he hinted that he would use African-American players (David Pietrusza, "The Continental League of 1921," *National Pastime* 13 [1993], 76–78). Neither the plan nor the league came to fruition, so many of the era's best players never played in the recognized major leagues and instead competed in the leagues now collectively known as the Negro Leagues.

In 1946 the Mexican League lured a number of well-known players from the major leagues. The circuit's promising start was quickly thwarted by financial and logistical problems. It survived until 1948 but by then had ceased to be a threat to the National and American leagues (Lee Lowenfish, *The Imperfect Diamond*, 158–159).

In the late 1940s and early 1950s the Pacific Coast League featured many Western players of major league caliber who preferred playing closer to home. There was serious talk that the PCL deserved to be considered a major league. The league's unique status was acknowledged with an unprecedented "open" classification. But any chance of major league recognition ended when the Giants and Dodgers moved west.

That same move prompted New York City mayor Robert Wagner to announce plans to start a Continental League after the 1958 season. The prospective new league gained credibility when Branch Rickey signed on as one of its leaders. The new circuit was scuttled by the National League's decision to grant New York an expansion franchise, but it demonstrated that a rival league didn't even have to play a game in order to improve the lot of ballplayers. Expansion naturally provided major leaguers with much greater job security. Charles P. Korr suggested that this paved the way for the increased militancy of the Players Association in the 1960s, which in turn allowed player salaries and benefits to soar (Charles P. Korr, *The End of Baseball as We Knew It*, 80).

There have been a few scattered efforts in the last thirty years to form a rival major league. A World Baseball Association was proposed in 1974. Donald Trump at one point made plans to launch The Baseball League. The United Baseball League was formed in 1994 with intentions of beginning play in 1996. None of these enterprises made it past the drawing board.

The National League's first major rival was actually none of the above. The International Association, formed in 1877, was the logical successor to the loosely organized National Association. This league has been denied "major league" status due to its loose organization and lack of a fixed schedule.

That decision is, to be blunt, an example of the fact that history is usually written from the perspective of the victors, if not actually by them. The idea that a fixed schedule is a litmus test of major league status is very difficult to justify, especially since the National League didn't have one in 1876. Loose organization is an even more nebulous claim.

When more important criteria are considered, little doubt is left of the league's status. The International Association competed with the National League for players and featured players of comparable quality. It proved its strength with competitive results in head-to-head games against the National League.

The International Association lasted for four years, though it changed its name midway through. On February 19, 1879, the league became known as the National Association because it no longer had any Canadian entries. Whether it is officially recognized or not, the International Association was the first rival of the National League.

18.4.2   **Leverage.** The basic economic principle of supply and demand has always exerted a powerful influence on player salaries. The presence of a rival major league, in particular, has invariably driven up salaries and related forms of compensation. The threat of jumping to an "outlaw" minor league has also afforded valuable leverage to a discontented ballplayer.

Until the 1879 adoption of the reserve clause (see **18.2.1**), the players had the ultimate form of leverage. Since they were all free agents at the end of each season, players could get market value for their services by threatening to jump to a rival club. Some found ways to artificially inflate the demand; according to Tim Murnane, after pitching a no-hitter in 1875 Joe Borden was "cute enough to lay up for the rest of the season" and thereby secured a three-year contract for much more than his value (*Boston Globe*, February 19, 1900).

The reserve clause changed everything, because owners could take advantage of their exclusive rights to use a "take it or leave it" approach. Suddenly the only leverage players had was to threaten a change of profession. Player salaries were low enough in the 1880s to make such threats plausible, but even then most baseball players were relatively well paid and were unlikely to be able to make similar amounts in another line of work.

But some at least did have legitimate alternatives. In particular, management found that a "take it or leave it" approach would not work with collegians of the era. Yale star Bill Hutchison received his diploma in 1881 but turned down all baseball offers to pursue business. Only financial reversals prompted him finally to return to baseball in 1886. Columbia Law School graduate John Montgomery Ward was said in 1893 to be "making the customary mid-winter bluff of the ball player of retiring from the diamond. As usual in such cases, it will not amount to anything" (*Sporting News*, January 21, 1893). But Ward did indeed retire after the 1894 season to practice law.

Others realized there was no harm in bluffing, a tactic that became especially associated with Deacon White. White's threats to retire had begun in the 1870s and became annual events after the adoption of the reserve clause. The *Cincinnati Enquirer* observed before the 1885 season, with only slight exaggeration: "Deacon Jim White is working his annual racket of coquetry with the management of the Buffalo Club. He says that it is not likely that he will play ball the coming season, as his farm near Corning, N.Y., needs his undivided attention. Jim has made this same little speech every winter for the past thirteen years, and about the time the salary is raised to a figure that meets his views he concludes that the cows, watermelons, turnips and such can take care of themselves another year anyhow and signs a contract" (*Cincinnati Enquirer*, reprinted in *Sporting Life*, January 7, 1885).

Less educated players had more limited options, but they still tried to cultivate them. Some of these efforts were quite transparent; in 1894 it was reported that "Silver King has decided that after all ball playing is preferable to 'laying brick'" (*Sporting Life*, March 31, 1894). But others were more successful. For example, John McGraw and Wilbert Robinson operated a profitable tavern in Baltimore that enabled the pair to hold out in 1900 and eventually gain generous contracts.

The spiraling salaries of recent years have largely rendered leverage obsolete. Most players could not say with a straight face that they were thinking of pursuing a more lucrative career. There is still one exception that is even built into major league bonus rules: if a player is a legitimate prospect in another sport, usually football, a major league team is allowed to offer him bonus payments that are spread out over several years.

18.4.3   Salary Caps. On October 17, 1885, the National League and the American Association jointly announced a $2,000 maximum player salary to begin the following season. Most major league owners found ways around the rule, rendering it largely ineffective. Nonetheless the announcement had an enduring influence, since baseball's first union (see **18.3.1**), the Brotherhood, was formed within days. The threat of salary caps and labor unrest have gone hand in hand ever since.

Salary caps were widely attempted in minor leagues of the era, where it seemed that they might have a greater chance of success. After all, minor leaguers had virtually no leverage, so the caps could be announced openly: "The New England League . . . has fixed a salary limit" (*Boston Globe*, June 6, 1886). Yet these were invariably scuttled when one owner broke the rules to give himself a better chance of winning, which forced others to follow suit. It became proverbial that "no salary limit rule can be devised so air tight that any manager can't blow through it any time he really tries" (*Sporting News*, January 2, 1913).

On November 21, 1888, the National League passed the Brush Classification Plan. This plan, proposed by Indianapolis owner John T. Brush, classified all players as A, B, C, D, or E, with prescribed salaries for each grouping. The maximum player salary for the top group was $2,500, far lower than what many players were then making. The rule was announced three days after Johnny Ward, head of the Brotherhood, had left for Australia as part of an around-the-world tour. The extremely unpopular rule was one of the main causes of the formation of the Players' League.

The idea of a salary cap has continued to emerge sporadically. During World War II the government imposed salary and price controls. Major league teams were instructed that a player's 1943 salary could not be lower than the lowest-paid member of the team had received in 1942, nor higher than the top salary paid by the team in 1942. Recent years have seen the owners frequently push for some form of salary cap, with the players staunchly opposing any such restrictions.

18.4.4 Minimum Salaries. Minimum salaries entered baseball with the National Agreement (see **18.2.3**). In the Tri-Partite Agreement of 1883, the fifth clause guaranteed minimums of $1,000 per year to players reserved by the National League and American Association, and $750 to those reserved by the Northwestern League. The same minimums were retained by the 1884 National Agreement, with the Eastern League subsequently being added with an $800 minimum.

Even the efforts of owners to limit player salaries in ensuing years retained this feature. The 1885 attempt to institute a salary cap (see **18.4.3**) continued the $1,000 minimum. The Brush Classification Plan, introduced in 1889, guaranteed a minimum salary of $1,500. Experience eventually taught owners that ceilings were more easily evaded than were minimum salaries. Accordingly, wage controls of all sorts dropped out of baseball for many years.

This feature was permanently reintroduced in 1946, when a $5,500 minimum salary was established as part of the owners' efforts to avert the formation of a player's guild.

18.4.5 Free Agency. Baseball entered the free-agency era in 1975, but the concept of free agency is a much older one. Before the introduction of the reserve clause (see **18.2.1**) in 1879, all baseball players had access to free agency, since they had the same freedom enjoyed by workers in any industry—the prerogative to sign with another club at the expiration of their contracts. The reserve clause removed this right by enabling clubs to continue to hold exclusive rights to players after the expiration of their contracts. It remained an ongoing bone of contention between owners and players for almost a century.

As discussed in the entry on "Leverage" (see **18.4.2**), most players expressed their discontent by holding out or threatening to retire. There have always been a few, however, who made more direct challenges, and some of these players have succeeded in attaining free agency. Owners have always seemed willing to compromise on an individual case if it helped preserve their ability to reserve most players.

Jim O'Rourke, one of the star players of the day and a law student on the side, may have been the first such player. A 1910 review of his career, apparently told by O'Rourke, gave this account:

"When Harry Wright asked him to sign with Boston [for 1880], O'Rourke said, 'Sure, I'll go, if you promise not to reserve me.' Wright had to promise, and he stood by smiling at O'Rourke's sharpness as the boy signed the contract. Each year thereafter, before he signed, both in Boston and Buffalo, O'Rourke forced his employers to waive the reserve clause.

"O'Rourke was the only player in base ball smart enough to succeed in doing this, and he got away with it for seven years. He even played in or [sic] the famous John B. Day, owner of the New York Nationals. It was in 1884 that Day went to the farm home of O'Rourke to sign him.

"'Name your figure,' said Day, 'and it will be paid, because I've got to have you.'. . .

"'I will sign for $4,500 a year for three years,' said O'Rourke, 'if you waive the right to reserve me at the end of that time.' Day promised, and from 1885 to 1887 young O'Rourke was the pet of base balldom.

"'But when my three-year contract expired in 1887,' said O'Rourke, 'I noticed none of the managers were bidding for me, even though I was un-reserved.

"'I knew then there was a deal on whereby I would have to go back to Day, even if he had not reserved me, so I went to him and said, 'Well, John, you fellows have caught up to me at last, and nobody seems to want me. I would like to play for you.'

"'Delighted to have you,' said Day, and he doubled O'Rourke's salary" ("Forty Two Years of Base Ball: Wonderful Life Story of Jim O'Rourke," *Kalamazoo Evening Telegraph*, February 26, 1910).

The Union Association was founded on September 12, 1883, as a direct challenge to the reserve clause. One of its initial resolutions was the bold statement that "we cannot recognize any agreement whereby any number of ball-players may be reserved for any club for any time beyond the terms of their contract with such club." The "outlaw" circuit lasted only one year.

Joe Gerhardt signed a one-year contract with Louisville in 1884 with the reserve clause removed. He signed to play with New York the next season (Ralph L. Horton, "Joe Gerhardt," in Frederick Ivor-Campbell, Robert L. Tiemann, and Mark Rucker, eds., *Baseball's First Stars*, 67).

In 1885 the Brotherhood of Professional Base-Ball Players was formed with star player and law student John Ward as its leader. The Brotherhood en-abled the players collectively to voice their opposition to the owners' strong-arm measures, including the reserve clause. In 1890 the players formed their own league, which was explicitly based upon free agency. Cap Anson claimed, "Any player who was dissatisfied with his location could apply to the board to be transferred without the payment of anything to the club losing his services" (Adrian Anson, *A Ball Player's Career*, 291). But the Players' League folded af-ter one year, and the subsequent merger of the National League and the American Association left the owners with more power than ever.

Players did not, however, entirely abandon their desire for free agency. John Ward retired following the 1894 season, but New York continued to reserve him. Ward appealed for free agency, though he had no intention of returning to the playing field. The owners may have suspected that he was setting the stage for a lawsuit, and they headed him off by finally granting him his release in February 1896.

Giants pitcher Amos Rusie sat out the 1896 season and then sued Giants owner Andrew Freedman for $5,000 and his release. The other league owners were worried that the suit might bring down the reserve clause, and paid the $5,000 to Rusie. Rusie thereby made $2,000 more for not pitching that season than he would have done by pitching.

Although entirely forgotten today, Mike Griffin was the Curt Flood of the 1890s. Brooklyn's captain and a veteran star center fielder, Griffin became involved in a contract dispute with the club after the 1898 season. When the club tried to alter the contract that had already been signed, Griffin balked; his contract was transferred to Cleveland and then St. Louis. Neither club would honor his original contract, so Griffin retired and successfully sued Brooklyn. But his career was over at age thirty-three.

After a long holdout, John McGraw and Wilbert Robinson signed contracts with St. Louis on May 8, 1900. According to McGraw, "Both Robbie and myself refused to sign a contract which would hold us over another year, regardless of our wishes. . . . The reserve clause was stricken from our contracts. This made us free agents at the end of the season, giving us the right to go to another club or anywhere we pleased" (John McGraw, *My Thirty Years in Baseball*, 123–124). McGraw accordingly claimed that he and Robinson were not contract jumpers when they signed with the American League.

Johnny Evers and Hugh Fullerton indicated that the National League responded to such threats by passing a new rule that stated: "Where the contract does not contain a reservation clause, every club, nevertheless, has a right to reserve a player unless the contract itself contains a written stipulation that the player is not to be reserved" (John J. Evers and Hugh S. Fullerton, *Touching Second*, 51–52).

The issue receded into the background for a decade and a half but resurfaced in 1914 with the emergence of the Federal League. A limited form of free agency was granted by the National Commission on January 6, 1914, in an attempt to avert the challenge of the Federal League. Robert Burk explained, "Ten-year major league veterans, in a change dubbed the 'Brown rule' in honor of the veteran pitcher [Mordecai 'Three-Finger' Brown], received the right of unconditional release" (Robert Burk, *Never Just a Game*, 197).

After the Federal League folded, the National Commission was quick to take this concession away. The Commission took an ad in the *Sporting News* to emphasize that "A non-reserve clause in the contract of a major league player without the approval of the Commission shall not be valid" ("Ball Players," *Sporting News*, February 17, 1916). In a November 1916 memo, clubs were informed: "The Commission has reason to believe that some major league players, whose expired contracts did not contain a renewal clause, will decline to concede further claim of their respective clubs to their services on the ground that at the expiration of their contracts they become free agents. ... With full realization that the reserve rule is not only a bulwark of professional base ball, and of inestimable benefit to the players, in assuring them as a class, regular employment at salaries adequate to their expertness, the Commission will hold in all such cases that the major league club, to which a player was under contract at the close of last season is entitled to retain him for 1917, if it so desires, and will not countenance the claim of any other club to such player that is not predicated on his purchase or release from his 1916 Club. The Commission will not approve or recognize any contract not in the new form and without change or modification of any of its provisions in any particular" (*Outside the Lines*, Fall 1999). This return to the previous way of doing business was included in the new player contract, which was made public on December 2 (I. E. Sanborn, "New Contract of Majors Has Ten Day Clause," *Chicago Tribune*, December 3, 1916).

The reserve clause was finally brought to the Supreme Court in 1922, where Justice Oliver Wendell Holmes, Jr., wrote a ruling that held that baseball was not interstate commerce and was therefore exempt from antitrust laws. While the legal basis of this finding struck many as dubious, baseball players had no choice but to accept it. With the courts against them and no rival league to turn to, most players came to view the reserve clause as a necessary evil, with some even defending it against periodic challenges.

Nonetheless Commissioner Kenesaw Mountain Landis, in his crusade against farm systems, declared many players free agents. Most were minor leaguers, but there were some major leaguers, such as Benny McCoy. When he was declared a free agent after the 1939 season, ten teams bid for his services. Hall of Famer Rick Ferrell was declared a free agent by Landis shortly before his rookie season of 1929, and signed a lucrative contract with the Browns that included a $25,000 bonus (Bob Matherne, "Free Agents Profiting by Landis Action," NEA wire service story, *Frederick* [Md.] *Post*, April 3, 1929).

The tide began to turn when Curt Flood was traded from the Cardinals to the Phillies in October 1969 but chose instead to challenge the reserve clause. His case went all the way to the Supreme Court, where he lost in a 5 to 3 ruling. In writing the majority opinion, Justice Harry Blackmun offered tepid support for the reserve clause by acknowledging: "If there is an inconsistency and illogic in all this, it is an inconsistency and illogic of long standing that is to be remedied by the Congress and not by this Court."

Players Association executive director Marvin Miller became convinced that the rule would finally fall if he had a test case to take to grievance arbitration (see **18.4.10**). But he needed a player to complete an entire season without signing a contract, and the owners did their best to preclude this from happening. Ted Simmons played much of the 1972 season without signing his contract, but in August he received an offer that he couldn't refuse. Five players began the 1973 campaign without contracts and seven more in 1974, but each eventually got an offer that was too tempting, so Miller still did not have his test case (John Helyar, *Lords of the Realm*, 131–135).

Catfish Hunter was awarded free agency on December 13, 1974. The issue, however, was the nonfulfillment of his contract by Oakland owner Charles O. Finley. As a result, it didn't set a precedent regarding the reserve clause.

The following season, Andy Messersmith and Dave McNally finally gave Marvin Miller his test cases by completing the season without signing contracts. Their grievance led to them being declared free agents by a three-man arbitration panel on December 23, 1975. The owners immediately fired arbitrator Peter Seitz, but they were too late to prevent the free-agency era from beginning.

18.4.6 Collusion. This point overlaps with a number of other entries in this section, but it bears repetition. Between 1986 and 1988 major league owners conspired to devastate the free-agent market by agreeing not to make offers. In 1990 they were found guilty of collusion and agreed to pay $280 million in damages.

What needs to be emphasized is that there is nothing new, or necessarily illegal, about collusion among owners. Indeed it can be argued that the unique nature of baseball's reliance upon the success of competitors has always made collusion essential. Simply honoring the reserve clauses of competitors can be construed as collusion. As described in the entry on the "Reserve Clause" (see **18.2.1**), an important preliminary step was an agreement by National League owners to limit advance signings. The blacklists went much further, since they placed restrictions on players who were not under contract at all. There were also informal blacklists or "gentlemen's agreements" that were imposed on players for a variety of reasons.

Jim O'Rourke claimed to have been a victim of the same practice for which the owners paid so heavily a century later. In the passage that appeared in the preceding entry, he indicated that he was free to sign with any club after the 1887 season but "noticed none of the managers were bidding for me, even though I was unreserved. I knew then there was a deal on" ("Forty Two Years of Base Ball: Wonderful Life Story of Jim O'Rourke," *Kalamazoo Evening Telegraph*, February 26, 1910).

The Brush Classification Plan of 1888 extended such restrictions to the entire league. The *Chicago Tribune* noted, "The general settlement appears to be that the classification scheme is illegal. It places a limit on the value of every classified player's services, which is opposed to the rulings of the

United States Supreme Court. Some lawyers say it is a clear case of conspiracy, nothing more or less" (*Chicago Tribune*, April 29, 1889).

But it didn't really matter whether it was conspiracy or not. As long as representatives of baseball's owners—first the National Commission and then the commissioner—determined baseball law, there was nothing illegal about conspiracy. As Johnny Evers and Hugh Fullerton observed, "Only the bitter rivalry between club owners, and the desire to satisfy players and keep them satisfied in order that they will do their best work, prevents wholesale horizontal decreases of salaries in the major leagues, where the combination is most powerful" (John J. Evers and Hugh S. Fullerton, *Touching Second*, 53–54).

That only changed when the owners agreed to characterize certain collusive activities as illegal. A clause added to the 1976 Basic Agreement specified, "Players shall not act in concert with other Players and Clubs shall not act in concert with other Clubs." Lee Lowenfish noted: "Ironically, it was the owners in 1976 who insisted on this language because they were worried that a players' agent might get his clients to act in concert" (Lee Lowenfish, *The Imperfect Diamond*, 263). Charles P. Korr suggested that memories of the Koufax-Drysdale joint holdout of 1966 (see **18.4.9**) impelled the owners to take this course (Charles P. Korr, *The End of Baseball as We Knew It*, 63).

It was under this provision that the Players Association filed a "collusion" grievance. The word "collusion" thereby entered the language of baseball and continues to exert its influence. John Helyar quoted an unnamed baseball man as saying, regretfully, "There was no collusion like old-style collusion" (John Helyar, *Lords of the Realm*, 95).

It is also worth noting in this regard that there is still a very fine line between legal and illegal forms of collusion. A perfect example is the current practice of "slotting," by which the major leagues have driven down the market value of draft choices by recommending bonus amounts for each slot in the amateur draft. While this seems to smack of collusion, Alan Schwarz explained, "Some people have mentioned the word 'collusion' in both the [Landon] Powell case and in referring to [Major League Baseball Executive Vice President of Baseball Operations Sandy] Alderson's predraft pep talk, but baseball's collusion rules apply only to major league free agents. Clubs are free to set a common strategy with respect to the draft" (*Baseball America*, October 2–15, 2000).

18.4.7   Big Market / Small Market Disparities. A familiar contention of ownership in recent years is that escalating salaries have created disparities between large- and small-market clubs. The idea that there is something new about such disparities is laughable. In fact, despite frequent protestations to the contrary, the evidence suggests that parity has steadily increased over time.

Take for example this complaint: "Chicago and New York are now able to handicap all other cities by paying men salaries of such magnitude as to make it impossible for their smaller-quartered competitors to get them." That was written in 1883! (*Cleveland Herald*, reprinted in *Perry* [Iowa] *Pilot*, July 11, 1883).

An 1884 *Sporting Life* article noted the complaint of the Cleveland owner that salaries were "clean out of sight." As a result, it claimed that "the richer, and naturally the larger cities, have gradually strengthened their teams, while the poorer, and, just as naturally, the smaller cities, have not only lost ground by the loss of old men by various means, but have been unable to pay the ruinous prices demanded by the new men" (*Sporting Life*, December 3, 1884). The article indicated that the rich clubs were Chicago, New York, Boston, and Providence, while the poor ones were Cleveland, Detroit, Philadelphia, and Buffalo.

Longtime baseball man James A. Williams wrote in 1891, "When professional base ball was young and its managers new the system of small percentages to visiting clubs and meagre guarantees, barely sufficient to pay traveling expenses, were adopted. This soon developed the fact that certain clubs were bound to make big money under the system, while others either made no money at all or lost. Then the latter demanded a great percentage in order that they, too, might reasonably expect some return for their investment and labors, but that spirit of cupidity and selfishness that has been the bane of the business almost since its inception came to the front and was able for years—13 in the league and 8 in the Association I think—and by skillful legislation was able to prevent any change to a fair division of receipts. In the meantime the smaller cities in each organization put up their money, labored hard to keep up with the procession, but dropped by the wayside" (*Sporting Life*, October 31, 1891).

In 1913 the president of the St. Louis Browns said, "Under the present system in the major leagues it's extremely hard for tailend clubs to edge into the first division. The winning clubs make big money, and for that reason they pay big money for talent. They sometimes pay fabulous and senseless prices for promising men. The owner of a losing club would go bankrupt trying to compete against the winners, figuring that a few of the high priced individuals would fail to deliver" (*New York Sun*, September 14, 1913).

In recent years Commissioner Bud Selig has advanced the idea that clubs now, for the first time in baseball history, go to spring training without any reasonable hope of winning. The commissioner might find it interesting to read an article that appeared in *Sporting News* before the 1913 season. In it,

Boston Braves captain Bill Sweeney predicted that his Braves would fight it out for fifth with the Cubs that year (*Sporting News*, March 27, 1913).

18.4.8　Holdouts. It is usually reported that the first holdout was Charles Sweasy of the 1870 Red Stockings, who demanded a raise from $800 to $1,000 and ultimately received it. But it is debatable whether Sweasy was really a holdout since he could have signed with another club.

The first post-reserve-clause holdouts were George Wright and Deacon White. Wright's case was discussed under the entry on the reserve clause (**18.2.1**). Deacon White also held out at the beginning of the 1880 season but eventually came to terms. Thereafter White voiced his opposition to the reserve clause by threatening retirement so many times that the *Cincinnati Enquirer* observed in 1888, "Deacon Jim White has just succeeded in making his forty-second annual retirement and is about ready to go to work again. The 'Deacon,' in his great act of 'How Not to Retire,' can knock [opera singer Adelina] Patti, [actress Sarah] Bernhardt et al., with their 'stolen diamond' stories all into a cocked hat when it comes to getting a big lot of advertising without putting up a cent for it. White has sprung the chestnut about going to work on his Corning farm in New York State once too often. It doesn't go with people who know him" (*Cincinnati Enquirer*, March 25, 1888).

Holdouts remained a major part of baseball for close to a century. Since the implementation of salary arbitration in 1973, holdouts have become very rare.

18.4.9　Joint Holdouts. Sandy Koufax and Don Drysdale held the most famous and most influential (see **18.4.6** "Collusion") joint holdout before the 1966 season. Dodgers owner Walter O'Malley expressed his displeasure: "Baseball is an old-fashioned game with old-fashioned traditions" (quoted in John Helyar, *Lords of the Realm*, 23). But Koufax and Drysdale's tactic was far from new.

In 1900 John McGraw and Wilbert Robinson owned a profitable tavern in Baltimore. When the Orioles franchise folded, their contracts were transferred to St. Louis. They jointly held out until after the start of the season, when they got an offer they couldn't refuse. McGraw claimed that not only did they get astronomical salaries, but that the reserve clause was removed from their contracts (John McGraw, *My Thirty Years in Baseball*, 123–124).

Ed Delahanty and Napoleon Lajoie held a joint holdout in Philadelphia that same year (Mike Sowell, *July 2, 1903*, 27–28; Jerrold Casway, *Ed Delahanty and the Emerald Age of Baseball*, 178–179). Batterymates Bill Killefer and Grover Cleveland Alexander used a similar tactic in 1917, with the great pitcher agreeing to "a compact with Killefer whereby the two are to stand together in their dealings with the Philadelphia Club" (*Sporting Life*, February 3, 1917).

18.4.10 Arbitration. For much of baseball history, the absence of impartial arbitration meant that owners could issue ultimatums during negotiations, while holdouts were the only means by which players could draw their own line in the sand. There are two basic forms of neutral arbitration that have been added by the Basic Agreement: grievance and salary arbitration. Each was introduced in the early years of Marvin Miller's tenure as executive director of the Players Association, and each has had a dramatic impact on the game. Neither, however, was remotely a new concept.

The Tri-Partite Agreement of 1883 created an Arbitration Committee, which consisted of three representatives of each of the three leagues that signed it (*Reach's Official Base Ball Guide, 1883,* 52). The Arbitration Committee was retained in the National Agreement that succeeded it, as was its partisan makeup (*Reach's Official Base Ball Guide, 1884,* 39). This provided players with a forum for grievances but not one that was as impartial as they would have liked. It appears that few players brought appeals to it, and the ones that did were either turned down or saw the matters referred back to the league in question.

When the Players' Protective Association was founded in 1900, its initial list of grievances included a request for a Committee of Arbitration that would consist of one representative from each side and a neutral third member. The idea proved to be well ahead of its time, with *Sporting Life* editor Francis Richter later commenting that "if adopted the game would become demoralized by endless appointments of and squabbles with arbitration committees" (Francis C. Richter, *Richter's History and Records of Base Ball,* 162–164). Association president Chief Zimmer eventually agreed to drop the idea.

Once the American and National leagues reached a peace agreement, players were granted a form of arbitration. The three-man National Commission began to hear grievances regularly, and the details of these cases were usually published in the sporting press, which gave wronged players some hope for redress in cases of rank injustice. But since all three members of the National Commission represented ownership, it was in no way an impartial system.

In 1910 Johnny Evers and Hugh Fullerton modestly suggested that allowing players to present a defense and holding public hearings would improve the system. With a touch reminiscent of *Alice in Wonderland*, they questioned the fairness of instances where "the Commission, or one member of it, states weeks in advance of a hearing what the decision will be" (John J. Evers and Hugh S. Fullerton, *Touching Second,* 55).

Accordingly they presented these demands: "an impartial court of three or five men not vitally interested in baseball, men who have no baseball connections, especially no financial ones. The players desire that this court shall codify and print all existing laws, and submit them to all members of the agreement for ratification. Finally, they demand that the court shall sit openly at stated intervals to hear causes, and take the evidence on both sides" (John J. Evers and Hugh S. Fullerton, *Touching Second*, 55).

It is hard to find anything unreasonable in these requests, yet owners continued to resist impartial hearings. They did replace the National Commission with a single commissioner after the 1920 season, but the commissioner remained an employee of the owners. As a result, one of the planks of Robert Murphy's unsuccessful effort to form a guild in 1946 was, "Arbitration in the event player and management cannot agree on salary" (*Sporting News*, June 5, 1946).

Once Marvin Miller became head of the players' union in 1965, he pushed hard for grievance arbitration, a staple of other industries. The owners were at first adamantly opposed to this concept but gradually yielded ground. The 1968 Basic Agreement included a grievance procedure that represented a compromise between the two positions. The fact that spelling out the procedure took up five pages of the twenty-four-page document indicates how painstakingly this middle ground was mapped out. The owners felt reassured by the role retained for the commissioner while the players took heart from knowing they now had a viable recourse when they felt wronged (Charles P. Korr, *The End of Baseball as We Knew It*, 71–73).

In 1970 the players pressed for eliminating the commissioner from the process altogether, and ownership again conceded ground. John Helyar indicated that Commissioner Bowie Kuhn was finally won over by the arguments of his adviser Lou Hoynes and owners' negotiator John Gaherin. Kuhn's basic objection was that the powers of his office should not be diminished. Hoynes and Gaherin contended that arbitrators would handle "nuts and bolts" issues, such as inspecting a hotel to decide if it was first-class. They persuaded the commissioner that getting involved in such disputes only diminished his prestige, and that he could retain control of issues that involved the "integrity of the game" and "public confidence" while ceding lesser matters to the arbitrator (John Helyar, *Lords of the Realm*, 113–114).

Kuhn later commented, "While I thought the change was neither necessary nor beneficial, and though it could not have been made without my consent, I reluctantly went along. There had never been a commissioner whose fairness in disputes between clubs and players could be questioned, and if anything they had probably been more sympathetic to the players' side of disputes. But provisions of this kind were commonplace in American collective bargaining agreements and could not realistically be resisted by sports managements—nor have they been. So the clubs and I concurred" (Bowie Kuhn, *Hardball*, 141).

As a result, impartial grievance arbitration—with the one important exception that the commissioner could intervene if the "integrity of the game" was involved—was incorporated into the 1970 Basic Agreement. The first case to be arbitrated involved whether Alex Johnson could be placed on the disabled list for psychological problems (Jonathan Fraser Light, *The Cultural Encyclopedia of Baseball*, 32).

Three years later the players received the right to salary arbitration. The owners' negotiators sold the plan to the owners as a minor concession that would cost relatively little money and would have the additional benefit of ending holdouts. More important, it would give an appearance of fairness that would lessen the effectiveness of Marvin Miller's calls for free agency. The owners approved "final offer arbitration" by a 22 to 2 vote, and it was added to the new Basic Agreement on February 25, 1973 (John Helyar, *Lords of the Realm*, 160–161).

The first player to go to salary arbitration was Minnesota pitcher Dick Woodson, whose case was heard on February 11, 1974. Woodson won his case and, while the amounts were not officially released, it was generally reported that he received $29,000 instead of the $23,000 being offered by the Twins. This seemed a small price to pay.

Within a few years both forms of arbitration would have extraordinary consequences. The grievance arbitration process made free agents first of Catfish Hunter, then of Andy Messersmith and Dave McNally, and, finally, of any player who played out his option. The salary arbitration process had initially led to modest increases because it compared players to others with similarly limited options. After the advent of free agency, the salaries commanded by free agents began to set the standard for arbitration cases.

This in turn pushed the value of free agents still higher. From the owners' perspective it was a vicious cycle that led to skyrocketing salaries. The players instead saw it as proof that their salaries had been artificially limited all along.

(v) Contracts

As we shall see in this entry, the provisions in players' contracts have always been closely tied to the threat of rival leagues.

18.5.1 Contracts. Although professionalism was not acknowledged until 1869, researcher Greg Rhodes reports that at least a few members of the Red

Stockings of Cincinnati had signed contracts in 1868 (*New York Clipper*, March 13, 1869). Once the game entered the era of open professionalism, contracts quickly became part of the game. John Thorn tracked down a 650-word contract for the 1871 season by which Cap Anson committed himself, among other things, "to conduct himself, both off and on the Ball Ground, in all things like a gentleman . . . to abstain from profane language, scuffling and light conduct, and to discourage the same in others . . . to practise at least two and a half hours per day . . . to use his best endeavours to perfect himself in play. Always bearing in mind that the Object in view in every game is to win."

18.5.2 Player Threats to Sue over a Contract. Researcher Richard Hershberger found that Dave Eggler sued the Philadelphia Club for his unpaid 1874 salary and was awarded $337.57 (*New York Clipper*, October 7, 1876).

18.5.3 Contract Perks. After the completion of the National League's first season in 1876, the owners addressed the issues of the expenses incurred by players while on the road. But if the players were expecting generous per diems, they were sadly mistaken. The owners instead decided that a thirty-dollar charge would be assessed for the cost of the player's uniform. Another fifty cents a day would be *deducted* from his contract for traveling expenses for each day the club was away from home (*New York Clipper*, December 23, 1876). These were far from trivial amounts, and players were similarly expected to pay to clean their uniforms and to purchase any equipment they would need (John Glasscock, quoted by John E. Wray in the *St. Louis Post-Dispatch*, reprinted in *Sporting News*, November 8, 1917; *New York Clipper*, January 10, 1880).

Needless to say, players were disgruntled about these duns. Jim O'Rourke declined to re-sign with Boston in 1879 in part in protest over the assessment (Bernard J. Crowley, "James Henry O'Rourke," in Frederick Ivor-Campbell, Robert L. Tiemann, and Mark Rucker, eds., *Baseball's First Stars*, 125). O'Rourke returned to Boston a season later, but he and his brother John threatened not to sign their 1880 contracts unless the offensive clauses were removed. Boston refused to do so, and an impasse was averted only when club supporters volunteered to pay for the expenses (*New York Clipper*, January 10, 1880).

Owners continued steadfastly to resist the concept of reimbursing players for even direct out-of-pocket expenses. In 1900 the Players' Protective Association requested the owners pay the doctor bills of a player who was injured during play. The idea was rejected by the owners (Francis C. Richter, *Richter's History and Records of Base Ball*, 162–163). The cost of players' travel and lodgings on road trips was also deducted from their paychecks ("The Great National Game in Dollars and Cents," *Washington Post*, May 9, 1909).

It was the formation of the Players' Fraternity in 1912 that finally brought relief. While the owners rejected the Fraternity's more far-reaching demands, they did make some concessions. Two of these points were the re-imbursement of some preseason travel expenses and finally the dropping of the $30 charge for uniforms (though players continued to pay for their own shoes) (Francis C. Richter, *Richter's History and Records of Base Ball*, 168–171). By 1917 players received $1 to $1.50 in meal money per day while on the road, which was a reasonable approximation of the typical cost (Jack Glass-cock, quoted by John E. Wray in the *St. Louis Post-Dispatch*, reprinted in *Sporting News*, November 8, 1917).

More generous per diems originated in 1946 for a similar reason—Robert Murphy's attempt to form the Players' Guild. In order to prevent the formation of anything resembling a union, the owners gave ground on a lot of minor issues, including this one. The per diems accordingly became known as "Murphy money," a term still in use.

18.5.4 Multi-year Contracts. With almost all issues involving contracts, the terms that owners were willing to grant varied with the amount of com-petition for the players' services. This is particularly true with long-term contracts.

Harry Wright seems to have pioneered the multi-year contract in the mid-1870s. In 1875 he offered George Latham a three-year contract if he played well (Harry Wright correspondence; quoted in William J. Ryczek, *Blackguards and Red Stockings*, 201). Pitcher Joseph Borden signed a three-year contract with Boston in 1876 (Tim Murnane, *Boston Globe*, February 19, 1900; Lee Allen, *The Hot Stove League*, 106). The *Washington Post* claimed in 1884: "Harry saddled [Joseph Borden] on the Bostons with a three years' contract. Some way he was not so phenomenal as he should have been, and after gazing upon the games from the grand stand of the Boston Club for a couple of months he pocketed a couple of thousand dol-lars [and left town]" (*Washington Post*, March 16, 1884). That was followed by reports of "a sort of regular army enlistment made by Lewis J. Brown for four years in Harry Wright's corps" (*Chicago Tribune*, December 3, 1876). Wright also extended a four-year contract to John Morrill and ap-pears to have given a three-year deal to Jack Manning (*Chicago Tribune*, August 27, 1876). None of the five was an established performer, and only Morrill would go on to stardom.

Signing so many unproven players to long-term contracts seems a fool-hardy move on the part of the usually canny Wright. One possibility is that he overreacted to having lost four of his stars to Chicago after the 1875 season, since all but the Latham contract came in the wake of this calamity. Baseball historian William J. Ryczek suggested that the contracts were not entirely guaranteed, with Boston retaining the right to release the players at any time, so that it was only the players who were making a long-term commitment (William J. Ryczek, *Blackguards and Red Stockings*, 201).

Yet there is plenty of evidence to support the suggestion of the *Washington Post* account that at least Borden's contract was guaranteed. Researcher David Arcidiacono reported that Boston tried unsuccessfully to buy out Borden's contract and to "make him work so hard [as a groundskeeper] that he would be forced to give up his contract, but . . . he cheerfully obeys any and all orders" (*Hartford Times*, September 20, 1876; quoted in David Arcidiacono, *Grace, Grit and Growling*, 58). Tim Murnane, who was signed on the same day as Borden, confirmed this version of events. According to Murnane, Borden's contract was finally bought off in 1877 after the club had failed "to discourage him by ordering him to report at the grounds twice a day, playing a lone hand most of the time" (*Boston Globe*, September 6, 1875; Tim Murnane, *Boston Globe*, February 19, 1900). Researcher David Ball found contemporary documentation of this buyout and similarly concludes that at least some of the contracts were guaranteed (*Cincinnati Enquirer*, February 15, 1877). So it appears that Wright simply miscalculated and that at least Borden's contract was guaranteed, as may have been the case with some of the others.

Frank Flint and John Ward both had two-year contracts covering the 1880 and 1881 seasons (*New York Clipper*, October 16, 1880; Bryan Di Salvatore, *A Clever Base-Ballist*, 136). The fact that two of the thirty original reserved players chose that moment to sign two-year contracts is puzzling. Ward, at least, was far too astute to sign a contract that benefited only his employer. And yet it seems even more unlikely that clubs would have guaranteed two years of a contract when the standard contract guaranteed only ten days. My guess is that their respective clubs offered them some financial inducement to sign up for an extra year.

The owners were in the ascendancy for most of the 1880s. The lone exception was the chaos initiated by the Union Association in 1884, which enabled Fred Dunlap to sign a record-breaking two-year contract calling for $3,200 in 1884 and $4,000 in 1885 (*Philadelphia Item*, quoted in *Washington Post*, March 16, 1884). But the upstart league didn't even last as long as Dunlap's contract, with the result that there were few if any long-term contracts for the remainder of the decade. Jim O'Rourke, as described in the entry on free agency (see **18.4.5**), claimed to have had a three-year contract that began in 1885. But if he did, he had relatively little company. By 1885 the National Agreement prohibited multi-year contracts, though a few star players were still demanding and receiving them.

The advent of the Players' League in 1890 brought short-lived hope to the players. All its players signed three-year contracts, but that turned out to be three times as long as the league lasted. The National League and the American Association fought back by offering three-year contracts that year. By the time these had expired, the National League had eliminated both its rivals and embarked upon a decade-long austerity movement (Robert F. Burk, *Never Just a Game*, 108, 124).

The pendulum swung again when the American League was formed in 1901. Soon there were regular reports of multi-year contracts. A 1903 report observed: "Fred Parent is the only player who is bound to the Boston Club for more than one season. He has two years to run. Criger, Young and Ferris are the only [other] players signed for another season" (*Sporting Life*, October 24, 1903). Fred Clarke signed a three-year, $22,500 contract in 1904 (*Sporting Life*, February 3, 1906). By 1907 the Chicago Cubs had Three-Finger Brown, Jimmy Sheckard, and Carl Lundgren signed to three-year contracts and Johnny Evers to a two-year contract (*Sporting Life*, April 20, 1907).

When the Federal League emerged as a rival to the National and American leagues following the 1913 season, many players used the sudden demand for their services to demand multi-year contracts that would lock in the higher salaries. For the two years of the Federal League's existence, the players remained in the driver's seat. But by the end of the 1915 season it was clear that would change.

Sportswriter H. T. McDaniel of the *Cleveland Leader* observed: "Signs of the coming of economical measures have not been lacking, but it has remained for the bosses of the Chicago Cubs to come out with the flat-footed announcement that hereafter they'll give no player a long contract.

"Hereafter no player will be tendered a contract for longer than two years, and that will be only in exceptional cases. The rank and the file must be satisfied with one-year contracts.

"Ostensibly the reason for this switch back to old principles is that long agreements give players ample opportunity to shirk. That's one reason, and undoubtedly a good one, but there is another cause, and that is when a player loses form and slides in ability there is no protection for the owner who has given a long contract.

"The Federal League's greatest trouble right now is that it is tied up with three and five-year contracts to players who have seen their best days. National and American League owners are also up against the same proposition, though to a lesser degree than the outlaws.

"With one-year contracts in vogue there'll be no hesitancy in slicing salaries or in attaching the tinware [i.e., releasing him] when a player slips. With long-time agreements this protection for the owners is impossible"

(H. T. McDaniel, *Cleveland Leader*; reprinted in *Sporting News*, December 2, 1915).

The Federal League signed a peace treaty with the other major leagues a few weeks later. With the players' bargaining power thus curtailed, long-term contracts soon became very rare. *Sporting Life* observed, "The long term contracts have been abolished for all time. The club owners were forced to give such contracts three years ago because of the fight with the Federal League. But the behavior of some of the star players who tied up their employers for three consecutive seasons has put an end to the custom. . . . Feeling sure of their salaries they did not extend themselves. They regarded base ball as a secondary consideration and thought more about automobile driving and tango teas than their duties on the field" (*Sporting Life*, February 3, 1917).

The last poignant reminder of the Federal League's penchant for multi-year contracts was a player named Rupert Mills, who had signed a two-year contract before the 1915 season. When the league folded a year later, Mills, who had studied law at Notre Dame, saw no reason why his contract should not be honored. Club owner Pat Powers thought he could deter Mills by suggesting sarcastically that he ought to perform in order to be paid. This tactic proved no more effective than had the attempt nearly four decades earlier to discourage Joe Borden. Mills began showing up for work at the empty park each morning and practicing baseball drills. He explained to the press, "I report every morning at 9:30 o'clock for morning practice and work out until 11 o'clock. I do mostly pitching in the morning to get wise to my curves for the afternoon game and when the umpire—that's me too—calls 'Play' I just go out and bang the ball around the lot." Eventually, Powers gave in and bought out his contract (Cappy Gagnon, *Notre Dame Baseball Greats*, 73; Irwin Chusid, "The Short, Happy Life of the Newark Peppers," *Baseball Research Journal* 20 [1991], 44–45).

In the aftermath of the Federal League's demise, it was several years before long-term contracts came back into vogue. Appropriately, Babe Ruth led the way, signing a three-year contract in 1919 and a five-year deal in 1922. The prosperity of the 1920s enabled a few other stars to land multi-year pacts, such as Edd Roush, who signed three-year contracts in both 1924 and 1927 (Eugene Murdock, *Baseball Between the Wars*, 140, 153).

The Great Depression again made multi-year contracts rare. Marty Marion signed a four-year contract in 1936 and claimed that this was one of the first long-term contracts (William Mead, *Even the Browns*, 43). In fact it was just the latest revival of a sporadic tradition that was sixty years old.

The dawn of the free-agency era in 1976 placed a renewed emphasis on multi-year contracts. Many clubs, led by the Kansas City Royals, sought to lock up their best players and avoid the threat of losing a star to free agency. But the tactic proved a double-edged sword, often locking a club into a contract that lasted much longer than the player's effectiveness.

Whether to sign a player to a long-term contract remains a crucial dilemma for general managers. At least, however, they no longer have to worry whether the players will be distracted by tango teas.

18.5.5 Guaranteed Contracts. In the nineteenth century, player contracts were guaranteed only for ten days. The 1879 adoption of the reserve clause (see **18.2.1**) accordingly meant that players were committed to the ball clubs in perpetuity while being assured only of payment for ten days if they were ill, injured, or playing poorly. This naturally struck the players as unjust, but it reflected the reality of baseball's shaky financial status, which dictated that no one in the game had much assurance of what the future would bring. Minor league clubs routinely went belly-up in midseason and left their players without an income, so there was limited sympathy when a similar fate befell an unproductive player.

The early twentieth century saw baseball make great strides toward financial stability, which made the persistence of the ten-day clause all the more irksome to players. After the 1902 season Ed Delahanty signed a contract with New York that called for him to be paid even if he were injured or enjoined by the courts from playing for New York. But Delahanty was a star with the leverage of a rival league; most players continued to enjoy no such security.

As discussed under "Pay for Injured Players" (**18.5.6**), by the early twentieth century there was an unwritten understanding that clubs should not release a player who was injured in the course of play. In 1916 the National Commission finally guaranteed the right of injured players to be paid for the balance of their contracts. But this still left players vulnerable to being released, traded, or sent to the minors with payment at the prior rate continuing only for ten days. In addition, the National Commission's apparent generosity was further undercut by its simultaneous efforts to eliminate long-term contracts.

The inequity of the ten-day clause was one of the themes of Robert Murphy's 1946 attempt to form a player's guild. In order to thwart Murphy, the owners agreed to extend the period to thirty days (Robert F. Burk, *Much More Than a Game*, 93; *Chicago Tribune*, September 17, 1946).

In the free-agent era, increased player leverage has brought a new level of security to contracts. They are still not entirely guaranteed, however, and players like Ron Gant and Aaron Boone have been released for being injured in the course of prohibited activities.

18.5.6   Pay for Injured Players. Early baseball had such razor-thin profit margins that early contracts were guaranteed only for ten days. Players with serious injuries were routinely released, and this did not offend the sensibilities of the period. In 1880 the *New York Clipper* commended William Hague, who "had the misfortune to lame his arm, and, finding that he could not throw with his usual precision, he honorably asked to be released after playing in fifty championship games" (*New York Clipper*, October 23, 1880).

An exception occurred in 1879: "The Stars of Cincinnati at a recent meeting passed a resolution to allow both Miller and Houtz (two of their players who are disabled, and likely to be for some months) their full salary, and furnish men to play in their positions" (*New York Clipper*, July 5, 1879). But it is hard to know whether this club acted out of magnanimity or to ensure that it did not lose these players to rival teams.

Moreover such generosity was far from universal. Ross Barnes was the National League's leading hitter in 1876 but missed most of the following year due to illness. Chicago withheld his salary, and Barnes sued but lost his case. In reporting the result, Henry Chadwick argued for a middle ground in such cases: "If illness is induced by the work of his services on the ballfield, then a player's salary should not be stopped on that account. But, if it arises from ordinary causes, it is rather hard upon a club to demand pay for the time lost" (*New York Clipper*, December 7, 1878).

This position will seem harsh to today's ears, but it is not unreasonable in the context of the era. Concepts such as worker's compensation and sick pay were still emerging or in the future, and baseball was not in a position to be more generous than other American employers.

When Cap Anson suffered a serious liver ailment in 1879, it revived the issue: "A nice point is likely to arise out of Anson's retirement. It will be remembered that Ross Barnes was in 1877 a member of the Chicago team, but became afflicted almost in the same way as Anson is, so that he was unable to play for the remainder of that season. He was denied his salary, and had to sue for it. The courts decided against him. Now Barnes wants to know whether the Chicagos will pay Anson in full this season, so as to keep him next year. Barnes says if they do they must also pay him. He will have a voice in the matter, being still a stockholder of the Chicago Club" (*New York Clipper*, September 13, 1879).

By the 1880s players had begun to take precautions. When Detroit's Jimmy Manning broke his arm in 1886, the *Detroit Free Press* reported, "Every member of the Detroit team carries an accident policy. The boys also have a mutual benefit association. A portion of his salary will be paid by the club and, all in all, Manning will receive about $75 a week" (*Detroit Free Press*, June 5, 1886).

An infielder named John Pickett was released by Baltimore in the middle of the 1892 season. Since his contract did not include the usual ten-day clause, Pickett sued for the balance of his 1892 salary. Baltimore contended that they should not have to pay because the ballplayer "was slow in his movement, and had a sore arm which incapacitated him from being of service to the club." Pickett won his case but never played in the major leagues again (Robert Burk, *Never Just a Game*, 124; Jim Charlton, ed., *The Baseball Chronology*, 96).

A few years later Baltimore took a different tack with John McGraw by continuing to pay his salary while he recovered from typhoid. The ostensible reason was that "Baltimore always appreciates the services of faithful, hustling players like McGraw" (*Boston Globe*, July 2, 1896). It seems more likely, however, that the real difference was that McGraw was a star, and the Orioles were unwilling to risk losing his services to a rival.

In 1900 Philadelphia tried to have it both ways by suspending injured Harry Wolverton (*Sporting Life*, August 22, 1900). Fortunately the advent of the American League the following season again gave players some leverage. The players came to expect fairer treatment in the ensuing years, though there were still exceptions. In 1904, for example, "The news of the release of Pat Carney, the Boston Nationals' outfielder and emergency left-handed pitcher, came as a great surprise to Boston fans. . . . As Carney was injured in the middle of the season, while actually playing for the Boston management, his release is entirely against the ethics of the National League. Players generally are not released when laid up in service" (*Washington Post*, September 9, 1904). Both Pittsburgh and Chicago offered contracts to Carney, but he indicated a preference for making "the Boston magnates 'come across' with the balance of his salary" (*Washington Post*, September 24, 1904).

In 1908 Ty Cobb demanded a clause that would guarantee his contract in the case of injury. August "Garry" Herrmann, chairman of the National Commission, responded: "That's a very peculiar demand Cobb makes. Our base ball contracts protect a player for a reasonable period if he is injured while playing. But such a clause is hardly necessary. Every club will protect its players. I have never heard of one that would not."

Herrmann cited several examples of injured players who had been retained by their club. He continued, "Of course, a club reserves the right to release a player when he becomes absolutely useless. But you look back over base ball, and you will find that mighty few deserving men have ever been treated shabbily. . . . It is patent that no club is going to run the risk of losing a player by cutting off his salary because he is injured" (*Sporting News*, February 6, 1908).

On December 2, 1916, the National Commission approved a new wording for player contracts that made explicit an injured player's right to be paid for the remainder of his contract. The owners maintained that this merely ratified what was already customary, while the players felt there were still exceptions (I. E. Sanborn, "New Contract of Majors Has Ten Day Clause," *Chicago Tribune*, December 3, 1916).

18.5.7 Pay for Spring Training. The general sentiment in the nineteenth century was that players ought to report for the start of the season in condition. Ownership felt that if the players required time to get into shape, they had no right to be paid for that time.

By the twentieth century, spring training had become customary (see 24.2.2 and 24.2.3) and the issue of payment for this period began to be controversial. Johnny Evers and Hugh Fullerton wrote in 1910, "One constant source of friction is the rule governing reporting for spring training. Many players have other business interests and object to spending six weeks training, without pay, when the time might be profitably occupied" (John J. Evers and Hugh S. Fullerton, *Touching Second*, 54). In 1912 the new baseball Fraternity requested that the players' salaries include spring training. Tigers owner Frank Navin indignantly responded that he had no intention of paying players to get in shape (*Sporting Life*, November 30, 1912).

In the face of mounting pressure from the players, the owners pled poverty. In 1915, in order to cut costs, the National League mandated that training camps could open no earlier than March 1. The *Sporting News* showed why it was becoming known as the owners' mouthpiece by writing: "Base ball is the only business where a highly paid employe is prepared for his work at the expense of the employer and the club owners are beginning to acknowledge the sense of the argument that it is a burden that they should not be expected to shoulder. Within the next few years, and a pin may be stuck in this prediction, players will be ordered to report to their managers a week or ten days previous to the opening of the season for instruction in team drills and signals. It will be required of each player that he shall be in physical condition to do his best, and if he is not, suspension without pay will follow until he is in that condition" (*Sporting News*, March 4, 1915).

A seemingly inevitable showdown was averted when it became apparent that large crowds would pay to watch spring training games. It slowly became clear that neither the owners nor the players needed to bear the costs since the fans were more than happy to do so. By 1923 the *Sporting News* had changed its tune and now editorialized that it was unfair for owners to make money off spring training exhibition games without paying players (*Sporting News*, March 1, 1923).

My understanding, however, is that the owners never did concede the point, and the players settled for higher salaries and spring training expense money.

18.5.8   Year-round Pay. Early contracts usually ran for six months, which meant that the owners' financial obligations to their players began on Opening Day and ended as soon as the season ended. As players took advantage of this to engage in lucrative barnstorming tours, owners began to reconsider. Chris Von der Ahe, in particular, was concerned that his players were getting injured during these games.

Jonathan Fraser Light explained that matters came to a head in 1899 when a player named George Wrigley tried to join a major league club after his minor league club's season ended. As a result, language that became known as the Cincinnati Agreement was added to the standard playing contract. It read: "The Club's right of reservation of the Player, and renewal of this contract as aforesaid, and the promise of the Player not to play otherwise than with the Club or an assignee thereof, have been taken into consideration in determining the salary specified herein and the undertaking by the Club to pay said salary is the consideration for both said reservation, renewal, option and promise, and the Player's service" (Jonathan Fraser Light, *The Cultural Encyclopedia of Baseball*, 612; see also *Sporting News*, January 13, 1900).

This prevented players from joining other clubs, but it did not stop barnstorming. Some clubs tried twelve-month contracts in 1910 (Robert Burk, *Never Just a Game*, 183). S. E. McCarty noted after the 1915 season that owners were again considering twelve-month contracts to eliminate barnstorming (*Pittsburgh Leader*, reprinted in *Sporting News*, November 4, 1915).

18.5.9   Pay for Performance. The idea of paying players based upon performance is a very old one. As early as 1878 it was reported that Indianapolis owner William Pettit "proposed at a recent meeting of that club a scheme for grading the salaries of professional players in 1879, which is decidedly unique" (*New York Clipper*, April 20, 1878). Pettit's idea involved having the league secretary rank the players based on their performance and their being paid accordingly.

A 1911 article reported, "Chief Bender of the Athletics has had a peculiar contract to sign for the last several seasons." It explained that, beginning in 1908, "Connie Mack, instead of giving the Indian a big salary, as he deserves, has him sign a blank contract, and at the end of the season he puts in a bonus which he thinks pays for the Indian's work" (*Mansfield* [Ohio] *News*, September 23, 1911).

While such a system would appear to have many advantages, it is easy to see how it could lead to hard feelings, especially if tried on a large scale.

18.5.10   Signing Bonuses. Giving an "advance" to a player who signed a contract was a common practice in nineteenth-century baseball. As the word implies, it was supposed to be repaid, but that didn't always happen.

The National League did its best to get rid of advances entirely. A rule prohibiting them was adopted at the same 1879 meeting at which the reserve clause (see **18.2.1**) was introduced (*New York Clipper*, October 11, 1879). But this proved impractical because players were not paid during the offseason, and many of them needed the advances to report. Thus advances had some similarity to signing bonuses, yet owners resisted the concept of overtly paying a player for his signature.

As noted in the entry on rival major leagues (**18.4.1**), Dan Fletcher's 1910 attempt to compete with the existing major leagues was based entirely on signing bonuses. The established leagues remained reluctant to adopt this practice but eventually did so.

In 1927, for example, St. Louis Browns owner Phil Ball offered Ty Cobb a $40,000 contract plus a $10,000 signing bonus (*Sporting News*, February 17, 1927). Cobb turned it down and signed with the Athletics instead. It is not clear who was the first player to accept a signing bonus, but it couldn't have been long past Cobb's refusal since the "bonus baby" era is generally considered to have started with the $20,000 premium paid to Charley Devens in 1932.

18.5.11   Incentive Clauses. Before the 1869 season the Mutuals of New York announced they would take advantage of the National Association of Base Ball Players' recognition of professional ball and begin to pay salaries. The club added: "Premiums will be paid to those who excel in the special departments of the game as shown by regular statistics at the close of the season" (*National Chronicle*, February 27, 1869).

While incentives were thus part of professional baseball from its outset, they remained rare in early contracts. Early players could be fined for a wide variety of offenses, but rarely were they rewarded. This is nicely illustrated by a story that, even if apocryphal, is highly symbolic. Cincinnati catcher Larry McLean had a clause in his 1910 contract stipulating a fine for drinking liquor. In 1911 it is said that he requested the team pay him a bonus for each time he turned down a drink (H. Allen Smith and Ira L. Smith, *Low and Inside*, 72–73).

Ironically, at least a few nineteenth-century players appear to have had such a clause: "[John] Fox, of the Alleghenys, gets $500 extra if he does not drink for the season" (*Washington Post*, April 13, 1884). The *Brooklyn Eagle* claimed that it applied to his teammates as well: "One of the inducements offered by the Allegheny Club, of Pittsburg, to keep the players from drinking is an additional $500 salary at the close of the season. This is money well invested" (*Brooklyn Eagle*, April 13, 1884). Ed Williamson reportedly had two separate incentive clauses in his 1888 contract. One called for an $800 bonus if he abstained from drinking, and the second provided for another $200 if he kept his weight below 190 pounds (*Boston Globe*, April 7, 1888).

18.5.12 Performance Bonuses. Performance bonuses were also uncommon in the nineteenth century, though there were a few exceptions. In 1884 the *Brooklyn Eagle* reported, "Should the Louisvilles win the championship, the players of the team are each to receive a handsome cash bonus, and [Guy] Hecker will be given a house and a lot" (*Brooklyn Eagle*, August 10, 1884). Bonuses became still rarer in the penurious nineties as owners took advantage of the single major league to pinch pennies. An exception was made for captains, who were given bonuses for fulfilling their duties.

A 1907 article in the *Detroit Times* showed that the practice of performance bonuses had begun to emerge: "In 1906 Cleveland originated the [bonus] system by offering its pitchers added money to the amount of $500 for the ones that won 20 games or over. Cleveland had a winning ball club that season, led the league for a good share of the time, made a lot of money and finished well up in the race. In 1907 the bonus system was discarded and Cleveland couldn't quite reach the top all season, in spite of her great team. Also her finish, considering her opportunities, was far from being a brilliant one.

"In 1907 the Detroit Tigers furnished the material for the bonus experiment. The team went ahead with a wonderful burst of speed, won the pennant and improved its position from a bonusless sixth in 1906 to the honor of a championship when the twirlers were working for that extra money" (*Detroit Times*, reprinted in *Sporting News*, December 5, 1907).

In spite of these impressive results, the article noted that Tigers owner Frank Navin was mulling over whether to continue the bonuses in 1908. For one thing, American League president Ban Johnson was opposed to the whole concept. In addition, it did not seem fair to give bonuses to pitchers but not to hitters. Yet extending the bonuses to all players would be difficult to do fairly and would amount to a general salary increase.

As owners continued to experiment with bonuses, they learned how difficult it is to unring a bell—once the precedent had been established, players came to expect bonuses. A 1917 article observed: "Club owners in the major leagues are beginning to feel that they have been making mistakes in offering players bonuses and making them presents at the end of the season for exceptionally good work. Those who have done it have had more trouble signing their players to new contracts than any others. From the *Philadelphia Ledger*, we learn that the Philadelphia National League Club furnishes one instance of how much the players appreciate these gifts. Last season Al Demaree was promised a bonus for winning a certain number of games. On the day he won a double-header he was presented with a $100 bill for his work, and as he accepted it, the cartoonist [Demaree] reminded President [William] Baker not to forget there was a bonus coming to him."

After providing additional examples, the writer concluded, "It would be a good thing if a rule were passed prohibiting gifts and bonuses in the future, as there would be less haggling over salaries each year" (*Sporting Life*, March 10, 1917).

18.5.13 No-trade Clauses. NFL players were obtaining no-trade clauses by 1965, but baseball players had a harder time gaining similar guarantees (*New York Times*, January 28, 1965). Requests for such clauses by Frank Howard and Rusty Staub in the early 1970s were refused (*Sporting News*, April 17, 1970, and March 18, 1972). Thus baseball's first no-trade clauses may have been the ones in the ten-and-five rule (see **13.2.7** "Vetoed Trades"), which was included in all contracts as part of the Basic Agreement of February 25, 1973.

Owners continued to oppose extending no-trade clauses to players with less tenure, a course that had unintended consequences. The Dodgers' refusal to grant Andy Messersmith's no-trade request in 1974 led Messersmith to play out his option and bring the grievance that toppled the reserve clause (see **18.4.5** "Free Agency") (Charles P. Korr, *The End of Baseball as We Knew It*, 148). No-trade clauses gradually became common during the free-agent era.

(vi) Commercialization

The incursion of commercialization into the national pastime is not nearly as recent a phenomenon as might be imagined.

18.6.1 Commercialization. Determining when baseball became commercialized is not possible, since elements of commercialism began to creep in very early. In particular, early clubs were not shy about asking local businessmen for financial support.

In 1866, for instance, the *Kalamazoo Telegraph* gave readers this little nudge: "the ball-players of this place have never received assistance or encouragement from the citizens, in the way of defraying expenses on match days or providing them an [sic] uniform, as almost every town is doing or has done" (*Kalamazoo Weekly Telegraph*, October 3, 1866).

Two years later an Omaha, Nebraska, player was more direct: "Our late defeat by the Marshalltown Base Ball Club, Aug. 6th, has called forth a good deal of comment by our citizens generally, and it is hoped that the defeat will be the means of giving a renewed life, vitality and interest in this community to the game, to make this club a success. It will require the good will and pecuniary indorsement of our people. We are all laboring young men. We believe the game in Omaha is beneficial to all young men whom we can interest therein. We know it to be an honorable game—of national reputation—encouraged by all, disparaged by none, except it be Omaha, whose citizens, excepting a few, have ever given us the cold shoulder, and from them have received no word or act of encouragement. When the Marshalltown club, the champions of Iowa, determined to play us, we endeavored to collect sufficient funds from our citizens to entertain them while here; we found it impossible to raise the sum of $100. No subscription exceeded five dollars, and only four that amount, a few of two dollars, and the balance of one dollar donations; and this in a flourishing city of 17,000 inhabitants. Compare this with the little city of Marshalltown toward its club—a city of 3,000 inhabitants. They donated $500 to the club, furnished its members with uniforms, sent their Mayor with them to this city, and many of their most wealthy and influential citizens with their wives, daughters and friends of the members, accompanied them here and out of the grounds, to cheer and encourage them.

"We were beaten, yet there is not a member of the Marshalltown club but acknowledged that our boys are superior players, *individually*. But a want of funds has, until the present, prevented a substantial organization. This was the cause, and the only one, of our late defeat" (*New England Base Ballist*, August 20, 1868).

While the Omaha club no doubt wanted both "the good will and pecuniary indorsement of our people," there can be little doubt from this account that financial support was a higher priority. This new reality caused efforts to solicit funds to gradually become more organized during the 1870s. A newspaper in Marshall, Michigan, hinted in 1872 that "a committee from the Pastime will be calling on businessmen this week to enlist honorary members" (*Marshall Statesman*, June 5, 1872). A Muskegon paper went straight to the point: "business men of our city are invited to give the club a helping hand. In Grand Rapids the clubs are largely aided by those interested in the game, and our citizens are probably aware that the Muskegons are deserving of their support. The Club desire to return thanks to Messrs. Hackley & Co., & C. Davis & Co., for lumber, and to Dr. Marvin, Harry Pillsbury, and others, for substantial donations" (*Muskegon News and Reporter*, July 28, 1877).

A Saginaw journal reported in 1878 that the local club "naturally expect some assistance from the business men of our city, which will undoubtedly be rendered. The club have resolved to present a subscription paper to the merchants for their approval, and if a liberal response is made a number of fine games will be contested in this city with the best nines in the state" (*Saginaw Daily Courier*, August 23, 1878). The following year a Kalamazoo resident urged, "as a citizen of Kalamazoo, I ask that the public turn out in good numbers to see these games in the future as the management will give up the nine if it is not a good deal better patronized. . . . Encourage them in every way possible and one of the most effective ways is to give them money. Don't let this nine go to pieces for want of patronage. It deserves success. Tell the management by your gifts that you appreciate their efforts to conduct the game honorably this year, paying every bill and furnishing interesting games" (*Kalamazoo Telegraph*, June 24, 1879).

Before long, clubs began to seek tangible ways of recognizing businessmen who responded to these appeals. Researcher David Arcidiacono discovered an 1875 article noting that the officers and stockholders of the Elm City Club of New Haven were open to the possible leasing of the ballpark fence for advertisements: "The subject of allowing the fence to be used for advertising purposes was discussed, and steps will be taken to lease the fence" (*New Haven Evening Register*, March 4, 1875).

By 1886 the idea had come to fruition: "An enterprising Washingtonian business firm has hired a section of the ball park fence for advertising purposes, and will give $25 to the first player on the home team who strikes it with a batted ball" (*Detroit Free Press*, April 24, 1886). John Thorn reports that the Polo Grounds had advertising by Opening Day that year. An advertising fence was also erected at Detroit's Recreation Park that year in order to prevent spectators from watching the game from outside the park (*Detroit Free Press*, June 4, 1886).

A few early clubs went much further, with some of them starting down the road toward the much more recent trend of selling naming rights to stadiums. The 1877 Hop Bitters of Rochester of the International Association bore the name of a patent medicine. It just so happened that team owner Asa T. Soule was also the president of the Hop Bitters Manufacturing Company. Henry Chadwick was appalled by the concept. Much as some current broadcasters try to avoid using commercialized stadium names, Chadwick referred to the club as "the nine organized and run by a firm in Rochester, N.Y., for advertising purposes" (*New York Clipper*, November 15, 1879).

When the Hop Bitters disbanded in 1879, he remarked acidly, "The Hop Bitters team experiment has simply been a mere advertising dodge, and now that the manager has accomplished all the advertising benefit from them he can expect, he comes out in his true colors, disbands one team, and announces the other as a mere gate money exhibition team" (*Brooklyn Eagle*, July 22, 1879).

They were not the last such club, as the *St. Louis Post-Dispatch* felt obliged to remind its readers in 1889, "Clubs having names of an advertising nature will not be advertised in this column" (*St. Louis Post-Dispatch*, April 13, 1889). The Page Fence Giants, a top African-American barnstorming club, found time during games to promote the Monarch Bicycle Company and the club's namesake, the Page Fence Wire Company (Jerry Malloy, ed., *Sol White's History of Colored Base Ball*, xxxii; Michael E. Lomax, *Black Baseball Entrepreneurs, 1860–1901*, 136–137). A nine in Jacksonville, Florida, agreed to wear uniforms bearing the name of a bookstore in exchange for a suit of clothes for each player. Their decision prompted a local paper to lament: "that young persons, growing up in a community where shortly they expect to take the honorable places of their fathers and elders, should so compromise their gentlemanly dignity is certainly matter for profound regret. It hurts the pride of every other amateur who hears of it; it matters not who or what the thing advertised may be, whether a great patriarchal trades house or a petty tenement shop; the loved name of amateur, which touches the better part of man, his pride of physical and mental excellence, his love of art for art's sake; of science, for its benefits to man; of skill, for the beauty which displays itself in deft movements, is outraged and abused when it is made merchandise for gain and greed, or betrayed to the common uses of the advertiser" (quoted in Kevin M. McCarthy, *Baseball in Florida*, 10. McCarthy's footnote cites the *Florida Times-Union*, a Jacksonville paper, of May 19, 1883. But his in-text reference gives the year as 1893).

Other manifestations of commercialism in baseball also evoked outraged protests. The *Chicago Tribune* complained in 1877 that the International Association's booklet of constitution and rules was "not a creditable publication, because it is defaced on every page with the cards of some uniform-manufacturers. It has almost lost its proper character as a book of rules, and become a mere manufacturers' circular" (*Chicago Tribune*, May 13, 1877).

Thus it is clear that the process of commercialization was beginning to manifest itself in a number of forms by the end of the nineteenth century. It is equally evident that it was continuing to be met with stout resistance.

18.6.2 Endorsements. The earliest commercial endorsement by a ballplayer that I'm aware of appeared in an 1877 ad in the *Chicago Evening Journal* which read, "The Chicago Base Ball Club delight in drinking mead at Gunther's." The mead being referred to was moxie mead, a soft drink of the time (*Chicago Evening Journal*, April 30, 1877; quoted in *Baseball in Old Chicago*, 38).

18.6.3 Hit Sign, Win Suit. The most famous of all the "Hit Sign" fence advertisements was the "Hit Sign, Win Suit" sign at Brooklyn's Ebbets Field.

Brooklyn clothier Abe Stark sponsored this advertisement from the early 1930s until the Dodgers' move to Los Angeles.

Gimmicks of this type date back to the nineteenth century, with an 1886 example at Washington's Swampoodle Grounds being cited in the entry on "Commercialization" (18.6.1). Gerard S. Petrone suggested that they gradually evolved from generous offers by local businessmen into more sophisticated advertising ploys (Gerard S. Petrone, *When Baseball Was Young*, 43).

The most famous campaign was the "Hit the Bull" ads sponsored by the American Tobacco Company from 1911 to 1913. The firm erected large wooden bulls to advertise their Bull Durham brand and placed them deep in the outfields—but within the field of play—of stadiums all over the country. A fifty-dollar prize went to any batter who hit one, but the promotion does not appear to have been very costly to the tobacco company. Four Kitty League clubs had the signs but in 1911 only one batter managed to hit one, and in 1912 "all attempts by the players to drive the ball into some part of Mr. Bull's anatomy proved fruitless" (John T. Ross, *Sporting News*, December 12, 1912).

They also proved a menace to outfielders, and Joe Jackson was knocked unconscious when he ran into the bull in a game on September 12, 1913. The injury cost Cleveland its slim chance in the pennant race (Gerard S. Petrone, *When Baseball Was Young*, 43–44). As noted earlier (see 14.4.12 "Bullpens"), the bulls on the outfield grass may have also been responsible for the term "bullpen" becoming the name of the area where pitchers warm up.

18.6.4   Publicly Owned Ballpark. In 1913 the *Sporting News* reported, "So successful has been the plan of the city owning the ball park in Dubuque, where the Three-I League team plays, that a similar scheme is suggested in Rock Island and the city authorities seem favorable. It is the idea that they shall buy the Rock Island ball park, one of the best equipped in the minor leagues, and lease it for a nominal sum to a club which will secure a franchise either in the Western League, the Three-I or the Central Association" (*Sporting News*, August 28, 1913).

The following month *Sporting Life* reported the results: "Rock Island voted, by a comfortable majority, to indorse the project to purchase a ball park and put the city back on the base ball map with a league team, a canvass of returns from the election showed on Saturday. Five hundred women, voting for the first time under the new Illinois suffrage law, were nearly unanimous in favor of base ball for Rock Island and swelled the majority. The fact that the $20,000 bond issue approved provides for the purchase of six acres outside the park for a municipal athletic field made the proposition specially attractive to women voters. With the ball park privately owned by the Rock Island Base Ball Association, league base ball was not a paying venture in Rock Island" (*Sporting Life*, September 20, 1913). *Sporting News* reported that Rock Island was the first city to have held a special election for such a purpose (*Sporting News*, September 25, 1913).

The first major league park to be publicly owned was Cleveland Municipal Stadium in 1932. Two years later the city of Syracuse found a new angle by making use of Federal Emergency Relief Association (FERA) funds to build a ballpark (*Sporting News*, December 20, 1934).

18.6.5 Corporate Ownership. When Anheuser Busch purchased the St. Louis Cardinals in 1953, it was the first time the major leagues had had a corporate owner, and this development disturbed many observers. Many of their concerns involved the commercialization of the game.

Columnist Ira Seebacher noted that this new phenomenon was causing speculation as to "whether the club will be run strictly as a sporting proposition with no idea of enhancing the new owners' product." He wondered if the brewery would permit opponents to sell broadcast time on games involving the Cardinals to rival beer companies. He even speculated that the Budweiser eagle might replace the traditional Redbird as the team's logo. He suggested that "the best thing that could happen would be for Ford Frick to step in right from the start and rule that it is undignified to connect too closely any commercial product with baseball. Baseball has dignity and its dignity must not be too brazenly trampled even by such wealthy men as now own the Cards" (*New York Morning Telegraph*, reprinted in *Sporting News*, March 4, 1953).

18.6.6 Naming Rights. Shortly after Anheuser Busch bought the Cardinals in 1953 and became the major league's first corporate owners, president August Busch announced plans to rechristen Sportsman's Park as "Budweiser Stadium." After a public outcry, the name Busch Stadium was selected instead. *Sporting News* editorialized that Busch "is to be congratulated on having quickly abandoned his intention to rename Sportsman's Park Budweiser Stadium in favor of Busch Stadium" (*Sporting News*, April 22, 1953). The next year the crafty Busch unveiled Busch Bavarian beer.

There was renewed controversy in 1964 when CBS purchased the New York Yankees. Sportswriter Leonard Koppett noted, "There was talk of conflict of interest; antitrust action seemed possible; for weeks the papers were full of stories about why the deal might be a bad thing" (Leonard Koppett, "The Ex-National Sport Looks to Its Image," *New York Times*, December 20, 1964). Eventually the sale went through, and the concept of corporate ownership came to be taken for granted. In the process, however, onlookers such as Koppett maintained that baseball lost its special status with many fans.

Chapter 19

VARIANTS

BASEBALL AS PLAYED by the Knickerbockers borrowed elements from several bat-and-ball games and established a single way of playing. Thus there were actually variants of baseball before there was regulation baseball, in the form of games known by such names as trapball, rounders, one o' cat, stoolball, roundball, and town ball.

The Knickerbockers' version initially tended to drive out its competitors, most notably the Massachusetts game, also known as roundball. Eventually, however, variant methods of playing the game reemerged. While none have seriously threatened baseball as a spectator sport, some have long and interesting histories. Others sounded like good ideas at first, only to quickly prove otherwise.

Selecting the entries for this chapter was not easy. I have tried to mention any version that became very popular or seemed historically significant. Other games were included because they were revived elements of the earliest days of baseball, or even harkened back to the bat-and-ball games that preceded the Knickerbockers. These criteria are admittedly arbitrary, and many other variants could just as easily have been selected.

19.1 Indoor Baseball. In 1897 an unnamed Chicagoan gave this account of the origins of indoor baseball:

"Indoor baseball originated in Chicago in the old Farragut Club, formerly the greatest aquatic club in the country, but now a matter of history, and came about through a frolic among the members of the club on Thanksgiving Day in 1887.

"The fellows were throwing an ordinary boxing glove around the room, which was struck at by one of the boys with a broom. George W. Hancock suddenly called out: 'Boys, let's play baseball!'"

"The boys divided into two teams and took their positions. The boxing glove was used for a ball and the broomstick for a bat. They commenced their sport, using no rules farther than the kind small boys follow on the prairie, but there was great fun. When the afternoon had closed Hancock gathered the members around him and said: 'I believe this affair can be worked into a regular game of baseball, which can be played indoors, and if you all come down Saturday night I'll make up some rules and have a ball and bat which will suit the purpose of the sport and do no damage to the surroundings.'

"And it was thus that Hancock gained the title of 'Father of Indoor Baseball.' He went home and thought out some rules that would equalize the different points of the game. A large, soft ball and a small bat were made, that being the central idea evolved from the boxing glove and broomstick and the material distinction between the new game and its prototype. From this the rest of the scheme was elaborated smoothly enough" (*Detroit Free Press*, December 17, 1897). Paul Dickson has noted that Hancock's claim to be the game's inventor has never been challenged or disputed (Paul Dickson, *The Worth Book of Softball*, 48).

Indoor baseball presented some new hazards, and its inventor did his best to solve them. An 1891 article noted, "George Hancock has invented a bat with a pneumatic tip, which will prevent it slipping from the hand, thus avoiding the liability of accident to spectators" (*Chicago Tribune*, October 25, 1891).

Hancock also published his rules, which—as had been the case with baseball (see 1.3)—helped the new game to spread rapidly. By that winter the game was being enjoyed in lodge halls, gymnasiums, and even dance halls all over Chicago (Paul Dickson, *The Worth Book of Softball*, 48). Indoor baseball had become popular in St. Louis by 1891 and quickly caught on in other cities (*Sporting News*, January 24, 1891). By the late 1890s the game had become widely popular, but before long it moved back outdoors and evolved into softball. By 1915 the indoor version had become rare enough that Jake Stahl invented a new version of indoor baseball using outdoor bats and balls in which the ball was hit into a canvas (*Chicago Tribune*, February 9, 1915).

Although George Hancock's version of indoor baseball was the one that gained popularity and eventually became softball, he wasn't the first to conceive the idea of playing baseball indoors. An 1884 article noted, "The managers of the Institute Building, Boston, are quite enthusiastic over the prospect of indoor base ball games. The inclosure is about 100 yard long by 30 wide, amply enough for an indoor foot ball field. The ball will be manufactured especially for this occasion, and will be smaller than the regulation size, and the base lines will be shortened" (*Sporting Life*, December 3, 1884). The scarcity of indoor facilities of this size naturally restricted this game's growth potential.

19.2 Softball. Softball was derived directly from indoor baseball. It was not long after indoor baseball caught on before the game was brought back outdoors. In 1895 Lewis Rober of Minneapolis was one of the leaders in convincing others of its suitability for outdoor play. Since Rober played for a team named the Kittens, the game was initially known as kitten ball. It was rechristened softball in 1926 by Walter Hakanson of Denver. Paul Dickson has observed that this was a peculiar choice of a name, since it was coined at a time when the ball used was "large and light, but not at all soft" (Paul Dickson, *The Worth Book of Softball*, 48).

19.3 Slow Pitch. Softball was originally played with fast pitching. Slow pitch first emerged around 1933 but did not become the dominant form until the 1950s. This change exemplified the curious tendency of softball to retrace baseball's history in reverse. Another notable case in point is the Chicago style of softball, which, like early baseball, is played without gloves and with a twelve-inch (rather than a ten-inch) ball that becomes mushy as the game progresses. Columnist Mike Royko was so passionate about these features that he sued to prevent the use of gloves (Paul Dickson, *The Worth Book of Softball*, 122–123).

19.4 Over the Line. Over the Line is one of the many variants of softball, which is distinguished by being played on beaches and usually without baserunning. Like so many offshoots of softball, it has also brought back one of the features of the very early days of baseball by having pitches gently tossed to the batter (Paul Dickson, *The Worth Book of Softball*, 124–125).

19.5 Muffin Baseball. Muffin baseball might not sound like a variant because it was not played by any particular rules. But its disdain for rules was the whole point of it.

By the early 1860s, clubs were being divided up into first nines, second nines, and third nines. These last groups were often referred to as "muffin" nines, because instead of fielding the ball cleanly they usually muffed it. Rather than taking this name as an insult, the players adopted it as a badge of honor.

With baseball being taken increasingly seriously, muffin games were a way of restoring the fun. They did so by reviving the spontaneity and some of the customs of the earlier, looser way of playing baseball. At the same time they specifically parodied the excesses of professional baseball, such as arguing with umpires and importing outside players.

In their heyday during the 1860s and 1870s, muffin games attracted crowds and newspaper coverage that often surpassed professional matches.

The players were often made up of prominent members of the community, such as politicians, doctors, and policemen, since unfamiliarity with the rules was an asset rather than a liability. The phenomenon of muffin baseball is described at much greater length in "'Breaking Fingers and the Third Commandment': How Muffin Games Helped Renew a Sense of Belonging," a chapter in my book *Baseball Fever*.

19.6 Baseball on Ice. With baseball and ice-skating both enjoying popularity in the early 1860s, it was inevitable that someone would try to combine them. The success of the experiment was mixed.

The earliest game thus far documented was discovered by researcher Priscilla Astifan. The game occurred on Irondequoit Bay in Rochester, New York, on January 1, 1861, and featured two local clubs, the Live Oaks and Lone Stars. A crowd of more than two thousand witnessed "spirited play" and the added bonus of a triple play (*Rochester Evening Express*, January 2, 1861, also *Rochester Union and Advertiser*, January 2, 1861; cited in Priscilla Astifan, "Baseball in the Nineteenth Century," *Rochester History* LII, No. 3 [Summer 1990], 19).

On February 4, 1861, the Atlantics of Brooklyn beat the Charter Oaks 36-27 in front of a large crowd. The *Brooklyn Eagle* reported, "It will be readily understood that the game when played upon ice with skates is altogether a different sort of affair from that which the Clubs are familiar with. The most scientific player upon the play ground finds himself out of his reckoning when he has got the runaway skates to depend on, and the best skater is the best player" (*Brooklyn Eagle*, February 5, 1861). Atlantics shortstop Dickey Pearce, however, was said to excel on ice, just as he did on land (*New York Clipper*, February 14, 1861; reprinted in James L. Terry, *Long Before the Dodgers*, 94).

A similar game was almost immediately played in Detroit, eliciting this response: "A very interesting game of base ball on skates was played at the park, day before yesterday morning. Quite a large number of spectators were present to witness the sport, it being the first game of the kind ever played, in this city, on the ice. The playing was somewhat mixed on account of some of the best players being the poorest skaters and some of the poorest players the best skaters. The ice was in prime condition, but a pretty sharp breeze which blew all the morning somewhat impeded the game" (*Detroit Free Press*, February 23, 1861).

The novelty of baseball on ice seems to have worn off fairly quickly. By 1865 the *Brooklyn Eagle* wrote, "We hope we shall have no more ball games on ice. . . . If any of the ball clubs want to make fools of themselves, let them go down to Coney Island and play a game on stilts" (*Brooklyn Eagle*, December 18, 1865; reprinted in James L. Terry, *Long Before the Dodgers*, 94).

While the crowds dwindled, the game continued to attract participants well into the 1880s. Over time, certain modifications to the rules were made when the game was played on ice. "A game on ice is played under rules which admit of five innings as a complete game, though more can be played if there is time. Then, too, only the square pitch or toss of the ball to the bat is allowable, no throwing the ball to the bat by the pitcher being admissable [sic]. The bound catch of a fair ball, too, counts; and each base runner makes every base simply by overrunning the line of the base, he being exempted from being put out in returning by turning to the right after crossing the line of the base. A very dead ball is used. The best skaters are required for the in fielders, and fast skaters for the out fielders. Ten players on each side make a game, there being right short stops as well as the regular short stops" (*Brooklyn Eagle*, January 9, 1887).

The rule changes were not the only element of baseball on ice that evoked early versions of baseball. Similar to muffin baseball, there were regular reminders that the activity could not be taken too seriously. An article in *Harper's Weekly* assured readers that "it is safe to let loose one's laughter on such an occasion, for even the most enthusiastic of professionals—even he whose daily bread depends upon the game—feels that he is in a position in which he can trifle with the game because of the abnormal conditions under which it is being played" (*Harper's Weekly*, January 26, 1884; reprinted in James L. Terry, *Long Before the Dodgers*, 95).

Baseball on ice became very rare, or at least was attracting far less attention by the 1890s, but it did not entirely vanish. In 1912 it became so popular in Cleveland that plans were announced to form a league if Lake Erie froze over (*Washington Post*, January 1, 1912). *Baseball Magazine* included a photo of the game in its April 1916 issue.

As noted under "Overrunning Bases" (1.8), Jimmy Wood believed that baseball on ice was responsible for the rule change that allowed base runners to overrun first base.

19.7   Roller Skates. Baseball on roller skates was also tried during the 1880s, though with disappointing results: "The experiment of playing base ball on roller skates was tried at the Knickerbockers Roller Skating Rink at the American Institute, New York, last week, but it was not very successful. A network is required to protect spectators who sit forward of the home base line, and a soft three ounce ball is another requirement. No bases are needed, as a three foot line—as in playing the game on ice—is all that is necessary. The ball can be delivered in any way. Small bats not over two inches in diameter, and not over thirty inches in length, should be used. The batsman should stand so as to have one foot on each side of the home base line, the home base being a painted square on the floor, with a four-foot line drawn through it. A skater in running bases has only to cross the line of each base and then turn to the right and return to the base. Fair balls caught on the bound count" (*Sporting Life*, January 7, 1885).

19.8 Freight-train Baseball. A freight-train brakeman told the *Chicago Herald* in 1886 of a new craze for freight-train baseball. He explained, "We don't do any batting, but we're great on fielding. The head brakeman stands on the front car, the rear brakeman in the middle of the train, and the conductor gets aboard the caboose. Then we play pitch, with the fireman for referee. There ain't many errors, now let me tell you. An error means a lost ball, and the man that lets it get away from him has to buy a new one. The feller that makes a wild throw, or the one that fails to stop a fair-thrown ball is the victim. The craze has run so high that I'll bet there ain't a dozen cars running out of Chicago that don't carry a stack of base balls along in their caboose. They would all say they didn't if you asked 'em, 'cause they don't want the bosses to get onto 'em, but just wait till they get out into the country, and if you're where you can see, you will see how freight-train base ball is played. Fellows that play ball on the ground may think they're having great sport, but if you want fun, and want to have the blood run pretty lively in your veins, just take a hand in a game on top of a freight train going twenty to twenty-five miles an hour" (*Chicago Herald*, reprinted in the *Boston Globe*, June 7, 1886).

The incentive of the men to deny this game's existence makes it difficult to know how long it lasted, and it was probably short-lived. But it may be the most bizarre setting in which baseball was ever played.

19.9 Punchball. Bill Mazer described punchball as having "amounted to 'The Official Sport of Brooklyn'" during the 1930s. The game had several advantages that made it well suited to the city streets. Most important, it could be played with minimal equipment—not even a bat—and with little chance of breaking a window or losing the ball. Many of the improvisations were reminiscent of the earliest days of baseball.

To begin with, the game was played with a soft ball: usually a beat-up tennis ball, a "pimple ball," or a "spaldeen," a bouncy rubber ball made by the Spalding Company. Catchers, pitchers, and bats were dispensed with entirely; instead the batter bounced the ball and punched it with his fist to begin the action. In addition, the number of players was flexible: "What also made the game so good was the fact that all you needed for a good game of punchball was four guys: two on each side. Invariably more kids would soon appear on the scene and you could change the team size at will."

Another touch that evoked the early days of baseball was the adaptability of the game to the terrain. Mazer explained: "The punchball 'court' consisted of home plate and three bases. Home plate was an iron sewer cover sitting in the middle of the street. First base would be off to the right, chalked into the pavement alongside the curb about 20 yards or so from home. Second base would either be another sewer top or, if they were too far apart, another chalked base. Third was chalked alongside the left curb opposite first." As described in the entry on "Home Plate" (14.3.2), the use of the iron sewer cover for home plate was particularly reminiscent of the early days of baseball.

The unique terrain meant that the game had a language of its own: "'Hitting a sewer,' for example, was the highest praise you could achieve on the block. Hitting a sewer meant that you were able to stroke the ball all the way past second base and on to the next sewer cover and to hell and gone down the street. Since the distance between sewer covers wasn't uniform throughout Brooklyn, there were legends about punchball players who were able to hit two sewers!"

Yet another feature similar to baseball's early days was regional variations in the rules: "Brooklyn featured two versions of punchball. In the Williamsburgh game, a chalked line was drawn across the street from first to third. Any ball that fell in front of the line was considered an out, just as any ball that landed on the sidewalk was ruled out. The Crown Heights version eliminated the 'out line' and allowed for the batter to hit grounders" (Bill Mazer, *Bill Mazer's Amazin' Baseball Book*, 104–106).

19.10   Stickball. Stickball was preferred to punchball by those for whom the greater resemblance to baseball compensated for the risk of lost balls and broken windows. The earliest reference I have found to the game occurred in 1934, when George Daley observed, "Stick ball is a new name to me. . . . [It] is a third cousin to baseball, played with a soft ball and a broomstick on the streets of New York. It is one of the most popular pastimes of boys gathered in various settlement houses. With sand lots getting scarcer and scarcer the youth still find a way to emulate Babe Ruth and get their start in baseball" (*New York Herald-Tribune*, April 19, 1934). Stickball would later become famous as Willie Mays's other favorite game.

19.11   Water Baseball. George L. Moreland reported that a game of baseball was played in the surf at Nantasket, Massachusetts, in 1881: "The contestants were clad in bathing costumes and the water was just deep enough to impede the progress of attempts at lively base running. The pitching and batting were quite creditable, but when a run was attempted the result was decidedly ludicrous" (George L. Moreland, *Balldom*, 278).

Early in the twentieth century the game was attempted in deeper water. A 1905 account noted that the game had originated the previous summer at schoolboy's camps and was usually played with five players a side: a pitcher, a catcher, and three basemen. It explained: "Each player stands on a square float and a rubber ball is used. When the batter makes a hit he swims for first base and advances as in the regulation game" (*Sporting Life*, April 1, 1905).

The *Detroit Free Press* indicated in 1907 that water baseball had originated in Atlantic City. The article said the game had been brought to Michigan in 1905 and become very popular at St. Clair Flats that year, drawing crowds of up to a thousand. After little activity in 1906, the game was again proving popular that spring. It provided this description: "Water baseball is played in a way similar to baseball, bases being used in the shape of floats set out in the same fashion as seen on the diamond, there being first, second and third. There are but two outfielders and no shortstop. The runner must be touched at each base" (*Detroit Free Press*, April 3, 1907).

Another effort was made in the 1930s when James Reilly, the swimming coach at Rutgers University, "invented a water game based on the diamond sport, but with six players on each team. Instead of batting the ball, players throw it from the diving board and the batter paddles 45 yards to first base. If he gets there before he is tagged or the base touched, he waits for the next man to bring him around by the same method. A catcher, 2 basemen and 3 fielders complete the line-up" (*Sporting News*, April 19, 1934).

19.12 Ten-man Baseball. As a result of the gaping holes that resulted when the fair-foul forced the first and third basemen to play close to their respective bases, the idea of adding a tenth fielder in the form of a right shortstop often arose. This was often combined with the idea of adding a tenth inning, for symmetry. A letter writer to Henry Chadwick's *The Ball Player's Chronicle* asked in 1867 if it was necessary to play ten innings if a tenth fielder were used, and the response was "Certainly not" (*The Ball Player's Chronicle*, June 27, 1867).

Chadwick apparently rethought his position. Before the 1874 season he confidently announced in his annual guides and weekly columns that baseball would henceforth be played with ten players and ten innings. The change, however, was not adopted by the National Association or any major clubs.

Nonetheless some clubs in isolated areas assumed that the new ten-man game had become standard. Not only did these clubs adopt it, but a few continued to use it for several years afterward. In Ypsilanti, Michigan, for instance, ten-man baseball was the version almost invariably played between 1874 and 1879, though it was very rare elsewhere in the state. The ten-man game was also the norm in Cuba for much of the nineteenth century, though it is not known how and why the extra player was added (Roberto Gonzalez Echevarria, *The Pride of Havana*, 104).

Henry Chadwick remained convinced that the ten-man version was the future of baseball and wrote after the 1874 season: "That this rule will ultimately prevail, we have not the least doubt. It took us over five years to teach the fraternity the value of the 'fly games' over that of the old rule of the bound catch, and probably it will be nearly as difficult to remove the prejudice against this later proposed improvement in the game" (undated clipping, Chadwick Scrapbooks).

In succeeding years he continued to advocate ten-man baseball, but after the fair-foul was eliminated in 1877 his calls increasingly fell upon deaf ears. Before the 1878 season the *Chicago Tribune* wrote sarcastically, "It must be getting pretty near the time when the *Clipper* annually brings out its 'ten runs and ten innings' plan. It would be a glorious scheme to rope that new Association into adopting this 'improvement'" (*Chicago Tribune*, February 3, 1878). Undeterred, Chadwick was still advocating ten-man baseball in the early 1880s (see, for example, *New York Clipper*, January 29, 1881).

19.13 No Man Left Behind. After the close of the 1878 season, the Chicago club tried to attract spectators to an exhibition game against Milwaukee by using "the new-fangled scheme of playing the men back on the bases on which they were left in the previous inning." The game was not an artistic success, as base runners had little incentive to take risks. Nor did it create excitement as Chicago won by a lopsided 26-3 margin. Most important, it was a commercial failure, and "the few people on the ground were at a loss to know how to score this new wrinkle" (*Chicago Tribune*, October 4, 1878).

19.14 Wiffle Ball. In 1953 Dave Mullany, Sr., wished there were a way for his son to throw a curve ball without hurting his arm. He also wanted it to be possible for his son to play baseball in the backyard without breaking windows. So he glued together two plastic cosmetic cases and sliced holes in them to create air resistance. He called the result the Wiffle Ball, because its curving action caused batters to whiff. The Mullany family still manufactures Wiffle Balls.

A somewhat similar idea had been put forward half a century earlier. A 1902 account reported that "Ted Kennedy, the once noted ex-pitcher, has, he claims, invented a special curving base ball which enables a pitcher to mechanically produce an inshoot, out-curve, jump and drop ball" (*Sporting Life*, February 8, 1902).

19.15 Two Swings. Roger Kahn recalled playing a version of baseball called "two swings." When no one was available whom both sides trusted to call balls and strikes, the batter would instead be allowed two swings (Roger

Kahn, *The Head Game*, 42). This was therefore a throwback to the days when umpires did not call balls and strikes.

19.16 Donkey Baseball. The original incarnation of donkey baseball occurred in 1861 and did not use actual donkeys. Instead its name was derived from "donkey races," a silly type of contest.

The *Brooklyn Eagle* gave this description of donkey baseball: "Yesterday afternoon a very amusing, and perhaps the most novel match ever played, took place upon the grounds of the Star Club, South Brooklyn. It being on the plan of a 'Donkey Race,' and but for the cold and chilly weather, the affair passed off pleasantly. The conditions of the game were, the nine making the LEAST runs should gain the victory and the player scoring the MOST runs to get the ball" (*Brooklyn Eagle*, November 16, 1861). Although Henry Chadwick noted the following spring that a "series of the 'Donkey Matches'" were planned, interest in these exhibitions does not appear to have been sustained.

The surprising thing is that donkey baseball was revived many decades later as an equally lighthearted game, but this time using actual donkeys. The *St. Louis Post-Dispatch* offered this description: "all participants, excepting the catcher, the pitcher and the batsman are astride donkeys. After hitting the ball it is necessary for the hitter to get on the back of a donkey and make his way to first base before the fielders, also on donkeys, retrieve the ball" (*St. Louis Post-Dispatch*, June 8, 1934).

19.17 Old-fashion. Colin Howell has documented a fascinating game called "old-fashion" that was played by the Mi'kmaq Indians of Atlantic Canada as recently as the 1940s. Old-fashion preserved an intriguing number of remnants of ball games of the pre-Knickerbockers era, including no foul ground, one out per inning, soaking (see **1.22**), and soft, homemade balls. Based on the accounts gathered by Howell, another resemblance to early baseball was the flexibility of the rules (Colin Howell, *Northern Sandlots*, 186–189).

Chapter 20

INCLUSION

THE FITFUL and still unfinished story of the acceptance of minorities and women into baseball admits of no brief summary. It has produced moments of triumph where baseball has symbolized the broader struggle for equality and set an example for society. But it has also yielded moments of shame where baseball has lagged even behind the rest of the country in the recognition of the universality of human rights, dreams, and ambitions.

It is tempting to say that the one thing this story has never been is dull. But the entry on African-American umpires (**20.1.16**) suggests that even that generalization may be false. It is accordingly wisest to let the entries speak for themselves.

(i) African Americans

20.1.1   African-American Clubs. The Unknown Club of Weeksville, New York, was playing as early as 1859. The *New York Anglo-African* published an account on December 10, 1859, of a match the Unknowns had played on November 15. Their opponents were the Henson Base Ball Club of Jamaica, New York, who won by a score of 54-43. The racial makeup of the Hensons was not specified in this article, but other references to the club make clear that they were African Americans (Michael E. Lomax, *Black Baseball Entrepreneurs, 1860–1901*, 1, 11). An account of the match and a box score are reprinted on page 35 of Dean Sullivan's *Early Innings*.

The involvement of African Americans in baseball during the game's first great expansion in the 1860s is difficult to measure. The number of documented African-American and integrated clubs during the decade is small, but there could be more that are lost to history. Early box scores and game accounts almost always referred to players by their surnames only, making identification difficult or impossible. In addition, it cannot necessarily be assumed that the presence of African-American and white players on the same club would have drawn attention.

The factors that restricted African-American participation in the 1860s are also tricky to assess. Racial prejudice may have played a role, but it seems more likely that practical considerations were paramount. Most notably, baseball was slow to spread to the South while the African-American population had not yet begun to move north in great numbers. Additionally, baseball was a sport that relied upon leisure time during daylight hours and ready access to an appropriate piece of land, both of which were in short supply for African Americans of the era.

20.1.2 Match Between African-American Clubs. The 1859 match mentioned in the preceding entry was one of the earliest between African-American clubs. But it is unlikely that it was the first, since the game account referred to it as "another victory for the Henson."

Matches among African-American clubs appear to have remained rare for the next few years. In 1862 the *Brooklyn Eagle* printed an account of a game between the Unknowns of Weeksville and the Monitor Club of Brooklyn and observed, "This is the first match to our knowledge that has been played in this city by players of African descent" (*Brooklyn Eagle*, October 17, 1862; reprinted in Dean Sullivan, ed., *Early Innings*, 35–36).

20.1.3 Integrated Matches. Dean Sullivan reported that some sort of baseball game involving players of both races took place on July 4, 1859. An account in the *New York Anglo-African* indicated that Joshua R. Giddings, an abolitionist white congressman, participated in the game. Since Giddings was sixty-four at the time, it can safely be assumed that the competition was not heated (*New York Anglo-African*, July 30, 1859; Dean Sullivan, ed., *Early Innings*, 34).

20.1.4 Integrated Clubs. The 1859 match mentioned in the preceding entry appears to have been a special event, with the two sides being improvised. The difficulties of identifying the race of individual players make it especially hard to pinpoint the first club to include both African-American and white players. That distinction most likely belongs to one of the clubs mentioned in earlier entries, or one of their contemporaries.

It can be said with certainty that an integrated club existed in Northampton, Massachusetts, in 1865. Brian Turner and John S. Bowman, in their excellent history of baseball in that town, demonstrated that Luther B. Askin, first baseman of the Florence Eagles in 1865 and 1866, was of African-American descent. While Askin was light-skinned, Turner and Bowman cited an account by the club's captain to show that he was aware of Askin's race.

What makes this particularly noteworthy is that Turner and Bowman had to unearth the fact. They explained that Askin was known as "Old Bushel Basket" for his catching skills and "was also cited on at least one occasion for 'heavy' hitting. Left unmentioned, however, was the extraordinary fact that he was an African American on a white team" (Brian Turner and John S. Bowman, *Baseball in Northampton, 1823–1953*, 14–15).

The Northampton club was probably not the first integrated club, but it does prove that this first occurred no later than 1865. Moreover the lack of attention paid to this "extraordinary fact" suggests that contemporaries did not view it as all that extraordinary, which means that there could easily have been earlier integrated clubs.

20.1.5 African Americans in Collegiate Baseball. College play would prove an important means of access for African Americans to baseball and many other areas, since it was more difficult to apply racial stereotypes and prejudices to a highly educated man. Intervarsity baseball competition did not become organized until the late 1870s, but baseball clubs were thriving on campuses in the 1860s and 1870s. Some of these clubs competed solely against one another, but many colleges had nines that played outside competition.

Ohio's Oberlin College featured a club called the Resolutes in the late 1860s that included two African Americans, Simpson Younger and J. T. Settle. The Resolutes played several matches each year against semipro and professional clubs. Phil Dixon and Patrick J. Hannigan reported that the club won ten of their thirteen matches while Younger was on the club. All three losses came at the hands of the Forest City Club of Cleveland, a top professional club that was a charter member of the National Association (Phil Dixon and Patrick J. Hannigan, *The Negro Baseball Leagues*, 41).

20.1.6 African Americans in Organized Baseball. Bud Fowler (born John Jackson) played in both the International Association and the New England League in 1878. While there were periods when he played outside of organized ball due to racism, Fowler was still playing in the minor leagues as late as 1895.

In the 1880s Fowler had a good deal of company in organized baseball. (Bob Davids compiled a list of African Americans in organized baseball in the nineteenth century that appears as an appendix in Jerry Malloy, ed., *Sol White's History of Colored Base Ball*, and in Phil Dixon and Patrick J. Hannigan, *The Negro Baseball Leagues*.) By the 1890s the insidious color barrier (see **20.1.9**) was beginning to take its toll. It is often reported that Bill Galloway, who played for Woodstock of the Canadian League in 1899, was the last African American in organized baseball before Jackie Robinson in 1946 (see, for example, Phil Dixon and Patrick J. Hannigan, *The Negro Baseball Leagues*, 80).

In fact there were a few scattered exceptions during those years. Some African Americans were able to pass as white. Dick Brookins, who appears to have been a light-skinned man of mixed race, was able to play in various Class D leagues between 1906 and 1910 (Bill Kirwin, "The Mysterious Case of Dick Brookins," *National Pastime* 19 [1999], 38–43). Jimmy Claxton, who was born in Canada to a white mother and a father of French, African-American, and Indian heritage, played briefly in the Pacific Coast League in 1916 after being introduced as an Indian. His release corresponded to the surfacing of rumors that he was actually an African American (William J. Weiss, "The First Negro in Twentieth Century O. B.," *Baseball Research Journal* 8 [1979], 31–35).

Others, however, attempted to play openly. William Clarence Matthews, an African American who starred for Harvard, played briefly for Burlington of the Vermont League. An African American named Bill Thompson played in the Twin State League of Vermont and New Hampshire throughout the 1911 season. Although his race was no secret, researcher Seamus Kearney reported that Thompson encountered no resistance (Seamus Kearney, "Bill Thompson, Pioneer," *National Pastime* 16 [1996], 67–68). Unfortunately, as noted under "Color Line" (**20.1.9**), within two years the mood in the Twin State League had changed.

20.1.7   African-American Major Leaguers. Jackie Robinson broke baseball's long-standing color barrier in 1947, yet he was far from the first African American to play major league baseball.

During the research for this book, with help from SABR colleagues Stefan Fatsis, Bruce Allardice, and Richard Malatzky, I was able to confirm that the first man of African-American heritage to play in the major leagues was William Edward White, the son of a white Confederate soldier and one of his slaves. White was a student at Brown University in 1879 and helped his school earn recognition as collegiate champions. When Providence first baseman Joe Start was injured that summer, White filled in for the next game, handling twelve chances flawlessly and getting one hit. Nonetheless it was White's only major league game (Stefan Fatsis, "Mystery of Baseball: Was William White Game's First Black?," *Wall Street Journal*, January 30, 2004, 1).

The next was Moses Fleetwood "Fleet" Walker, who debuted with Toledo of the American Association on May 1, 1884. His brother Welday became the third African-American major leaguer when he joined Toledo in July. The Walker brothers had both attended Oberlin College and the University of Michigan, meaning that the only three African Americans known to have played major league baseball in the nineteenth century had attended prestigious colleges.

There is compelling evidence that at least one more nineteenth-century player, pitcher Charles Leander "Bumpus" Jones, was an African American who passed as a white. Jones pitched a no-hitter in his major league debut on October 15, 1892, yet would win only one more major league game despite three twenty-win seasons in the minors (Chris Rainey, "A Cincy Legend: A Narrative of Bumpus Jones' Baseball Career," Dick Miller and Mark Stang, eds., *Baseball in the Buckeye State*, 7).

In 1901 John McGraw attempted to pass an African-American man named Charley Grant off as an Indian named Chief Tokahoma. His ruse was not successful, and the accepted version of history has it that there were no more serious attempts to break the major league's color barrier until the signing of Jackie Robinson in 1946.

The reality is more complex, due to the influx of Latin players in the intervening years. According to Roberto Gonzalez Echevarria, "Roberto (El Tarzan) Estalella and Tomas de la Cruz, both of African descent, had already played in the majors in the thirties and forties, protected by the American confusion over race, color and nationality" (Roberto Gonzalez Echevarria, *The Pride of Havana*, 45).

Symbolic of that confusion, at least three other Cubans—Pedro Dibut, Oscar Estrada, and Ramon Herrera—played in both the white major leagues and the Negro National League. Quite a few other Cuban-born major leaguers played for clubs like the Long Branch Cubans, which barnstormed with African-American clubs (Dick Clark and Larry Lester, eds., *The Negro Leagues Book*, 255–257).

Peter Bjarkman cited several other Cubans and Puerto Rican Hi Bithorn as other major leaguers who may have been of African descent. He suggested that their omission from the traditional version means that "the full story of baseball's gradual and fitful racial integration has never been accurately told or popularly accepted" (Peter Bjarkman, "Cuban Blacks in the Majors Before Jackie Robinson," *National Pastime* 12 [1992], 58–63).

20.1.8 African-American Tours. The first extensive trip by an African-American baseball club may have occurred when the Bachelor Club of Albany, New York, traveled to Philadelphia to play two Philadelphia clubs in 1867. The first multi-city tour seems to have taken place in 1870 when the *New York Tribune* reported: "The Mutuals, a colored Club of Washington, are on a tour and are now in Western New York" (*New York Tribune*, August 26, 1870). The club played matches in Lockport, Niagara Falls, Buffalo, Rochester, Utica, Canajoharie, and Troy (*New York Clipper*, September 3, 1870; quoted in Michael E. Lomax, *Black Baseball Entrepreneurs, 1860–1901*, 28).

In the mid-1890s the Page Fence Giants of Adrian, Michigan, bought their own railroad car. Researcher Jerry Malloy reported that "the sixty-foot-long, gilt ornamented car was fitted with a lavatory, private manager's office, a state room, kitchen, and a combined dining-setting-sleeping room. Capable of sleeping 20, the car sported leather seats and a Belgian carpet. The coach was staffed with a cook (who pitched in one game) and a porter-barber" (Jerry Malloy, ed., *Sol White's History of Colored Base Ball*, xxxiv). Not only did this innovation make touring cheaper and easier, it spared the club many of the indignities of segregation. Phil Dixon and Patrick J. Hannigan point out that Negro League clubs are strongly associated with endless bus trips. They note that in fact the clubs traveled almost exclusively by train until the mid-1920s (Phil Dixon and Patrick J. Hannigan, *The Negro Baseball Leagues*, 26).

20.1.9   Color Line. The color barrier that kept most African Americans out of organized baseball until the appearance of Jackie Robinson generally took the form of an unwritten "gentlemen's agreement." When the issue was pushed, however, the prohibition was expressed more openly.

After the 1867 season the African-American Pythian Club of Philadelphia applied for membership in the Pennsylvania Association of Amateur Base Ball Players; the response was ominous. Pythians representative Raymond Burr was advised "to withdraw [rather] than to have it on record that [the Pythians] were blackballed." He declined at first but eventually did so when defeat was inevitable. In a scene that would become all too familiar, Burr found that all the delegates "expressed sympathy for our club" but that only a handful were willing to cast votes in favor of the club. The others claimed that they would "in justice to the opinion of the clubs they represented be compelled, against their personal feelings, to vote against [the Pythians'] admission" (Michael E. Lomax, *Black Baseball Entrepreneurs, 1860–1901*, 22–24).

Two months later the Pythians applied for membership in the National Association of Base Ball Players. That body's nominating committee unanimously recommended that clubs not be admitted if they were "composed of one or more colored persons" (*The Ball Player's Chronicle*, December 19, 1867; reprinted in Dean Sullivan, ed., *Early Innings*, 68–69). The Pythians withdrew their nomination.

An article in Henry Chadwick's *Ball Player's Chronicle* commented that the nominating committee pursued that course in order "to keep out of the

Convention the discussion of any subject having a political bearing, as this undoubtedly had" (*The Ball Player's Chronicle*, December 19, 1867; reprinted in Dean Sullivan, ed., *Early Innings*, 68–69). That insidious reasoning—effectively creating a ban without having to take responsibility for having done so—presaged an ugly pattern that would become all too familiar in the 1880s.

As shown in the preceding entries, as baseball developed in the late 1860s and throughout the 1870s African Americans made their way into collegiate, semipro, and professional baseball. In 1875 the Mutual Base Ball Club of Washington, D.C., became the first African-American club admitted to the National Amateur Association of Base Ball Players (*St. Louis Globe-Democrat*, April 12, 1875). While African-American ballplayers of this period undoubtedly encountered some hostility, there do not appear to have been any outright bans on interracial play before the mid-1880s.

There are several plausible interpretations for why the 1870s' apparent progress toward racial harmony was succeeded by a backlash. The one that seems most compelling to me is that white ballplayers felt threatened not so much by the prospect of playing against African Americans as by the fear of losing to them. The improved level of African-American baseball made this an increasingly likely occurrence in the mid-1880s. For example, when the Cuban Giants' application to join the Eastern League was rejected, the *Meriden Journal* admitted that "the dread of being beaten by the Africans had something to do with the rejection of the application of the Cuban Giants" (*Meriden Journal*, quoted in *Trenton Times*, July 23, 1886; reprinted in Michael E. Lomax, *Black Baseball Entrepreneurs, 1860–1901*, 58).

Whether it was this specific fear or the decade's general deterioration of interracial relationships, the 1880s saw the specter of a color bar begin to loom over baseball. When Fleet Walker signed to play for Toledo of the Northwestern League in 1883, one delegate offered a resolution that would ban African Americans from the league. After a spirited debate the resolution was withdrawn, and the delegate took the curious course of asking that references to his resolution be removed from the minutes (*Grand Rapids* [Mich.] *Times*, March 16, 1883).

The National League and the American Association were able to avoid confronting the issue directly by having no acknowledged African Americans under contract after 1884. Their absence was generally ignored by the press, but occasionally a candid journalist such as John B. Foster would draw attention to the tacit agreement: "Many National League managers sigh because they could not sign [Fleet Walker]. There is no rule against the signing of colored players by National League clubs, but personalities are apt to arise if the experiment is tried, and managers are loth to tempt trouble" (John B. Foster, "Buckeye Boys," *Sporting News*, December 28, 1895).

The International League became their refuge, and the presence of eight African-American players in the league by 1887 made it impossible to pursue the familiar course of a gentlemen's agreement. Several ugly incidents occurred, the most notorious when Chicago's Adrian "Cap" Anson refused to play an exhibition game against Newark if African American George Stovey pitched (David Zang, *Fleet Walker's Divided Heart*, 54–55). The International League felt obliged to address the issue but, like earlier leagues, chose to do so as coyly as possible. The *Newark Journal* reported that the league's board of directors had held a "secret meeting" and instructed the league secretary "to approve of no more contracts with colored men" (quoted in Jerry Malloy, "Out at Home," in John Thorn, ed., *The National Pastime*, 235).

Obviously a meeting that was reported in the next day's papers could not have been much of a secret. The results that ensued from the meeting are also somewhat curious. The next year the league had only three African-American players, and in 1889 only Fleet Walker. When he left at the end of the season, the circuit remained lily-white until Jackie Robinson joined Montreal in 1946. So it appears that the course taken by the International League was not overtly to ban the entire race but instead to grandfather the current players and sign no new ones.

Not all whites were reticent about expressing racist views. The players on the St. Louis Brown Stockings refused to play an exhibition game against an African-American club because "they drew the color line strongly" (*Philadelphia Sunday News*, quoted in *St. Louis Post-Dispatch*, September 13, 1887). The *Detroit Free Press* observed that there were several African-American players who "would prove a boon to some of the weak clubs of the league and association, but if there is one thing the white ball player insists on doing it is drawing the color line very rigidly" (*Detroit Free Press*, December 4, 1887). Two Syracuse players refused to pose for a team picture because of the presence of an African American (quoted in Jerry Malloy, "Out at Home," in John Thorn, ed., *The National Pastime*, 228–229).

The following year Welday Walker read that the Tri-State League planned to ban African Americans. He wrote an open letter to the league president, arguing that such a rule "casts derision at the laws of Ohio—the voice of the people—that say all men are equal" (*Sporting Life*, March 14, 1888; reprinted in Dean Sullivan, ed., *Early Innings*, 69–70). Walker's reasoning is so straightforward and compelling that a logical rebuttal would be impossible, which helps explain why an indirect course was again pursued.

Apparently the Tri-State League had no intentions of actually passing a color bar. But the number of African Americans in the league fell from four to one that year, and to none the following year. Once again a tacit color line had been created without having to deal with the controversy that would have ensued from an explicit prohibition. The same pattern occurred in other leagues, with the result that the number of opportunities for African Americans in the minor leagues fell dramatically. By the end of the nineteenth century, organized baseball was able to have it both ways—it had made the game lily-white without the appearance of any conscious effort to attain that end.

For nearly fifty years organized baseball clung with equal stubbornness to the color bar and to the myth that it didn't have one. One can find a few rare admissions that such a prohibition did in fact exist. Brian Turner and John S. Bowman have documented a fascinating instance in the Twin State League in 1913.

It is important to stress that the Twin State League had not signed the National Agreement and was technically outside of organized baseball. But the league maintained a good working relationship with organized baseball (Brian Turner and John S. Bowman, *Baseball in Northampton, 1823–1953*, 42).

The Twin State League would have appeared to be the perfect place for an African American to play. Two years earlier an African American named Bill Thompson had spent the entire season in the league without encountering opposition. Nonetheless when the Bellows Falls club attempted to use African-American pitcher Frank Wickware in an August 26, 1913, game against the Northampton Meadowlarks, the Larks refused to take the field.

The controversy that ensued produced some unusually forthright admissions of prejudice. The *Northampton Gazette* wrote: "The color line is drawn in organized baseball. The Twin State league recognizes orders from that commission, refuses to play a ball player when ordered not to, [so] why not in drawing the color line." At a September meeting the directors voted to bar African Americans from the league by a 5 to 1 vote.

As we have seen, such candid acknowledgments of the existence of a color line were rare, which enabled a few African Americans to play in the minor leagues in the early twentieth century. But this decision by a league in which African Americans had been accepted two years earlier made it clear that the color barrier was very real and increasingly inflexible.

In the 1930s professional football attempted to follow baseball's example. While there had been African Americans in the National Football League from its inception, their numbers began to dwindle in the 1930s. By 1933 only Joe Lillard of the Chicago Cardinals remained, and he was let go at season's end. His coach, Paul Schissler, explained that opposing players "took it out on" Lillard and his teammates; accordingly, "We had to let him go, for our own sake, and for his, too" (quoted in Thomas G. Smith, "Outside the Pale: The Exclusion of Blacks from the National Football League, 1934–46," *Journal of Sports History* 15, No. 3 [Winter 1988], 255–281; reprinted in Robert W. Peterson, *Pigskin*, 179).

From 1934 to 1945 there were no African Americans in the NFL—but the league followed baseball's evasive path and never passed a ban. The extent of the denial is suggested when Chicago Bears owner George Halas claimed in the late 1960s: "Probably it was due to the fact that no great black players were in colleges then. That could be the reason. But I've never given this a thought until you mentioned it. At no time has it ever been brought up. Isn't that strange?" (quoted in Myron Cope, *The Game That Was*; reprinted in Robert W. Peterson, *Pigskin*, 169).

By the 1930s the myth that there was no color line in baseball was becoming increasingly difficult to sustain. The success that barnstorming Negro League clubs had against white clubs could not be explained away. Efforts were made to reduce the number of such games, but the questions persisted.

When reporters pressed the matter, a few Negro League stars were given sham tryouts (Jules Tygiel, *Baseball's Great Experiment*, 30–46). But no strategy could continue to obscure the increasingly obvious fact that baseball had a color line.

Longtime Commissioner Kenesaw Mountain Landis was still claiming in 1942, "There is no rule, formal or informal, or any understanding—unwritten, subterranean, or sub-anything—against the hiring of Negro players by the teams of organized baseball" (quoted in Jules Tygiel, *Baseball's Great Experiment*, 30). Yet there were more and more cracks in this façade as, under pressure, baseball people came out as either opposed to or in favor of a color barrier that supposedly didn't exist (Jules Tygiel, *Baseball's Great Experiment*, 38–42).

In fact it probably didn't make much difference which side an individual was on; it was the tacit concession that there *was* such a prohibition that mattered. The acknowledgment of overt racial prejudice—at the same time African Americans were fighting in a world war to preserve the freedoms they shared in so unequally—was enough. Once it was generally admitted that baseball actually had a color barrier, it was not long before that barrier fell. That, I believe, is no coincidence.

20.1.10 All African-American / Latin Lineup in the White Major Leagues. On September 1, 1971, with Philadelphia in town, Pittsburgh manager Danny Murtaugh handed in this starting lineup: Rennie Stennett, 2b; Gene Clines, cf; Roberto Clemente, rf; Willie Stargell, lf; Manny Sanguillen, c; Dave Cash, 3b; Al Oliver, 1b; Jackie Hernandez, ss; Dock Ellis, p. The Pirates won by a score of 10-7, but what was more significant was that not one of their nine starters would have been able to play in the major leagues twenty-five years earlier.

Even after baseball began to integrate, there continued to be rumors that quotas were the latest manifestation of the "gentlemen's agreement." Roger

Kahn, for example, observed, "There existed in 1953 what John Lardner called the 50 percent color line; that is, it was permissible for a major league team to play only four black men out of nine. The ratio, five whites to four blacks, substantiated white supremacy. But to have five blacks playing with four whites supposedly threatened the old order" (Roger Kahn, *The Boys of Summer*, 166–167). It was not until July 17, 1954, that the Dodgers fielded a starting lineup with a majority of African Americans (Jonathan Fraser Light, *The Cultural Encyclopedia of Baseball*, 96).

Thus the symbolic importance of the Pirates lineup on September 1, 1971, was considerable.

20.1.11   African-American Managers. The first African American to manage in the minor leagues was Stanislaus Kostka "S.K." Govern, a native of the Virgin Islands who had been involved with the Cuban Giants since the club's inception. In 1889 the Cuban Giants were members of the Middle States League, earning Govern the distinction. In late June a second African-American club, the Gorhams of New York, managed by Benjamin Butler, briefly joined the Middle States League (Michael E. Lomax, *Black Baseball Entrepreneurs, 1860–1901*, 89–90, 98–102).

Frank Robinson was the first African American to manage a major league team, being named player-manager of the Cleveland Indians on October 3, 1974. His historic managerial debut took place on April 8, 1975, and he homered to lead Cleveland to a 5-3 victory.

Bill Deane noted that at least a couple of African Americans had filled in on a one-game basis before then. Willie Horton was named "manager for a day" by Detroit pilot Mayo Smith on September 19, 1968, and the Tigers beat the Yankees 6-2. On May 8, 1973, Ernie Banks served as acting manager of the Chicago Cubs after Whitey Lockman was ejected (Bill Deane, "How 'Bout That," *Baseball Research Journal* 20 [1991], 90).

20.1.12   African-American Coaches. Buck O'Neil was the first African American to serve as a major league coach, holding that position for the Chicago Cubs in 1962. The promotion came after O'Neil had spent seven years in the Cubs organization as a scout and spring training instructor. Although the announcement came during the period when the Cubs were using a rotating head coaching system, O'Neil was not included in the rotation (Richard Dozer, "Cubs Sign Negro Coach," *Chicago Tribune*, May 30, 1962). It is sometimes contended that Rube Foster informally served as a pitching coach for the New York Giants in the early twentieth century, but there is little evidence to support that contention.

20.1.13   African-American General Managers. Bill Lucas was named director of player personnel for the Atlanta Braves on September 19, 1976. He held the position until his premature death on May 5, 1979, and fulfilled the functions normally associated with a general manager. Braves owner Ted Turner was nominally the club's general manager, but star outfielder Dale Murphy later commented, "I always thought of [Lucas] as the general manager. I'm surprised to hear that he wasn't the general manager." Lucas's untimely death prevented him from seeing the fruits of his labor when the team whose nucleus he had built captured the 1982 National League West division title (Mark Bowman, "Lucas Left Impression on Braves," article on mlb.com website, February 4, 2003).

Bob Watson became the first African American to hold the title of general manager of a major league club when he was hired by the Houston Astros following the 1993 season. His tenure proved ill-omened; Watson was diagnosed with cancer, and the 1994 season was ended prematurely by a strike. Watson later became general manager of the Yankees and helped the club capture the 1996 World Series, but he resigned in 1998 citing burnout.

20.1.14 African-American Professional Teams. After the 1875 season the Blue Stockings of St. Louis formed a joint stock company in hopes of raising $1,000 to fund the club for the 1876 season. They quickly raised half the amount, but it is not known what happened after that (*St. Louis Globe-Democrat*, November 16, 1875). In 1882 the *Cincinnati Enquirer* noted that "Philadelphia has a nine of colored professionals," which may have been a club known as the Orions. Several other African-American clubs appear to have operated as professionals over the next couple of seasons (Robert W. Peterson, *Only the Ball Was White*, 34).

The first successful African-American professional team was one formed by Frank P. Thompson in 1885. The club soon became known as the Cuban Giants and became one of the most famous African-American clubs of the nineteenth century, but its exact origins are much less clear.

Baseball researcher Jerry Malloy concluded that Sol White, the first important historian of African-American baseball, was responsible for the confusion. White played on the team and later recalled that when Thompson was head waiter at the Argyle Hotel in Babylon, New York, he "chose the best ball players from among his waiters, and organized a base ball club to play as an attraction for the guests of the hotel." The players proved very talented, and Thompson took them on the road when the hotel season ended in September (Jerry Malloy, ed., *Sol White's History of Colored Base Ball*, 8).

Sol White was also the source of the most usually cited story of the origin of the inappropriate Cuban Giants name. In a 1938 interview he explained that "the version which came to him is that when that first team began playing away from home, they passed as foreigners—Cubans, as they finally decided—hoping to conceal the fact that they were just American

Negro hotel waiters, and talked a gibberish to each other on the field which, they hoped, sounded like Spanish" (*Esquire*, September 1938; reprinted in Jerry Malloy, ed., *Sol White's History of Colored Base Ball*, lix–lx).

Malloy argued that these picturesque tales are of dubious authenticity. He observed that there is no contemporary documentation of pseudo-Spanish being spoken and questioned the likelihood that such a ploy would fool any-one. Malloy also uncovered a very different account of the club's origins that appeared in the *New York Age* in 1887.

This article, written by J. Gordon Street but likely emanating from an interview with Frank P. Thompson himself, indicated that Thompson or-ganized the club as the Keystone Athletics in Philadelphia in May 1885. The club spent most of the summer in Babylon, Long Island. In August they merged with clubs from Washington and Philadelphia and assumed the name of the Cuban Giants (J. Gordon Street, "The Cuban Giants," *New York Age*, October 15, 1887; reprinted in Jerry Malloy, ed., *Sol White's His-tory of Colored Base Ball*, 134–135).

Malloy pointed out several elements of Street's account that make it more credible than White's. First, it appeared in 1887 while the club was still in its prime, while White did not join the club until several years later. Sec-ond, the account implies that the players' primary obligation during the summer in Babylon was to entertain guests with their ball-playing. This seems far more plausible than White's version in which a large number of talented ballplayers happened to be working at the same hotel.

Finally, Malloy pointed out that Street's version accounts for manager S. K. Govern becoming involved with the Cuban Giants. Govern had been managing the Manhattans of Washington, one of the three clubs that was in-volved in the merger. Malloy also uncovered evidence that the Manhattans had previously toured Cuba, which may account for the name assumed by the club (Jerry Malloy, ed., *Sol White's History of Colored Base Ball*, lx–lxi).

20.1.15 Leagues of African-American Teams. In 1884 the *Washington Post* reported talk of a "league of colored baseball clubs" that would include teams in Washington, Baltimore, and Pittsburgh. Nothing appears to have materialized (*Washington Post*, February 24, 1884).

The Southern League of Colored Base Ballists was organized in 1886 with three clubs in Jacksonville, two clubs in Memphis, two clubs in Savan-nah, and one club each in Atlanta, Charleston, and New Orleans. The sea-son was scheduled to run from June 7 to August 25, but details of the league's activities remain very sketchy. No standings are known to have been pub-lished, and only the *New Orleans Times-Picayune* ran box scores. Researcher Bill Plott noted that the *Jacksonville Leader* was designated as the league's official organ and suggested that further research into that newspaper's files might be productive (Bill Plott, "The Southern League of Colored Base Ballists," *Baseball Research Journal* 3 [1974]; reprinted in *Baseball Historical Review* 1981, 75–78).

That fall, Walter S. Brown of Pittsburgh announced plans for the National Colored Base Ball League with teams in Philadelphia, Baltimore, Pittsburgh, Washington, Louisville, and Cincinnati. Franchises in New York and Boston were later added while Washington and Cincinnati were dropped. The league was granted protection under the National Agreement and opened play on May 5, 1887, but disbanded before the end of the month (Michael E. Lomax, *Black Baseball Entrepreneurs, 1860–1901*, 63–70; Jerry Malloy, "Out at Home," in John Thorn, ed., *The National Pastime*, 220–222).

Over the next thirty-three years, barnstorming African-American players built the popularity of their game. The potential for remunerative tours left the best clubs with limited incentive to pin themselves down to a league. This did not change until 1920 when the Negro National League, the first of the leagues now collectively referred to as the Negro Leagues, was formed. The league was organized at a meeting at the YMCA in Kansas City, Missouri, on February 13, 1920.

20.1.16 African-American Umpires. In 1882 the *Grand Rapids* (Michigan) *Democrat* reported matter-of-factly that "a Mr. Pierson, colored, of Port Huron," had umpired the previous day's game between clubs representing Grand Rapids and Port Huron (*Grand Rapids Democrat*, September 9, 1882). No additional comment on his race or umpiring was made, which raises the intriguing possibility that there were other African-American umpires at this time. If so, however, their names are lost to history.

Emmet Ashford became the first African American who is known to have umpired in the minors when he was hired by the Southwestern International League in 1951. It took Ashford fifteen long years before he was hired by the American League on February 20, 1966, and thereby became the first African-American umpire in major league history.

When Wayne Beasley was hired by the Carolina League in 1972, he became the first African-American umpire in a Southern league. There were still only four African-American umpires in professional baseball at the time, and combining the position's onerous duties with becoming a racial pioneer was a volatile mix. It therefore came as no great surprise when Beasley resigned in June.

What did raise eyebrows was the reason cited by Beasley: boredom. He said that racial incidents had been few but explained, "I am despondent. I can't find enough to do during the days. I have read all the books I can and

I still can't find enough to keep me busy." Supporting Beasley's contention, another African American was hired to replace him (Jim L. Sumner, *Separating the Men from the Boys*, 133).

20.1.17 African-American Announcers. In 1965 Jackie Robinson was unveiled by Roone Arledge as one of three "interpretive" commentators who would work the regional telecasts of ABC's Game of the Week (*Sporting News*, March 27, 1965).

20.1.18 African-American Pension Recipients. William Buckner served as the trainer of the Chicago White Sox from 1908 until shortly before the start of the 1918 season. Among the obstacles he had to overcome was that during spring training tours of the South "he was not able to get around to see much of the boys in the hotels" (*Chicago Tribune*, March 31, 1908). After Buckner was dismissed in 1918, it was sometimes reported that team captain Eddie Collins asked for his firing, but this makes little sense as Collins was still captain when Buckner returned in 1922. Sportswriter I. E. Sanborn attributed Buckner's dismissal to pitcher Dave Danforth, a Southerner (*Chicago Tribune*, September 19, 1923).

After Buckner returned to the White Sox he remained the club's trainer until 1933 (*Chicago Tribune*, January 29, 1922; *Mexia Evening News*, March 23, 1922; *Washington Post*, April 21, 1933). He continued to work for the club for several more years and became the first African American to collect a pension from a major league ball club (Phil Dixon and Patrick J. Hannigan, *The Negro Baseball Leagues*, 65).

20.1.19 White in Negro Leagues. Eddie Klep pitched for the Cleveland Buckeyes of the Negro American League in 1946.

(ii) Women

20.2.1 Women Spectators. As noted in the entry on "Ladies' Days" (**16.1.7**), during the early days of baseball the presence of women was believed to ensure a higher class of spectators and better behavior. As a result the presence of women spectators at early baseball games was actively sought, and newspaper accounts almost invariably mentioned their presence. Clubs went to great trouble to make them feel welcome, arranging special seating sections for their convenience and usually admitting them without charge.

The amount of attention lavished on this theme reflected the pedestal upon which women of the era were placed. Being so honored may be flattering at first, but it soon becomes uncomfortable. In addition, the flattery was often mixed with a large dollop of condescension. By the 1870s and 1880s the sporting press was regularly running items that recounted the ill-informed comments of female spectators. For example, the *Milwaukee Journal* remarked in 1884, "The attendance of ladies at the ball park yesterday was large, although less than a dozen understood the game. However, they applauded heartily at each play, not waiting to discriminate between good and bad work" (*Milwaukee Daily Journal*, June 27, 1884).

Nonetheless the presence of women spectators at baseball games has always been strongly encouraged.

20.2.2 Women Players. Women who sought to *play* baseball received a very different response. The dominant theme of the treatment of women in the Victorian era was to restrict them to a narrow, well-defined sphere. As long as they remained within that sphere—as for example by being spectators at baseball matches—they were praised. But actually playing baseball brought attention to women's bodies in ways that were deemed inappropriate, and their participation in the sport was therefore discouraged.

The response to women who tried to play baseball can best be compared to how parents treat children who want to experiment with something beyond their years. Plan A is to watch indulgently and hope the child will tire of it. If that doesn't work, Plan B is executed, which is to suppress the activity with increasing forcefulness.

In my history of early baseball in Michigan I reported on five baseball clubs formed in the state by women between 1867 and 1878. None was treated with outright hostility, but none lasted long. There is thus no way to be certain how often, if at all, Plan B had to be implemented (Peter Morris, *Baseball Fever*, 195–198).

Baseball fared somewhat better at women's colleges, whose isolation undoubtedly made the prospect of athletic women less threatening. In 1866 two baseball clubs were formed at Vassar. The sport was revived there in 1876, and the school's clubs competed against nines from Smith College, Mount Holyoke, Wellesley, and Barnard. Amy Ellis Nutt observed: "Played inside the confines of those campuses, women's baseball was allowed to flourish" (Amy Ellis Nutt, "Swinging for the Fences," in Lissa Smith, ed., *Nike Is a Goddess*, 35).

As Nutt's formulation implies, there was more resistance at coeducational colleges. A female team named the Dianas was formed at Northwestern in 1869. The Dianas were even challenged by a male team, though they declined (*Chicago Times*, October 22, 1869; quoted in Robert Pruter, "Youth Baseball in Chicago, 1868–1890: Not Always Sandlot Ball," *Journal of Sport History*, Spring 1999, 6).

Unfortunately this was a rare exception. In 1904 the participation of five women in a pick-up baseball game at the University of Pennsylvania prompted campus officials to ban women from playing baseball (Amy Ellis Nutt, "Swinging for the Fences," in Lissa Smith, ed., *Nike Is a Goddess*, 36).

The response to women who tried to play baseball professionally was much harsher. Two touring clubs of women known as the Blondes and the Brunettes played several games in 1875, beginning with a match at Springfield, Illinois, on September 11. The Blondes won 42-38, and a contemporary newspaper described it as the first game "ever played in public for gate money between feminine ball-tossers" (quoted in Lois Browne, *Girls of Summer*, 15).

But if the clubs expected a supportive attitude to continue, they were sadly mistaken. When they met again in St. Louis the following week, a local paper sniffed: "There were bases, a ball, a bat, and an umpire, but otherwise the game more resembled 'puss-in-the-corner' than base ball. . . . The whole affair was a revolting exhibition of impropriety, possessing no merit save that of novelty, and gotten up to make money out of a public that rushes to see any species of semi-immorality" (*St. Louis Republican*, September 19, 1875).

In 1879 another tour was mounted by two clubs of professional women baseball players billing themselves as the Blondes and the Brunettes. They were presumably not the same players, but the response they evoked was similar.

They were initially met with fairly gentle but unmistakable mockery. According to the *Washington Post*, "the audience roared itself hoarse" at a game in New York. The account made clear that the activity could not be taken seriously: "The players wore small jockey caps atop of their top knots and plaits, and whenever the hats came off, which they always did, all thoughts of ball were, pro tempore, dismissed till the disaster was repaired."

The descriptions of the action were similarly insistent on stressing the appearance of the players: "The blue catcher wore her hair down, and when the umpire had called three strikes on her, she dashed off in a nebulous state, pursued by the ball and generally made her base, since the ball was thrown wide in fear of hitting somebody. The hitting was unique. The bat was held above the head as nearly perpendicular as might be, and brought down with the grace and force that adorn an act of domestic discipline administered with a broom. Naturally almost every ball hit was grounded" (*Washington Post*, May 12, 1879).

Instead of discouraging the women, such accounts stimulated a larger attendance. More than five thousand spectators turned out for a July 4 game in Philadelphia. The newspapers responded by emphasizing that it was not the skill of the players that provided the attraction. It was reported that when the tour passed through New England, "The spectators tease them unmercifully, sometimes trip them up as they run, and even seize and kiss them" (*Muskegon News and Reporter*, August 13, 1879). A newspaper in Adrian, Michigan, crowed, "let's have the women here . . . it's better than a circus" (*Adrian Times and Expositor*, August 18, 1879).

As the tour continued, the ridicule became increasingly mean-spirited. The *Detroit Post and Tribune* wrote: "It is a remarkable comment upon the popular taste that the largest crowd assembled at Recreation park since this beautiful resort was thrown open to the public was that attracted Saturday afternoon by the announcement of a base ball match between two female nines, who are making a professional tour through the country. It was the worst burlesque upon the national game imaginable, and not even funny. The females were neither comely, shapely nor graceful, and their awkward antics demonstrated that while there are many things a woman can accomplish playing base ball is not one of them. It is not her great specialty. It does not enable her to do justice to herself. The women of America may do a great many things with impunity, but when she essays base ball she should be kindly but firmly suppressed. It may be mentioned incidentally that after the trouble was all over it was discovered that the young women with red stockings had vanquished the maidens in blue hose by a score of 20 to 19" (*Detroit Post and Tribune*, August 18, 1879).

Things grew still worse at a stop in Louisville on August 25: "The spectators were very noisy and boisterous, and when the women left the ground they were stoned" (*New York Clipper*, September 6, 1879).

In succeeding years, accounts of women's professional baseball players became still harsher. The *New York Clipper* wrote that winter: "There are some things that women can't do. The teachings of centuries have established the fact that a woman can't play baseball . . . though a woman may rule the universe, she can't play baseball" (*New York Clipper*, March 20, 1880). In 1884 a *Sporting Life* correspondent chimed in: "Females can't play base ball even a little bit, and all attempts to organize and run such clubs must end in disaster. Let us hear no more of female base ball clubs. The public wants none of it" (*Sporting Life*, May 28, 1884). Lest there be any doubt, another correspondent was even more blunt two years later: "The only decent public connection women can have with the game is as spectators" (*Sporting Life*, September 18, 1886; quoted in Jean Hastings Ardell, *Breaking into Baseball*, 104).

Whenever possible, newspapers reinforced this message with condescending accounts that emphasized the players' appearances rather than their play. An 1880 article about two clubs of young women in Cambridge, Massachusetts, for example, centered upon the "common walking dress" worn by the players (*New York Clipper*, March 6, 1880).

If these not-too-subtle hints still didn't work, the press resorted to the ultimate form of suppression by linking female baseball players to sexual improprieties. An Associated Press account of a female club that played in Albany, Georgia, alleged: "The girls are from 15 to 19 years of age, jaunty in style, brazen in manner, and peculiar in dress. When they reached this place their agent obtained room for them at the Artesian Hotel. It was not long before the proprietor discovered that the character of his house was suffering. All the swells of the city were around the place like a swarm of bees. The proprietor promptly ejected the ball players, and they had to amuse themselves for several hours at the depot until the train arrived. . . . Their conduct was of such a character that respectable ladies got off the cars and waited for the next train" (*Sporting Life*, December 24, 1884).

In 1891 a *Sporting Life* correspondent wrote: "The sentence of Sylvester Wilson, or Franklin, to five years in Sing Sing at hard labor for abducting a sixteen-year-old girl and inducing her to travel with his ladies' base ball team, will likely put an end to all female base ball clubs. For this relief much thanks" (*Sporting Life*, October 31, 1891).

This hostility had its desired effect: professional play by women became scarce in the late nineteenth century. One team that did attempt a tour was met with the headline: "Chase Them: Another Female Troupe to Disgrace Base Ball" (*Sporting Life*, May 5, 1894). In the early twentieth century, with women making strides toward equality, women's professional baseball was revived in the form of the Bloomer Girls and other successful touring teams. A few women even endeavored to break into organized baseball.

20.2.3 Women in Organized Baseball. No woman has ever played in the major leagues, and the few appearances by women in the minor leagues have been very brief.

Lizzie Stroud pitched an inning for Reading of the Atlantic League against Allentown on July 5, 1898, under the name Lizzie Arlington. She allowed two hits but no runs. On September 7, 1936, Sonny Dunlap played right field for the Fayetteville Bears of the Arkansas-Missouri League, going hitless in three at bats.

Other women did not even make it onto the field. Pitcher Jackie Mitchell was signed by the Chattanooga Lookouts in 1931, but Commissioner Kenesaw Mountain Landis voided the contract. In 1950 Fort Lauderdale of the Florida International League tried to sign All-American Girls Baseball League star Dorothy Kamenshek. She declined, apparently fearing it was a gimmick. Harrisburg of the Inter-State League signed a woman named Eleanor Engle on June 21, 1952, but her contract was disallowed and a ban on women players announced. Near the end of the 1971 season, Raleigh-Durham general manager Walter Brock announced plans to sign

Jackie Jackson. The league office talked him out of the idea (Jim L. Sumner, *Separating the Men from the Boys*, 131).

In recent years a few women have broken into professional baseball, all in the independent leagues. Ila Borders pitched in the Northern League and Western Baseball League for four seasons, beginning in 1997. She was followed by Kendra Haynes, an outfielder who played in the Frontier League. Kendall Burnham played very briefly in the Central League in 2003, where she was a teammate of her husband Jake.

20.2.4 Women in Exhibitions Versus Major Leaguers. Lizzie Murphy, one of the best women professionals of the day, played first base for a major league all-star team in an exhibition game at Fenway Park on August 14, 1922.

Jackie Mitchell, a seventeen-year-old female who had attended Kid Elberfeld's baseball school, pitched in an exhibition game against the New York Yankees on April 2, 1931. She pitched only two-thirds of an inning but made headlines by striking out Babe Ruth and Lou Gehrig consecutively.

It is often contended that the Yankee stars were just playing along with a publicity stunt. But Amy Ellis Nutt noted that "Mitchell, until her death in 1987 at the age of seventy-three, maintained that her fanning of Ruth and Gehrig was not a stunt on their part. She claimed that the only instruction given to the Yankee hitters about how to handle her pitches was not to hit the ball directly back at the young girl" (Amy Ellis Nutt, "Swinging for the Fences," in Lissa Smith, ed., *Nike Is a Goddess*, 44).

The great multi-sport athlete Babe Didrikson pitched a scoreless inning for the Philadelphia Athletics against the Brooklyn Dodgers in a spring training game on March 20, 1934. Two days later she pitched for the Cardinals against the Red Sox but allowed three runs in the first inning.

20.2.5 Women Touring Overseas. The Philadelphia Bobbies, a successful barnstorming club of the 1920s, toured Japan at the end of the 1925 season. The club played games against men's teams in Tokyo, Osaka, Kyoto, and Kobe before a shortage of funds prevented them from continuing on to Formosa (Jean Hastings Ardell, *Breaking into Baseball*, 106–108).

20.2.6 Women on Men's Collegiate Baseball Teams. At least five women have played for a men's collegiate baseball team. According to Gai Ingham Berlage, a young woman named Margaret Dobson played second base for Vanport College in Portland, Oregon, in a 1951 game against Clark Junior College (*South Bend Tribune*, April 14, 1951; quoted in Gai Ingham Berlage, *Women in Baseball*, 110). Susan Perabo played a single game for Division III Webster College in Missouri in 1985. Julie Croteau played first base for St. Mary's College in Maryland, another Division III school, in 1989. She met with harassment and eventually dropped out of school (Amy Ellis Nutt, "Swinging for the Fences," in Lissa Smith, ed., *Nike Is a Goddess*, 44). Jodi Haller pitched for NAIA St. Vincent's College in Pennsylvania in 1990. Ila Borders broke new ground by becoming the first woman ever to earn a baseball scholarship in 1994. She pitched for NAIA Southern California College for three seasons and then went on to a professional career (see **20.2.3** "Women in Organized Baseball") (Jean Hastings Ardell, *Breaking into Baseball*, 92–95).

20.2.7 Women Drafted by the Major Leagues. The White Sox selected Carey Schueler, the daughter of team general manager Ron Schueler, in the forty-third round of the 1993 amateur draft. She never played professionally.

20.2.8 Women Coaches. In 1995 Julie Croteau became the first woman to coach for a Division I college baseball program when she was hired by the University of Massachusetts–Amherst.

20.2.9 League of Women. *Sporting Life* reported that a league of female players had been formed in Los Angeles on July 26, 1905 (*Sporting Life*, August 5, 1905).

On February 20, 1943, Philip K. Wrigley announced plans for the All-American Girls Softball League. Wrigley's intention was to have a backup in case the war necessitated the shutdown of major league baseball. Although that did not happen, the women's circuit went ahead and soon gained a life of its own. The league eventually switched to a smaller ball and overhand pitching and lasted for twelve years as the All-American Girls Baseball League.

The players' short skirts were a far cry from the uniforms of earlier women ballplayers. What hadn't changed was the tendency for the players to be judged on their appearance rather than their performance. Lois Browne cited the following example of the press coverage the league was apt to receive: "[Chicago Colleens manager Dave Bancroft] had to consult the chaperon of his charges to find out if his charges felt fit (after a rather long afternoon visit to the beauty parlor) to take the mound against the Muskegon Lassies. Fortunately, the pitcher was ready and willing and looking cute, with long, fluffy hair billowing from under her green cap" (quoted in Lois Browne, *Girls of Summer*, 147).

The All-American Girls Baseball League disbanded after the 1954 season and soon faded into obscurity. It was brought back to the public's attention in the early 1990s by the film *A League of Their Own*, which brought deserved recognition to these pioneers. Curiously, when interest in the

league revived it came to be known as the All-American Girls Professional
Baseball League.

20.2.10 Women Owners. George Van derbeck's wife briefly became owner
of the Detroit franchise in the Western League during the couple's divorce
proceedings in the mid-1890s.

The first woman to own a major league team was Helene Hathaway Robison Britton. She was thirty-two when she inherited the St. Louis Cardinals on March 24, 1911, upon the death of her uncle, Matthew Stanley
Robison. In 1916 she and her husband separated, and she assumed his role
as team president. In 1912 Milwaukee Brewers owner Charles Havenor
died, leaving control of the American Association team to his widow Agnes
(*Sporting News*, May 23, 1912). The Brewers won the American Association
pennant in 1913. Two female owners, Effa Manley and Olivia Taylor, played
prominent roles in the Negro Leagues.

On January 4, 1931, Lucille Thomas purchased the Tulsa franchise in
the Western League from St. Louis Browns owner Phil Ball. She became the
first woman actually to buy a professional baseball team as opposed to in-
heriting one, and the development attracted considerable interest. Mrs.
Thomas was a former schoolteacher who had studied the organ at the American Conservatory of Music in Chicago before marrying wealthy oil operator C. R. Thomas and establishing herself as a successful businesswoman in
her own right.

She faced a formidable task: the Tulsa franchise had no stadium and accordingly had played its home games in Topeka, Kansas, in 1930. The depression was at its height, and Lucille Thomas had barely three months to
raise the funds necessary to build a suitable home for the club. She immediately announced plans for a new stadium that would allow night ball, and en-
ergetically began the difficult task of finding investors.

Media interest focused on her gender, and she fielded plenty of imperti-
nent, stereotypical questions. She responded as patiently as possible because
she realized that the attention might make it easier to raise funds: "If this
business of being a woman owner is so novel that I can capitalize on the publicity, I'll do it." She indicated, for example, that she intended to have an im-
maculately clean ballpark and would like to hire female ushers, but she
denied rumors that her players would be required to study etiquette (*Sporting News*, January 22, 1931).

Unfortunately her fund-raising efforts were unsuccessful. Jittery investors were reluctant to back the new stadium, and as Opening Day approached it became clear that one would not be built. Eventually Lucille
Thomas conceded the inevitable and surrendered the franchise (*Sporting
News*, April 16, 1931).

20.2.11 Women Umpires. Researcher Mark Alvarez discovered that a Mrs. Doolittle signed the Knickerbockers' scorecard as the umpire of a game on June 8, 1847. Little is known about her (Jean Hastings Ardell, *Breaking into Baseball*, 138). *Sporting Life* reported in 1905 that Mrs. M. G. Turner of Cleveland had recently umpired a Lower Peninsula Lake League game at Lake Orion, Michigan (*Sporting Life*, February 25, 1905). (The fact that this note ran in February makes me skeptical.)

That same season saw seventeen-year-old Amanda Clement of Hudson, South Dakota, begin to umpire semiprofessional games in Iowa and South Dakota. By 1911 she had earned enough money to attend Yankton College in South Dakota. She went on to a career as a physical education instructor and coach.

During her six years of umpiring, she gained renown across the country. In 1905 *Sporting Life* described Amanda Clement as "probably the only girl in the country who is an umpire of professional base ball games. . . . She has received pay for her services. The ball players, though gallant toward women, frequently criticised her decisions quite as emphatically as they would those of a man. On such occasions she has had no hesitancy in talking back, and on half a dozen occasions has ordered players from games" (*Sporting Life*, October 7, 1905).

Clement herself told a somewhat different story in 1906: "Do you suppose any ball player in the country would step up to a good-looking girl and say to her, 'You color-blind, pickle-brained, cross-eyed idiot, if you don't stop throwing the soup into me I'll distribute your features all over your countenance!' Of course he wouldn't" (*Cincinnati Enquirer*, no date given; reprinted in Amy Ellis Nutt, "Swinging for the Fences," in Lissa Smith, ed., *Nike Is a Goddess*, 40).

In spite of these differing versions, there is no dispute that Clement did earn the respect of the men whose games she umpired. She received frequent commendations for her competence and impartiality (Gai Ingham Berlage, "Women Umpires as Mirrors of Gender Roles," *National Pastime* 14 [1994], 36–37). Nonetheless it was more than fifty years before another woman followed in her footsteps, and her experience was much less pleasant.

Bernice Gera graduated from an umpiring school in Florida in 1967 and began a long struggle to become a professional umpire. After years of litigation she finally became the first woman umpire in organized baseball history when she officiated a New York–Penn League game on June 24, 1972. Several disputes occurred, and she resigned between games of the doubleheader.

Christine Wren umpired in the Northwest League in 1975 and 1976 and in the Midwest League in 1977. She was considered a good umpire by the Midwest League president, but took a leave of absence at season's end and was able to find a better-paying job (Tom Gorman as told to Jerome Holtzman, *Three and Two!*, 167–168). Perry Barber officiated in the independent Atlantic League and also served as the league's director of umpiring (Jean Hastings Ardell, *Breaking into Baseball*, 150). Pam Postema umpired in the minors for thirteen years before being released after the 1989 season. She later filed suit against major league baseball for discrimination and received an out-of-court settlement.

Teresa Cox umpired in the Southern League periodically from 1988 to 1992 and in the Arizona Fall League in 1989 and 1990. Ria Cortesio Papageorgiou and Shanna Kook are currently umpiring in the minor leagues.

20.2.12   Women Sportswriters. The paradox that women were welcomed by baseball as spectators but not accepted in other capacities applied even to writing about the game, a sad reality that was thoughtfully explored by Jean Hastings Ardell in a chapter of her recent book (Jean Hastings Ardell, *Breaking into Baseball*, 190–213). Ardell noted that a woman named Ella Black served as a correspondent for *Sporting Life* in 1890, and her work attracted favorable comment. Nonetheless, for the next century women who tried to break into sportswriting were all too often patronized or met with outright hostility.

Polite condescension was the preferred method until the 1970s. Women who attempted to write about baseball found that they themselves were the story, which effectively prevented them from having their work judged on its merits. Nowhere was this more evident than in the headlines affixed to their submissions, which it seems safe to assume were the handiwork of male headline writers. Ella Black's work appeared under such headlines as "Only a Woman: But She Has Some Ideas about the Make-Up of the Pittsburg Clubs" and "The First Game: As Viewed by One of the Weaker Sex"; early-twentieth-century sportswriter Ina Eloise Young's writing ran beneath such titles as "Eying Dresses and Hats as Well as Worlds' [sic] Series Games: Characteristic of Her Sex, Miss Young Notes How Wives of Champion Ball Players Dress" and "Petticoats and the Press Box"; and during World War II, Jeane Hoffman's byline appeared beneath the likes of "No 'End' to Jokes, Girl Finds, in Yankee Stadium Press Box" (*Sporting Life*, April 12, 1890; April 26, 1890; *Trinidad* [Colo.] *Chronicle-News*, October 15, 1908; *Baseball Magazine*, May 1908; *New York Journal-American*, December 3, 1942; all quoted in Jean Hastings Ardell, *Breaking into Baseball*, 192, 195, 256). Obviously such headlines would have made it difficult to take the accompanying articles seriously.

The second half of the twentieth century saw more women pursuing careers as sportswriters, and their presence was met with increasingly vehement resistance, much of which concentrated on the appropriateness of allowing women in the locker room. Yet the fact that accredited female journalists also had a hard time being allowed to sit in the press box with their fully clothed male colleagues suggests that there were underlying issues (Jean Hastings Ardell, *Breaking into Baseball*, 190–191, 200–201, 206–208). Pioneering sportswriter Anita Martini reported that she was initially not allowed to eat in the press dining room at the Astrodome (Melvin Durslag, *Sporting News*, November 11, 1978). In the past decade or two, this resistance has finally begun to disappear.

20.2.13   Women Broadcasters. In 1938 golfer Helen Dettweiler was hired by the General Mills Company to act as a sort of goodwill ambassador by touring the country and broadcasting local games ("Helen Dettweiler to Become Woman Baseball Announcer," *Washington Post*, June 19, 1938). An article in *Sporting News* later that summer reported that she had already visited twenty cities and that her play-by-play accounts "are authoritative and have gained her much commendation." It added, "Until she entered the field, play-by-play accounts of games had been confined to men, but Miss Dettweiler has succeeded in breaking down that barrier, under the auspices of General Mills, and with the aid of a charming personality and thorough knowledge of the game has brought sample broadcasts from a woman's point of view to thousands of listeners" (*Sporting News*, August 25, 1938).

In the early 1950s actress Laraine Day hosted a fifteen-minute pregame television show entitled "Day with the Giants" while the Giants were managed by her husband, Leo Durocher (*Washington Post*, May 21, 1950). At the tailend of the 1964 season, Charles O. Finley assigned Betty Caywood to broadcasts of Kansas City Athletics games. Finley made no bones about his intention to exploit her for ratings: "The idea is that by putting a woman on staff we'll appeal to the dolls" (*New York Times*, September 17, 1964).

In 1971 Wendie Regalia began broadcasting Giants pregame shows. She conducted interviews all season long but quit at season's end to break ground in another endeavor—as an agent representing five prominent members of the San Francisco 49ers (AP: *Lima* [Ohio] *News*, December 12, 1971). Five years later Houston sportswriter Anita Martini earned the distinction of being the first woman to broadcast a National League game (Jean Hastings Ardell, *Breaking into Baseball*, 202).

After the 1976 season the White Sox engaged Mary Shane as the first regular female play-by-play announcer (*Chicago Tribune*, December 22, 1976). According to fellow broadcaster Jimmy Piersall, even pioneer club owner Bill Veeck was lukewarm about the novel concept. As one of four White Sox broadcasters, it was easy to reduce Shane's role. After brief appearances on thirty-five home games, mostly on the radio, she was phased out. Piersall recollected: "She never had a chance. Even a bad baseball player gets at least one full season to see if he'll come around. But because of all the in-bred prejudice against a woman covering a baseball team, Mary didn't even get that. It was a real shame because I think she had what it takes to make it, and some day the idea of a woman bringing a woman's perspective to baseball broadcasting will be a tremendous innovation somewhere." Shane went on to success as an NBA beat reporter (Jim O'Donnell, "Death Stirs Memories of Broadcast Pioneer," *Chicago Herald*, November 5, 1987).

20.2.14 Women Public Address Announcers. Sherry Davis was hired as the public address announcer of the San Francisco Giants in 1992, becoming the first female to hold such a post for any major American professional team. She described her job in considerable detail to George Gmelch and J. J. Weiner in their book *In the Ballpark*. Since 2000 the Giants have employed Renel Brooks-Moon in that capacity.

20.2.15 Women Scouts. The husband-and-wife team of Roy and Bessie Largent scouted the South for the Chicago White Sox in the 1930s, finding such players as Zeke Bonura, Smead Jolley, and Hall of Famer Luke Appling. Researcher Rod Nelson of the SABR Scouts Committee reported that both of their names appear on many, though not all, of the contracts and other official club documents.

An article in *Sporting News* noted, "Mrs. Largent is as much a scout as Roy and it is often her judgment that determines whether a prospect should be obtained or rejected. . . . Mrs. Largent made all the trips with Roy until last year, when her health failed, but she has since fully recovered and again is shouldering her half of the work. He gives her much credit for his success and claims she knows more ball players than any woman in the world" (*Sporting News*, January 10, 1935).

Edith Houghton, who had toured Japan with the Philadelphia Bobbies as a thirteen-year-old in 1925 (see **20.2.5** "Women Touring Overseas"), was hired as a Phillies scout in 1946. According to Phillies owner Bob Carpenter, "She just kept pestering me, and I've always had a weakness for anyone with drive and initiative. She said, 'Just give me a chance.' So I did . . . she went out and signed some players for us. None of 'em made the big leagues, but they were okay. She knew a ballplayer when she saw one" (Kevin Kerrane, *Dollar Sign on the Muscle*, 77). Houghton scouted in Pennsylvania and Ohio for about five years (Jean Hastings Ardell, *Breaking into Baseball*, 108).

The recent trend away from traditional scouting and toward a greater reliance on video clips has provided more opportunities for women to break into the profession. Major league baseball's Scouting Bureau now employs a number of women.

20.2.16   Bloomer Girls. Researcher Barbara Gregorich indicated that the first club to be known as Bloomer Girls originated around 1892 (Barbara Gregorich, "Jackie and the Juniors vs. Margaret and the Bloomers," *National Pastime* 13 [1993], 9). Bloomer Girls became a generic name used by many touring teams of the early twentieth century and often included one or two men disguised by wigs.

20.2.17   African-American Women. The All-American Girls Baseball League never integrated, though two African-American players tried out with South Bend in 1951. But at least three African-American women—Toni Stone, Connie Morgan, and Mamie "Peanut" Johnson—played in the Negro Leagues in the 1950s, with Stone having the most distinguished career. Twenty years earlier, Isabel Baxter had become the first woman to play in the Negro Leagues when she played a single game for the Cleveland Giants in 1933 (Jean Hastings Ardell, *Breaking into Baseball*, 110).

(iii) Other Minorities

20.3.1   Jewish Major Leaguers. Lipman Pike starred for numerous clubs in the 1860s and '70s and had a reputation as one of the era's most powerful hitters. He is also credited with being the first Jewish manager, serving as playing captain for Hartford in 1874 and briefly having that role for Troy in 1871 and for Cincinnati in 1877. As was the custom of the day, his heritage was frequently remarked upon. I have found no evidence that he faced the prejudice encountered by later Jewish players such as Hank Greenberg.

20.3.2   Hispanic Major Leaguers. Cuban-born Esteban Bellan played for Troy in 1871, the first year of the National Association.

The first Hispanic to play in the National League was Vincent Nava, a prominent catcher in the early 1880s. Nava's dark skin attracted a great deal of comment, much of it ill-informed. He was often referred to as being either Cuban or African American. In fact, as Joel S. Franks has shown and my research has confirmed, Nava was born in California to a British father and a Mexican mother (Joel S. Franks, *Whose Baseball?*, 46).

Intriguingly, Nava's real name was Vincent Irwin, and that was the name he took while playing ball in his native San Francisco. When he first came east in 1882 he was initially referred to as Vincent Irwin, but that was soon replaced by Nava (*Cleveland Leader*, March 25, April 12, and April 14, 1882). He became known as Nava in baseball circles, but Californians still clung to the earlier name, referring to him as "Vincent Nava, known on this coast as 'Sandy' Irwin" (*San Francisco Examiner*, January 10, 1887).

The reasons for his name change are not known. Franks speculated that Nava may have been motivated by pride in his heritage but also noted that he could have been trying to make clear that he was not of African-American descent.

The color line also restricted the access of Hispanics to major league baseball. Cuban-born Chick Pedroes played two games for the Cubs in 1902, but little is known about him. Cincinnati signed two Cubans in 1911, and they were reported to be "two of the purest bars of Castilian soap ever floated to these shores" (quoted in Mark Rucker and Peter C. Bjarkman, *Smoke*, 43). Light-skinned Cubans regularly gained admission to the white major leagues in the ensuing years, but this was not the case for ballplayers from other regions of Latin America.

A rare exception was Louis Castro, who had a brief major league career and a long minor league career. There is contradictory evidence as to whether Castro was born in the United States or Venezuela, but both his parents were from South America. Castro learned to his chagrin just how seriously race is taken in the United States: "Manager Lou Castro of the Portsmouth team of the Virginia League just for a joke told Southern scribes that former president [Cipriano] Castro of Venezuela was his uncle. Then when he learned that President Castro has negro blood in his veins he wished he could recall the joke" (*Sporting News*, February 20, 1913).

Once the color line was abolished, major league scouts began to hunt for talent in Latin America. Ever since the 1950s, the region has produced a disproportionate amount of talent, including such superstars as Luis Aparicio, Roberto Clemente, Juan Marichal, Rod Carew, Roberto Alomar, Pedro Martinez, and Sammy Sosa.

Lou Castro managed in the minors, and Mike Gonzalez was a longtime major league coach. But the first major league manager of Hispanic origin was Preston Gomez with the San Diego Padres in 1969.

20.3.3   Native American Major Leaguers. The first Native American to play major league baseball was Tom Oran, who played for one of the two St. Louis entries in the National Association in 1875. Joe Visner and James Toy had brief major league careers with several clubs in the late 1880s and early 1890s. Louis Sockalexis became the first prominent Native American major leaguer for Cleveland in 1897, and there is controversy about whether the nickname of the Indians was a tribute to him. Chief Bender was the first Native American elected to the Hall of Fame.

20.3.4   Japanese Major Leaguers. In 1964 Masanori Murakami became the first Japanese player to make the jump to this country's major leagues. He pitched effectively for the San Francisco Giants for two seasons and then returned to his homeland, where there had been some disapproval of his decision to play in the United States.

There had been earlier Japanese ballplayers who were apparently denied the opportunity to play major league baseball by racial prejudice. Sportswriter William F. H. Koelsch reported in 1905: "Shumza Sugimoto, the Japanese ball player, who is now at Hot Springs, and may be taken by [Giants manger John] McGraw, does not like the drawing of the color line in his case, and says he will remain a semi-professional with the Creole Stars of New Orleans if his engagement with the Giants will be resented by the players of other clubs" (*Sporting Life*, February 25, 1905). Before the 1911 season, McGraw attempted to sign another Japanese star named Togo Hammanoto (Larry Mansch, *Rube Marquard*, 73).

20.3.5 Deaf Major Leaguers. The distinction of being the first deaf major leaguer most likely belongs to Paul Hines, who starred in the majors from 1872 to 1891 despite a severe loss of hearing. Hines was not deaf from birth, and the extent of his hearing loss is not entirely clear. But it did plague him for much of his career, with the *New York Clipper* stating in 1879 that he was "as deaf as a post" and *Sporting Life* in 1883 calling him the "deaf centre-fielder" (*New York Clipper*, October 18, 1879; *Sporting Life*, July 22, 1883).

Another candidate is Doug Allison, the catcher of the Red Stockings of Cincinnati. Researcher David Arcidiacono discovered a couple of references to Allison's being partially deaf, including an 1876 article that his deafness resulted from his Civil War service: "Allison was a gunner in Fort Sumpter [sic] during the late war, and is the only survivor of three batches of gunners of six men in each batch. His service during the war accounts for his impaired hearing" (*Boston Globe*, March 24, 1876). Allison was in fact a Civil War veteran, but he enlisted in 1864 and his regiment saw no combat duty, so this account must be taken with a grain of salt.

Hines and Allison were succeeded in professional baseball by several products of the Ohio School for the Deaf in Columbus. The school had a prominent baseball team in the 1870s and 1880s, and went on a tour of the state in 1879. Several of its players made the leap to professional baseball. When the school reopened for the 1883–1884 academic year, the school newspaper noted matter-of-factly that students John Ryn and Ed Dundon had spent their summer vacations playing baseball (*Mutes Chronicle*, September 6, 1883).

Dundon had in fact played in the major leagues that summer. His stay in the majors was undistinguished, as was that of Gallaudet student Tom Lynch, who pitched a single game for Chicago in 1884. But 1888 saw the debut of Ohio School for the Deaf alumnus Billy Hoy, who collected more than two thousand major league hits while playing for such woeful teams that the *Washington Post* once quipped that "a pitcher and catcher and Mr. Hoy constitute the Washington Baseball Club. The other six men who accompany them are put in the field for the purpose of making errors" (*Washington Post*, May 11, 1888).

Hoy modestly downplayed the handicaps he had to overcome: "While at school I played catcher and third base as well as outfielder, but in the professional game I have always been in center field, because my deafness is less of a handicap there than it would be as an infielder." He added that there was even less disadvantage when batting: "I can see the ball as well as others and my team mates tell me whether a ball or strike is called by using the left fingers for balls and the right fingers for strikes. In base running the signals of the hit and run game and other stratagems are mostly silent, and the same as for the other players. By a further system of sign [sic] my team mates keep me posted on how many are out and what is going on around me. . . . So it may be seen the handicaps of a deaf ball player are minimized" (*Grand Valley* [Moab, Utah] *Times*, July 12, 1901).

Nor did Hoy's handicap earn him any concessions from opponents. During his second season the Cleveland Spiders recognized that a deaf man would be peculiarly vulnerable to the hidden ball trick and began to scheme. With Hoy on second base, three Cleveland players handled the ball until second baseman "[Cub] Stricker got hold of it and crept up behind Hoy, hoping that the latter would step off his base. The mute was onto the little game, and when Stricker stood beside him he smacked the hand that held the ball, and the dogskin rolled several feet away. Before Stricker realized what had happened Hoy was safe on third base. Captain [Jay] Faatz made a vigorous kick, but Umpire [Lon] Knight held that there was no rule to cover such a play. It was simply a case of dog eat dog. [Patsy] Tebeau captured the ball during the dispute and concealed it under his arm with the intention of getting even with the mute. The latter was wide awake as usual, and deliberately squatted down on the base and would not move until he saw the ball returned to [Henry] Gruber, who was pitching" (*Sporting Life*, September 11, 1889).

Hoy's success paved the way to the major leagues for R. C. Stephenson, George M. Leitner, William Deegan, Luther Taylor, Dick Sipek, and Curtis Pride. Major leaguers with substantial hearing impairment have included Hines, Allison, Pete Browning, Frank Chance, and Bobby Jones.

Chapter 21

PARTICIPANTS

A LARGE PART of the appeal of the pre-1850 prototypes of baseball was that they were flexible enough to include any number of participants. If twelve children were playing and three more showed up, this created no serious problem. Melville McGee, for instance, offered these recollections about how baseball was played in the 1830s: "It seems to me now as I look back and recall those early days that the young people enjoyed their sports and games and entered into them with far more zest then young people do at the present day. There was no feeling of envy or superiority, or the feeling that you don't belong to my set. All were on a level, and everyone was just as good as any other" (Melville McGee, "The Early Days of Concord, Jackson County, Michigan," *Michigan Pioneer and Historical Collections* 21 [1892], 430).

Of all the elements that the Knickerbockers added to baseball, perhaps the most fundamental was exclusion. Once their rules had been fine-tuned, a baseball match included eighteen players and no more. A game lasted nine innings, and once started, latecomers were excluded. Nonparticipants were excluded from the playing field. Then enclosed fields were adopted, meaning that nonparticipants couldn't even watch without paying admission. The game had changed from an inclusive activity to an exclusive one.

As baseball prospered, the pendulum began to swing back the other way. Clubs discovered a variety of roles for nonplayers, and the ranks of those involved in baseball again started to swell. Not all these people were immediately paid for their work, and many of them wore multiple hats; yet each addition increased the sense that the game was again trying to include a cross-section of Americans.

In 1883 *Harper's Weekly* reported that one stadium had a game-day staff of forty-one people: seven ushers, six policemen, four ticket sellers, four gatekeepers, three fieldmen, three cushion renters, six refreshment boys, and eight musicians (*Harper's Weekly*, May 12, 1883). While I have not tried to ascertain the identity of the first cushion renter, I have tried to explain how and when several new types of baseball people were added.

21.1   Security Personnel. A security force was on hand for an 1858 game at the Fashion Race Course in New York. Coincidentally—or maybe not—this was also the first game at which an admission fee was charged.

21.2   Ticket Takers. In the 1860s and 1870s it was not uncommon for spectators to find their tickets being taken by the home club's extra player. This practice originated for two reasons, one obvious and the other less so.

The obvious reason was that budgets were tight and everyone was expected to help out wherever possible. The more subtle reason dated back to the mid-1860s, when players were successful with their unprecedented demand for a share of the gate proceeds. In order to ensure that they weren't being gypped by the owners of the parks, "the players then appointed one of their number—the extra man—to count tickets" (James Wood as told to Frank G. Menke, "Baseball in By-Gone Days, Part 3," syndicated column, *Indiana* [Pa.] *Evening Gazette*, August 17, 1916).

21.3   Ushers. The usher had begun to make the lives of spectators easier as early as 1872, when a Cleveland newspaper reported: "The grounds have been 'fixed up' in capital style, having been made quite level and thoroughly rolled. Joe Murch is superintendent. He will have some great improvements made and is making several arrangements for the convenience of those who go to see matched games. Among other changes, ice water will be furnished free to spectators, an usher will be employed to seat ladies, no intoxicating liquors will be sold, lemonade, confectionery, ice cream and fruits may be obtained at the grand stand" (*Cleveland Plain Dealer*, April 20, 1872).

21.4   Vendors. Vendors seem to attract notice only when they are the subject of a complaint. An Adrian, Michigan, newspaper grumbled in 1879, "Hereafter the vending of peanuts, lemonade, etc., in the grand stand at Blissfield, should be prohibited. People purchase seats there to see the game and not to gaze on the oft-appearing form of the peddler, who is sure to stand just in front of you when a fine play is being made. An indignant public will gratefully remember the manager who will ban these bores from all grand stands forever" (*Adrian Daily Times and Expositor*, August 23, 1879).

An Ohio newspaper echoed the theme in 1898: "Fakirs climbing across the stands during the play are also another unpleasant thing. Of course 'butchers' must hustle and people get thirsty, but when the score is a tie or one run to the good a kid asking if you wish lemonade, gum or pop is a nuisance" (*Youngstown Vindicator*, April 4, 1898).

In 1952 owner Paul Fagan of the San Francisco Seals tried to ban peanuts because he concluded that it cost the club more to clean them up than they made by selling them. Fans were outraged and promised to bring peanuts into the stadium and make more of a mess than ever. An ambassador from a South American peanut-producing country even called the owner to voice his concerns. Fagan had to concede the point (Dick Dobbins and Jon Twichell, *Nuggets on the Diamond*, 246; Red Smith, March 23, 1952, reprinted in *Red Smith on Baseball*).

21.5 Official Scorers. In early baseball each club had its own scorer. The position was deemed highly important, and scorers had their own seating area. Nonetheless, until statistics began to develop, their main function was to keep track of the score, and even on this they sometimes disagreed.

As statistics became an important part of baseball, a single person assumed the function of official scorer. It was not long before onlookers were second-guessing his decisions. The *Cincinnati Enquirer* noted in 1878, "The Cincinnati 'official scorer' gets more and more demoralized every day. His score of Wednesday's League game is full of errors" (*Cincinnati Enquirer*, May 3, 1878).

Soon players began to complain as well. In 1885, George "Orator" Shafer reportedly told his team's owner, Henry Lucas, that he wanted to play elsewhere because his base hits were being incorrectly ruled as errors. Lucas asked, "Am I to blame because a reporter makes a mistake?" Shafer replied, "You employ the official scorer that's downing me" (*St. Louis Post-Dispatch*, July 9, 1885).

21.6 Batboys. The earliest mention of batboys I have encountered is an 1880 reference to "Al. Pierce, the colored youth who used to officiate as bat carrier of the St. Louis Browns" (*New York Clipper*, August 14, 1880). In 1884 the American Association passed a rule permitting the use of a bat boy or girl. Henry Lucas also used a batboy at St. Louis's Union Grounds that season: "A colored boy in uniform takes the bat from each sticker, and hands it to him when his time to go to the bat comes" (*Cincinnati News-Journal*, May 13, 1884).

21.7 Groundskeepers. The very tight budgets of early baseball meant that the groundskeeping was often done by someone with other responsibilities. August Solari owned and operated St. Louis's Grand Avenue diamond in the 1860s and later became the full-time groundskeeper for several St. Louis teams. When the pitching arm of Joe Borden went dead in 1876, he became the Boston groundskeeper. In the early 1880s Detroit hired groundskeeper John Piggott who could be used as an extra player in case of injury (*Detroit Post and Tribune*, March 30, 1882).

The *St. Louis Post-Dispatch* reported in 1883: "The games played [in New Orleans] now don't draw much more than enough people to pay the salary of the ground-keeper" (*St. Louis Post-Dispatch*, December 24, 1883). The note is significant because it simultaneously demonstrates that groundskeeping was becoming a full-time position and that it remained touch and go whether clubs could afford this added salary.

By the late 1880s the position was so involved that there was no alternative to having a full-time groundskeeper. In 1887 the *Detroit Free Press* provided a fascinating look at his routine: "Uncle Billy Houston [is] without doubt the best base ball ground keeper in the country. . . . Almost anybody can roll and mow a lawn, but the putting of a diamond into the proper condition is an entirely different matter. Uncle Billy has a mysterious method of procedure which he refuses to divulge to anybody. This much he tells of his modus operandi. He uses three or four different kinds of earth, the top layer being black. He sifts all the earth he puts on the runways in order that nothing may be left there that would injure a man in sliding to a base. Mixed in with the top layer of earth is a sort of fluffy weed, which Billy says imparts a springy quality to the runway. As a result of the work he has so far done the runways and spots where the infielders stand are as near perfection as possible, being so level a ball will roll on them like a billiard table. By sprinkling the earth is kept at the proper consistency and the runways are kept so smooth and springy it seems possible for anybody to steal a base. . . . He watches closely during a game, and if a ball takes an erratic shoot after striking the ground Billy notes the spot, and remedies the defect at the earliest opportunity" (*Detroit Free Press*, May 16, 1887).

And in 1893 the *Sporting News* gave this description of the daily routine of Pittsburgh groundskeeper James Pridie: "Every day the club is home the ground is rolled with five ton rollers, and the field is thoroughly sprinkled with water; then the ground-keeper goes over the entire infield with a rake and levels the ground, fills up all the ground, and every little defect is looked after. Then the ground is rolled again. After the work has all been attended to the pitcher and batter's box is chalked, then the base lines, the coachers' and the outside boundary lines are all lined with chalk. After every game the pitcher's and batter's boxes are covered over with large tarpaulins, in case it should rain before the next game, and to keep the ground from dew" (*Sporting News*, December 9, 1893).

In addition to these arduous duties, groundskeepers often wore extra hats. Their responsibilities were apt to include security, crowd control, fire and safety inspections, and other miscellaneous chores. A St. Louis groundskeeper even spied on team owner Chris Von der Ahe and testified at one of his divorce trials (*Sporting Life*, April 6, 1895).

21.8   Batting Practice Pitchers. In early baseball, batting practice was usually just fungo hitting, despite the regular protests of Henry Chadwick. Even once it became a little more organized, it was usually pitched by anyone available who could get the ball over the plate.

The position began to gain a little more prestige when clubs started seeking batting practice pitchers who could simulate a type of pitching that was likely to give the club trouble. In the late 1880s the Detroit Wolverines had a lot of left-handed hitters who tended to struggle against southpaws. In response they often used a left-handed pitcher named Howard Lawrence to pitch batting practice (*Boston Globe*, May 21, 1886).

For many years batting practice was thrown by a member of the staff who was between starts. This was changed in the late 1920s by Cubs pitcher Henry Grampp. Sportswriter Edward Burns observed, "All other major league clubs rotate the job of pitching in batting practice among pitchers several days away from any possible turn to pitch. Not so the Cubs—that's Hank's job 154 days of the season" (Edward Burns, "Henry Grampp's in Town, So All Cubs Feel Fine," *Chicago Tribune*, January 31, 1929).

It was Grampp's "talent for impersonation" that made him so valuable (Edward Burns, "Henry Grampp's in Town, So All Cubs Feel Fine," *Chicago Tribune*, January 31, 1929). Sportswriter James S. Collins explained, "If the Cubs are to face Carl Mays, for instance, Mr. Grampp goes out there and throws up a few underhand balls to the Cub sluggers. If [Grover Cleveland] Alexander is expected to be the opposing pitcher, we are told, he gives an imitation of Alexander's style" (James S. Collins, "Almost the Naked Truth," *Washington Post*, March 21, 1929).

Grampp was with the Cubs from 1927 until 1929, yet appeared in only three major league games during these years. Collins observed dryly that the umpire's cry of "Play Ball" was "Grampp's cue to call it a day and hie himself to the showers. Next to managing the Phillies, Mr. Grampp's seems the most unattractive job baseball has offered since an unsung hero filled a line on the Giants' pay roll as keeper of the late 'Bugs' Raymond" (James S. Collins, "Almost the Naked Truth," *Washington Post*, March 21, 1929). In 1930 Grampp returned to the minor leagues.

Eric Nadel and Craig R. Wright claimed that Grampp was ambidextrous, but I have found no evidence of this (Eric Nadel and Craig R. Wright, *The Man Who Stole First Base*, 14). Burns stated that Grampp "works a half shift when a left hander is slated by the opposition," which doesn't seem to suggest that he threw left-handed (Edward Burns, "Henry Grampp's in Town, So All Cubs Feel Fine," *Chicago Tribune*, January 31, 1929).

Eventually teams began to have left-handed pitchers on hand specifically for this role. Tony Gwynn noted that when he wanted to practice a specific hitting approach in 1988, "I came out early and had our left-handed batting practice pitcher throw to me" (George F. Will, *Men at Work*, 220).

21.9 Ticket Scalpers. Ticket scalpers were plying their trade at baseball games as early as 1886, when the *Boston Globe* reported, "Ticket fakirs made a harvest at yesterday's game. Ten cents was the advance asked on the regular price" (*Boston Globe*, June 1, 1886).

21.10 Trainers. In 1887 Brooklyn president Charles Byrne referred to "our experienced trainer, Mr. McMasters" (*Brooklyn Eagle*, March 23, 1887). Jack McMasters was one of the earliest baseball trainers and may well have been the first man to fill that position full time. A 1900 article reported, "It is not generally known that Jack McMasters, the well-known trainer at Harvard, is the first man who regularly trained a professional baseball team. He was engaged by the late Charles H. Byrne of the Brooklyn club to look after the players of that organization from 1886 to 1890. Previous to that time McMasters had been the trainer for the Williamsburg Athletic club" (*Milwaukee Journal*, April 3, 1900). Lee Allen reported that McMasters had also previously worked with boxers (Lee Allen, *The Hot Stove League*, 114).

A few other clubs followed suit, with the Phillies in 1889 employing both a trainer and a team physician (Jerrold Casway, *Ed Delahanty and the Emerald Age of Baseball*, 35). Nonetheless the practice appears to have died out in the wake of the costly 1890 war between the players and the owners.

In 1898, with trainers having become a prominent feature of several other sports, a *Sporting News* correspondent lambasted baseball for falling behind the times: "It is an accepted axiom among athletes of the higher order that no man can train himself. They know nothing of a trainer around base ball teams." He offered a scathing comparison between cyclists and ballplayers: "From the first day the racer goes into training until the last day of the season he is never out of the trainer's sight. The trainer eats, walks, drinks and sleeps with his man. He says at what hour he shall arise and at what minute he shall retire. . . . Now for your base ball player. Every spring he is taken from the North to the South with from 25 to 40 other men of all classes. He has no one to control or direct him. He is free to train himself. I fancy that when Byron wrote that sarcastic line, 'Lord of himself, that heritage of woe,' he had in mind a base ball player in training."

The correspondent continued: "I wager that if [New York pitchers Amos] Rusie and [Jouett] Meekin were put in the hands of a competent trainer . . . those great pitchers would be fit as a fiddle on April 1. But the New York club has not got any trainers and it will pay Rusie and Meekin for a month's sitting on the bench. Their combined salaries for that month would pay a good trainer for the season" ("Dan Irish," "System Is Bad: Ball Players Not Properly Trained," *Sporting News*, February 19, 1898, 2).

Cincinnati owner John T. Brush seemed unimpressed by this reasoning, commenting: "I have often heard the writers confound training with practice. They should make some distinction. A prize fighter trains and a ball player practices" (*Sporting News*, February 26, 1898). Yet within weeks he reversed his course and hired a graduate of a Stockholm medical school: "President Brush has engaged Dr. M. A. Frey, a Swedish massage professor, to look well to the arms and legs of the player. . . . Not only in training, but through the entire season he will be with the team, treating their sore muscles at home and when traveling" (*Sporting Life*, March 5, 1898). Frey, who weighed a mere ninety pounds, quit the position after two years to become a jockey (Lee Allen, *The Hot Stove League*, 114).

In spite of Frey's defection, the use of trainers was recognized as an idea whose time had come. The following year the *Chicago Post* reported that Tom Burns, manager of the Chicago Orphans, was attempting to hire a doctor to perform the same duties. The *Cincinnati Enquirer* confirmed that the expense of a trainer was more than offset by the savings that resulted: "There can be no doubt that the scheme as tried by Cincinnati last year was productive of much good. When 'Buck' Ewing came to Chicago with his victorious Porkopolis players, he emphatically declared that it was the constant care and supervision exercised by Dr. Frey that kept his men in good condition. The doctor, he said, was worth all he cost and many times more. Some of the Orphans last year were in the habit of visiting a Turkish bath establishment to be attended by a skillful masseur and doctor. Their bills were invariably quite steep, and the club paid them without much of a protest. It is thought that the services of a doctor to follow the men would cost little in proportion to what he might save the Chicago Club. 'A rub or two in time might keep some player in the game who might otherwise be out of service for several weeks,' said Jimmy Callahan" (*Cincinnati Enquirer*, January 15, 1899).

Within the space of two years, the perception of the trainer changed from an expensive luxury to a virtual necessity. Tim Murnane observed in 1900, "The need of a trainer, or a rubber, is now keenly felt by [Boston] manager [Frank] Selee. . . . Few up-to-date clubs dream of starting to train for a season's hard work without a skilled trainer. In this respect the Boston club has not advanced one inch, sticking still to the methods in vogue in 1876, when every man was his own trainer and rubber. As players are valuable assets for the big clubs it seems only reasonable that they would take every precaution to keep the boys in the pink of condition by having a man over them who has made the game a life study. This is what Selee believes and would like to see come about as soon as possible" (*Boston Globe*, April 2, 1900).

In 1907 the *Detroit News* reported, "Each year, in the game of base ball, the need of an expert trainer grows more apparent. Foot ball would be thought impossible without the trainer, track athletics would be a joke, but base-ball has grown and prospered with never a thought of a trainer until a few years ago when 'rubbers' were secured to rub down the men. Detroit has taken the first step toward the proper training of the players [by hiring trainer Tom McMahon]. The Tigers will not have a 'rubber' this year. They will have a trainer in every sense of the word" (*Detroit News*, March 13, 1907).

Even after trainers became common, respect for their professional status was slow in coming. Reportedly, early-twentieth-century trainers were expected to look after the team's baggage on road trips (Gerard S. Petrone, *When Baseball Was Young*, 28).

21.11 Team Doctors. The idea of referring all the players on a baseball team to one doctor seems to have originated very early. The team rules of the 1872 Forest Citys of Cleveland included one that stated, "No member of the club will be excused from practice or play unless upon a written certificate from Dr. N. B. Prentice, and said certificate must state the cause" (*Cleveland Leader*, March 11, 1872). It is less clear when doctors began to be added to clubs' payrolls. As noted in the preceding entry, the Phillies had a team physician in 1889, and in 1892 the *Brooklyn Eagle* mentioned "Dr. McLean, the Brooklyn club's physician" (*Brooklyn Eagle*, June 8, 1892). But the extent of their duties would be difficult to determine.

21.12 Public Address Announcers. In early baseball, umpires called out the day's batteries. Of course their cries were inaudible to much of the audience unless the umpire was particularly leather-lunged.

Famed concessionaire Harry Stevens began to extend the practice at the Polo Grounds during the 1890s: "Hustling Harry's innovation of announcing the batteries before the game starts and also calling out the names of players substituted in the middle of a contest has caught the crowd" (*Sporting Life*, May 5, 1894).

When Washington's American League Park opened in 1901, the scorecard concession was awarded to a man named E. Lawrence Phillips who decided that letting fans know the batteries and substitutions would help his business. Megaphones had just been popularized as a result of the prominent role they played in the Spanish-American War. Phillips bought one, and umpires soon allowed him to take over the duty of calling out names (Mike Sowell, *July 2, 1903*, 140).

These early announcers with megaphones stood on the field to address the crowd. Chicago Cubs announcer Pat Pieper continued this tradition until the 1960s.

21.13 Clubhouse Attendants. After winning the 1913 city series over the crosstown Cubs, the White Sox voted a full share to "'Billy,' the boy who takes care of their uniforms and has charge of the clubhouse" (*Chicago Tribune*, October 14, 1913).

21.14 Commissioners. Baseball's first commissioner, Judge Kenesaw Mountain Landis, was appointed on November 12, 1920, and commenced his term on January 12, 1921. The creation of the office is often characterized as being simply a reaction to the Black Sox scandal, but there were other factors involved.

Since 1903 baseball had been governed by a three-man National Commission made up of the two league presidents and one owner. This worked quite well for a while, but by the late 1910s this body's decisions were becoming increasingly controversial. In 1918 Connie Mack refused to accept one of its rulings and obtained a court injunction. Early in 1920 Chairman Garry Herrmann, the only owner to have ever served on the commission, resigned. Herrmann angrily suggested that no club owner was impartial enough to serve on the governing board.

Throughout the year the owners tossed about ideas for replacing the commission. After the Black Sox scandal came to light in September, these ideas began to focus around a three-man board of nonbaseball men known for their impeccable integrity. One of the names that emerged was Judge Landis, best known for his later-reversed decision fining Standard Oil $29 million. The owners no doubt considered the fact that Landis had heard the Federal League's antitrust lawsuits and had delayed his ruling until the Federal League was forced to settle.

The owners went back and forth about whether they wanted a three-man commission or a single commissioner, but eventually decided to offer sole authority to Landis. On November 12, 1920, a party of eleven owners and their representatives traveled to Landis's courtroom to offer him the position. David Pietrusza has observed that the owners probably expected him immediately to recess court in order to hear their offer. Instead he continued his session, and when the restless baseball men made too much noise, the no-nonsense judge threatened to clear the courtroom.

When the case concluded, Landis was offered the position of commissioner. After being assured that he would not have to resign his federal judgeship, he accepted (David Pietrusza, *Judge and Jury*, 161–172).

21.15   Team Psychologists. Sports psychologist Coleman Robert Griffith was hired by Philip K. Wrigley in 1938 to work with the Cubs and lasted two seasons. In 1950 Wrigley protégé Bill Veeck hired David F. Tracy, a psychologist and hypnotist, to help improve the St. Louis Browns' self-image. The team got off to an 8-25 start and Tracy was let go on May 31. It was not until the 1980s that the role was permanently revived. Dr. James McGee was hired as the Orioles team psychologist around 1982 and counseled players on a variety of issues, including stress and substance abuse. A 1986 article reported that he was still the major league's only psychologist but that other organizations were looking into creating similar positions (AP: *Frederick* [Md.] *Post*, March 13, 1986).

21.16   Traffic Spotters. When the Houston Astrodome opened in 1965, one of its novel features was a weather station some two hundred feet above the field, from which the air conditioning was controlled. Owner Judge Roy Hofheinz took advantage of this perch to add a novel type of employee—"a traffic spotter, who will radio warnings of potential tie-ups to police stations as far as five miles away" (Robert Lipsyte, "Johnson Attends Opening of Houston's Astrodome," *New York Times*, April 10, 1965). The hope was that this would ease fans' commutes to the ballpark.

Chapter 22

COMPETITION

THE SEARCH for a viable and durable mode of competition has played a major role in the history of baseball. Its importance is easily forgotten because the format used by the major leagues to determine a champion remained essentially unchanged from the introduction of the Brush Rules in 1905 until 1969. The controversy caused by more recent changes, particularly the addition of wild card teams to the playoffs, makes it especially important to understand that the system introduced in 1905 was the result of a long process of trial and error.

(i) Determining a Champion

The earliest popular mode of competition was the challenge system, by which an aspirant challenged the champions to a two-out-of-three series. This worked well if the champions sportingly accepted the gauntlet that had been thrown down. If they didn't, there were, well, problems.

In 1870 two Nevada clubs, the champion Silver Stars of Carson and the challenging Striped Stockings of Elko, were unable to agree upon a basis for a series. So they wrote to Henry Chadwick, who replied that "there is no rule governing the question of sending or receiving challenges. . . . The customary rule here in vogue is for the challenged club to name a day and ground, but it is, of course, optional with the challenging club to accept or not" (reprinted in Robert A. Nylen, "Frontier Baseball," *Nevada*, Volume 50, Number 2 [March/April 1990], 56). Others were more categorical, such as Fred Delano of the Brother Jonathans of Detroit, who asserted: "A challenge to a game of base ball, as to anything else, gives the challenged party choice of time and place" (*Detroit Free Press*, June 14, 1863).

Such rules naturally made it easy for a champion club to avoid defending its title. The two Nevada clubs never did meet, and many other championships were retained by default.

Tournaments proved a popular alternative to the challenge system, and they often generated tremendous interest and excitement. But, as noted in this chapter's first entry, they too were plagued by problems.

Disputes about the mode of competition often masked a still more troubling underlying issue. Anyone who sought to make money by operating a baseball club looked to the model of capitalism, but unchecked capitalism creates the kind of disparities that ruin a competitive sport. Gross disparities in talent eliminated what was referred to in the nineteenth century as the "glorious uncertainty of base ball," and when the outcome was a foregone conclusion, opposing clubs became "demoralized" and spectators found better things to do.

22.1.1 Tournaments. Noting plans to hold a baseball tournament at the 1865 Michigan State Fair, the *New York Clipper* wrote, "We have had almost every other kind of tournament but base ball, but this exception, it appears, is not to be for long" (*New York Clipper*, August 8, 1865).

That tournament was held in Adrian on September 20–21, and while it generated considerable interest it also showed the limitation of the format. Detroit, then as now, was far and away the state's biggest city and sent a club that included two eastern players, at least one of whom was almost certainly a professional (see **18.1.5** "Players Lured West by Money"). Clubs from small towns like Salem withdrew, and Detroit easily won the four-team tournament (Peter Morris, *Baseball Fever*, 96–101).

Tournaments remained an important part of baseball for the next few years, but the difficulty of adapting them to baseball became increasingly evident. Their intention was to include every club that wished to participate, but it seldom worked out that way. The number of entrants almost never corresponded to the number of clubs that appeared. If the number of entrants was not a power of 2 (2, 4, 8, 16, etc.), byes were necessary, which was intrinsically unfair. Limited daylight made it difficult to play more than two games a day; rain could ruin things entirely.

Moreover, even if everything miraculously ran smoothly, only one club could emerge victorious. All the other clubs were thus inclined to grumble, whether they had a legitimate cause or not. Consequently while tournaments invariably began with great enthusiasm, they often ended with general dissatisfaction. Worse, the grievances were often aired in the newspapers for weeks afterward, leaving a bitter taste in everyone's mouth.

Thus John B. Foster, in an 1895 account of the history of baseball in northern Ohio, remarked: "In years gone by base ball tournaments were quite numerous and popular. Now and then such a tournament is held in this part of the State, but they are not as common as they once were" (John B. Foster, "Buckeye Boys," *Sporting News*, December 28, 1895).

22.1.2 Handicaps. One way to address competitive imbalance is to devise some sort of handicap or tiered system. Baseball certainly tried this approach.

Tournaments soon began to offer multiple brackets in order to stimulate competition. Sometimes these worked well, but it was impossible to ensure that clubs entered the appropriate division. Far too often a lower tier was won by a club that should have been in a higher division, which only exacerbated hard feelings.

Efforts were made to address these problems. One of the most popular methods was to have separate brackets for junior clubs, which usually featured players eighteen and under. Unfortunately this led to early versions of overage Little Leaguer Danny Almonte and endless tedious complaints by junior clubs that they had faced allegedly junior opponents who were "bearded like the pard" (*Jackson* [Mich.] *Citizen*, September 18, 1874).

Other clubs advertised for opponents whose average weight was below a certain figure. Still other efforts focused on dividing clubs into arbitrary classes. Obviously these were even more open to chicanery.

Another approach was for a weaker club to be allowed to use extra players and/or have five or six outs per inning when the sides seemed particularly uneven. Cap Anson reported that when his Marshalltown club appeared at a tournament in the late 1860s, opposing clubs refused to play them unless they were allowed six outs per inning (Adrian C. Anson, *A Ball Player's Career*, 38).

A ballplayer named Frank A. Deans recalled many years later that the Actives of Wellsboro, Pennsylvania, were desperate for competition in 1871 but had no worthy rivals. Eventually they convinced a local junior nine called the Red Hots to play them by "conditioning that the Red Hots should put but one Active out for each inning, while the Actives should put out of the Red Hots the usual three at an inning." Two games were played in this fashion, but the results were still so lopsided in favor of the Actives that another game was played "on the same conditions, and Actives playing with but six men (no outfielders—didn't need any)" (*Wellsboro Agitator*, August 14, 1901).

When professional clubs were involved the need for such handicaps was all the more evident, but an 1874 game in Jackson, Michigan, demonstrated why they were doomed to failure. Harry Wright's Red Stockings of Boston won four straight National Association pennants from 1872 to 1875 by increasingly lopsided margins. The game's still shaky economics meant that the club relied heavily upon filling in the gaps in their schedule with matches against semipro and amateur clubs. But with the Red Stockings dominating the National Association, there was no hope that these games would be competitive.

In 1873 the Red Stockings played fourteen games against semipro and amateur opponents and won by a cumulative margin of 524-48. While these contests still drew large crowds, it seemed unlikely that they would continue to do so year after year. Moreover locals resented any sign that the Red Stockings were not putting forth their best effort. After a game in Jackson in 1873, one onlooker complained that the visitors were "simply toying" with their hosts (*Adrian Daily Press*, August 22, 1873; quoted in Peter Morris, *Baseball Fever*, 298).

Accordingly, in 1874 Harry Wright determined to allow all amateur clubs five outs per inning. This didn't prevent the Red Stockings from winning easily, but it kept the scores a little more respectable. When Boston returned to Jackson, Wright explained these terms, and the home captain reluctantly conceded the point. But the club's first baseman, Hugh Ernst, flatly declared that he would not agree to accept any handicap. The game was finally played on even terms, and the home team was proud of the 19-4 loss (*Jackson Citizen*, July 8, 1874).

This margin was indeed impressive by comparison with the scores by which the Red Stockings were beating their National Association opponents. Unfortunately it also underscored the fact that handicap systems were not a solution to the problems caused by competitive imbalance.

22.1.3 Leagues. A league is a lot of things, but its essence is a group of teams that have agreed on a method of selecting a champion. Developing the first baseball league was a process of trial and error that benefited from earlier failed efforts.

During the 1860s the challenge system was considered the basis of determining the country's best club. For the first half of the decade, the club so designated was usually deserving. In the second half of the decade, the competition became increasingly contrived.

In 1866 the Atlantics of Brooklyn retained the championship because their best-of-three series with the Athletics of Philadelphia was not completed. In 1867 and 1868 the New York clubs froze out outside clubs by scheduling matches in such a way that a challenger could never complete a series in time to claim the title. Matters got downright silly when the Red Stockings of Cincinnati went undefeated in 1869, beating every top club along the way, and yet were still not officially recognized as the national champions.

The challenge system was further undermined by accusations of "hippodroming," a term that meant that the outcomes were predetermined.

After the first gambling scandal rocked baseball in 1865, one of the guilty players, Thomas Devyr, explained that co-conspirator William Wansley told him, "We can lose this game without doing the club any harm, and win the home and home game" (quoted in Dean Sullivan, ed., *Early Innings*, 51). The unfortunate result was that whenever the first two games in a series were split, there were rumors that the clubs had deliberately set up a lucrative deciding game.

By the end of the 1860s, as James L. Terry noted, the system was so obviously broken that newspapers "would refer to various teams as the 'nominal' championship club" (James L. Terry, *Long Before the Dodgers*, 73). As a result, when every major club had at least four losses in 1870, there were numerous claimants to the national championship and no fair way to sort them out.

It was against this backdrop that the National Association of Professional Base Ball Players was formed on March 17, 1871. The historic meeting took place at Collier's Rooms, a saloon located at the corner of Broadway and Thirteenth in New York City. It is sometimes said that the meeting was called by Henry Chadwick. But Chadwick specifically noted, "The origin of this convention should be placed on record, viz., Mr. N. E. ["Nick"] Young, the efficient Secretary of the Olympic Club of Washington" (*New York Clipper*, March 25, 1871; William J. Ryczek, *Blackguards and Red Stockings*, 11–14).

The ten clubs that attended the meeting agreed on a fairly simple format. Every club wishing to compete for the championship was to play a five-game series with every other club, thus determining the champion by head-to-head play. Clubs were responsible for their own scheduling. Each entrant was to submit a ten-dollar entry fee, and the money would be used to purchase a pennant that the champion would fly.

The new league debuted on May 4, 1871, and its historic first game was scheduled to feature Boston and Washington in the nation's capital. Instead that game was rained out, and the first game took place in Fort Wayne, Indiana. It was a symbolic beginning for a league in which things would rarely go as anticipated (David Nemec, *Great Encyclopedia of Nineteenth Century Major League Baseball*, 8).

This was especially true with the format for determining the champion. By mid-season, there were differing opinions as to whether the champion was determined on the basis of series won or games won. This was compounded by disputes over player eligibility and unplayed games. To top it all off, the Great Chicago Fire destroyed the home park and all the possessions of one of the main contenders, the White Stockings of Chicago (William J. Ryczek, *Blackguards and Red Stockings*, 55–63).

The deciding game of the season saw the White Stockings face the Athletics of Philadelphia under bizarre circumstances. The game had to be played at a neutral site in Brooklyn, so only five hundred people attended. The White Stockings wore piebald uniforms borrowed from other clubs, and were without two players who had left the club after the fire.

Adding to the sense of anticlimax, it was generally agreed that a Philadelphia win would make them champions but that if Chicago won the champion might end up being Chicago, Boston, or Philadelphia, depending on the resolution of several claimed forfeits. That was avoided when Philadelphia won the game, but it was clear there was a lot of room for improvement in determining a champion (William J. Ryczek, _Blackguards and Red Stockings_, 55–63).

The National Association lasted five years and never again had a dispute over its champion. This wasn't a good thing—the Red Stockings of Boston captured the pennant by increasingly large margins, finally going 71-8 in 1875, in the circuit's final season. Its open-entry policy accentuated the competitive imbalance as each season began with co-op entries that were soundly thrashed and then withdrew.

In 1876 Chicago president William Hulbert led a coup that created the National League. When almost all the National Association's viable franchises jumped to the new entity, baseball's first major league quietly passed into history. As implied by the word "league," the new circuit was based far more upon the centralized leadership of the club owners.

A number of new policies introduced by the National League were important in ensuring baseball's financial well-being. These included entry criteria and territorial rights (see **18.2.4**), a predetermined league-wide schedule (see **22.1.4**), the turnstile (see **14.5.1**), and the reserve clause (see **18.2.1**). Unfortunately these undeniably significant innovations were later used by major league baseball's Special Records Committee to make the self-serving decision that the National League was the first "major league."

22.1.4   Schedules. The first league-wide schedule was adopted by the National League on March 22, 1877. Before then, clubs arranged the dates and locations of matches by themselves.

22.1.5   Playing Out the Schedule. Until 1908 it was not customary to make up rainouts and other canceled games. That season the Tigers finished with a 90-63 mark, and the Indians compiled a 90-64 record. It hardly seemed fair that a rainout had helped determine the pennant, so the American League mandated the following year that clubs had to complete their schedule if the pennant hung in the balance.

(ii) Postseason Championships

In the nineteenth century, what we now call the regular season was often referred to as the championship series. As is often the case, the choice of words
was indicative of an essential truth: that having labored long and hard to arrive
at a satisfactory way to determine a champion, there was no thought of un-
dermining the outcome with additional games. When viewed from that perspective, what is peculiar is the current tendency of almost all sports to have a
long season and then have the same clubs compete again in the playoffs.

Consequently baseball's earliest postseason series came about because of
the unique circumstance of having two major leagues that were willing to
play each other.

22.2.1 World Series. Despite the rivalry of the International Association
and the National League in the late 1870s, there is no evidence of any effort
to match the leagues' champions.

The idea did emerge as soon as the American Association was formed in
1882. Even though the two leagues were at war, National League champion
Chicago and American Association pennant winners Cincinnati began a series on October 6, 1882. Researcher Frederick Ivor-Campbell concluded
that "no one in 1882 saw them as more than exhibition games" (Frederick
Ivor-Campbell, "Postseason Play," *Total Baseball* IV, 281).

Nonetheless the games did attract attention. After the teams had split
two games, the series was abruptly abandoned. Many histories state that the
series ended because the American Association threatened to expel Cincinnati. But David Nemec argued that scheduling conflicts were more likely the
reason (David Nemec, *The Beer and Whisky League*, 38).

Before the next season the two leagues signed a peace treaty known as
the Tri-Partite Agreement (see **18.2.3** "National Agreement"). Preliminary
efforts were made to organize a postseason series between the American Association champion Athletics of Philadelphia and the National League
champions from Boston. But interest in such a match waned when the Athletics lost several postseason exhibition games against other National
League teams (David Nemec, *The Beer and Whisky League*, 54).

The first completed series between the two league champions took place
in 1884, with Providence representing the National League and New York
the American Association. The series had no official status, but Providence
manager Frank Bancroft boldly declared that the series was for "the championship of America" and that the winner would "fly a pennant next year as
champions of America" (*Providence Evening Telegram*, October 17, 1884;
reprinted in Frederick Ivor-Campbell, "Extraordinary 1884," *National Pastime* 13 [1993], 19).

Providence earned that right by winning the first two games of the three-game series. The third game was played nonetheless, and Providence won that one too. *Sporting Life* commented: "the result clearly proclaims the Providence Club 'Champions of the World'" (quoted in Frederick Ivor-Campbell, "Extraordinary 1884," *National Pastime* 13 [1993], 22).

The series became an annual event and was held every year through 1890. The annual Spalding and Reach guides began referring to the event as the "world's championship series" and the "world's series." When the two leagues merged in 1892 to form a twelve-team league, several efforts were made to create a valid postseason series. These are discussed in the next entry.

After the American League declared itself a major league in 1901, it spent two years at war with the National League. When peace came in 1903, the idea of a world's series was revived, and Boston of the junior circuit up-ended the National League's representatives, the Pittsburgh Pirates. It is important to emphasize, however, that the series had no official sanction.

In 1904 the New York Giants won the National League pennant, but Giants manager John McGraw and owner John T. Brush declined to play the American League champions from Boston. Their refusal was widely denounced by the press and the public. McGraw and Brush were portrayed as being motivated either by cowardice or by the well-publicized feuds that both men had waged with American League president Ban Johnson.

As discussed in the other entry for "World Series" (see **16.2.6**), McGraw and Brush also had a legitimate basis for their stance. But they were so clearly in the minority that John Brush rethought his position over the off-season and helped put together the Brush Rules, which would thereafter form the basis of the World Series.

22.2.2 Intramural Playoffs. As noted earlier, a postseason series between the champions of rival leagues has a natural and obvious appeal. A postseason series between clubs that have competed all season, though unquestioningly accepted today, is a much more dubious concept. It has the inherent risk of diluting what is now called the "regular season" and fan interest in those contests.

The concept was first tried in 1892, the first season after the National League and American Association had merged into a twelve-club entity. The new league adopted a split-season format, with the first-half winner meeting the second-half champion in a postseason series. Cleveland and Boston played a classic first game that ended in an eleven-inning scoreless tie. The remainder of the series was less dramatic as Boston swept the next five games. The format was abandoned at season's end.

Two years later a postseason series was revived when Pittsburgh businessman William Temple offered the Temple Cup to the winner of a best-of-seven series between the league's first- and second-place finishers. The Temple Cup was contested for four years and always featured the tempestuous Baltimore Orioles.

But the series were all lopsided, with none requiring more than five games. Additionally, the second-place finisher won three of the four matchups, leaving it debatable which club was the true champion. It appears that the fans cast the deciding vote on the fate of the Temple Cup, for dwindling attendance in 1897 led to the demise of the series.

In 1900 the concept was revived for one year when the *Pittsburgh Chronicle-Telegraph* sponsored a series between runner-up Pittsburgh and first-place Brooklyn, which was won by Brooklyn. The birth of the American League again made possible a postseason series between clubs that had not faced each other that year. It was accordingly not until 1969 that the championship format again featured rematches of in-season contests.

22.2.3 Neutral Sites. Many athletic competitions, including the Super Bowl and most NCAA tournaments, are deliberately held at neutral sites. It has been a long time since this was done in baseball, but it was attempted. In 1885 the final three games of the World's Series between Chicago and St. Louis were played in Pittsburgh and Cincinnati. The 1887 Series between Detroit and St. Louis was a fifteen-game extravaganza that included ten neutral-site games in eight different cities. In 1888 games in the series between New York and St. Louis were played in Brooklyn and Philadelphia. Attendance at neutral sites was generally lower, and the experiment has never been repeated.

22.2.4 Best-of Series. In most early postseason series, the number of games was predetermined and all were played even if one side amassed an insurmountable lead. This was based on the same reasoning that led to the bottom of the ninth being played in baseball games even if the team that batted last was ahead—that baseball was a spectacle, not a competition (see **1.25** "'Walkoff' Hits"). But by doing so, a basic reality was being disregarded. Baseball was a competition, whether that fact was acknowledged or not, which meant that players and spectators lost interest in games that were played after the champion was determined.

There was a more insidious problem associated with playing out meaningless games. As noted under "Fixed Games" (**11.1.1**), there was a strong tendency to assume that a game was fixed when one club staved off elimination. The best way to fend off such rumors was to offer prize money to the winners (see **22.3.5**) and announce beforehand that the series would end when one club had clinched the championship. The 1889 World's Series was the first to do the latter, with a best-of-eleven format that was scheduled to end as soon as one club won six games (Jerry Lansche, *Glory Fades Away*, 157).

The number of games in these series varied in early years. Although a best-of-seven format was used as early as 1885, it was not permanently adopted until 1922.

22.2.5 City Series. It may seem surprising today, but postseason series between clubs representing the same city in rival leagues once competed with and sometimes even outstripped the series between the champions of the respective leagues.

In 1882 Cleveland of the National League beat Cincinnati of the American Association in a postseason series to determine the top club in Ohio. Peace was made between the two leagues the following year, which led to similar series that capitalized upon natural rivalries in Philadelphia and New York (Frederick Ivor-Campbell, "Postseason Play," *Total Baseball* IV, 281).

This concept was revived in 1903 when the war between the National and American leagues ended. Over the next fifteen years, intracity series in Philadelphia, St. Louis, and Chicago capitalized on deep-seated local interest and became fan favorites. As is evident throughout Ring Lardner's Jack Keefe stories, the event that Keefe called the "city serious" was especially popular in Chicago.

Although canceled when one of the clubs was in the World Series as well as for the First World War and occasional other reasons, the Chicago city series was contested twenty-six times between 1903 and 1942. Researcher Emil Rothe reported that "The dominance of the White Sox in these autumn affairs defies logic," as the Sox won nineteen series while the Cubs won six times, with one tie (Emil H. Rothe, "History of the Chicago City Series," *Baseball Research Journal* 8 [1979], 16).

22.2.6 Shaughnessy Playoffs. The Shaughnessy Playoffs were a simple and highly effective solution to the complex problems faced by minor league baseball during the Great Depression. Montreal president Frank Shaughnessy proposed that the only way to keep fans interested in the regular season was a postseason playoff among the top four teams. The top team would face the fourth-place team, while the second- and third-place finishers would square off, with the winners meeting for the league championship.

Montreal Herald sportswriter Al Parsley reported that Shaughnessy had borrowed the idea from hockey: "Frank Shaughnessy of the Montreal Royals had to beat down stiff opposition in selling the play-off idea to the International League and American Association magnates. But, as he insisted at the meetings early in the year and as he still maintains, 'something had to be done to protect our baseball investment. Under the old system baseball, from the standpoint of this city's experience, must be considered a poor investment. I am supported in this statement by practically every owner of a Double A club. Here in Montreal we have $1,800,000 sunk into a stadium and club and have been losing money steadily because of waning interest by the 1st of August. With the play-offs, it is confidently believed that we can keep up interest just as they do in hockey. Hockey's success is enough proof that the thing will do in baseball'" (*Montreal Herald*, reprinted in *Sporting News*, February 16, 1933).

There was concerted resistance to the idea because of the obvious fact that the Shaughnessy Playoffs watered down the regular season. Nonetheless there was a dire need to sustain fan interest, and it was hard to dismiss an idea with the potential to increase revenues. In spite of efforts by minor league "czar" William G. Bramham to halt the Shaughnessy Playoffs, they were implemented in the International League and Texas League in 1933.

Fans thronged to the games, and other leagues rushed to adopt them. Their success was such that baseball historian Robert Obojski concluded that it is "generally acknowledged to have saved the minors from total financial ruin in the depression-ridden 1930s" (Robert Obojski, *Bush League*, 46–48). That being the case, even purists had to reluctantly accept the Shaughnessy Playoffs.

Major league baseball added intramural playoffs in 1969 and a wild-card team in 1995. (The wild card would have debuted in 1994 if not for the strike.) Like them or hate them, the wild cards and multi-tier playoffs now used by the major leagues are the logical culmination of the Shaughnessy Playoffs.

(iii) Bling Bling

Quick Quiz:

(1) What is the name of the trophy awarded to the champions of the National Hockey League playoffs?
(2) What is the name of the trophy awarded to the winners of baseball's World Series?

If you correctly answered the Stanley Cup to the first question, it doesn't necessarily mean that you're a diehard hockey fan. On the other hand, even a very knowledgeable baseball fan is likely to struggle with the second question. The Commissioner's Trophy simply hasn't captured the public's imagination. That paradox is all the more puzzling because, as this section will show, tangible rewards for championships have played a major role in baseball history.

22.3.1 Trophies. The earliest baseball trophy was the game ball presented by the losers to the winners of each challenge match, as specified by the 1857 rules. The Spalding Collection of the New York Public Library includes a photograph of the trophy case in which the Atlantics of Brooklyn proudly collected and displayed the baseballs they had captured (James L. Terry, *Long Before the Dodgers*, 77).

Less famous clubs preserved these symbols of their triumphs with equal care. Catcher William Stirling of the Red Herrings of Eaton Rapids, Michigan, a successful club of the 1870s, collected a boxful of souvenir balls, "but went even further than that. He was very handy with the old quill and pen, and after the game the ball was cleaned thoroughly—the name of both teams, the score, place and date were printed on it in a very neat and attractive manner. After the ink dried the ball was given a coat of light-colored varnish to preserve it" (W. Scott Munn, *The Only Eaton Rapids on Earth*, 250–251).

Similarly, a member of an 1864 amateur club in Albany, New York, wrote to a friend after a victory: "The ball is a very nice Hardwood. We shall have it varnished and lettered in the following manner: Won by 1st Nine Hiawatha B. B. C. from 1st Nine Alpine B. B. C. Sept 24th 1864. Score 34 to 25" (quoted in Scott S. Taylor, "Pure Passion for the Game: Albany Amateur Baseball Box Scores from 1864," *Manuscripts* LIV, No. 1 [Winter 2002], 7). E. H. Tobias, who chronicled the earliest days of St. Louis baseball, confirmed that these trophies were "afterwards gilded and the date and the score of the game painted thereon in black letters" (E. H. Tobias, *Sporting News*, November 2, 1895).

This custom was usually enacted at the end of a match with a great display of sportsmanship in which both sides gave three cheers and a tiger to their opponents. But disputes became common enough that the National Association of Amateur Base Ball Players issued specific instructions for "Furnishing the Ball" (*Bay City* [Mich.] *Journal*, July 30, 1872).

Although this ritual is generally recalled as a quaint feature of antebellum baseball, it persisted much longer than that. John H. Gruber noted that once it became customary to use multiple balls during the game, "the winning club demanded and got every ball that had been in play. This led to much wrangling as the players of the losing team were unwilling to give up balls that could be used in practice." Accordingly, the rules were changed in 1887 so that the winners kept only the final ball. Gruber claimed that the custom of awarding the ball at game's end was still in effect in 1915, but by then it was being overshadowed by gaudier trophies (John H. Gruber, "The Ball and the Bat," *Sporting News*, November 11, 1915).

While the game ball was the earliest trophy, it was not long before additional forms of recognition were being awarded. When the Live Oaks of

Rochester, New York, were triumphant at the Monroe County Agricultural Society Fair on September 16, 1858, they were invited to have tea with the society's managers and to help in the judging process. The club also received a pennant that was later described as "nothing more or less than an American flag" with the club's name inscribed and its emblem, a wreath of green oak, embroidered upon the stripes (Priscilla Astifan, "Baseball in the Nineteenth Century," *Rochester History* LII, No. 3 [Summer 1990], 7, 17).

By the 1860s jewelers were sculpting elaborate trophies for the winners of prestigious championships. A silver ball was offered to the club recognized as the national champion by the Continental Club of Brooklyn in 1861 and 1862. Frank Queen, the editor of the *New York Clipper*, attempted to revive this tradition in 1868 (James L. Terry, *Long Before the Dodgers*, 35, 37, 73).

Similar rewards were soon being offered at local competitions. In 1862 the proprietors of the Walton House in Rochester, New York, donated a silver ball to go to the winner of a baseball game on ice (*Rochester Evening Express*, January 10, 1862; quoted in Priscilla Astifan, "Baseball in the Nineteenth Century," *Rochester History* LII, No. 3 [Summer 1990], 7). In 1864 John A. Lowell offered a silver ball to the champion team of New England. The trophy was first awarded on September 27, 1864, and remained the subject of heated competition for several years (*New England Base Ballist*, August 13, November 5, 1868). Indeed the competition became so intense that it was decided to melt the ball in a crucible and present smaller balls to several clubs (*Boston Journal*, February 20, 1905).

Beginning in 1865 a goblet was offered to the champions of the state of Michigan, consisting of "a silver cup, mounted on three miniature bats. The lid of the cup is of oval shape, and in a depression carries a silver ball, the emblem of success. Between the bats, constituting the standard, are also placed fac similes of the square and circular bases. The prize is thus very appropriate, in addition to being of a novel model" (*Detroit Advertiser and Tribune*, September 13, 1865).

That same year saw clubs in Connecticut begin to compete for a miniature bat made from the state's famous Charter Oak. The bat was engraved with a picture of the celebrated tree and was kept in a rosewood case (David Arcidiacono, *Grace, Grit and Growling*, 5). A similar prize was offered by the New England Association two years later in the form of a bat that was reportedly "composed of pieces of wood from the John Hancock house on Benson street, the Lincoln cabin, the old Boston elm, the apple tree under which Gen. Lee surrendered at Appomattox and the battleships Kearsarge and Alabama" (*Boston Journal*, February 22, 1905).

At an 1866 tournament in Rockford, Illinois, clubs vied for the championship of the Northwest and a ball "of full regulation size, two and three-quarters inches in diameter, of eighteen carat gold, and put up in a satin-lined Morocco case," and a bat "of solid rosewood, elaborately mounted with the same quality of gold, and cased the same as the ball" (*Detroit Advertiser and Tribune*, June 21, 1866; reprinted in Peter Morris, *Baseball Fever*, 110). Many similar trophies are described in my history of early baseball in Michigan.

Colorado ballplayers also had an impressive piece of jewelry to aim for by 1867: "The silver ball which is to be presented by Mr. Anker to the champion base ball club of Colorado, may now be seen at his store, on F street. It is a very beautiful piece of workmanship, being the same size and weight of the regulation ball, and ornamented with crossed bats on either side. It bears the following inscriptions: 'Champion Base Ball of Colorado' 'Presented to Champion Base Ball Club of Colorado by M. Anker'" (*Rocky Mountain* [Denver] *News*, June 4, 1867).

Other trophies being competed for by 1868 included a gold ball for the champions of Western and Central New York, a silver ball awarded to the best club in Maryland, a gold ball denoting the championship of Wisconsin, and another silver ball for the top club in Maine (James L. Terry, *Long Before the Dodgers*, 73–74; Will M. Anderson, *Was Baseball Really Invented in Maine?*, 2–3). Canadian clubs were following suit by 1880, commissioning "A model base ball bat in silver" from Peck & Snyder of New York to symbolize the national championship (*Woodstock* [Ont.] *Sentinel Review*, June 4, 1880).

The earliest trophy for a league championship that I am aware of was a parian vase offered to the National League champion in 1881. (Parian is a type of china known for its ivory tint.) This vase was almost certainly one of a pair created by Trenton, New Jersey, pottery makers for the 1876 U.S. Centennial celebrations. The pair was described as follows: "Round the foot of each vase, and standing on the supporting pedestal, are arranged three figures of base-ball players, modelled after a thoroughly American ideal of physical beauty, embodying muscular activity rather than ponderous strength. . . . A series of clubs belted round with a strap ornaments the stem of the vases, and some exquisitely wrought leaves and berries are woven round the top. The orifice is covered by a cupola or dome, composed of a segment of a base-ball, upon which stands an eagle" (Jenny J. Young, *The Ceramic Art: A Compendium of the History and Manufacturing of Pottery and Porcelain* [New York, 1878]; quoted in James M. DiClerico and Barry J. Pavelec, *The Jersey Game*, 200).

The two vases were eventually separated, and one was given to the National League to be used as a symbol of the league championship. According to James M. DiClerico and Barry J. Pavelec, this occurred in 1887, but in fact the vase was first mentioned in 1881 (*Detroit Free Press*, July 31, 1881).

So either the vase was offered for several years or DiClerico and Pavelec were mistaken about the year.

In 1988 art historian Ellen Paul Denker found one of the pair in the Detroit Historical Museum and the other in the New Jersey State Museum. She was able to reunite them for an exhibition at the Metropolitan Museum of Art (James M. DiClerico and Barry J. Pavelec, *The Jersey Game*, 200).

The first postseason trophy seems to have been a silver trophy presented by Metropolitans president Erastus Wiman to the St. Louis Brown Stockings following the 1886 World's Series. In 1887 actress Helen Dauvray offered the first permanent trophy for the world champions. Manufactured by Tiffany's, the Dauvray Cup was awarded until 1893, when it was succeeded by the Temple Cup.

22.3.2 Individual Awards. At early baseball tournaments it was common to award medals or other jewelry to individual players for a wide variety of accomplishments. Usually these were for Field Day–type events like running and throwing contests. Sometimes other categories were added, such as best captain, most home runs, and best catcher. I even found one occasion on which an award was given to the best umpire (Peter Morris, *Baseball Fever*, 296).

To mark the opening of Brooklyn's Union Grounds, a handsome bat and ball were offered to the player scoring the most runs (*Brooklyn Eagle*, May 12, 1862). In later years, individual awards became a popular way to bring attention to a new or unappreciated statistical measurement. As noted earlier, Henry Chadwick offered an engraved bat in 1868 to publicize the category of base hits (see **17.3**).

In 1879 the McKay Medal attracted considerable attention. The *Buffalo Courier* explained that a local man named James W. McKay was offering "a medal to the League player who makes the best combined average in batting and fielding during the season of 1879. . . . He thinks this will induce the heavy batters to look more to their fielding averages, and the fine fielders to do something in the way of hitting. It will be called the McKay Medal, and any player who wins it this year shall own it. The medal will be of solid gold, five inches high and two broad, and will weigh twenty-five pennyweights. On the top bar will be the words 'McKay Medal'" (*Buffalo Courier*, quoted in *Chicago Tribune*, April 6, 1879).

It was pointed out to McKay that this format would give a significant advantage to first basemen, so he eliminated fielding and decided to give it to the player with the highest batting average in seventy or more games. At season's end there was a dispute as to whether Cap Anson or Paul Hines had the highest average, but since only Hines had played in the requisite seventy games, he was awarded the medal (*New York Clipper*, November 22, 1879).

22.3.3 Most Valuable Player Awards. Bill Deane noted that in 1875 Jim "Deacon" White received a silver trophy donated by a wealthy spectator that was engraved with the words "Won by Jim White as most valuable player to Boston team, 1875" (Bill Deane, *Award Voting*, 5–6).

Before the 1878 season, General Thomas S. Dakin, a star pitcher for the Putnam Club of Brooklyn in the 1850s, offered a "splendid gold mounted willow bat" to the best player on the championship-winning team. A committee of three was to make the decision (*New York Clipper*, January 5, 1878). Unfortunately, Dakin died suddenly a few months later, and the idea did not resurface for another thirty years.

When it did, it was once again under rather bizarre circumstances. In 1910 the Chalmers Automobile Company had offered a car to the American League's batting champion. On the last day of the season the St. Louis Browns' third baseman played far too deep, allowing Nap Lajoie to beat out a series of bunt hits in his attempt to catch Ty Cobb and win the automobile. To preclude such shenanigans, it was decided that a vehicle would in the future be given to the player in each league voted "the most important and useful player to his club and to the league at large in point of deportment and value of services rendered" (Bill Deane, *Award Voting*, 6).

The award was withdrawn after the 1914 season, but most valuable player awards returned in 1922 and have been a feature of major league baseball ever since.

22.3.4 World Series Rings. Helen Dauvray had gold medallions made for each member of the world champion team beginning in 1887.

When the World Series was made a permanent institution in 1905, the agreement between the two leagues called for all of the winning players to receive an "appropriate memento, in the form of a button." Within a few years it appears to have become customary for a small piece of jewelry to be given to World Series champions. According to Jonathan Fraser Light, these were initially stickpins (Jonathan Fraser Light, *The Cultural Encyclopedia of Baseball*, 390).

In 1918 the Red Sox and Cubs delayed the start of the fifth game of the World Series because of a dispute about the purse. As a result, the winning Red Sox received a letter from National Commission member John Heydler informing them that "each member of the team is fined the Series emblems and none would be given" (quoted in Ty Waterman and Mel Springer, *The Year the Red Sox Won the Series*, 271).

Harry Hooper of the Red Sox was particularly upset about this decision and unsuccessfully brought the matter to the attention of every baseball commissioner until his death in 1974. Finally in 1993 the Red Sox held a ceremony for the seventy-fifth anniversary of the championship and gave emblems to descendants of the players (Ty Waterman and Mel Springer, *The Year the Red Sox Won the Series*, 271–273).

As far as I can determine, the custom of awarding World Series rings began in the 1920s.

22.3.5   Cash. By the late 1860s match games for cash purses were becoming fairly common. The first such game in Michigan took place on July 4, 1866, for a $100 purse, and undoubtedly there were earlier such games in other states.

Players also sometimes received bonuses for special accomplishments. The Hartford players, for example, were offered bonuses if they won the 1875 pennant (David Arcidiacono, *Grace, Grit and Growling*, 28).

Formal monetary rewards for the World's Series winners were introduced in 1884, when $1,000 was donated by Al Wright of the *New York Clipper* (Jerry Lansche, *Glory Fades Away*, 37). The tradition continued the following year when St. Louis owner Chris Von der Ahe and Chicago owner A. G. Spalding put up $500 each to be split among the winning side. But when the series was officially declared a tie, the money was returned to the owners.

World's Series shares were thus actually awarded for the first time the following year, when the same two clubs met in a winner-take-all format. Curt Welch scored the series-clinching run on what became known as the "$15,000 slide" (though there is no evidence that he slid, and the total revenues were a little under $14,000).

In 1887 the American Association inaugurated prize money for the regular-season winner. Chris Von der Ahe had lobbied for such a purse, and his Browns claimed it. The National League had no corresponding prize, but Lady Baldwin later indicated that Detroit owner Frederick K. Stearns bought each player a new suit of clothes for winning the pennant and added a $500 bonus when the club won that fall's World's Series (*Indiana* [Pa.] *Gazette*, September 27, 1935).

(iv) Youth

Junior clubs were an important part of early baseball, fostering tournaments and other forms of competition. There was even an active national organization of junior clubs in the 1860s. Gradually, however, organized competition between youngsters faded, with the use of overage players being one of the prime reasons.

By the 1920s interest in major league baseball had reached unprecedented levels. In contrast, youth participation was dropping sharply, with a 1924 survey by the National Amateur Athletic Foundation showing a

50 percent decline. This prompted serious concerns about the future of the game, not unlike the ones that are often expressed today. Newspapers offered dire predictions that the game was dying as a participation sport, and the *New York Times* wrote with dark irony that baseball "continues to hold its supremacy as the game Americans most like to see others play" (quoted in Harold Seymour, *Baseball: The People's Game*, 84).

Into that void stepped a series of youth leagues in the succeeding years.

22.4.1 American Legion Baseball. Major John L. Griffith was executive vice president of the National Amateur Athletic Foundation in 1924 when that organization's survey showed a 50 percent decline in baseball participation among boys. Griffith was also a member of the American Legion and urged his fellow members to address the problem. The result was the first American Legion tournament, staged in 1926.

22.4.2 Little League. Little League baseball was started by Carl Stotz in Williamsport, Pennsylvania, in 1939 to address a couple of wrongs. Stotz's nephews and their friends were having a hard time finding a diamond on which to play. In addition, some elements of the game were ill-suited for boys. Stotz explained: "Nothing was geared to children. The pitcher was too far away to throw hard enough to be effective, so he simply aimed the ball over the plate. The catcher, without a mask, chest protector, or shin guards, stooped over near the backstop, when there was one. The ball usually came to him on a bounce, making him more of a retriever than a catcher" (Carl Stotz and Kenneth D. Loss, *A Promise Kept*; quoted in Talmage Boston, *1939, Baseball's Pivotal Year*, 239–240). So Stotz formed a three-team league for boys twelve and under with sixty-foot baselines and a forty-foot pitching distance that became the first Little League.

The concept spread rapidly and in 1947 Stotz convinced U.S. Rubber (now Uniroyal) to become the corporate sponsor of Little League. Representatives of U.S. Rubber eventually gained control of the Little League board of directors, and Stotz was ousted in 1955. He remained bitter for the rest of his life.

22.4.3 Little League World Series. The first Little League World Series was held in Williamsport on August 21, 1947, with the hometown Maynard Midgets winning.

22.4.4 Babe Ruth Baseball. Babe Ruth Baseball began in Hamilton Township, New Jersey, in 1951 with a single ten-team league for players aged thirteen to fifteen. In the years since, the scope and age range have grown enormously.

22.4.5   PONY Baseball. PONY Baseball, an acronym for "Protect Our Nation's Youth," began in Washington, Pennsylvania, in 1951. Originally for thirteen- and fourteen-year-old boys, it experienced rapid growth and now features seven age groups.

22.4.6   Travel Teams. Following the lead of basketball, many of the best eleven- and twelve-year-old baseball players have forsaken traditional forms of regional competition. Instead these promising youngsters join travel teams and compete in their own tournaments. The national championship of travel baseball is held in Cooperstown, New York, in late August, at the same time as the Little League World Series. The idea was conceived by Lou Presutti on a visit to Cooperstown with his father in 1975.

Allan Simpson explained, "Youth baseball is essentially divided into two levels of competition: recreation leagues and travel leagues. Little League represents the former, and other longstanding organizations like Babe Ruth and PONY Baseball fall on that side of the fence. Membership is structured, with strict eligibility guidelines and rules governing where teams can draw players from, field dimensions and length of season. The competition may be purer, but rec leagues focus more on age than ability. . . . High-powered travel teams, who often play 120 games a year, can load up on players from all over the country" (*Baseball America*, October 27–November 9, 2003).

(v) Is Competition Necessary at All?

While capitalism was the model on which early professional clubs and leagues were based, it seemed most ill-suited to promoting the game. Whenever one club became dominant, it forced its competitors out of business and thereby hurt its own economics. Accordingly, some asked whether competition was necessary or at least sought to restrain competition.

As noted under "Leagues" (see **22.1.3**), clubs that were playing best two-out-of-three series were among the first to show an awareness of this reality. It became proverbial that the first two games of such a series would be split so that the clubs could make more money and the fans would have added excitement. In time, more ambitious schemes were proposed to move baseball away from being a competition and toward being a spectacle.

22.5.1   Socialism in Baseball. Notwithstanding its status as the American national pastime, baseball has a long tradition of socialistic practices. As much as it goes against the instincts of the successful capitalists who own baseball clubs to consider revenue sharing, professional sports as a business uniquely depends upon the success of one's rivals. Even George Will has allowed that "the great American game needs something un-American: socialism" (George F. Will, "Baseball and Socialism," June 18, 1981, reprinted in George F. Will, *Bunts*).

In the first major league, the National Association (1871–1875), many of the clubs were cooperative ventures in which the players split the revenues in lieu of collecting a salary. The co-ops competed against clubs run as stock companies, which were backed by local citizens who had each put forth a modest sum in return for a season ticket. The capital thus generated allowed these clubs to pay their players fixed salaries and thereby to corral better players. They thrashed the co-op clubs, most of which disbanded quickly, sometimes without ever playing a road game.

The advent of the National League brought a system more akin to capitalism to the fore. Although undermined by collusive practices (see **18.4.6**), competition between adversarial magnates remained the league's basic manner of conducting business until the 1890 season.

In that year, with three leagues fighting for survival, major league baseball drifted far from traditional capitalistic practices. This was most obvious in the Players' League where the players owned stock, but there were examples in the other leagues as well. In the American Association the other seven teams agreed to supply the new Brooklyn team with at least one quality player, though only two complied (David Nemec, *The Beer and Whisky League*, 188–189). Meanwhile several National League owners loaned John B. Day money to save the New York Giants from bankruptcy (the ramifications of this event are discussed in the next entry) (A. G. Spalding, quoted in *New York Clipper*, February 5, 1895; reprinted in *Spalding's Official Base Ball Guide, 1895*, 123).

The twentieth century also saw occasional examples of socialistic practices in baseball. When John McGraw and Andrew Freedman stripped the Baltimore Orioles in the middle of the 1902 campaign, other American League owners donated players to keep the league intact. After the 1939 season, at the urging of league president Will Harridge, every American League team agreed to offer one player off their roster for sale to the woeful Browns (William Mead, *Even the Browns*, 65). The basis of the All-American Girls Baseball League was socialistic, with players being drawn from a single pool and often shifted to help a weak franchise. After airplane travel became extensive in 1958, both major leagues adopted a disaster plan that called for a redistribution of talent if a team were to suffer a catastrophic accident.

In recent years, major league owners have agreed to revenue sharing of income from certain sources, yet have staunchly resisted such tendencies in other areas.

22.5.2 Syndicate Ownership. In 1883 and 1884 the Metropolitan Exhibition Company, of which John B. Day was president, owned the New York franchises in both the National League and the American Association. Day orchestrated at least one highly dubious transfer of players when the Association Metropolitans released Tim Keefe and Dude Esterbrook, and the two players then signed to play for the National League team.

David Nemec suggested that Columbus and Pittsburgh of the American Association may have been under the same ownership in 1884. He also noted that Brooklyn owner Charles Byrne bought the Cleveland club in 1885 and transferred its best players to Brooklyn. Two years later Byrne bought the Metropolitans and again pillaged the club's best players for his Brooklyn squad (David Nemec, *The Beer and Whisky League*, 72).

This destructive practice accelerated in the 1890s. In July 1890 New York Giants owner Day told his fellow National League magnates that he had to have $80,000 or he would be forced to sell his franchise to the Players' League. A. G. Spalding, John T. Brush, and other owners chipped in to keep him afloat (A. G. Spalding, quoted in *New York Clipper*, February 5, 1895; reprinted in *Spalding's Official Base Ball Guide, 1895*, 123). The precarious financial position of the National League after the threat from the Players' League led to several owners having at least a share of more than one franchise. In the American Association, St. Louis Brown Stockings owner Chris Von der Ahe acquired a controlling interest in the Cincinnati franchise.

The potential for conflicts of interest raised by these situations was nothing compared to what happened on the eve of the new century. The 1899 season saw two different dual-ownership situations in the twelve-team National League, with Harry von der Horst owning Baltimore and Brooklyn while the Robison brothers owned St. Louis and Cleveland. Baltimore manager John McGraw's canny maneuvers enabled the Orioles to remain respectable in spite of the transfer of several key players to Brooklyn. Cleveland, however, compiled a 20-134 record and spent the second half of the season on the road because the home fans wanted no part of the sorry spectacle. Several other owners had interests in rival clubs, and the public understandably became deeply cynical about the game's integrity.

Three years later another equally farcical situation occurred. John McGraw was managing Baltimore's entry in the American League but had a running feud with league president Ban Johnson. Eventually he helped New York Giants owner Andrew Freedman to buy a controlling interest in the Orioles. Freedman promptly released most of Baltimore's players and then signed many of them and McGraw for the Giants.

These fiascoes led to a 1927 rule banning ownership of more than one major league club. That rule was disregarded in the series of dubious transactions that led to the purchase of the Montreal Expos by the other twenty-nine club owners in 2001.

22.5.3 National Baseball Trust. The *reductio ad absurdum* of the era of syndicate ownership was a proposal made in 1901 by New York Giants owner Andrew Freedman. Under Freedman's plan the National League would be transformed into a holding company for the league's eight franchises. Each owner would receive a specified share of the whole league, thus jeopardizing the concept of competition.

Freedman and three other owners, John T. Brush, Frank Robison, and Arthur Soden, concocted the plan at a secret meeting at Freedman's estate at Red Bank, New Jersey, in July. It was leaked to the *New York Sun*, which broke the story on December 10 and 11, 1901, and inaugurated a heated controversy. With four owners on each side, a bitter deadlock ensued that was characterized by bizarre machinations.

Eventually the trust was defeated, but not before it had damaged the National League and helped the American League become established as a major league. One element that helped doom the plan was that Freedman assigned himself 30 percent of the stock, more than twice as much as any other owner.

(vi) Other Modes and Types of Competition

22.6.1 Interleague Play. While interleague play debuted in 1997, the idea had been around much earlier. Cubs president William Veeck (father of the innovative owner Bill Veeck) proposed interleague play in the major leagues on August 22, 1933. Veeck died suddenly six weeks later, and the idea was shelved.

Beginning in the 1950s the idea of interleague play was raised on a regular basis, usually coinciding with a scheme for expansion. The American League suggested interleague play on November 22, 1960, as part of a scheme to allow each league to add one expansion team. On July 31, 1962, the National League rejected Commissioner Ford Frick's proposal for interleague play in 1963. Red Smith wrote in 1973 that the idea had never succeeded because one league or the other was opposed, but that it was again gaining support (Red Smith, May 28, 1973; reprinted in *Red Smith on Baseball*). Several other instances were enumerated in the Spring 1997 issue of *Outside the Lines*, the newsletter of the SABR Business of Baseball committee.

The two Triple A minor leagues, the American Association and the International League, experimented with interleague play between 1988 and

1991. In the end it was decided that the added expense of travel outweighed the benefits.

22.6.2   Tripleheader. There have been three tripleheaders played in the major leagues, all in the National League: Brooklyn and Pittsburgh on September 1, 1890; Baltimore and Louisville on September 7, 1896; Pittsburgh and Cincinnati on October 2, 1920.

Quite a few tripleheaders were played in the minor leagues between 1878 and 1910, for a variety of reasons. The first took place on July 4, 1878, when New Bedford and Hartford sought to capitalize on the traditionally large Independence Day crowd by playing three games in three different cities—New Bedford, Taunton, and Providence. The Saginaw–Bay City Hyphens, the first and probably last team named in honor of a punctuation mark, hosted Montreal for three games on July 4, 1890, one in Bay City and two in Saginaw.

Making up postponed games was a more common reason for such exhibitions. A list of such games appears in George L. Moreland's *Balldom* (George L. Moreland, *Balldom*, 258–259; the list has a number of errors). At least two quadrupleheaders were played for this reason, both of which were sweeps. Researcher Mike Welsh reported that Sioux City beat St. Joseph 6-1, 15-7, 12-5, and 7-4 on September 15, 1889, while researcher Bill Deane found that Hudson topped Poughkeepsie by scores of 2-1, 6-4, 3-1, and 4-2 on September 20, 1903.

Manchester and Portland of the New England League played six games on September 4, 1899, for a different reason. It was the last day of the season, and Manchester was trying to catch Newport for the second-half title. Manchester did indeed win all six games, but the league office threw out all but one of them.

Regardless of the motive, such events had the obvious potential to make a farce of the game. George L. Moreland brought up the issue at the 1910 meeting of the National Association of Baseball Clubs, and a resolution was passed that banned clubs from playing more than two games in a day (George L. Moreland, *Balldom*, 259).

22.6.3   Day-Night Doubleheader. Major league baseball's first day-night doubleheader was played on September 27, 1939, when the Chicago White Sox hosted Cleveland. Separate admissions were charged.

22.6.4   Triangular Doubleheader. Greg Rhodes and John Snyder observed that the Reds scheduled four doubleheaders in 1899 where they hosted two different teams: Louisville and Cleveland on June 11 and September 10;

Louisville and St. Louis on August 6 and September 3. Since then there have been only two such doubleheaders played, on September 9, 1913, in St. Louis, and on September 25, 2000, in Cleveland (Greg Rhodes and John Snyder, *Redleg Journal*, 129).

22.6.5 Intercollegiate Match. Amherst College defeated Williams College 73-32 on July 1, 1859, in a match played by the looser rules of the "Massachusetts game." On the previous day the two schools had squared off in a chess match. The Williams students were let out of classes to watch the match, and nearly the entire student body was in attendance. Dean Sullivan's *Early Innings* includes a newspaper account of the match.

Clubs formed at colleges were a major part of the expansion of baseball during the 1860s, though intercollegiate competition was slowed by the fact that most colleges let out for the summer. By the late 1870s the college championship was being contested, and varsity baseball clubs began to proliferate in the 1880s.

22.6.6 College World Series. The University of California defeated Yale 8-7 to win the first College World Series in 1947.

22.6.7 Olympics. Baseball and the Olympics might seem a perfect match, but that hasn't proven to be the case, despite numerous efforts.

Two exhibition games were played at the 1912 Olympics in Stockholm. One featured a Swedish team against a team of American Olympians from other sports, and the other featured two squads of Americans (Pete Cava, "Baseball in the Olympics," *National Pastime* 12 [1992], 2–8).

Another exhibition game was staged at the 1936 Olympics in Berlin. The contestants were two American amateur teams, and they played in front of a crowd that was estimated at close to 100,000. The German spectators did not understand baseball very well, and the loudest applause was accorded to pop flies. By the end of the game the crowd had thinned considerably (M. E. Travaglini, "Olympic Baseball 1936: Was Es Das?," *National Pastime* 5 [1985], 46).

A Finnish game named Pesapello was demonstrated at the 1952 Olympics in Helsinki. The game was derived from baseball, but Red Smith was not impressed: "It was invented by Lauri Pihkala, a professor who wears a hearing aid and believes his game was modeled on baseball. Somebody must have described baseball to him when his battery was dead" (Red Smith, August 2, 1952, reprinted in *Red Smith on Baseball*).

The 1956 Games in Melbourne featured an exhibition game between an American and an Australian team. As the game progressed, the stadium began to fill up to its capacity of 114,000 as spectators arrived for the track and field events that were to follow the game. Thus the game may have been witnessed by the largest crowd in baseball history.

After another exhibition at the 1964 Olympic Games in Tokyo, baseball finally became a demonstration sport at the 1984 Games. The first medals in baseball were awarded at the 1992 Olympics in Barcelona.

22.6.8   Old-timers Games / Senior Professional Baseball Association. Obviously it took a few years before old-timers games could be played, but it was sooner than might be expected. Researcher John Thorn noted that in 1869 the Excelsiors of Brooklyn played a game against their 1859 first nine (cited in Eric Nadel and Craig R. Wright, *The Man Who Stole First Base*, 145).

Such games soon became a popular feature of nineteenth-century baseball. On April 13, 1896, old-timers games were played all over the country for Harry Wright Day, an event that commemorated the first anniversary of Wright's death.

The first attempt to transform the interest that such games generated into an ongoing venture was made in 1935. *Sporting News* reported that "A traveling baseball school, made up of old-time stars who will play games in connection with their instruction classes, has been announced for the coming summer by Walter J. Foley of Framingham, Mass" (*Sporting News*, January 10, 1935). A nineteen-game tour was planned that would feature such stars of the past as Cy Young, Rube Marquard, and Harry Hooper. The tour proved to be a fiasco, and Young had to dip into his own pocket to pay for the food and lodging of his fellow players (Reed Browning, *Cy Young*, 199–200).

A similar plan was inaugurated on May 31, 1989, when the Senior League was founded for players thirty-five and over. The league lasted one full season and part of a second one.

22.6.9   Winter Baseball. As noted in the entry on "Baseball on Ice" (**19.6**), it was quite common in the 1860s for the game to be played on ice during the winter months. John Thorn informs me that Hick Carpenter and Jimmy Macullar of the 1879 Syracuse Stars were the first active major leaguers to play winter ball in the Caribbean when both men played for the Colon Club of Cuba in the winter following the 1879 season.

For many years the most prominent form of professional baseball played over the fall and winter was barnstorming. Winter baseball thrived in California from the 1920s through the 1940s. The now popular fall instructional leagues began in 1957 when the Cardinals, Phillies, Tigers, and Yankees sent teams to Tampa (Kevin M. McCarthy, *Baseball in Florida*, 126).

Chapter 23

SPREADING
THE WORD

(i) The Writer's Game

As discussed under "Mass-circulated Rules" (1.3), the connection between early baseball and the written word was so intimate that Tom Melville concluded that "baseball was the first game Americans learned principally from print." Melville noted that town ball was "handed down from generation to generation orally" while baseball was learned by reading "printed regulations" (Tom Melville, *Early Baseball and the Rise of the National League*, 18).

This connection was symbolized most prominently in the custom of maintaining a written scorebook of a club's activities and matches. Previously the score, if kept at all, was maintained by someone making notches on a stick. Frank Pidgeon recalled that the Eckfords of Brooklyn were so excited when they scored their first run in their first match game against the Unions of Morrisania that some of their players "ran to the Umpire's book, to see how it looked on paper" (*Porter's Spirit of the Times*, January 10, 1857; quoted in George B. Kirsch, *The Creation of American Team Sports*, 111).

The years that followed would expand and deepen the connection between baseball and the written word.

23.1.1 Newspaper Account of a Game. Researcher George A. Thompson, Jr., discovered brief articles published in New York newspapers on April 25, 1823, that made mention of a recent game of "base ball." The one in the *National Advocate* reported "a company of active young men playing the manly and athletic game of 'base ball' at the Retreat in Broadway (Jones')." Neither this article nor the one in the *New-York Gazette and General Advertiser* mentioned a score or described the play in any detail (George A. Thompson Jr., "New York Baseball, 1823," *National Pastime* 21 [2001], 6–8).

The first known lengthy account of a baseball game appeared in the *New York Morning News* on October 22, 1845, and is reprinted in Dean Sullivan's *Early Innings*, pages 11–13.

23.1.2   Baseball Poem. John Thorn discovered a poem published in the *National Daily Baseball Gazette* in 1887 that was said to have first been published some fifty years earlier (*National Daily Baseball Gazette*, April 20, 1887). The poem was sent in by a man named Walter Colton Abbott, of Reading, Michigan, who said that it had originally appeared in the *New York News and Courier* around 1838. It read:

> Then dress, the dress, brave gallants all,
>   Don uniforms amain;
> Remember fame and honor call
>   Us to the field again.
> No shrewish tears shall fill our eye
>   When the ball club's in our hand,
> If we do lose we will not sigh,
>   Nor plead a butter hand.
> Let piping swain and craven jay
>   Thus weep and puling cry,
> Our business is like men to play,
>   Or know the reason why.

A note pointed out that "butter hand" was a precursor to butterfingers.

If Abbott's dating of the poem is accurate, it is likely the earliest baseball poem.

23.1.3   Baseball Reporters. Henry Chadwick is often considered to be the first reporter to write regularly about baseball, but he did not start doing so until 1856. William Rankin accordingly maintained that the first baseball reporter was William Cauldwell, who was secretary of the Unions of Morrisania and one of the proprietors of the *New York Sunday Mercury*. During 1853 he published periodic accounts of the club's activities (*Sporting News*, January 14, 1905).

23.1.4   Writers' Association. According to Francis C. Richter, the first baseball writers' association was a local group formed in Philadelphia in 1885 (Francis C. Richter, *Richter's History and Records of Base Ball*, 422). The first such organization of national scope, the Base Ball Reporters' Association of

America, was formed in Cincinnati on December 9, 1887, with George Munson of the *Sporting News* as president and Henry Chadwick as vice president. Its objectives were to "promote the welfare of the National Game, and to bring about a thorough and regular system of base ball scoring" (*Spalding's Official Base Ball Guide, 1888*, 97–98). The organization lasted three years.

The Baseball Writers Association of America was organized during the 1908 World Series with the less ambitious aim of ending "the overcrowding of the press box" by nonwriters that often occurred at big games (William G. Weart, writing in A. H. Spink, *The National Game*, 350). The organization survives to this day.

23.1.5 Interviews. Historian Paul Starr reported that the interview genre was developed in the 1860s by American newspapermen. He noted that it did not catch on in England and France for another two decades. He suggested that "America's more egalitarian, less deferential culture fostered the invention of a mode of journalistic inquiry that subjected important people to questioning by mere reporters." Even in the United States, many businessmen and politicians regarded an interview as "an impertinence" (Paul Starr, *The Creation of the Media*, 148).

Interviews of baseball players began to appear in the 1870s, but some of the subjects took an equally dim view of their interrogators. The earliest published interview I have found was conducted with Chicago captain Jimmy Wood in 1875. In it Wood bluntly informed the *Chicago Tribune* reporter that "there are thousands of people who buy the papers simply for the reports of the games, and who would not otherwise think of looking at a newspaper" (*Chicago Tribune*, June 18, 1875).

23.1.6 Baseball Guide. The first baseball guide was the *Beadle's Dime Base-Ball Player*, an annual edited by Henry Chadwick. It first appeared in 1860.

23.1.7 Baseball Periodical. The first American periodical devoted entirely to ball sports was Henry Chadwick's *The Ball Player's Chronicle*. The premier issue proclaimed, "for the first time in the annals of the game, the fraternity can now boast of an 'organ' of their own" and hailed the development as a sign that "base ball is a permanently established institution" (*The Ball Player's Chronicle*, June 6, 1867). The end of the playing season represented a major challenge to the fledgling periodical. On January 2, 1868, it changed its name to the *American Chronicle of Sports and Pastimes*, but the apparent effort to attract a larger readership was unsuccessful, and it folded in June.

23.1.8 Hardcover Book. In 1868 Henry Chadwick published a book that, depending on whether one believes the title page or the page headers, was entitled either *The Game of Base Ball* or *The American Game of Base Ball*. As late as 1888 the scarcity of books about baseball was attracting notice: "Universal as has been the baseball mania, it is an astonishing fact how little literature has sprung up in connection with the game" (*Outing*, November 1888). That would change.

23.1.9 Dictionary of Baseball Jargon. Henry Chadwick compiled a list of baseball terms and definitions for the 1868 book mentioned in the preceding entry. He put together a more comprehensive glossary of terms for the British during an 1874 tour of England by top American baseball players. These last four entries should give some indication of the extent to which Chadwick single-handedly framed the early experience of baseball.

23.1.10 Baseball Novels. Jonathan Fraser Light suggested that the first work of fiction with a baseball theme may have been an 1868 novel entitled *Changing Base* by William Everett (Jonathan Fraser Light, *The Cultural Encyclopedia of Baseball*, 101). As late as 1890 a publisher remarked: "It's a wonder to me that nobody has yet written a baseball novel. I should think that such a venture would meet with a large and ready sale, if it did not become a craze with the horde of admirers of the game" ("A Baseball Novel Wanted," *New York Tribune*, July 20, 1890; reprinted in the *National Pastime* 25 [2005], 126). The oversight was soon addressed, and novels about baseball rapidly became popular.

23.1.11 Books by Ballplayers. In 1884 John F. Morrill wrote an instructional book called *Batting and Pitching, with Fine Illustrations of Attitudes* (Jonathan Fraser Light, *The Cultural Encyclopedia of Baseball*, 102). John Montgomery Ward's *Base Ball: How to Become a Player* followed in 1888.

23.1.12 Autobiographies by Ballplayers. The first autobiography of a baseball player was Mike Kelly's 1888 *Play Ball*, which like many subsequent ones was ghostwritten. The subtitle of the work was either *Stories of the Ball Field* or *Stories of the Diamond Field*, depending on whether the cover or the title page is to be believed (Marty Appel, *Slide, Kelly, Slide*, 129).

23.1.13 Baseball Encyclopedia. George L. Moreland's 1914 *Balldom* and Ernest J. Lanigan's 1922 *The Baseball Cyclopedia* were incomplete but important early attempts to compile historical records of baseball clubs and players. S. C. Thompson and Hy Turkin came out with the first attempt at a comprehensive book of this sort in 1951. Macmillan entered the fray in 1969 with *The Baseball Encyclopedia*, which was also the first book of any kind to be typeset by computer. Pete Palmer and John Thorn brought out the first edition of their monumental *Total Baseball* in 1989.

(ii) Baseball in Other Media

Baseball enthusiasts have attempted to bring their favorite game into a surprising number of media, with mixed results.

23.2.1 Photographs. Connie Mack claimed that a photograph of boys playing baseball on Boston Commons appeared in Robin Carver's 1834 *The Book of Sports* (Connie Mack, *My Sixty-Six Years in the Big Leagues*, 213). This was, in fact, just a woodcut (David Block, *Baseball Before We Knew It*, 197).

Baseball and photography both began to develop in earnest in the 1840s. But early photographs were ruined by any sort of movement, and only a few images of baseball before 1860 are known to exist. Mark Rucker noted that only "a daguerreotype, a few ambrotypes, and some salt prints" have been discovered. By the early 1860s, however, photographs of baseball players became much more common due to the popularity of "cartes de visite." Rucker's wonderful book, *Base Ball Cartes*, offers many stunning examples.

Tom Shieber attempted to pinpoint the earliest baseball photograph. While he acknowledged that dating photos from the mid-nineteenth century is an inexact science, he settled upon one that featured the 1855 Atlantic Base Ball Club of Brooklyn (Tom Shieber, "The Earliest Baseball Photography," *National Pastime* 17 [1997], 101–104).

Researcher John Thorn reports that the earliest halftone reproduction of a photograph to appear in a newspaper was printed in an issue of the *New York Graphic* in 1880. The first photographs of baseball players in action to appear in a newspaper are believed to have been the ones in a set that was published in the *New York World* on April 29, 1886. It was not until the 1890s that it became common for newspapers to print photographs of baseball players.

23.2.2 Songs. In early baseball it was quite common for clubs to walk to the ballpark singing the team song. The Knickerbocker club was joined by the Gotham and Eagle clubs at a dinner on December 15, 1854, at Fijux's restaurant in New York. James Whyte Davis of the Knickerbocker club composed a song for the occasion called "Ball Days," which was so well received that it was printed. In 1858, J. Randolph Blodgett, a player for the Niagaras of Buffalo, published the sheet music for a piece called "The Base Ball Polka." The first published pieces with words appear to have been "The Bat and Ball" and "Base Ball Fever," both in 1867.

The All-American Girls Baseball League revived this tradition by having a victory song.

23.2.3   Records. "Slide Kelly Slide," a popular song about Mike Kelly, was recorded as early as 1893 but not widely distributed. "Jimmy and Maggie at a Baseball Game" became the first baseball recording to receive extensive distribution in 1906.

23.2.4   Symphonies. No baseball team seems better suited for epic treatment than the Brooklyn Dodgers. Perhaps that is what inspired composer Robert Russell Bennett, even though he was a Giants fan, to write a 1941 composition entitled *Symphony in D for the Dodgers*.

The symphony was first played on WOR in New York City on May 16, 1941, and was then staged at Lewisohn Stadium on August 3. It was conducted by Hans Wilhelm Steinberg and consisted of four movements. The joyful opening sonata sought to depict "the bedlam and wonderful nonsense exuded by the citizens of Brooklyn when the beloved bums win one." This was succeeded by a dirge that conveyed the city's gloom following a Dodger defeat.

The third movement portrayed the efforts of energetic Brooklyn president Larry MacPhail to acquire Bob Feller. Sportswriter Bob Considine commented that MacPhail was "typically in brass. He is in the form of a scherzo, threaded with hunting horn tootles. Seems the guy is out looking for talent to buy. Beneath the hunting horn ta-ra'ing can be heard a scraping sound which could either have been a carpenter working on the foundation of [Hans] Steinberg's podium or the symbolic sound of the Brooklyn stockholders walking the floor at night, worrying about the way MacPhail is treating O. P. M., which, of course, means other people's money. MacPhail gets into the dag-dangest session with Alva Bradley, owner of Bobby Feller, that you ever heard emanate from a tuba. But even though MacPhail pleads for Feller through the good offices of 17 clarinets, 14 oboes, 83 bull fiddles and a boat load of refugee French horns, Bradley, the louse, turns him down. 'No,' Bradley answers with 64 saxophones, a mouth organ and comb wrapped in tissue paper" (Bob Considine, "Symphony in D for the Dodgers," *Washington Post*, August 6, 1941, 18).

Despite this disappointment, the symphony ended on a high note. Dodgers broadcaster Red Barber strode from the wings for the final movement and, backed by orchestral music, described Dolph Camilli beating the Giants with a dramatic home run.

The symphony was not a critical success, with the *New York Times*'s Noel Straus observing: "Much was expected of this work with its rich opportunities for wit and excitement. But in reality it fell rather flat on the ears of the moderate-sized audience present. One rather anticipated that the woodwinds would go in for a lot of wild pitching, that there would be barrages of hits by the kettle-drums, and that the brasses would smack at least a few homers over the distant bleachers . . . but nothing of the sort materialized" (Noel Straus, "Stadium Premiere for Baseball Epic," *New York Times*, August 4, 1941).

23.2.5   Operas. In 1888 John Philip Sousa wrote the score for a comic opera entitled *Angela, or The Umpire's Revenge*. The plot revolved around a pitcher whose complaints about an umpire's calls prompt the latter to retaliate by interfering with the pitcher's romance (H. Allen Smith and Ira L. Smith, *Low and Inside*, 221).

23.2.6   Motion Picture. Jonathan Fraser Light reported that Thomas Edison released a fragmentary series of baseball images in 1898. Eight years later Edison created the first movie about baseball with a story line, entitled *How the Office Boy Saw the Ball Game*. In 1911 the National Commission negotiated to sell rights to film the World Series, but there are conflicting reports as to whether a movie was made (Jonathan Fraser Light, *The Cultural Encyclopedia of Baseball*, 466). The first footage from an actual baseball game was taken in 1903 during a postseason game between Cleveland and Cincinnati (Lonnie Wheeler and John Baskin, *The Cincinnati Game*, 50). The first ballplayer to appear in a film was Hal Chase in 1911.

(iii) Broadcasting Refinements

Chapter 16 on marketing told of how new methods of broadcasting had to overcome initial resistance. In this section we note some significant advances in radio and television broadcasting.

23.3.1   Pregame Shows. Red Barber called his first Brooklyn Dodger game on Opening Day of the 1939 season, bringing to an end a pact between the three New York teams that prohibited radio broadcasts. For the historic event, Barber was able to convince radio station WOR to give him extra time beforehand to interview managers Bill Terry and Leo Durocher (Bob Edwards, *Fridays with Red*, 61).

23.3.2   Taboos Against Mentioning a No-hitter. Long before radio was invented, it was traditional for teammates not to mention a potential no-hitter in the dugout. Ernest Lanigan explained in 1913, "One sure way to spoil a no-hit game for a pitcher is to remark, particularly in the ninth inning,

'Well, they haven't made a hit thus far.' That almost invariably brings forth one or more bingles" (*Sporting Life*, August 7, 1913).

Red Barber explained how this superstition was transferred to announcers: "This hoodoo business started in the dugouts with a fairly reasonable premise—a teammate would not mention a possible no-hitter for fear of putting undue pressure on his pitcher, who just might be pitching away blissfully unaware of what he was doing. Then, before radio came along, this hoodoo, or jinx, got up to the press box, and the writers turned silent whenever the occasion presented itself. When radio got going, the hoodoo spread into the broadcasting booths. Not mine" (quoted in Bob Edwards, *Fridays with Red*, 76).

Indeed, in the first major league game that Barber broadcast, Lon Warneke had a no-hitter broken up with one out in the ninth inning. Barber mentioned that no-hitter during the game because he was unaware of the taboo, but he continued to defy the convention throughout his career.

23.3.3 Athletes-turned-broadcasters. The first ballplayer to become a broadcaster was Jack Graney, who called Indians games from 1932 to 1954. Not everyone was receptive to the idea. When Graney was invited to announce the 1934 World Series, Commissioner Kenesaw Mountain Landis forbade him from doing so on the grounds that the former American Leaguer would be partisan to the junior circuit. Graney wrote tersely to Landis, "my playing days are over. I am now a sportscaster and should be regarded as such." He was allowed to call the 1935 Series (Ted Patterson, "Jack Graney, The First Player-Broadcaster," *Baseball Research Journal* 2 [1973], reprinted in *Baseball Historical Review* 1981, 52–57). Graney's smooth transition to the airwaves paved the way for others, including Harry Heilmann, Waite Hoyt, and Gabby Street, and eventually for broadcasting to become a popular second career for ballplayers.

23.3.4 TV Commercials. Red Barber delivered three commercial messages during the first telecast of a major league game. Red later recounted, "In the middle of the agreed inning, I held up a bar of Ivory Soap and said something about it being a great soap . . . a few innings later I put on a Mobil Gas service-station cap, held up a can of oil, and said what a great oil it was . . . and for Wheaties? This was a big production number. Right on the camera, right among the fans, I opened a box of Wheaties, shook out a bowlful, sliced a banana, added a spoon of sugar, poured on some milk—and said, 'That's a Breakfast of Champions'" (Red Barber, *The Broadcasters*, 134).

23.3.5 Color Television. The first major league game to be telecast in color aired in New York City on CBS Channel 2 on August 11, 1951, and featured the Brooklyn Dodgers and the Boston Braves. Although viewers had to have a homemade converter in order to see the action in color, a CBS spokesman estimated that some one thousand sets were tuned to the game, with ten thousand fans watching the historic event. Special guests at Gimbel's Department Store and at CBS headquarters also watched the telecast (*New York Times*, August 12, 1951).

Red Smith wrote favorably of the experiment the next day but noted: "There was some slight running of colors. When Charley Dressen, the Dodgers' resident djinn, stood on the bare base path to chat with one of his runners, his white uniform was as immaculate as a prom queen's gown. But the camera followed him as he returned to the coach's box beside third, and against this background of turf he turned green, like cheap jewelry.

"Light blues ran a good deal, too, washing across the picture. The Braves' gray traveling uniforms took on an unnatural bluish cast, and when the camera swept the shirtsleeved crowd one had the impression that all the customers had been laundered together with too much bluing in the water. The dark blue of the Dodgers' caps, however, remained fast and true" (Red Smith, August 12, 1951, reprinted in *Red Smith on Baseball*).

Thus for all Tommy Lasorda's claims to have bled Dodger blue, he was not the first Dodger manager to do so.

23.3.6 Instant Replays. According to Jonathan Fraser Light, the first use of instant replay in a baseball game took place on WPIX-TV in New York on July 17, 1959 (Jonathan Fraser Light, *The Cultural Encyclopedia of Baseball*, 372). But it was not until the 1965 season that major league baseball agreed to let ABC use instant replays as a regular feature of baseball telecasts.

Many doubted that the innovation would be good for the game. On the eve of the 1965 season an AP wire service piece noted: "The television people have promised to train the isolated camera on any and all dramatic, close and controversial plays, thereby enabling the viewer to ascertain immediately whether his first impression of the umpire was correct—that he was nothing but a blind Tom." Players like Jim Gentile expressed concern that umpires would respond to this scrutiny by becoming "overcautious" (AP: *Frederick* [Md.] *Post*, March 30, 1965).

Others felt that the effects on umpires would be worse than that. Columnist Ed Nichols suggested that the Men in Blue would no longer get the benefit of the doubt on close plays: "Everyone in the country will be in position to second guess them . . . there are sure to be a lot of humiliating moments for the umpires" (Ed Nichols, "Isolated Camera Tough on Umps," *Salisbury Times*, December 23, 1964).

The new technology was first used in an ABC broadcast on April 17, 1965 (Bucky Summers, "Still Baseball on TV," *Frederick* [Md.] *Post*, April 20,

1965). Before long it became clear that the initial fears were unjustified. Umpire Joe Paparella later explained, "CBS [sic] had been televising the [American League] games and then wanted permission to use the replays. [American League president] Mr. [Will] Harridge, [umpire] Cal Hubbard, and I talked about it. CBS showed us some slides of what they would use. They said they were not going to try to embarrass an umpire but just show a close play and let the viewers decide. I'm tickled to death that we approved it for the simple reason that it has shown that umpires are right 99 percent of the time. It has been a shot in the arm to umpires because the public now realizes what a good job umpires do" (quoted in Larry R. Gerlach, *The Men in Blue*, 145).

Sportswriter Arthur Daley reached a similar conclusion: "When television came up with an invention called 'instant replay,' most officials—baseball as well as football—regarded it fearfully as a device of the devil. It would expose their every mistake to the second guessers. They need not have worried. Only with the rarest exceptions does instant replay do anything but confirm the astonishing accuracy of every call" (Arthur Daley, "The Human Factor," *New York Times*, December 20, 1968).

The prominence of instant replays in the 1965 season does appear to have had one notable effect on the umpiring profession. Sportswriter Joseph Durso suggested that the men in blue, fearful of being made to look bad, were becoming more willing to consult with colleagues and reverse a call if necessary. Umpire Tom Gorman commented: "Maybe umpires are consulting each other more. If they are that's good umpiring. You know, if a man can't see a play clearly, he ought to ask somebody's advice, but never on a judgment play or for any reason related to cameras" (Joseph Durso, "The Magic Eye," *New York Times*, August 3, 1965).

23.3.7 Slow-motion Replays. Slow-motion replay was first used during an Army-Navy football game on December 31, 1964 (Jonathan Fraser Light, *The Cultural Encyclopedia of Baseball*, 727). Two months later ABC president Tom Moore announced plans to bring the technique to baseball along with instant replay: "We don't feel baseball has been adequately covered on TV in the past. We propose to use multi cameras, including the instant replay, stop action and slow motion. We intend to apply some of the techniques that have been used so effectively in football. And there are many more opportunities to do it in baseball. For example, while the manager is on the mound we might analyze the situation that confronts him" (Sid Ziff, "TV and Baseball," *Los Angeles Times*, February 28, 1965).

At the initial telecast on April 17, 1965, the slow-motion feature was deemed a disappointment: "The slow motion sequences that were used were taken by the same camera which originally shot the play so that the audience was still the same distance from it and the distance was fuzzy." This was blamed on the fact that it was more difficult for a baseball producer to predict where the action would occur than was the case in football (Bucky Summers, "Still Baseball on TV," *Frederick* [Md.] *Post*, April 20, 1965). The technique was refined and reintroduced by NBC for the 1966 World Series (*Zanesville Times Recorder*, October 6, 1966).

23.3.8   Split Screen. Red Smith said that split screens were introduced because of Jackie Robinson's daring baserunning, so that television viewers could see both the pitcher and Robinson poised to take off from first base (Red Smith, October 25, 1972, reprinted in *Red Smith on Baseball*). If so, the practice did not become common for many years. A 1967 *New York Times* article reported that split screens had occasionally been used in baseball but that ABC was now introducing split-screen instant replay to football (Jack Gould, "TV: A.B.C. Football, Coverage Scores," *New York Times*, December 4, 1967).

23.3.9   Game of the Week. National telecasts of a featured game began when ABC's *Game of the Week* debuted on June 6, 1953.

23.3.10   Satellite Broadcasts. Baseball was first broadcast overseas on July 23, 1962, as part of a groundbreaking experiment with the Telstar satellite. Viewers in Europe were able to watch twenty minutes of live clips from all over the United States, including ninety seconds of action from a game at Wrigley Field between the Cubs and Phillies. The innovation caused *Chicago Tribune* reporter Edward Prell to wonder whether the Europeans who interrupted their dinner to watch the game had become the first witnesses of night baseball at Wrigley Field (*Chicago Tribune*, July 24, 1962).

Chapter 24

TRAVELING MEN

THE LINK between baseball and traveling is profound. Early visiting clubs often had to overcome considerable hardship just to get to the game. For example, a 36-0 loss by the Blue Belts of Leland, Michigan, to the White Stars of Traverse City in an 1876 game was mitigated by the fact that the Blue Belts "walked six miles and came the rest of the way in a rough wagon" (*Grand Traverse* [Mich.] *Herald*, September 7, 1876). Needless to say, visiting clubs were no-shows for a wide variety of reasons, including "choppy seas" (*South Haven Sentinel*, August 11, 1877). It is no coincidence that professional baseball and the building of a national network of railroads in the 1860s and 1870s were near-simultaneous developments. Indeed there is good reason to believe that the railroads saved baseball.

(i) Getting from Game to Game

24.1.1 Tour. The Excelsior club of Brooklyn left on June 30, 1860, for a twelve-day, thousand-mile tour of New York State that saw them beat clubs in Albany, Troy, Buffalo, Rochester, and Newburgh-on-the-Hudson. The point of the excursion was not so much the competition as providing a showcase for the game, by allowing spectators outside the New York City area to see baseball played with a new degree of skill and finesse. One account noted: "no such ball playing was ever before witnessed in Buffalo. The manner in which the Excelsiors handled the ball, the ease with which they caught it, under all circumstances, the precision with which they threw it to the bases, and the tremendous hits they gave into the long field made the optics of the Buffalo players glisten with admiration and protrude" (*Brooklyn Eagle*, July 9, 1860; quoted in James L. Terry, *Long Before the Dodgers*, 31).

Later that summer the Excelsiors accepted an invitation from a Baltimore club of the same name to travel to Maryland for a game. The emphasis was again on ceremony rather than competition: "It was not thought that the Baltimore Club had *the least show to win*, it was to be a game of instructions" (William Ridgely Griffith, *The Early History of Amateur Base Ball in the State of Maryland*; reprinted in *Maryland Historical Magazine* Vol. 87, No. 2 [Summer 1992], 204).

After the Civil War the rapid expansion of the railway system made far more ambitious tours possible. The Nationals of Washington became the first Eastern team to venture west of the Allegheny in 1867 when they made a three-thousand-mile excursion that included stops in Columbus, Cincinnati, Louisville, Indianapolis, St. Louis, and Chicago. The 1868 Red Stockings of Cincinnati were the first club from what was then known as the West to make an extensive tour of the East. The following year the Red Stockings again crisscrossed the country and took advantage of the newly completed transcontinental railroad to become the first club to venture out to California.

In 1874 Albert Goodwill Spalding organized the first international tour, taking the Athletics of Philadelphia and the Red Stockings of Boston to England and Ireland for a tour (see A. G. Spalding, *America's National Game*, Chapter 13, and Adrian C. Anson, *A Ball Player's Career*, Chapter 9, for the descriptions of two participants. Peter Levine's *A. G. Spalding and the Rise of Baseball*, 17–20, provides a more objective account). Frank Bancroft took the first team of Americans to Cuba in 1879. The first around-the-world tour took place following the 1888 season, when Spalding escorted the Chicago team and an all-star team on a trip to Australia, with stops in Egypt and Europe on the way home (see A. G. Spalding, *America's National Game*, Chapter 18, and Adrian C. Anson, *A Ball Player's Career*, Chapters 18–31, for descriptions by two participants. Peter Levine's *A. G. Spalding and the Rise of Baseball*, 99–109, again provides a more objective account). Pacific Coast League magnate Mike Fisher took a team on a three-month tour of Japan, China, and the Philippines beginning on November 3, 1908. Another around-the-world tour took place following the 1913 season (see James E. Elfers's *The Tour to End All Tours* for a first-rate chronicle of this expedition).

24.1.2 Eating on the Run. Even today, eating appropriately while traveling can be difficult. For early ball clubs the challenge of arranging meals in a way that would allow them to play their best was daunting. This was compounded by the temptation to indulge in the feasts that host clubs often provided for their guests.

In time, clubs learned the benefits of moderation. When the Nationals stopped in Columbus, Ohio, during their 1867 tour, the local paper observed: "At the close of the game the players partook of a cold lunch, which had been spread in a tent on the grounds. The [host] Capitals, in this respect, followed the recommendation of the Nationals, and we think this plan is better than to get an elaborate meal at a hotel" (*Ohio State Journal,* August 9, 1867).

Cincinnati manager Harry Wright "had a regular diet for [the Red Stockings] while traveling, and the strongest stimulant they were permitted to imbibe was a very delicious drink commonly known as egg lemonade, which the veteran Henry christened the 'Red Stocking punch'" (R. M. Larner, "Beginning of Professional Baseball in Washington," *Washington Post,* July 3, 1904).

When Deacon White captained the Forest City club of Cleveland in 1872, teammate Al Pratt later recalled: "we were never allowed anything but a cold snack at noon. We always went to lunch right at 12 o'clock and then ate but a little cold meat. Some warm meat was imbibed, but everything else cold. White would as soon let us have eat poison as a heavy, warm meal at noon. Some young players of today may laugh at White's methods. I never did. I thought they were all right. I think so yet. That cold, light lunch kept our stomachs from being overworked, our head clear and our eyesight good. The best effect was on the eyes. White always claimed that a man who persisted in eating heavy and warm food at lunch would not have as clear an eye or as good a head for hours after as the man who took his food cold" (*Sporting Life,* April 15, 1905).

24.1.3 Trains. The popular image of early travel by baseball clubs, especially in the Negro Leagues and minor leagues, is of endless trips on the team bus. In fact trains were the virtually exclusive method of transportation for baseball players—regardless of race—from the dawn of professional baseball until the 1920s.

The railroads offered discounts to baseball clubs, though there was talk before the 1887 season that these would be discontinued due to interstate commerce laws (*Cleveland Leader and Herald,* March 13, 1887). But the reality was that there was no affordable alternative for transporting an entire team. Thus the only exceptions were for individual players who chose to travel on their own: "Some of the minor leaguers ride bicycles, or get the old man to take them to the next town in the buggy" ("The Great National Game in Dollars and Cents," *Washington Post,* May 9, 1909).

Rail travel remained a staple of baseball for more than half a century, and the comfort associated with train rides improved considerably over that period. As noted under "African-American Tours" (see **20.1.8**), some touring African-American clubs traveled in spacious touring cars in which they could sleep in comparative luxury. A 1916 article remarked that major leaguers now all had lower berths, as sleeping in an upper berth was "very 'bush league'" (Willis E. Johnson, "The Player's Life in the Major Leagues," *Sporting Life*, March 4, 1916). This led to the usual grumbling by old-timers. Early sportswriter T. Z. Cowles wrote in 1918: "Ball players of the long ago period were not like their fellows of 1918, born with gold spoons in their mouths. The epoch of princely salaries had not yet dawned. They traveled in ordinary sleeping cars at night, when they could get them. If not, they sat up. No special Pullmans for them" (T. Z. Cowles, *Chicago Tribune*, June 16, 1918).

24.1.4 Team Buses. Once buses were invented in the mid-1920s, owners soon found them to be cheaper and began to switch to them.

24.1.5 Automobiles. Car travel has never been a major part of baseball because of the need for multiple automobiles to transport a team. One of the rare exceptions left the players involved in little mood to repeat the experiment. Benton Stark noted that the New York Giants and Brooklyn Dodgers traveled to their 1904 season opener in a procession of automobiles, which were still a novelty. One of the vehicles collided with a horse-drawn wagon on the Brooklyn Bridge, and the players decided to continue the trip by train (Benton Stark, *The Year They Called Off the World Series*, 105–106).

24.1.6 Airplanes. On March 6, 1919, the New York Giants announced that they would fly to their season opener in Philadelphia. The *New York World* reported that since taking his first flight, Giants manager John McGraw "has never ceased to talk about the birdman stuff." Accordingly, the Curtiss Aeroplane & Motor Company offered to provide a plane to transport the entire team (*New York World*, March 16, 1919). They eventually took the train instead.

The Hollywood club of the Pacific Coast League flew to a game on July 15, 1928. Hollywood owner Bill Lane was convinced "that airplane travel for ball clubs will soon be the rule and not the exception in a few years and decided that he'd be the first club owner to give it a try" (*Los Angeles Times*, July 17, 1928).

The first major league team to fly to a game was the Cincinnati Reds, who flew from St. Louis to Chicago on June 8, 1934, in two Ford Tri-Motors chartered from American Airlines. The innovative Larry MacPhail authorized the flight because of a heat wave, but six Reds players chose a sweltering train ride instead.

There were a few more plane trips in the ensuing years. The Red Sox flew from St. Louis to Chicago on July 30, 1936, and Brooklyn flew the same route on May 7, 1940. But it was not until after World War II that plane travel became common.

On April 16, 1946, the Yankees announced plans to become the first club to travel exclusively by air (Cliff Trumpold, *Now Pitching: Bill Zuber from Amana*, 97). The first team to own its own plane was the Brooklyn Dodgers, who purchased a forty-four-passenger twin-engine plane on January 4, 1957.

24.1.7 Cross-country Trips. The Red Stockings traveled to California in 1869, but the trip west took nine days and the return trip eleven days, making such trips impractical on any kind of regular basis (Greg Rhodes and John Erardi, *The First Boys of Summer*, 66–69, 72).

The Los Angeles Bulldogs of the American Football League became in 1937 "the first West Coast professional team to host eastern rivals on a regular basis" (Robert W. Peterson, *Pigskin*, 123). Baseball owners were not unmindful of the westward shift of the population, but baseball's daily schedule made it far more difficult to accommodate games in California.

After the 1941 season, a deal to move the St. Louis Browns to Los Angeles was almost consummated. Ratification of the arrangement was scheduled to take place on December 8, 1941 (*Sporting News*, August 4, 1962). Fatefully, the attack on Pearl Harbor occurred on the day before. The ensuing wartime restrictions on travel eliminated any talk of major league play in California.

After the war the idea continued to percolate, but the general consensus was that it wouldn't be financially viable unless two clubs in the same league were located on the West Coast. Finally the Dodgers and Giants made the historic decision to move to California in 1957. Major league baseball was played on the West Coast for the first time when the Dodgers and Giants faced off at San Francisco's Seals Stadium on April 15, 1958.

24.1.8 International Travel. The first major league game played outside the United States took place on April 14, 1969, when the Montreal Expos hosted the St. Louis Cardinals.

24.1.9 Accidents. It was proverbial for many years that a way to ensure a safe train trip was to travel with a baseball club. Baseball clubs have used a wide variety of methods of transportation. While there have been accidents on all of them, the number has continued to be remarkably low considering the millions of miles traveled by baseball clubs. In particular, while individual players have perished in travel-related accidents, teams have been extraordinarily fortunate.

For example, in July 1911 the location of the St. Louis Cardinals' car was changed before a train trip from Philadelphia to Boston. Twelve passengers were killed and many more injured, but the St. Louis players escaped unscathed.

There have been a few tragic exceptions. Raymond Owens and Buster Brown of the Negro American League's Cincinnati Buckeyes were killed in a 1942 accident while returning from a game in Buffalo. On June 23, 1946, the team bus of the Spokane Indians went over a three-hundred-foot cliff in the Cascade Mountains, killing nine players. The team bus of the Duluth, Minnesota, team of the Northern League collided with a truck on July 24, 1948, killing four players and the manager. A 1901 trolley car accident injured six members of the Syracuse team, with future major leaguer Lee De-Montreville suffering a broken leg (*Sporting News*, June 8, 1901). One of the California Angels' team buses overturned on the New Jersey turnpike on May 21, 1992, with manager Buck Rodgers suffering serious injuries.

24.1.10   Beat Reporters. Henry Chadwick, who was then writing for *The Ball Player's Chronicle*, was one of the first reporters to travel with a ball club when he accompanied the Nationals of Washington on their historic 1867 tour.

24.1.11   Broadcasters. Radio announcers began traveling with teams around 1948. Before that year it was customary for announcers to recreate road games for their listeners based upon accounts of the game they received via telegraph.

24.1.12   Driven to Mound. In 1959 Milwaukee Braves general manager John McHale decided to speed up games by having relief pitchers driven from the bullpen to the mound. He selected a Harley-Davidson "Topper" motor scooter with a special sidecar because its light weight and large tires meant that "pitchers can be driven directly across the outfield turf to the mound. Heavier vehicles would have to take the longer route on the cinder path bordering the fences to the first-base dugout, where the pitcher would still have to walk to the center of the diamond" (*Virgin Island Daily News*, July 14, 1960). The motor scooter was first used on June 23, 1959, when relief pitcher Hal Jeffcoat was brought in from the bullpen by uniformed chauffeur John "Freckles" Bonneau (*Sporting News*, July 1, 1959).

(ii) Spring Training

There are many claims as to which club initiated the custom of spring training. It is not a case of conflicting accounts so much as the fact that anything resembling today's spring training would have been prohibitively expensive for early baseball clubs. If you had asked the captain of an early team if he planned to take his players south for a month to get in condition, he probably would have had a hearty laugh and told you that it sounded like a wonderful idea if you'd like to foot the bill.

As a result, while there was an awareness of all the elements of spring training from the early days of baseball, these components emerged in fits and starts. It was many years before formal training camps became customary, which means that the various elements of spring training are best considered separately.

24.2.1 Preliminary Workouts. It has of course always been appreciated that players in peak condition will play best.

As noted in the entry on "Muscle Building" (**2.4.1**), the Red Stockings of Boston conducted extensive workouts at a local gymnasium before the 1872 season. Tim Murnane reported that these endeavors began each year on March 15 and lasted until the weather allowed them to move outdoors (Tim Murnane, *Boston Globe*, April 19, 1896; February 19, 1900). Before the 1875 season, the New Haven club engaged in a serious workout: "First, each man runs a quarter of a mile, then gentle exercise upon the horizontal bar is taken, after which a trial at vaulting on the vaulting horse is indulged; then a series of Indian Club swinging, followed by the whole team pulling about one mile on the whole apparatus. After all this, the club retires to a bowling alley where they pass and strike balls" (*New York Sunday Mercury*, April 11, 1875; reprinted in Jim Charlton, ed., *The Baseball Chronology*, 27).

Undoubtedly every captain in the country would have liked to put his charges through similar workouts. But the reality was that clubs could not afford to pay players for such training drills, and players could not afford to quit their offseason jobs to exercise. As a result, unless most of the players had spent the winter in the area, preseason training in early baseball was primarily done by individuals without supervision. As discussed under "Trainers" (see **21.10**), that did not start to change until around 1898 when trainers began to assume control.

24.2.2 Southern Tours. Early clubs were equally aware that a trip through the South would be a wonderful way to prepare for the season. Yet again, the problem was finding an affordable way of doing so.

In 1868 the Atlantics of Brooklyn announced plans for an ambitious Southern tour that would take them to New Orleans, Mobile, Savannah, and other cities (*American Chronicle of Sports and Pastimes*, January 2, 1868). Cold weather postponed their departure several times, and the tour was eventually canceled due to the weather and what was tactfully described as an inability to "come to terms as to the share of receipts" (*American Chronicle of Sports and Pastimes*, February 13, 1868; February 27, 1868; March 5, 1868).

The Red Stockings of Cincinnati and the White Stockings of Chicago both traveled to New Orleans in April 1870 to play exhibition games and round into shape. The Mutuals of New York went to Savannah, Georgia, in 1871 to put the club in condition (*New York Globe*, reprinted in *Sporting Life*, March 31, 1906). In 1877 the Indianapolis entry in the League Alliance conducted a preseason tour that started in Texas and continued on to New Orleans, Memphis, and St. Louis. But such tours demanded great planning, and there were any number of obstacles.

One of the most daunting was that baseball enthusiasm in the South often lagged far behind the rest of the country. When Frank Bancroft tried to arrange a stop in Montgomery, Alabama, in 1880, he received a firm "no" and this discouraging explanation: "Several reasons might be assigned for this opinion of mine, but the first one is likely to be conclusive: *we have no local club*. For that matter we have *no ball ground*, and a personal experience justifies me in saying that our people have never shown the slightest enthusiasm over baseball as a fine art. You might get your work in quite profitably selling corn solvents or worm medicines; tame Indians, dressed simply in scalping knives and brass band, have been successful lately as advertising mediums, but shows requiring tickets are not looked upon with favor" (*New York Clipper*, January 24, 1880). Moreover, with the Civil War still a recent and bitter memory, Southerners in communities with baseball teams would not necessarily go out of their way to invite such tours. Consequently many clubs that would have liked to begin the season with a Southern tour ended up staying closer to home.

By the mid-1890s the idea of a Southern tour had gained widespread acceptance. Jack Rowe contended in 1895 that a club that went South gained a significant edge: "the managers who take their men into a warm climate are doing a sensible act . . . the experiments can be tried out, and the men will gradually learn to play together, which means much to a club" (*Spalding's Official Base Ball Guide*, 1895, 125). The *Brooklyn Eagle* solicited opinions on a number of topics from members of the local team before the 1896 season and published the responses. A Southern spring training trip was perceived as a competitive requirement. Pitcher Ed Stein's comments were typical: "I think a Southern trip is almost necessary on account of the warm weather. In the North it remains quite cold during the whole of March and outside practice would be almost impossible. The season starts so early that the players could hardly get in shape in time for practicing here" (*Brooklyn Eagle*, March 11, 1896).

24.2.3 Training Camps. In the mid-1880s the training camp as we know it today came into existence. As discussed in the previous entries, the desirability of collective spring workouts was already recognized. But it was only the growing prosperity of the game and specifically the owners' tightening contractual grip on the players that made formal training camps possible.

An 1887 article in the *Cincinnati Enquirer* noted: "Not over three years ago the idea of training ball players to get them in condition for the season's work was unheard of. Not a club in the country put the men through the preliminary paces in the gymnasium, and a ball-player was not required to report to duty until the team began actual work upon the field."

The piece credited Gus Schmelz with helping popularize the practice while managing Columbus in 1884. It observed that in three short years, "what a difference is noticeable. The comparison is striking. There is not a single club in either one of the leading base-ball organizations that does not require the members of its team to go through some form of training for from two to three weeks' time before the regular opening of the season. They are either taken on a Southern trip, where the weather is mild and will admit of outdoor practice, or are put in a gymnasium under the care and direction of a competent instructor" (*Cincinnati Enquirer*, April 3, 1887).

The inaugural issue of the *Sporting News* in 1886 editorialized, "The preparatory work now being done by two or three prominent clubs in the country marks one of the most sensible departures from the old rut in baseball that has ever been made." The publication asked rhetorically: "What has caused this important feature of training to be so long neglected? In the early days of the game no doubt the poverty of the club had something to do with it. But the main reason has been the protest of the players themselves to pull off the 'beef' and harden the muscles" (*Sporting News*, March 17, 1886).

In June 1891 Athletics owner J. Earl Wagner declared, "Our men are just beginning to get in condition. Two or three of them have not yet got their extra flesh off. The Bostons took a preparatory southern trip, and when the season opened felt like a lot of two-year-olds" (quoted in *Williamsport Sunday Grit*, June 7, 1891). Once it was perceived that holding spring training gave a club a large competitive advantage, and could even make the difference in winning a pennant, it naturally became standard for every club to conduct one. The benefits of preseason training became still more evident in the next few years, when, as noted under "Preliminary Workouts" (**24.2.1**), trainers began to assume control.

It became clear that these benefits were being noticed when minor league clubs began to follow suit. In 1909 the *Detroit Free Press* reported that "the southern training camp is no longer the privilege of the rich major leagues. The more important of the minors have taken up the spring practice tours" (*Detroit Free Press*, March 7, 1909).

24.2.4 Spring Training in Florida and Arizona. While major league clubs today all hold their spring training camps in either Florida or Arizona, those weren't the earliest sites. Both states were still sparsely populated, with swamps and deserts respectively limiting their appeal.

The first major league team to try Florida was Ted Sullivan's Washington club, which prepared for the 1888 season in Jacksonville. One report claimed that the state did not exactly open its arms to baseball, as "the hotel clerk insisted that the ballplayers not eat in the same dining room with the other guests, not mingle with them, and not even mention their profession to the guests" (Kevin M. McCarthy, *Baseball in Florida*, 141). That, however, sounds suspiciously like one of Ted Sullivan's exaggerated stories. One of the players on that club, backup catcher Connie Mack, seems to have had positive memories as his Athletics often trained in Jacksonville.

Bryan Di Salvatore suggested that John Ward began the practice of getting towns to pay to host teams for spring training in 1892 when he convinced Ocala, Florida, to give Brooklyn free use of its field and to pay for some of the team's travel (Bryan Di Salvatore, *A Clever Base-Ballist*, 344). The practice began to expand in the early twentieth century. In 1913 the *New York Times* reported, "President Charley Murphy of the Cubs has gone his colleagues one better in commercializing the advertising value of his ball club. Murphy has persuaded the business men of Tampa, Fla., to put up $4,700 in good cold cash to cover the expenses of the Cubs' spring training. The Tampa merchants want the Cubs to go there and have put up the money. . . . Mr. Murphy has generously consented to let the Tampa business men have the receipts of the games to partly reimburse them for handing out the $4,700" (*New York Times*, January 12, 1913).

By the end of the nineteenth century it was pretty much standard for clubs to train in the warmer climes. At first, clubs all chose the Southeast, but the 1899 season saw one pioneering team venture much farther west. A *Sporting Life* correspondent noted, "Chicago is the only team that will go West. They will train in New Mexico, and this experience will be watched with the closest attention by the club owners" (*Sporting Life*, March 25, 1899).

Texas became a popular spring training spot in the early twentieth century, but it was several decades before Arizona was tried. The first major league club to hold spring training there was the Detroit Tigers in 1929; it was not until 1947 that the Cleveland Indians became the first major league club to establish a permanent training base in Arizona.

24.2.5 Spas. The Chicago White Stockings were holding training camp at Hot Springs, Arkansas, in the mid-1880s. By the turn of the century this resort town had become the place to train and was hosting several other clubs. Pat Tebeau observed, "Rheumatics throw away their crutches after bathing two weeks at Hot Springs, and if there is another resort in the country where tired limbs can be restored, I want to know about it" (*Sporting News*, February

19, 1896). By that time, however, as noted in the next entry, clubs had begun to discover that many of the benefits of natural spring water could be reproduced elsewhere. This reality, coupled with complaints about poor grounds, overcrowding, and the consequent distractions, eventually led clubs to abandon Hot Springs and move farther south for spring training.

24.2.6 Steam Boxes. According to a 1900 article, Arthur Irwin appears to have introduced steam boxes to baseball before the 1896 season. Irwin was managing New York at the time and thought they could help his players lose weight. His players were not so easily convinced, but eventually pitcher Dad Clarke agreed to try the new device.

Unfortunately the attendant didn't fully understand the box's workings and turned on all the steam at once. Clarke came running out, screaming, "Turn the hose on me, I'm stewed." He apparently wasn't exaggerating much, as his skin was said to have come off in patches over the next month.

In spite of this less-than-auspicious debut, the concept caught on. The article continued, "The 'lobster pots,' as the players of the New York team persist in calling the steam boxes, have proved a most valuable adjunct to the training outfit being used daily at the Polo grounds. A player shuts himself in the box stripped to the buff. He seats himself on a shelf prepared for the purpose, shoves his head through the hole in the lid and shouts to an attendant 'Let 'er go.' There is a hissing of steam, a wild shriek from the player and then a gasp of contentment as the searching vapor gets in its parboiling work and locates the stiffness and soreness. Soon the perspiration begins to ooze from every pore and the winter kinks are gradually dissipated and the rusty knee and arm joints work on their hinges with rejuvenated vigor. A half hour's steaming and the player emerges from the box as rosy red as a Baldwin apple. An instant under the shower bath, a dash upstairs into the hands of the rubbers, who work the massage treatment as long as the victim will stand the punching and mauling, and the player is a new man, with all signs of soreness gone and a few pounds of superfluous weight left behind him" (*New York Journal*, reprinted in *Grand Valley* [Moab, Utah] *Times*, June 29, 1900).

As described in memorable fashion in Laura Hillenbrand's *Seabiscuit*, such quick weight-reduction methods became especially popular among jockeys, whose livelihoods directly depended on them (Laura Hillenbrand, *Seabiscuit*, 66–70).

24.2.7 Permanent Spring Training Homes. As late as 1899 a *Sporting Life* correspondent remarked, "Considering the number of years base ball teams have gone South, it seems strange that no club has yet selected a permanent place for spring practice. They wander around from one place to another down South like the Ponce de Leon looking for the fountain of eternal youth. . . . It is a rare occurrence for a team to train two successive seasons at the same place" (*Sporting Life*, March 25, 1899).

It was several more years before the Giants established the first long-term spring training base, returning to Marlin Springs, Texas, each year from 1908 to 1918. The club's decision to put down roots was facilitated by the skill of groundskeeper John Murphy, who was able to create a grass infield instead of the skin diamonds that had been the norm in arid climates.

Gradually other clubs began to follow the Giants' lead. Sid Mercer noted in 1910, "The establishment of permanent base ball training camps in the South by the New York and Pittsburg clubs of the National League and the advantages of holding preliminary practices on fields laid out to conform to big league standards is paving the way for a system of splendidly equipped base ball plants in Dixie" (*New York Globe*, reprinted in *Sporting News*, December 8, 1910).

Johnny Evers and Hugh S. Fullerton observed in 1912 that there was a movement "more and more toward permanent training camps, and against exhibition tours." They commented that this allowed clubs to use the winter to train and evaluate draftees (John J. Evers and Hugh S. Fullerton, *Touching Second*, 223–224).

Nevertheless a 1912 article noted, "Base ball teams have been traveling South for Spring practice for a great many years, but from the way they shift each season from one place to another it seems as though no club had yet found the ideal training spot." The piece quoted Connie Mack as explaining, "I can't say that I have ever found a place where everything is perfect. I guess our record will show that we have never gone to the same place two years in succession" (*Philadelphia Record*, reprinted in *Sporting Life*, March 9, 1912).

24.2.8 Pitchers and Catchers First. In February 1903 Connie Mack took a limited squad of players, primarily pitchers, to Jacksonville, Florida. It was explained that "The object of the early visit to the south is to try out the pitchers and get them in good condition for the preliminary games in April with the Phillies" (*Fort Wayne News*, February 25, 1903).

Nap Lajoie sent the Cleveland pitchers and catchers to Hot Springs two weeks before the squad of players in 1905. His reasoning was that the team's pitchers habitually got off to slow starts and he wanted them to be ready for the start of the season (Gerard S. Petrone, *When Baseball Was Young*, 22). This of course forced the catchers to report early as well since, as Casey Stengel famously observed, without a catcher the ball will just roll to the backstop.

Over the next few years this practice gradually went from being the exception to the rule. Sportswriter Joe S. Jackson noted in 1911 that Frank Chance planned to take his young battery members "South two weeks in advance of the team itself, so that he can start them as early as possible. This is a general custom" (*Washington Post*, January 21, 1911).

Chapter 25

AS AMERICAN
AS APPLE PIE

AS EARLY AS 1855, baseball was referred to by the Knickerbockers club secretary as "the national game of Base Ball" (minutes of the Knickerbocker Base Ball Club for August 22, 1855; quoted by Frederick Ivor-Campbell, *Nineteenth Century Notes*, 92:1 [April 1992], 5–6). It is possible that he simply meant that the game was being played nationally, but the *New York Clipper* left no room for doubt when it announced the following year that "the game of Base Ball is generally considered the National game amongst Americans" (*New York Clipper*, December 13, 1856). That was an extraordinarily bold statement considering that the Knickerbockers' version of the game had yet to travel beyond the New York City area. While baseball was unquestionably being played in many regions, it was still being played in so many different ways that it was not always recognizable as the same game.

Porter's Spirit of the Times was far more accurate when it stated that same year: "We feel a degree of old Knickerbocker pride at the continued prevalence of Base Ball as the National game in the region of the Manhattanese" (quoted in James M. DiClerico and Barry J. Pavelec, *The Jersey Game*, 25). But "the National game in the region of the Manhattanese" doesn't have quite the same ring as "the national game."

Other sources were similarly more precise in describing baseball as "a national game." A description of the first meeting of the National Association of Base Ball Players in 1857 noted that "Base ball has been known in the Northern States as far back as the memory of the oldest inhabitant reacheth, and must be regarded as a national pastime, the same as cricket is by the English" (*Spirit of the Times*, January 31, 1857; reprinted in Dean Sullivan, ed., *Early Innings*, 22–24). There is a big difference between describing base-ball as a national game and as *the* national game, but it is a distinction that is easily blurred.

That is exactly what many were willing to do in the late 1850s. Historian George B. Kirsch reported that "references to 'the national game of base-ball' appeared frequently in the daily and sporting press throughout the late 1850s," and that "All of the New York City sporting weeklies regularly pro-claimed baseball to be 'the national game of ball' before the Civil War" (George B. Kirsch, *The Creation of American Team Sports*, 92, 68).

There were many reasons for this insistence on nationalism. One of the most important was that Americans were quite conscious that cricket was the English national game, and anxious to have a game they could call their own. Walter Bagehot argued persuasively that the "principal thought of the American constitution-makers" was to avoid the shortcomings of the British constitution, specifically the tyranny of King George III (Walter Bagehot, *The English Constitution*, 199). Similarly, a recurring theme in early baseball was to ensure the game's distinctiveness from cricket.

And, while it might be argued that baseball has long since overcome the defensive urge to define itself by its differences from cricket, the issue occa-sionally resurfaces. A curious example occurred in 1946 when Leo Durocher was asked by Commissioner Happy Chandler to comply with a "good con-duct" rule. Durocher responded with a sarcastic reference to a cricket cus-tom: "When shall I serve tea, in the fourth inning, or the sixth?" (*Sporting News*, April 11, 1946).

The decision to style baseball as the national game created an impetus for the game as it spread across the country in the 1860s and 1870s. Instead of just being another newfangled New York fad, an activity billed as the na-tional game had prestige and had to be taken seriously.

In the years to come, baseball's connection to the national identity would manifest itself in an impressive number of different ways. In the process, baseball's right to bill itself by the once extraordinary title of "the national game" would be strengthened and deepened.

(i) Wrapping the Game in the Flag

25.1.1   Flags. Historian George B. Kirsch reported that a group of ladies in Danvers Centre, Massachusetts, presented the local ball club with the Stars and Stripes in 1859 (*New York Clipper*, August 20, 1859; cited in George B. Kirsch, *The Creation of American Team Sports*, 93). The first stadium to fly the American flag appears to have been the Carrol Park Grounds in Brooklyn, home of the Star and Excelsior clubs in 1862. During the season opener in late March, "the National ensign floated from the roof over the flag of the [Star] club" (*Brooklyn Eagle*, March 27, 1862). The flag was also featured two months later at the opening of the first enclosed baseball stadium, the Union Grounds in Brooklyn, and it soon became a familiar sight at baseball diamonds (James L. Terry, *Long Before the Dodgers*, 36).

25.1.2 National Anthem. A band performed "The Star-Spangled Banner" at the opening of Brooklyn's Union Grounds on May 15, 1862. The song, however, was not yet the national anthem, and other patriotic songs were sometimes substituted in the early years of baseball. When the Nationals of Washington visited Chicago on their historic 1867 tour (see **24.1.7** "Cross-country Trips"), a band tried to spur on the home nine by playing "Rally Round the Flags, Boys" (Henry Chadwick, *The American Game of Base Ball*, 96). In the ensuing years, "The Star-Spangled Banner" came to be regarded as the song of choice for patriotic occasions, though it did not officially become the U.S. national anthem until 1931.

A more imposing obstacle was that, in the days before public address systems, it was necessary to hire a band to perform music (see **14.5.12** and **14.5.13**). Despite the expense, "The Star-Spangled Banner" continued to be played on special occasions. As part of the Opening Day festivities in San Francisco in 1892, "the band played The Star-Spangled Banner" (*San Francisco Examiner*, March 27, 1892). At Brooklyn's home opener in 1903, "The flag was raised to the strains of 'The Star Spangled Banner'" (*New York Sun*, April 22, 1903). After that the anthem's performance on Opening Day became a regular occurrence (see, for example, Benton Stark, *The Year They Called Off the World Series*, 102; Jonathan Fraser Light, *The Cultural Encyclopedia of Baseball*, 474; *Washington Post*, April 23, 1920).

At the opening game of the 1918 World Series, with the nation's entry into the world war on every mind, "The Star-Spangled Banner" was played during the seventh-inning stretch. It received a heartfelt reception: "the ball players turned quickly about and faced the music. First the song was taken up by a few, then others joined, and when the final notes came, a great volume of melody rolled across the field. It was at the very end that the onlookers exploded into thunderous applause and rent the air with a cheer" (*New York Times*, September 6, 1918). The display was repeated at the remaining games of the Series, and in subsequent years it became customary to have it performed at the Fall Classic.

The advent of public address systems made it feasible to play recorded music at the ballpark. But it was not until World War II that it became customary for the national anthem to be played before every game.

After the tragic events of September 11, 2001, the seventh inning of baseball games began to be marked by the singing of "God Bless America."

This continued a pattern: "The Star-Spangled Banner" was first played at a baseball game during the Civil War; became a World Series tradition during World War I; and became a part of every game during World War II. "God Bless America" was added after 9/11.

25.1.3 Patriotic Club Names. Historian George B. Kirsch noted that many of the names of early baseball clubs had patriotic connotations, such as "Young America, Columbia, Union, Independent, Eagle, American, Continental, Empire, National, Liberty, and Pioneer. Others honored such heroes as George Washington, Alexander Hamilton, James Madison, Thomas Jefferson, Andrew Jackson, and Benjamin Franklin" (George B. Kirsch, *The Creation of American Team Sports*, 93).

25.1.4 President Throwing Out the First Ball. William Howard Taft began this tradition before Washington's Opening Day game against Philadelphia on April 14, 1910. Partisanship appears to have entered into the assessments of Taft's throw. The *Washington Post* rhapsodized that Taft "had done his part so nobly" and showed "faultless delivery" in opening "the season with a true presidential flourish" (*Washington Post*, April 15, 1910). An Associated Press account, however, was not quite as warm: "The president took the ball in his gloved hand as if he were at a loss what to do with it until [umpire Billy] Evans told him he was expected to throw it over the plate when he gave the signal. . . . Catcher [Gabby] Street stood at the home plate ready to receive the ball, but the president knew the pitcher was the man who usually began business operations with it, so he threw it straight to Pitcher Walter Johnson. The throw was a little low, but the pitcher stuck out his long arm and grabbed the ball before it hit the ground, while the insurgents in the bleachers cheered wildly" (AP: *Chicago Tribune*, April 15, 1910).

25.1.5 President to Attend a Major League Game. Benjamin Harrison attended a game on June 6, 1892, between Cincinnati and Washington.

(ii) Talking the Talk

The characterization of baseball as the national game has been justified by a wide variety of different arguments. They have not always been terribly persuasive.

Some have substituted rhetoric for fact. A notable example was A. G. Spalding, who drew support from the discredited notion that Abner Doubleday invented baseball and the questionable idea that the Civil War helped to spread the game: "A National Game? Why, no country on the face of the earth ever had a form of sport with so clear a title to that distinction. Base Ball had been born in the brain of an American soldier [i.e., Doubleday]. It received its baptism in bloody days of our nation's direst danger. It had its early evolution when soldiers, North and South, were striving to forget their foes by cultivating, through this grand game, fraternal friendships with comrades in arms. It had its best development at the time when soldiers, disheartened by distressing defeat, were seeking the solace of something safe and sane; at a time when Northern soldiers, flushed with victory, were yet willing to turn from fighting with bombs and bullets to playing with bat and ball" (A. G. Spalding, *America's National Game*, 92–93).

Others have used politics as the basis of imaginative analogies. A journalist wrote in 1859, "In the American game the ins and outs alternate by quick rotation, like our officials" (*New York Herald*, October 16, 1859). During World War I a British journalist was amazed by the way players argued with the umpire and reasoned: "If the Yanks are not bothered by the overwhelming dignity and autocratic authority of the umpire, they would have no trouble with the Germans" (quoted in Jonathan Fraser Light, *The Cultural Encyclopedia of Baseball*, 626).

Still others contradict each other. The *New York Herald* noted in 1859 that "the English game [of cricket] is so slow and tame, and the American [game of baseball] so full of life" (*New York Herald*, October 16, 1859). Jacob Morse added, "the American would not sacrifice a morning for a cricket game. He is quick and active, nervous and energetic, and he wants his sport to answer the requirements of his temperament. Base ball has suited his purpose admirably" (Jacob Morse, *Sphere and Ash*; reprinted in Dean Sullivan, ed., *Early Innings*, 157). William Wheaton of the Knickerbockers maintained that "The difference between cricket and baseball illustrates the difference between our lively people and the phlegmatic English" (quoted in *San Francisco Examiner*, November 27, 1887). Yet Roger Kahn suggested that "baseball's inherent rhythm, minutes and minutes of passivity erupting into seconds of frenzied action, matches an attribute of the American character" (Roger Kahn, *A Season in the Sun*, 8–9).

These both sound like plausible arguments, and they reflect the dramatic alteration in baseball's tempo that was discussed in Chapter 12. But it can't be true that the American temperament is ideally suited to both paces.

Henry Chadwick also had a rather peculiar take on the matter. He later claimed that while watching a baseball game in 1856 he had been "struck with the idea that base ball was just the game for a national sport for America" (*Brooklyn Eagle*, May 11, 1888). When the Red Stockings and Athletics toured England in 1874 he wrote that "the visit in question has resulted in setting at rest forever the much debated question as to whether we had a National Game or not, the English press with rare unanimity candidly acknowledging that the 'new game of base-ball' is unquestionably the American National Game" (quoted in Adrian C. Anson, *A Ball Player's Career*, 74–75). This raises the obvious question of how the English press would be in any position to determine America's national game.

Perhaps it is better just to feel that baseball is the national game and not to reason why.

25.2.1 National Association of Base Ball Players. Although writers have not always made convincing cases for why baseball is the national game, they have been much more effective in deflating grandiose claims of national significance. For example, when the National Association of Base Ball Players was formed in 1858, the *New York Clipper* wrote: "This document proposes to call the organization 'The National Association of Base Ball Players'—a misnomer, in our opinion, for the convention seems to be rather sectional and selfish in its proceedings, than otherwise, there having been no invitations sent to clubs in other States. . . . National, indeed! Why the association is a mere local organization, bearing no State existence even—to say nothing of a National one. The truth of the matter is—that a few individuals have wormed themselves into this convention, who have been, and are endeavoring to mould men and things to suit their own views. If the real lovers of the beautiful and health-provoking game of base ball wish to see the sport diffuse itself all over the country—as Cricket is fast doing—they must cut loose from those parties who wish to arrogate to themselves the right to act for, and dictate to all who participate in the game. These few dictators wish to ape the New York Yacht Club in their feelings of exclusiveness—we presume. Let the discontented, therefore, come out from among this party, and organize an association which shall be National—not only in name—but in reality. Let invitations be extended to base ball players everywhere to compete with them, and endeavor to make the game what it should be—a truly National one" (*New York Clipper*, April 3, 1858).

25.2.2 National League. The formation of the National League in 1876 evoked similar skepticism about the accuracy of the word "national." A *Brooklyn Eagle* reporter observed, "The League championship rules open with an error, inasmuch as they refer to their code as that of the championship of the 'United States.' It is nothing of the kind; it is simply for the championship of the League Stock Company Association. Suppose the New Haven Club should win a majority of the games played with the Association clubs, would that club not practically win the championship? It reminds me of the three Tailors of Tooley street, proclaiming themselves as 'We, the people of England'" (*Brooklyn Eagle*, March 27, 1876).

25.2.3 We Are the World. Not content to make debatable assertions of a national scope, some early aficionados of baseball went still further. As early as 1865, claims like this one were being made: "Game 40 to 28, Atlantic ahead, and still the champions of the world" (*Brooklyn Eagle*, August 15, 1865). As noted earlier (see **22.2.1**), by the 1880s the term "World's Series" had been coined.

Chapter 26

MISCELLANY

(i) Keeping Up Appearances

26.1.1 Beards and Mustaches. Facial hair on early ballplayers was not an unusual sight. The *Williamsport Sunday Grit* wrote in 1891 that twenty years earlier, "The players usually sported chin whiskers, muttonchops or heavy military moustaches" (*Williamsport Sunday Grit*, June 7, 1891). *Sporting Life* confirmed in 1910: "It was no uncommon thing, however, in the old days, to see bearded men playing ball" (*Sporting Life*, October 8, 1910).

By the time the National League was formed, clean-shaven mugs had become the norm. The beard worn by 1870s outfielder John Remsen was often cited as a novelty. One account claimed that Remsen wore the beard to protest the disputed 1876 presidential election, having "registered an oath not to let a hair-cutter lay hands on him until Tilden takes his seat" (*Louisville Courier-Journal*; reprinted in *Chicago Tribune*, June 3, 1877).

Facial hair had practically vanished by the 1880s. An 1888 article reported: "It is worthy of remark that the [American] Association since its organization never had a player in its employ who wore P. Rooney Galways or mutton chops, except one [Wesley] Blogg, who caught about two games for the Pittsburgs in 1883. He was short-lived, and when the wind from a few sharp foul tips dallied with his lilacs he threw up the job and quit" (*Williamsport Sunday Grit*, March 18, 1888).

In September 1891, piqued at continued references to his advancing years, Cap Anson appeared for a game in Boston wearing fake white whiskers and long white hair. He continued to wear the whiskers for the entire game and, in typically contentious fashion, told the umpire he intended to take his base if a pitched ball touched his whiskers (H. Allen Smith and Ira L. Smith, *Low and Inside*, 19).

In 1904 outfielder John Titus of the Phillies was reported to be the only National League player to wear a mustache (*Washington Post*, October 2, 1904). In 1908 *Sporting Life* remarked that "For several years Titus has been the only player to wear a 'soup strainer'" (*Sporting Life*, March 28, 1908). These accounts overlook Jake Beckley, who wore a mustache from time to time. In the middle of the 1906 season, Beckley "joined the ranks of the clean-shaven. John Titus is the only National leaguer wearing a mustache today" (*Grand Rapids* [Wisc.] *Tribune*, August 1, 1906). Beckley apparently regrew the mustache and then shaved it off again before the start of the 1907 season, prompting the observation that he no longer "shared with Titus of the Phillies the distinction of being the only major league players daring enough to wear coffee strainers in public" (*Chicago Tribune*, April 12, 1907). Baseball historian David Fleitz reported that Beckley was one of three players to sport facial hair in 1907 but does not specify who the third man was (David Fleitz, "Jacob Peter Beckley," Tom Simon, ed., *Deadball Stars of the National League*, 231).

Titus finally shaved his distinctive red mustache before the 1908 season, prompting one Philadelphia writer to wax eloquent about the breaking of a "link that bound the past to the present." He elaborated: "Philadelphia had for many years the companion piece to the Titus mustache. Monte Cross held on to his till 1904, but when it began to take on a gray tinge at the ends Monte thought it about time to change his disguise. Jake Beckley clung to the old-fashioned imperial for a long time, but even the German was forced to bow to modern customs. Once no big leaguer was complete without upper lip adornment. His mustache was only second in importance to his hat or glove. Photographs of the old-timers, Anson, Kelly, Brouthers, all show a fine piratical adornment. Some time in the early '90s the fashion changed. Some baseball modiste of that period decided that the mustache was no longer de rigueur. The edict was promptly obeyed and enough hair was shorn from the faces of ball tossers to stuff a mattress. To the younger generation of fans the Titus mustache was a survival of a remote period—a curiosity. Now even that is gone" (reprinted in the *Syracuse Herald*, April 1, 1908).

In the ensuing years, hirsute players became extremely rare. Players would occasionally sport a beard or mustache during spring training, but the kidding that resulted would usually lead them to part with it before the regular season began. Senators catcher John Henry wore one during spring training in 1917 but shaved before Opening Day (*Washington Post*, May 28, 1917). The Athletics' Wally Schang grew one after the regular season, but his teammates considered it a jinx and he finally removed it (*Atlanta Constitution*, June 18, 1917).

Before the 1918 season, Washington catcher Ed Gharrity's mustache prompted sports columnist Jack Keene to comment, "Bets are now in order as to how long Gharrity will be able to wear it and when he will crack under the strain. He will have to take a line of hoots from the fans that will make him bite his nails a bit. Somehow the fans can't abide a ball player in any sort of whiskers. The feeblest and least offensive of mustaches will have them screaming in fury. Wally Schang almost got stoned last season when he came forth with an embellished upper lip and then [sic] John Henry of the Senators tried to get by with the same idea. Neither went very far with it. The fans won't have it and there you are. It somehow doesn't seem natural" (*Lima* [Ohio] *News*, March 13, 1918). The issue became moot when Gharrity was drafted.

The uniformity of clean-shaven players during the 1920s made the beards worn by the barnstorming House of David ball club all the more distinctive. The next major leaguer to wear facial hair during the regular season appears to have been Allen Benson, a House of David pitcher who was signed by the Senators in 1934. Bill Deane noted that Benson was described as possessing the "novelty of being the first bearded pitcher to appear in the majors for years." It was reported that Benson had "vowed when he was signed by Washington that if he didn't win he would cut off his beard and try it with a mustache alone" (*Sporting News*, August 30, 1934). But Benson didn't get the chance as he was released after two unsuccessful starts.

Benson was followed two years later by Frenchy Bordagaray of the Dodgers. Deane found that Benson reported to training camp in 1936 sporting a mustache and even added a goatee at some point (*New York World-Telegram*, May 19, 1936). Bordagaray hinted that he intended to continue to wear it during the regular season, and Dodgers manager Casey Stengel voiced no objection (*New York World-Telegram*, March 6, 1936). He wore the mustache until late April, then shaved it off but regrew it. Bordagaray recalled that, part of the way through the season, "Stengel called me into his office and told me to get rid of it. He said, 'Frenchy, if there's gonna be any clown on this club, it's gonna be me'" (*New York Daily News*, April 25, 1971; thanks to Bill Deane for providing all these citations).

Bordagaray's experiment was followed by another long gap. Bill Deane has found evidence that Satchel Paige was wearing a mustache when he was signed by the Indians in 1948. But the 1950s saw the ascendance of the "organization man" in American society, and baseball players embodied that conformism. Throughout the turbulent 1960s, major leaguers remained clean-shaven to a man, and it became increasingly clear that this was much more than a grooming decision.

In 1966 Marvin Miller became the first executive director of the Players Association and brought the winds of change with him, in more ways than one. Charles P. Korr has noted that Miller's mustache was mentioned in a disproportionate number of articles about the union (Charles P. Korr, *The End of Baseball as We Knew It*, 272).

By the early 1970s Reggie Jackson and several other members of the Oakland A's brought facial hair back to major league baseball, with the encouragement of owner Charles O. Finley. Not every club was as supportive. Bobby Tolan filed a grievance against the Reds, with one of the issues being his refusal to shave his mustache when told to do so by manager Sparky Anderson (Charles P. Korr, *The End of Baseball as We Knew It*, 138). Tolan won the grievance on narrow grounds, but the Reds continued to enforce the team rule against facial hair for many years. The Yankees still have such a policy, which forced Johnny Damon to shave his trademark beard after signing with the club. And new manager Joe Girardi (a former Yankee coach) of the Florida Marlins in 2006 decreed that his club would be clean-shaven.

26.1.2 Glasses. Pitcher Will White, a star of the 1870s and 1880s, was the first bespectacled major leaguer. His success did not erase the stigma associated with wearing glasses.

Sportswriter Oliver Abel told this story about early-twentieth-century pitcher Ed Reulbach: "Reulbach was known as the wildest man out of captivity. There were times when his wildness made him the joke of the business. No one could understand his peculiar actions. He was charged with being 'yellow,' and every possible explanation excepting the true one was advanced.

"The truth was that Reulbach had one bad eye, an eye so bad that at times its weakness affected the other, and he lost sight of the plate entirely. When, in the heat and sweat of a hard game, his good eye failed him, he pitched at where he thought the plate was.

"Reulbach never was seen reading a newspaper, or even a score card, or the bill of fare at a table. One night Johnny Kling, who was rooming with him, entered the room and found Reulbach wearing a pair of glasses, reading a newspaper. Caught in the act, he confided in Kling the secret of his eye, and Kling never revealed the fact that the big pitcher's eye was defective. He got away with it for years. [Cubs manager Frank] Chance never knew why his star pitcher had those famous fits of wildness, and the other players never could understand it.

"Years afterward, Reulbach told the joke. But the fact is, the 'joke' was on him. In his effort to keep the others from suspecting that his eyesight was faulty, he over-strained the eye, and it was a long time after he quit the game before the weak eye yielded to treatment and regained part of its strength. Glasses would, perhaps, have made Reulbach the greatest pitcher baseball has ever known" (*Sporting News*, March 15, 1923).

Bespectacled pitcher Lee Meadows had a successful major league career that lasted from 1915 to 1929, but he was convinced that a position player with glasses could not be successful. He explained: "I have worn glasses while pitching for several years and know no reason why they should prove a handicap to any youngster who wants to pitch. There is no chance for him, though, in any other position on the team in my opinion. A spectacled youth cannot play the outfield because it is impossible for him to accurately judge a fly ball while running at full speed. He may not aspire to be a catcher because he cannot wear a mask and spectacles. He will be handicapped in the infield because of the ground he must cover for it is difficult to judge a line drive or a grounder if running at top speed while wearing glasses" (quoted in *Fort Wayne Sentinel*, July 27, 1916).

Meadows was proved wrong halfway through his career, when infielder "Specs" Toporcer reached the major leagues on April 13, 1921. Another landmark event occurred in 1931 when bespectacled Chick Hafey won the National League batting title. Sportswriter Grantland Rice wrote: "It will be interesting to observe whether the success of Chick Hafey in winning the batting championship of the National League last year breaks down the fear of 'four-eyes.' A lot of good ball players, and plenty of umpires, so they will tell you, would have been far better if they had had the nerve to wear glasses during business hours. Ball players have feared that the wearing of specs would give the hint that they were going back" (Grantland Rice, "The Sportlight," syndicated column, March 10, 1932).

26.1.3 Eye Black. It is sometimes said that baseball borrowed the use of eye black from football. But the first football player who is known to have used eye black was Andy Farkas, a Washington Redskins fullback who used it in a game against the Philadelphia Eagles in 1942. Baseball players were doing it much earlier, most notably outfielder Patsy Dougherty.

A 1904 note observed, "Pat Dougherty rubs mud or charcoal under his eyes, after the practice of many minor league ball players, who assert that it lessens the glare of the sun on a bright day" (*Sporting Life*, July 9, 1904). Sportswriter L. W. Herzog confirmed, "Some time ago I noticed an article stating that Ty Cobb always plastered mud under his eyes and that it was an old Indian trick. It's an old Irish trick, too, for Captain M'que Doherty [sic] has done it for years" (*Sporting News*, November 14, 1907). Sportswriter W. A. Phelon wrote in 1905, "Sandow Mertes tried that new sun field wrinkle here [Chicago] the other day—that trick of painting black circles round the eyes instead of wearing smoked glasses. It made Sandow look like an Apache on the warpath, and the only perceptible result was, that Sandow misjudged a long fly and let in the winning run" (*Sporting Life*, June 24, 1905).

(ii) Rituals

26.2.1 Married/Single. Games between teams of married and single men were common in early baseball. The earliest I have found was played between members of the Bedford Club of Long Island in 1855 (*Spirit of the Times*, September 29, 1855). The concept spread quickly to the rest of the country and became a common way for early clubs to divide into two squads; the *Detroit Free Press* of May 16, 1860, described such a game, as did the *Kalamazoo Gazette* of July 27, 1860. A game between married and single women was played in Rockford, Illinois, in 1870 (*New York Tribune*, August 26, 1870).

26.2.2 Fraternizing. There was no league rule against fraternizing in the early days of baseball, but individual clubs had rules against it. The rules of the Chicago White Stockings in 1883 included one that read: "After coming upon the field in uniform, players must not converse with reporters, scorers, acquaintances, or others in the audience" (*Fort Wayne Daily News*, April 10, 1883).

Joe Cantillon claimed in 1914 that there had been no need for such rules in the early days. He explained: "The players of 25 years ago . . . had far more interest in their play than the athletes of today. Formerly one never saw the members of the teams that were to play a series standing around together chatting and laughing and visiting before the game started. Every player in those days hated every man on the club to be played that day, and when the two captains came together to consult with the umpire it was like two bull-terriers turned loose from the benches, and once the game started it was for blood and not for averages" (*Minneapolis Journal*, reprinted in *Sporting News*, May 28, 1914).

26.2.3 Pregame Warmups. Pregame rituals were already taking a highly organized form in early baseball, with Cap Anson's Chicago White Stockings following a particularly regimented schedule when at home. The preliminary practice was controlled by a series of gongs.

The home team took the field first to warm up and toss the ball around. When the first gong sounded, the audience entered and the home team left the field and went to their clubhouse. The next gong went off twenty-five minutes before the game and was a signal for the visitors to take the field for their preliminaries.

The third sounding of the gong took place ten minutes before the start of the game, and Chicago retook the field. The fourth gong came eight minutes later and ended all warm-ups. The captains then flipped for choice of innings, and a fifth gong was sounded, at which time the members of the fielding team took their positions (*Fort Wayne Daily News*, April 10, 1883).

26.2.4   Weddings at Home Plate. Cincinnati business manager Frank Bancroft arranged the first wedding at home plate on September 18, 1893. When he heard that assistant groundskeeper Louis Rapp was planning to get married, Bancroft suggested that the ceremony take place at home plate at League Park. The newlyweds received gifts from the Reds, the visiting Orioles, and the fans (*Sporting Life*, September 23, 1893; Harry Ellard, *Base Ball in Cincinnati*, 192–195).

26.2.5   High Fives. Glenn Burke is believed to have invented the high five while playing for the Dodgers in the late 1970s.

(iii) Customs, Traditions, and Taboos

26.3.1   Nostalgia for the Good Old Days. In an 1868 article, old-time player Pete O'Brien (writing as "Old Peto Brine") cited the waiting game (see **2.3.1** "Waiting Out the Pitcher") as a prime example of how "they don't play ball nowadays as they used to" (*The American Chronicle of Sports and Pastimes*, January 9, 1868). There is also nothing new about nostalgia for the days when the only numbers mentioned on the baseball pages were the players' statistics. Sportswriter Bill Hanna observed, "I, for one, pine for the good old days when items about the knobby fingers and eagle batting eye of some diamond favorite filled the public prints, rather than contracts, commissions, injunctions and a hundred and one other matters tiresomely material and not base ball at all" (Bill Hanna, *New York Sun*; reprinted in *Sporting News*, March 4, 1915). Hanna was writing in 1915.

26.3.2   Reports That Baseball Is Dead. When baseball experienced its first great rush of popularity between 1865 and 1867, there was a widespread feeling that "baseball fever" was simply a fad that would soon abate. Accordingly, when the game struggled in 1868 and 1869, many journalists prematurely pronounced the game dead. It was far from the last time.

26.3.3   Custom That the Club That Leads on July 4 Will Win the Pennant. Sportswriter Frank Getty wrote in 1929: "Old Mr. McGillicuddy's diligent young men are in the spot customarily occupied by pennant winners on Independence Day" (*Washington Post*, July 5, 1929).

26.3.4   Sunday Baseball. The issue of Sunday baseball was a contentious and divisive one from the earliest days of baseball until well into the twentieth century.

As early as 1862 the police were becoming involved: "Officer Haslam yesterday espied in Greenpoint some half dozen boys who were engaged in a game of base ball. But the officer although an admirer of the noble game is also opposed to its practice on the Sabbath, so he arrested both the ins and outs and locked them up for the night. This morning Justice Colahan dismissed them with a warning to have their practice days changed" (*Brooklyn Daily Times*, April 28, 1862; reprinted in James L. Terry, *Long Before the Dodgers*, 19).

For the remainder of the nineteenth century, arrests for playing ball on the Sabbath continued to be a regular occurrence. It became proverbial that it took ten men to play on Sunday—nine to play and one to watch for the police (*Grand Rapids* [Mich.] *Times*, May 3, 1871).

Sunday baseball was illegal in the early days of the National League, though a few clubs disregarded the rule. The American Association became the first major league to regularly schedule Sunday baseball games during its initial season of 1882.

Sunday baseball is usually thought of as a moral issue, but, as with night baseball (see **14.1.3**), class also played a major role. Since working-class men had six-day work weeks and usually finished work too late for afternoon games, they had few opportunities to visit National League stadiums. This allowed the National League to try to cater to an upscale audience by charging higher admissions. In contrast, the American Association openly courted the working class by offering lower ticket prices, Sunday baseball, and alcoholic beverages.

The National League did not allow Sunday baseball until its merger with the American Association in 1892. Even then, local laws prevented most National League teams from playing Sunday games, and it was decades before some of them did. The state of Pennsylvania was the last holdout, with Pittsburgh and Philadelphia clubs not playing Sunday games in their own parks until 1934.

The major league's first Sunday night game did not take place until June 9, 1963, and only then because of the oppressive daytime heat in Houston. Charlie Bevis's *Sunday Baseball* gives a detailed history of the issue.

26.3.5 Sunday Ballparks. The first major league club to play Sunday games at a different park from their regular park was Syracuse, a National League club that defied the league's prohibition in 1879 and played Sunday games at Lakeside Park to avoid the Blue Laws in their home county. By the late 1880s, having a separate Sunday ballpark was a common practice (Michael Gershman, *Diamonds*, 34).

26.3.6 Numbering System for Scoring. The idea of assigning a number to each defensive position was suggested almost as soon as scorekeeping became part of baseball. But Henry Chadwick objected in 1861 that "if each player retained his position in the field throughout the game, this mode of record would do, clumsy as it is; but when scarcely a game is played wherein changes are not made, it of course becomes entirely unreliable, as it does not designate the fielder who put the striker out, but simply records the position on the field" (*Beadle's Dime Base-Ball Player*, 1861).

Since position in the batting order was the only constant, scorers had to use this number to designate a player. Unfortunately this meant that a scorer could not record the result of a play until he had checked the position in the lineup of each defensive player who had handled the ball. The resulting system was so cumbersome that it took Henry Chadwick some six pages to explain all its intricacies (Henry Chadwick, *The American Game of Base Ball*, 62–68). But there was little alternative.

By 1889 changes in position had become much less common and this prompted a writer in the *New York Mail and Express* to suggest that a single number be used for each defensive position. Chadwick explained the proposal: "The pitcher is numbered 1 in all cases, catcher 2, first baseman 3, second baseman 4, short stop 5, third baseman 6, right fielder 7, centre fielder 8, and left fielder 9. For example, if a ball is hit to third base and the runner is thrown out at first base, without looking at the score card it is known that the numbers to be recorded are 6-3, the former getting the assist, and the first baseman the put-out. If from short-stop to first, it is 5-3. If from the second baseman, it is 4-3. If a dropped third strike, and the runner is thrown out at first, it is K 1-2-3-K, indicating the strike out."

Chadwick believed this idea was "in no respect an improvement on the plan which has been in vogue since the National League was organized," citing a familiar objection: "if you name the players by their positions, and these happen to be changed in a game, then you are all in a fog on how to change them" (*Sporting Life*, May 29, 1889). Yet what Chadwick did not anticipate was that the legalization of substitutions, a gradual process that had begun that season (see **1.32** and **6.2.1**), would mean that the entry of new players into the game would become more common than swaps of position.

This eliminated the main benefit of the system that Chadwick had been using for so long. Moreover, it cannot have taken long for scorekeepers who experimented with the new method to see that it was much simpler to write 4-3 on a grounder to the second baseman than to have to check the position in the batting order of both defensive players.

The new idea appears to have caught on quickly, as researcher Keith Olbermann reports that an 1891 Giants scorecard included "Hints on Scoring" that are a word-for-word reprint of the instructions that had appeared in the *Mail and Express*. It is probably no coincidence that that was the same year in which unlimited substitutions became legal.

Readers may have noticed that the scoring system introduced around 1889 designated the shortstop as 5, the third baseman as 6, the right fielder as 7, and the left fielder as 9. As Keith Olbermann has explained, the change to today's numbering system occurred during the next twenty years, but what prompted the switches remains mysterious. Olbermann, however, recounts an intriguing explanation for the reversal of the third baseman and shortstop's numbers that has been handed down by credible sportswriters who believe it to be true.

This version pinpoints the early-twentieth-century World Series, for which *Sporting Life* editor Francis Richter and *Sporting News* editor Joseph Flanner were often named official scorers. The two men soon discovered they were using different numbering systems, and quarreled. Richter maintained that the shortstop was the infielder who played between the second and third basemen, so it was only logical to assign him the number between them. But Flanner thought it more appropriate to select a number that reflected the shortstop's traditional role (see **1.15** and **4.2.6**). Richter conceded the point, and Flanner's system has prevailed ever since, even though few fans today are aware that the shortstop was ever considered anything but an infielder (Keith Olbermann, "Why Is the Shortstop '6'?," *Baseball Research Journal* 34 [2005], 16–18).

26.3.7   K for Strikeout. Henry Chadwick did have more influence in shaping the abbreviations used in box scores. He pioneered the use of the letter K to denote a strikeout because "the letter K in struck is easier to remember in connection with the word than S" (*Outing*, July 1888, "Scoring Rules for College Clubs"; also *National Chronicle*, January 30, 1869). Chadwick could never have anticipated how his somewhat arbitrary decision would affect the lives of Roger Clemens's four children, Kody, Kory, Koby, and Kacy.

(iv) Legends and Shrines

26.4.1   Tinker to Evers to Chance. Franklin P. Adams's famous poem first appeared in his *New York Evening Mail* column, "Always in Good Humor," in 1910. According to researcher Cliff Blau, on July 11, 1910, Art Devlin of the Giants grounded into a 6-4-3 double play that saved a Cubs victory and inspired the verse. The next day Adams's column featured the eight-line poem under the heading "That Double Play Again." It was an immediate hit, with parodies appearing almost daily in the *Evening Mail* for the next week, and the *Chicago Tribune* also publishing responses. On July 18 the *Evening Mail* reprinted the poem under the more familiar title "Baseball's Sad Lexicon."

26.4.2 Casey at the Bat. Ernest L. Thayer's poem originally appeared in the *San Francisco Examiner* on June 3, 1888. DeWolf Hopper gave his first of some ten thousand public recitals of the poem the following year.

26.4.3 John Anderson Play. In the early twentieth century the phrase "John Anderson play" was widely used to describe a player who attempted to steal an already occupied base. A typical article explained, "The most famous species of 'bones,' no doubt, are the John Andersons. To be entitled to a place in the John Anderson Order, you must steal second with the bases full. A lesser degree is awarded if you steal third with a man occupying that bag" (*Sporting News*, November 16, 1916).

As Hugh Jennings observed, there was nothing fair about the term: "John Anderson has for years been held up as the leading example of dumb play in base ball because he tried to steal second with the bases filled, but many other players have made the same mistake and escaped criticism. A few years ago even Ty Cobb, admittedly best of all base runners, tried to steal third while Bobby Jones was on the bag" (Hugh Jennings, *Rounding Third*, Chapter 72).

John Anderson played in the major leagues from 1894 to 1908, and the term was already being used toward the end of his playing days. Nonetheless the origins of the term proved difficult to pin down. Rob Neyer's pursuit of the elusive game was described in the *1990 Bill James Baseball Book* (Bill James, *1990 Bill James Baseball Book*, 241).

I was finally able to find it as a result of an article that appeared in *Sporting News* on February 25, 1923. The piece reported that the play took place while Anderson was playing for the St. Louis Browns, and gave enough details that, with the help of the Retrosheet website, I was able to locate a game that seemed to match. The game in question was the first game of a doubleheader on September 24, 1903, with the Browns playing in New York.

The *New York Sun*'s account confirmed that "[Jack] Chesbro was in fine form, except for a short spell in the eighth inning, when the Browns had him on the grill. They made four hits in a row and would have done more damage but for a stupid play by Anderson. With all the bases occupied and only one out Anderson ran for second on a third strike and was doubled up unceremoniously" (*New York Sun*, September 25, 1903).

26.4.4 Norman Rockwell Painting. Norman Rockwell's famous painting of three umpires checking the sky appeared on the cover of the *Saturday Evening Post* on April 23, 1949.

26.4.5 Called Shot. Baseball has had many claims of "called" home runs over the years, with varying levels of documentation. The earliest such claim may have been made by a *Brooklyn Eagle* reporter in 1873. The called shot was alleged to have taken place in the first of three 1858 games between the best players from Brooklyn and New York City. According to the reporter, "John Holder, just before going to the bat, bet $75 that he would make a home run, and hitting the ball to centre field, he actually did score the coveted run and won the bet" (*Brooklyn Eagle*, July 16, 1873).

26.4.6   Hall of Fame. The first vote for the Baseball Hall of Fame in Cooperstown, New York, took place on February 2, 1936, with Ty Cobb, Babe Ruth, Honus Wagner, Christy Mathewson, and Walter Johnson being elected. The museum was opened on June 12, 1939.

The concept of a Hall of Fame had currency in baseball long before then, however. A 1903 article noted that "[National League] President [Harry] Pulliam proposes to establish a base ball 'Hall of Fame' at League quarters in New York" (*Sporting Life*, March 21, 1903). Pulliam seems to have intended more of a museum than anything else. He began it with a life-sized photo of 1902 batting champion Ginger Beaumont and planned to add a new photo each year. But 1903 batting champion Honus Wagner declined the honor because of his disappointment with his poor World Series (*Sporting Life*, April 2, 1904). Moreover, since Wagner captured six of the next seven National League batting titles, it would have been a rather monotonous display even had Wagner agreed to pose.

After this abortive effort, the term "Hall of Fame" became a figurative way of referring to anyone who achieved a great accomplishment. No-hitters were a prominent example; *Sporting News* reported in 1910, "[Chester Carmichael] earned a niche in the base ball hall of fame the other day by not allowing a single player to reach first base in an East League championship game" (*Sporting News*, August 18, 1910). Diverse other accomplishments prompted this description. For example, a sporting correspondent observed in 1913: "Sindler got himself into the 'hall of fame' last week by pitching a double-header against Kingston" (*Sporting Life*, August 30, 1913). And sportswriter Joe S. Jackson wrote in 1911, "Those Athletics, by the way, have brought forward a new candidate for the batting hall of fame," by which he meant achieving two hundred hits in a season (*Washington Post*, September 10, 1911). Bill James noted that "Hall of Fame" was also used as a metaphor for a sportswriter's all-time team (Bill James, *The Politics of Glory*, 5).

In 1922 the U.S. Commission of Fine Arts, an independent agency established by Congress twelve years earlier to offer advice on the architectural and artistic appearance of the nation's capital, recommended the building of a baseball monument in East Potomac Park. The American League liked the idea and budgeted $100,000 for it (*Sporting News*, August 10, 1922). The plan for a monument was pursued for a couple of years, with the intention of commemorating the winners of the most valuable player award, but eventually was abandoned.

26.4.7 The Doubleday Myth. The Doubleday Myth was initiated on December 30, 1907, by a group that has become known as the Mills Commission. This body was charged by A. G. Spalding with determining the origins of baseball and came to the preposterous conclusion that the game was invented by Abner Doubleday.

Robert Henderson is often credited with being the first to debunk the Doubleday Myth in the 1930s, as for example by Leonard Koppett in his introduction to the 2001 reprint of Henderson's _Ball, Bat and Bishop_. While Henderson did an especially thorough job, the gaping holes in the commission's conclusions were documented almost immediately. Sportswriter William Rankin repeatedly used his _Sporting News_ column to point out the flaws (_Sporting News_, April 2, 1908; _Sporting News_, September 9, 1909; A. H. Spink, _The National Game_, 54). Henry Chadwick also joined in the howl of protests. A writer named Will Irwin also addressed the issue in a 1909 _Collier's_ article entitled "Baseball: Before the Professional Game."

26.4.8 Washington Monument. Even before the Washington Monument had been dedicated in February 1885, the first attempt had been made to catch a baseball dropped from the top of it.

Sporting Life reported in January, "Paul Hines, [Charley] Snyder, [Phil] Baker and [Ed] Yewell are persevering, and have made several attempts to catch a base ball thrown from the Washington monument. In one instance a ball was thrown off for Snyder to catch, but he was unable to judge it correctly. Hines, who happened to be several yards distant, saw the ball coming his way, put up his gloved hand, but the sphere went through them like a flash, and made a deep indentation in the frozen ground. Phil. Baker captured the ball once unexpectedly, but he held it only momentarily. There seems to be no rule by which the ball falling from such a great distance can be judged" (_Sporting Life_, January 14, 1885).

An account the following week observed: "The impression among the resident ball players is that Baker and Ewell [sic] will catch it if they get under the ball; that Hines is now afraid to make the attempt since he has seen the velocity of the ball. Snyder insists and offers to back up his opinion that the ball will not be caught between this and the 1st of April. . . . Everybody is discussing the subject, and therefore everybody is anxiously awaiting results" (_Washington Herald_, reprinted in _Sporting Life_, January 21, 1885).

Paul Hines gave a somewhat different version in 1906: "A New York man engaged in the business of selling sporting goods made me an offer of $200 for the ball if I succeeded in catching it. The monument at that time was not finished, and the scaffolding built around the top to be used in placing the capstone rose some feet higher than the monument itself.

"I offered to pay Charley Snyder and some other players to go to the top and toss the ball to me, but none would venture, and I finally employed one of the workmen engaged there. I gave him three balls. The first one he tossed landed on top of a shed. The second dropped into a lake. The third was thrown some distance from where I stood, but I made a run for it, and the ball just tipped the ends of my fingers. Though I had no glove on (we didn't wear 'em then), the ball did not sting my hand as much as many I had caught in center field" (quoted in Gerard S. Petrone, *When Baseball Was Young*, 64).

It was another nine years before the first successful catch was made by Pop Schriver on August 24, 1894. Schriver was followed by Gabby Street on August 21, 1908, and Billy Sullivan on August 24, 1910 (Lee Allen, *The Hot Stove League*, 99; Jack Kavanagh, *The Heights of Ridiculousness*, 1–24).

(v) Injuries and Deaths

26.5.1 X-rays. Pete Cassidy of Louisville was the first ballplayer to receive the then-new x-ray technique on April 7, 1896. Cassidy had suffered a wrist injury, but doctors had been unable to pinpoint the exact problem. The x-rays revealed a loose piece of bone, which was then removed by surgery.

26.5.2 Knee Surgery. New York Giants shortstop Travis Jackson suffered a serious knee injury in 1932, when he was only twenty-eight and later recalled, "I went on the retired list and thought that was it." After a few months, he received a phone call from Giants manager Bill Terry who "wanted to know whether I would have my knees operated on if the Giants would pay for it. I told him, 'That's a silly question, Bill. I can't walk now and I'd do anything to get fixed up.'" Jackson missed an entire year but then returned to form and was eventually elected to the Hall of Fame (Walter M. Langford, *Legends of Baseball*, 101).

26.5.3 Tommy John Surgery. Braves pitcher Harry Hulihan had a tendon grafted from his thigh into his pitching shoulder in 1923. The surgery cured his pain, but he lost his velocity and his career ended (John Bennett, "Harry Hulihan," in Tom Simon, ed., *Green Mountain Boys of Summer*, 116). On July 17, 1974, surgeons transplanted a tendon from Tommy John's right forearm into the left-handed pitcher's throwing elbow. The success of the operation has given new hope to countless sore-armed pitchers since.

26.5.4   Ice on Pitching Arm. George F. Will claimed that the now common practice of icing the pitching arm after a start was originated in the 1960s by Sandy Koufax and Don Drysdale (George F. Will, *Men at Work*, 143). It's a difficult claim to substantiate because ice had been used for injuries for many years before then. Exactly who was the first to use ice as a precautionary measure rather than to treat a specific injury is probably impossible to determine, but Drysdale and Koufax do seem to have helped popularize the routine use of ice after a start.

26.5.5   Death Resulting from a Professional Game. Atlanta's Lou Henke died on August 15, 1885, from the effects of an injury he had sustained in a Southern League game the preceding day.

Ray Chapman of Cleveland is the only major league player to die as an immediate result of an on-the-field incident. On August 16, 1920, Chapman was hit in the head by a pitch from Carl Mays of the New York Yankees, and he died the next morning. While the Chapman tragedy is still remembered, the much more recent death of umpire Cal Drummond has been virtually forgotten. Drummond was struck in the mask by a foul tip while acting as plate umpire in a June 10, 1969, game between the Baltimore Orioles and California Angels. He completed the game, but his condition worsened and he spent a week in unconsciousness in a Baltimore hospital. The following spring he was one day away from returning to the major leagues when he collapsed while umpiring a minor league game in Des Moines and died four hours later. An autopsy attributed the death to the foul tip eleven months earlier (Larry R. Gerlach, "Death on the Diamond: The Cal Drummond Story," *National Pastime* 24 [2004], 14–16).

In addition, there have been a number of players whose deaths were attributed to accidents that occurred during major league games. Jimmy Rogers's death on January 27, 1900, was reported to have resulted from his being hit by a pitch while playing for Louisville (*Sporting Life*, January 27, 1900). Athletics pitcher Jim Crabb's major league career was cut short when he was hit in the chest with a line drive. The injury bothered him the rest of his life, and his 1940 death was believed to have resulted from complications from the injury (Jerry E. Clark, *Anson to Zuber*, 54). Athletics catcher Mike Powers died in 1909 while he was still an active player, and his death is sometimes said to have resulted from an injury in a game several weeks earlier. Former Pirates pitcher Jimmy Gardner's death in 1905 was attributed to the effects of a pitched ball that fractured his skull six years earlier (*Sporting Life*, June 24, 1905). Researcher Jack Daugherty discovered a 1912 obituary of former Braves and Giants outfielder Frank Murphy that attributed his death to his having been hit by a pitch during his playing career (*Tarrytown Press-Record*, November 7, 1912).

It is important to remember, however, that many if not all these claims reflect the imprecise medical knowledge of the time, especially regarding physical activity. An 1880 article, for instance, reported that an ex-player named Alexander Trope had died of "a cancer caused by a blow to the stomach by a baseball some five years ago" (*New York Clipper*, September 25, 1880). Another article in the same publication four years later indicated that minor leaguer John McDonough had died from consumption (tuberculosis) contracted from being hit by a foul ball (*New York Clipper*, August 2, 1884).

26.5.6   Player to Die of Lou Gehrig's Disease. Former Giants pitcher Claud Elliott, whom John Thorn pegged as the game's first relief specialist (see **6.2.9**), died of amyotrophic lateral sclerosis on June 21, 1923. That same week a young first baseman named Lou Gehrig made his major league debut. Eighteen years later Gehrig died of the same disease, and it was renamed in his memory.

(vi) Hodgepodge

26.6.1 Instant Rules. In theory, new rules may be enacted only at the annual meetings at the season's end. In practice, new interpretations are sometimes added in mid-season if there seems to be no rule covering a situation.

Eddie Onslow reported that Ty Cobb once deliberately kicked a ball that was lying in the base path. According to Onslow, there was no rule against this tactic, so one was made the next day (Eugene Murdock, *Baseball Between the Wars*, 113). Ed Wells claimed that the same thing happened when Joe Sewell made a trench to cause a bunt to roll foul (Eugene Murdock, *Baseball Between the Wars*, 74). Eddie Stanky's attempt to distract batters by jumping up and down was dealt with in the same summary fashion, as were the 1957 efforts to break up double plays (see **11.1.8** and **5.5.3**).

26.6.2   Twins. The Reccius brothers, who played in the 1880s, were long believed to be the first twins to play in the majors—until researcher Bob Bailey established that they weren't actually twins. As a result, the distinction now belongs to George and Bill Hunter, who had brief major league stints— George with Brooklyn in 1909 and 1910, and Bill with Cleveland in 1912.

26.6.3   Teams of Nine Brothers. There were quite a few teams of nine brothers in early baseball, including the Maddens in New England in 1878; the Grieshabers of St. Genevieve County, Missouri, in 1884; the Atkins of Mexico, Missouri, in 1888; the Karpens of Chicago in 1890; the McEntees and Lennons of Joliet, Illinois, in 1890; the Thompsons of Winchester, New

Hampshire, in 1898; the Whites of Hammond, Indiana, in 1903; and the Birkenmeyers of Wappingers Falls, New York, in 1904. At least a couple of these teams faced each other; the Lennon brothers beat the Karpens in 1890 and the Whites in 1903 (Charles W. Bevis, "Family Baseball Teams," *Baseball Research Journal* 26 [1997], 8; *Sporting Life*, October 10, 1903).

There continued to be a smattering of such clubs in the 1920s and 1930s, as Charles W. Bevis has documented. The last one may have been the Acerras of Long Branch, New Jersey, who were still playing as late as 1947 (Charles W. Bevis, "Family Baseball Teams," *Baseball Research Journal* 26 [1997], 8–12). Since then, declining family size has spelled the end of such clubs.

26.6.4   Father-Son Major Leaguers. Herm and Jack Doscher were the first father and son to both play major league baseball. Ken Griffey, Sr., and Ken Griffey, Jr., were the first father and son to be major league teammates.

26.6.5   Baseball-playing Couple. After the 1883 season, pitcher Bollicky Bill Taylor married one of the players on the "Brunettes," a touring women's team. The couple separated after only two months (Harold Dellinger, "Bill Taylor," in Frederick Ivor-Campbell, Robert L. Tiemann, and Mark Rucker, eds., *Baseball's First Stars*, 163).

26.6.6   Postponed Due to Sun. A game between Boston and Cincinnati on May 6, 1892, was called in the fourteenth inning because the sun was directly in the batters' eyes. The *Cincinnati Enquirer* reported the next day that both teams agreed with the umpire's decision (Lee Allen, "Called on Account of Sun," *Sporting News*, December 11, 1965; reprinted in *Cooperstown Corner*).

26.6.7   All Nine Positions. Bert Campaneris was the first to play all nine positions in a single major league game on September 8, 1965. The feat has since been accomplished by Cesar Tovar, Shane Halter, and Scott Sheldon. On August 31, 1974, the Portland Mavericks of the Northwest League rotated after every inning, so that all nine players played all nine positions. Portland won the game 9-8.

26.6.8   Athletes Referring to Themselves in the Third Person. Billy "Kid" Gleason told a reporter in 1894: "Your uncle [I] was after a $500 slice of the $2,400 [Ned] Hanlon paid Chris [Von der Ahe] for me, and I am not violating any confidence in assuring you that I got it. When Willie figures in a deal he makes it a point to see that his interests are not neglected" (*St. Louis Post-Dispatch*, September 22, 1894).

26.6.9   Extra-inning Games. It is sometimes claimed that there were extra-inning games played before 1857, but this is a misconception. Nine innings did not become the standard until 1857, and most matches before then were played to a specified score. Such games thus often took more than nine innings, but they were not extra-inning games.

Since early games were high-scoring affairs, extra-inning games were rare. The earliest one listed in Marshall Wright's *The National Association of Base Ball Players, 1857-1870* is a ten-inning game between the Hoboken Club and the Mutuals of New York on August 4, 1859. The extra frame allowed the Mutuals to pull out a 19-15 win.

Bibliography

BOOKS

1864 American Boy's Book of Sports and Games (New York, 1864; reprint New York, 2000)

Melvin L. Adelman, *A Sporting Time: New York City and the Rise of Modern Athletics, 1820–70* (Urbana, Ill., 1986)

Aetna Base Ball Association Constitution and By-Laws (unpublished logbook; Burton Collection, Detroit Public Library)

Lee Allen, *Cooperstown Corner: Columns from the Sporting News, 1962–1969* (Cleveland, 1990)

Lee Allen, *The Hot Stove League* (New York, 1955; reprint Kingston, N.Y., 2000)

David W. Anderson, *More Than Merkle* (Lincoln, Nebr., 2000)

Will Anderson, *Was Baseball Really Invented in Maine?* (Portland, Me., 1992)

Roger Angell, *Once More Around the Park: A Baseball Reader* (New York, 1991; reprint Chicago, 2001)

Roger Angell, *A Pitcher's Story: Innings with David Cone* (New York, 2001)

Roger Angell, *The Summer Game* (New York, 1972)

Adrian C. "Cap" Anson, *A Ball Player's Career* (Chicago, 1900; reprint Mattituck, N.Y., n.d.)

Marty Appel, *Slide, Kelly, Slide: The Wild Life and Times of Mike "King" Kelly, Baseball's First Superstar* (Lanham, Md., 1999)

Marty Appel, *Yesterday's Heroes* (New York, 1988)

David Arcidiacono, *Grace, Grit and Growling* (East Hampton, Conn., 2003)

Jean Hastings Ardell, *Breaking into Baseball: Women and the National Pastime* (Carbondale, Ill., 2005)

Gustav Axelson, *Commy: The Life Story of Charles A. Comiskey* (Chicago, 1919)

Walter Bagehot, *The English Constitution* (London, 1867)

Red Barber, *The Broadcasters* (New York, 1970)

The Barry Halper Collection of Baseball Memorabilia (New York, 1999)

Gai Ingham Berlage, *Women in Baseball: The Forgotten History* (Westport, Conn., 1994)

Charles W. Bevis, *Sunday Baseball: The Major Leagues' Struggle to Play Baseball on the Lord's Day, 1876–1934* (Jefferson, N.C., 2003)

David Block, *Baseball Before We Knew It* (Lincoln, Nebr., 2005)

Don Bollman, *Run for the Roses: A Fifty Year Memoir* (Mecosta, Mich., 1975)

Bill Borst, *Baseball Through a Knothole: A St. Louis History* (St. Louis, 1980)

Talmage Boston, *1939, Baseball's Pivotal Year: From the Golden Age to the Modern Era* (Fort Worth, Tex., 1994)

Jim Bouton, edited by Leonard Shecter, *Ball Four: My Life and Hard Times Throwing the Knuckleball in the Big Leagues* (New York, 1970)

Larry G. Bowman, *Before the World Series: Pride, Profits and Baseball's First Championships* (De Kalb, Ill., 2003)

James H. Bready, *Baseball in Baltimore* (Baltimore, 1998)

Eric Bronson, ed., *Baseball and Philosophy: Thinking Outside the Batter's Box* (Chicago, 2004)

Jim Brosnan, *The Long Season* (New York, 1960; reprint Chicago, 2002)

Warren Brown, *The Chicago Cubs* (New York, 1946; reprint Carbondale, Ill., 2001)

Lois Browne, *Girls of Summer: The Real Story of the All-American Girls Professional Baseball League* (Toronto, 1992)

Reed Browning, *Baseball's Greatest Season, 1924* (Amherst, Mass., 2003)

Reed Browning, *Cy Young: A Baseball Life* (Amherst, Mass., 2000)

Robert F. Burk, *Much More Than a Game: Players, Owners and American Baseball Since 1921* (Chapel Hill, N.C., 2001)

Robert F. Burk, *Never Just a Game: Players, Owners and American Baseball to 1920* (Chapel Hill, N.C., 1994)

J. P. Caillault, *A Tale of Four Cities* (Jefferson, N.C., 2003)

Bob Carroll, *Baseball Between the Lies* (New York, 1993)

Robin Carver, *The Boy's and Girl's Book of Sports* (Boston, 1834)

Jon David Cash, *Before They Were Cardinals: Major League Baseball in Nineteenth-Century St. Louis* (Columbia, Mo., 2002)

Jerrold Casway, *Ed Delahanty in the Emerald Age of Baseball* (Notre Dame, Ind., 2004)

David Cataneo, *Tony C.: The Triumph and Tragedy of Tony Conigliaro* (Nashville, 1997)

Henry Chadwick, *Chadwick's Base Ball Manual* (London, 1874)

Henry Chadwick, *The American Game of Base Ball* (aka *The Game of Base Ball. How to Learn It, How to Play It, and How to Teach It. With Sketches of Noted Players*) (1868; reprint Columbia, S.C., 1983)

Henry Chadwick, *Beadle's Dime Base-Ball Player* (1860) (reprint: Morgantown, Pa., 1996) (later editions are occasionally cited, but this guide changed little from year to year)

Henry Chadwick, *DeWitt's Base Ball Umpire's Guide* (various years)

Henry Chadwick, *Haney's Base Ball Book of Reference for 1867* (aka *The Base Ball Player's Book of Reference*) (New York, 1867)

James Charlton, ed., *The Baseball Chronology: The Complete History of Significant Events in the Game of Baseball* (New York, 1991)

James Charlton, ed., *Road Trips* (Cleveland, 2004)

Seymour R. Church, *Base Ball: The History, Statistics and Romance of the American National Game from Its Inception to the Present Time* (San Francisco, 1902; reprint Princeton, N.J., 1974)

Dick Clark and Larry Lester, eds., *The Negro Leagues Book* (Cleveland, 1994)

Jerry E. Clark, *Anson to Zuber: Iowa Boys in the Major Leagues* (Omaha, 1992)

Ty Cobb, *Bustin' 'Em and Other Big League Stories* (New York, 1914; reprint William R. Cobb, ed., Marietta, Ga., 2003)

Ty Cobb, *Memoirs of Twenty Years in Baseball* (1925; reprint William R. Cobb, ed., Marietta, Ga., 2002)

Mickey Cochrane, *Baseball: The Fans' Game* (New York, 1939; reprint Cleveland, 1992)

William Curran, *Big Sticks: The Phenomenal Decade of Ruth, Gehrig, Cobb, and Hornsby* (New York, 1990)

William Curran, *Mitts: A Celebration of the Art of Fielding* (New York, 1985)

Arthur Daley, *Inside Baseball: A Half Century of the National Pastime* (New York, 1950)

Bill Deane, *Award Voting* (Kansas City, 1988)

Jordan Deutsch, Richard M. Cohen, Roland T. Johnson, and David S. Neft, eds., *The Scrapbook History of Baseball* (Indianapolis, 1975)

Donald Dewey and Nicholas Acocella, *The Ball Clubs: Every Franchise, Past and Present, Officially Recognized by Major League Baseball* (New York, 1996)

Paul Dickson, ed., *Baseball's Greatest Quotations* (New York, 1991)

Paul Dickson, *The Hidden Language of Baseball: How Signs and Sign-Stealing Have Influenced the Course of Our National Pastime* (New York, 2003)

Paul Dickson, ed., *The New Dickson Baseball Dictionary* (New York, 1999)

Paul Dickson, *The Worth Book of Softball: A Celebration of America's True National Pastime* (New York, 1994)

James M. DiClerico and Barry J. Pavelec, *The Jersey Game: The History of Modern Baseball from Its Birth to the Big Leagues in the Garden State* (New Brunswick, N.J., 1991)

Bryan Di Salvatore, *A Clever Base-Ballist: The Life and Times of John Montgomery Ward* (New York, 1999)

Phil Dixon and Patrick J. Hannigan, *The Negro Baseball Leagues: A Photographic History* (Mattituck, N.Y., 1992)

Dick Dobbins and Jon Twichell, *Nuggets on the Diamond* (San Francisco, 1994)

Bert Dunne, *Play Ball!* (Garden City, N.Y., 1947)

Bob Edwards, *Fridays with Red: A Radio Friendship* (New York, 1993)

James E. Elfers, *The Tour to End All Tours* (Lincoln, Nebr., 2003)

Harry Ellard, *Base Ball in Cincinnati: A History* (1907; reprint Jefferson, N.C., 2004)

John J. Evers and Hugh S. Fullerton, *Touching Second: The Science of Baseball* (Chicago, 1910; reprint Mattituck, N.Y., n.d.)

David Falkner, *Nine Sides of the Diamond: Baseball's Great Glove Men on the Fine Art of Defense* (New York, 1990)

Federal Writers' Project, *Baseball in Old Chicago* (Chicago, 1939)

G. H. Fleming, *The Unforgettable Season* (New York, 1981)

Stephen Fox, *Big Leagues: Professional Baseball, Football, and Basketball in National Memory* (New York, 1994)

Joel S. Franks, *Whose Baseball? The National Pastime and Cultural Diversity in California, 1859–1941* (Lanham, Md., 2001)

Ford Frick, *Games, Asterisks and People: Memoirs of a Lucky Fan* (New York, 1973)

Cappy Gagnon, *Notre Dame Baseball Greats: From Anson to Yaz* (Charleston, S.C., 2004)

Larry R. Gerlach, *The Men in Blue: Conversations with Umpires* (New York, 1980)

Michael Gershman, *Diamonds: The Evolution of the Ballpark* (Boston, 1993)

A. Bartlett Giamatti, *Take Time for Paradise: Americans and Their Games* (New York, 1989)

Malcolm Gladwell, *The Tipping Point: How Little Things Can Make a Big Difference* (Boston, 2000)

George Gmelch and J. J. Weiner, *In the Ballpark: The Working Lives of Baseball People* (Washington, D.C., 1998)

Warren Goldstein, *Playing for Keeps: A History of Early Baseball* (Ithaca, N.Y., 1989)

Peter Golenbock, *Wrigleyville: A Magical History Tour of the Chicago Cubs* (New York, 1999)

Roberto Gonzalez Echevarria, *The Pride of Havana: A History of Cuban Baseball* (New York, 1999)

Tom Gorman, as told to Jerome Holtzman, *Three and Two!* (New York, 1979)

Guy W. Green, *Fun and Frolic with an Indian Ball Team* (1907; reprint Mattituck, N.Y., 1992)

Robert Gregory, *Diz: The History of Dizzy Dean and Baseball During the Great Depression* (New York, 1992)

Stephen Guschov, *The Red Stockings of Cincinnati: Base Ball's First All-Professional Team and Its Historic 1869 and 1870 Seasons* (Jefferson, N.C., 1998)

Dan Gutman, *Banana Bats and Ding-Dong Balls: A Century of Unique Baseball Inventions* (New York, 1995)

Dan Gutman, *It Ain't Cheatin' If You Don't Get Caught: Scuffing, Corking, Spitting, Gunking, Razzing, and Other Fundamentals of Our National Pastime* (New York, 1990)

Allen Guttmann, *Sports Spectators* (New York, 1986)

David Halberstam, *October 1964* (New York, 1995)

John Helyar, *Lords of the Realm* (New York, 1994)

Robert W. Henderson, *Ball, Bat, and Bishop: The Origin of Ball Games* (New York, 1947; reprint Urbana, Ill., 2001)

J. Thomas Hetrick, *Chris Von der Ahe and the St. Louis Browns* (Lanham, Md., 1999)

Laura Hillenbrand, *Seabiscuit* (New York, 2001)

Frank W. Hoffmann and William G. Bailey, *Sports and Recreation Fads* (Binghamton, N.Y., 1991)

Jerome Holtzman, *No Cheering in the Press Box*, revised edition (New York, 1995)

Arlene Howard, with Ralph Wimbish, *Elston and Me: The Story of the First Black Yankee* (Columbia, Mo., 2001)

Colin Howell, *Northern Sandlots* (Toronto, 1995)

Frederick Ivor-Campbell, Robert L. Tiemann, and Mark Rucker, eds., *Baseball's First Stars* (Cleveland, 1996)

Bill James, *The 1990 Bill James Baseball Book* (New York, 1990)

Bill James, *The Bill James Baseball Abstract* (various years)

Bill James, *The Bill James Guide to Baseball Managers: From 1870 to Today* (New York, 1997)

Bill James, *The New Bill James Historical Baseball Abstract* (New York, 2001)

Bill James, *The Politics of Glory: How Baseball's Hall of Fame Really Works* (New York, 1994)

Bill James and Rob Neyer, *The Neyer/James Guide to Pitchers* (New York, 2004)

Hugh Jennings, *Rounding First* (n.p., 1925)

Harry "Steamboat" Johnson, *Standing the Gaff* (Nashville, Tenn., 1935; reprint Lincoln, Nebr., 1994)

Lloyd Johnson, *Baseball's Book of Firsts* (Philadelphia, 1999)

Lloyd Johnson and Miles Wolff, eds., *The Encyclopedia of Minor League Baseball*, 2nd edition (Durham, N.C., 1997)

James M. Kahn, *The Umpire Story* (New York, 1953)

Roger Kahn, *The Head Game: Baseball Seen from the Pitcher's Mound* (New York, 2000)

Roger Kahn, *Memories of Summer* (New York, 1997)

Roger Kahn, *A Season in the Sun* (New York, 1977)

Mark Kanter, ed., *The Northern Game and Beyond: Baseball in New England and Eastern Canada* (Cleveland, 2002)

Lawrence S. Katz, *Baseball in 1939: The Watershed Season of the National Pastime* (Jefferson, N.C., 1995)

Jack Kavanagh, *The Heights of Ridiculousness: The Feats of Baseball's Merrymakers* (South Bend, Ind., 1998)

Jack Kavanagh and Norman Macht, *Uncle Robbie* (Cleveland, 1999)

Kevin Kerrane, *Dollar Sign on the Muscle: The World of Baseball Scouting* (New York, 1984)

George B. Kirsch, *The Creation of American Team Sports: Baseball and Cricket, 1838–72* (Urbana, Ill., 1991)

Charles P. Korr, *The End of Baseball as We Knew It: The Players Union, 1960–81* (Urbana, Ill., 2002)

Bowie Kuhn, *Hardball: The Education of a Baseball Commissioner* (New York, 1988)

Bruce Kuklick, *To Every Thing a Season: Shibe Park and Urban Philadelphia, 1909–1976* (Princeton, N.J., 1991)

Robin Tolmach Lakoff, *The Language War* (Berkeley, Calif., 2000)

F. C. Lane, *Batting* (1925; reprint Cleveland, 2001)

Walter M. Langford, *Legends of Baseball* (South Bend, Ind., 1987)

Ernest J. Lanigan, *The Baseball Cyclopedia* (New York, 1922; reprint St. Louis, 1988)

Jerry Lansche, *Glory Fades Away: The Nineteenth-Century World Series Rediscovered* (Dallas, 1991)

Irving A. Leitner, *Baseball: Diamond in the Rough* (New York, 1972)

Peter Levine, *A. G. Spalding and the Rise of Baseball: The Promise of American Sport* (New York, 1985)

Frederick G. Lieb, *The St. Louis Cardinals: The Story of a Great Baseball Club* (New York, 1944; reprint Carbondale, Ill., 2001)

Jonathan Fraser Light, *The Cultural Encyclopedia of Baseball* (Jefferson, N.C., 1997)

Michael E. Lomax, *Black Baseball Entrepreneurs, 1860–1901: Operating by Any Means Necessary* (Syracuse, 2003)

Lee Lowenfish, *The Imperfect Diamond: A History of Baseball's Labor Wars*, revised edition (New York, 1991)

Philip J. Lowry, *Green Cathedrals: The Ultimate Celebration of All 271 Major League and Negro League Ballparks Past and Present* (Reading, Mass., 1992)

Neil W. Macdonald, *The League That Lasted: 1876 and the Founding of the National League of Professional Base Ball Clubs* (Jefferson, N.C., 2004)

Connie Mack, *My Sixty-Six Years in the Big Leagues* (Philadelphia, 1950)

Jerry Malloy, ed., *Sol White's History of Colored Base Ball, with Other Documents on the Early Black Game, 1886–1936* (original version 1907; reprint Lincoln, Nebr., 1995)

Larry D. Mansch, *Rube Marquard: The Life and Times of a Baseball Hall of Famer* (Jefferson, N.C., 1998)

William Marshall, *Baseball's Pivotal Era, 1945–1951* (Lexington, Ky., 1999)

Christy Mathewson, *Pitching in a Pinch* (New York, 1912; reprint Mattituck, N.Y., n.d.)

Ronald A. Mayer, *Perfect!* (Jefferson, N.C., 1991)

Bill Mazer, with Stan and Shirley Fischler, *Bill Mazer's Amazin' Baseball Book* (New York, 1990)

Kevin M. McCarthy, *Baseball in Florida* (Sarasota, 1996)

Tim McCarver with Danny Peary, *Tim McCarver's Baseball for Brain Surgeons and Other Fans* (New York, 1998)

John J. McGraw, *My Thirty Years in Baseball* (New York, 1923; reprint Lincoln, Nebr., 1995)

Michael McKinley, *Putting a Roof on Winter: Hockey's Rise from Sport to Spectacle* (Vancouver, 2000)

William B. Mead, *Even the Browns* (Chicago, 1978)

Tom Melchior, *Belle Plaine Baseball, 1884–1960* (Belle Plaine, Minn., 2004)

Tom Melville, *Early Baseball and the Rise of the National League* (Jefferson, N.C., 2001)

Frank G. Menke, *The Encyclopedia of Sports* (New York, 1955)

Dick Miller and Mark Stang, eds., *Baseball in the Buckeye State* (Cleveland, 2004)

Stephen G. Miller, *Arete: Greek Sports from Ancient Sources* (Berkeley, Calif., 1991)

Leigh Montville, *Ted Williams: The Biography of an American Hero* (New York, 2004)

George L. Moreland, *Balldom* (Youngstown, Ohio, 1914; reprint St. Louis, 1989)

Peter Morris, *Baseball Fever: Early Baseball in Michigan* (Ann Arbor, Mich., 2003)

W. Scott Munn, *The Only Eaton Rapids on Earth* (Eaton Rapids, Mich., 1952)

Eugene Murdock, *Baseball Between the Wars: Memories of the Game by the Men Who Played It* (Westport, Conn., 1992)

Eric Nadel and Craig R. Wright, *The Man Who Stole First Base: Tales from Baseball's Past* (Dallas, 1989)

David Nemec, *The Beer and Whisky League* (New York, 1994)

David Nemec, *Great Baseball Facts, Feats and Firsts,* revised edition (New York, 1999)

David Nemec, *The Great Encyclopedia of 19th Century Major League Baseball* (New York, 1997)

David Nemec, *The Rules of Baseball* (New York, 1994)

Rob Neyer and Eddie Epstein, *Baseball Dynasties: The Greatest Teams of All Time* (New York, 2000)

Robert Obojski, *Baseball Memorabilia* (New York, 1992)

Robert Obojski, *Bush League: A History of Minor League Baseball* (New York, 1975)

Sidney Offit, ed., *The Best of Baseball* (New York, 1956)

Marc Okkonen, *Baseball Uniforms of the Twentieth Century: The Official Major League Guide* (New York, 1991)

Marc Okkonen, *Minor League Baseball Towns of Michigan* (Grand Rapids, Mich., 1997)

Marc Okkonen, *The Ty Cobb Scrapbook* (New York, 2001)

Michael O'Malley, *Keeping Watch: A History of American Time* (New York, 1991)

Preston D. Orem, *Baseball (1845–1881) from the Newspaper Accounts* (Altadena, Calif., 1961)

Danny Peary, ed., *Cult Baseball Players* (New York, 1990)

Danny Peary, *We Played the Game: 65 Players Remember Baseball's Greatest Era, 1947–1964* (New York, 1994)

Harold Peterson, *The Man Who Invented Baseball* (New York, 1969)

Robert W. Peterson, *Only the Ball Was White: A History of Legendary Black Players and All-Black Professional Teams* (New York, 1970)

Robert W. Peterson, *Pigskin: The Early Years of Pro Football* (New York, 1997)

Gerard S. Petrone, *When Baseball Was Young* (San Diego, 1994)

Charles Peverelly, *The Book of American Pastimes* (New York, 1866)

David Pietrusza, *Judge and Jury: The Life and Times of Judge Kenesaw Mountain Landis* (South Bend, Ind., 1998)

David Pietrusza, *Lights On! The Wild Century-Long Saga of Night Baseball* (Lanham, Md., 1997)

David Pietrusza, *Minor Miracles: The Legend and Lure of Minor League Baseball* (South Bend, Ind., 1995)

David Pietrusza, Lloyd Johnson, and Bob Carroll, eds., *Total Baseball Catalog: Great Baseball Stuff and How to Buy It* (New York, 1998)

Joseph V. Poilucci, *Baseball in Dutchess County: When It Was a Game* (Danbury, Conn., 2000)

Murray Polner, *Branch Rickey* (New York, 1982)

R. E. Prescott, *Historical Tales of the Huron Shore Region* (Alcona County, Mich., 1934)

Richard A. Puff, ed., *Troy's Baseball Heritage* (Troy, N.Y., 1992)

Martin Quigley, *The Crooked Pitch: The Curveball in American Baseball History* (Chapel Hill, N.C., 1988)

Reach's Official Base Ball Guide, various years

Greg Rhodes and John Erardi, *The First Boys of Summer* (Cincinnati, 1994)

Greg Rhodes and John Snyder, *Redleg Journal* (Cincinnati, 2000)

Francis C. Richter, *Richter's History and Records of Base Ball* (Philadelphia, 1914; reprint Jefferson, N.C., 2005)

Branch Rickey, *Branch Rickey's Little Blue Book* (New York, 1995)

Lawrence S. Ritter, *The Glory of Their Times* (New York, 1966; reprint New York, 1984)

Mark Rucker, *Base Ball Cartes: The First Baseball Cards* (Saratoga Springs, N.Y., 1988)

Mark Rucker and Peter C. Bjarkman, *Smoke: The Romance and Lore of Cuban Baseball* (Kingston, N.Y., 1999)

Babe Ruth, *Babe Ruth's Own Book of Baseball* (New York, 1928)

William J. Ryczek, *Blackguards and Red Stockings: A History of Baseball's National Association, 1871–1875* (Jefferson, N.C., 1992)

William J. Ryczek, *When Johnny Came Sliding Home: The Post–Civil War Baseball Boom, 1865–1870* (Jefferson, N.C., 1998)

Tony Salin, *Baseball's Forgotten Heroes: One Man's Search for the Game's Most Interesting Overlooked Players* (Indianapolis, 1999)

Alan Schwarz, *The Numbers Game: Baseball's Lifelong Fascination with Statistics* (New York, 2004)

Michael Seidel, *Ted Williams: A Baseball Life* (Lincoln, Nebr., 2000)

Harold Seymour, *Baseball: The Early Years* (New York, 1960)

Harold Seymour, *Baseball: The Golden Age* (New York, 1971)

Harold Seymour, *Baseball: The People's Game* (New York, 1990)

Bruce Shlain, *Oddballs: Baseball's Greatest Pranksters, Flakes, Hot Dogs and Hotheads* (New York, 1989)

Tom Simon, ed., *Deadball Stars of the National League* (Washington: 2004)

Tom Simon, ed., *Green Mountain Boys of Summer: Vermonters in the Major Leagues 1882–1993* (Shelburne, Vt., 2000)

George Sisler, *Sisler on Baseball: A Manual for Players and Coaches* (New York, 1954)

Marshall Smelser, *The Life That Ruth Built: A Biography* (New York, 1975; reprint Lincoln, Nebr., 1993)

Curt Smith, *Voices of the Game*, revised edition (New York, 1992)

H. Allen Smith and Ira L. Smith, *Low and Inside: A Book of Baseball Anecdotes, Oddities, and Curiosities* (Garden City, N.Y., 1949; reprint Halcottsville, N.Y., 2000)

Red Smith, *Red Smith on Baseball* (Chicago, 2000)

Robert Smith, *Baseball* (New York, 1947)

Dennis Snelling, *A Glimpse of Fame: Brilliant but Fleeting Major League Careers* (Jefferson, N.C., 1993)

Burt Solomon, *Where They Ain't* (New York, 1999)

Mike Sowell, *July 2, 1903: The Mysterious Death of Hall-of-Famer Big Ed Delahanty* (New York, 1992)

Mike Sowell, *The Pitch That Killed* (New York, 1989; reprint Chicago, 2003)

Albert Goodwill Spalding, *America's National Game: Historic Facts Concerning the Beginning, Evolution, Development, and Popularity of Base Ball, with Personal Reminiscences of Its Vicissitudes, Its Victories, and Its Votaries* (New York, 1911; reprint Lincoln, Nebr., 1992)

Spalding's Official Base Ball Guide, various years

Alfred H. Spink, *The National Game* (St. Louis, 1910; reprint Carbondale, Ill., 2000)

Sporting News, *Baseball: A Doubleheader Collection of Facts, Feats and Firsts* (New York, 1992)

Benton Stark, *The Year They Called Off the World Series: A True Story* (Garden City Park, N.Y., 1991)

Paul Starr, *The Creation of the Media* (New York, 2004)

Vince Staten, *Why Is the Foul Pole Fair? (Or, Answers to Baseball Questions Your Dad Hoped You'd Never Ask)* (New York, 2003)

Dean Sullivan, ed., *Early Innings: A Documentary History of Baseball, 1825–1908* (Lincoln, Nebr., 1995)

Dean Sullivan, ed., *Late Innings: A Documentary History of Baseball, 1945–1972* (Lincoln, Nebr., 2002)

Dean Sullivan, ed., *Middle Innings: A Documentary History of Baseball, 1900–1948* (Lincoln, Nebr., 1998)

Jim L. Sumner, *Separating the Men from the Boys: The First Half-Century of the Carolina League* (Winston-Salem, N.C., 1994)

James L. Terry, *Long Before the Dodgers: Baseball in Brooklyn, 1855–1884* (Jefferson, N.C., 2002)

John Thorn, ed., *The Armchair Book of Baseball* (New York, 1985)

John Thorn and Pete Palmer, with David Reuther, *The Hidden Game of Baseball* (Garden City, N.Y., 1984)

John Thorn, ed., *The National Pastime* (New York, 1988)

John Thorn and John Holway, *The Pitcher* (New York, 1987)

John Thorn, *The Relief Pitcher* (New York, 1979)

John Thorn and Pete Palmer, et al., *Total Baseball*, various editions

Robert L. Tiemann and Mark Rucker, eds., *Nineteenth Century Stars* (Kansas City, 1989)

Cliff Trumpold, *Now Pitching: Bill Zuber from Amana* (Middle Amana, Iowa, 1992)

Brian Turner and John S. Bowman, *Baseball in Northampton, 1823–1953* (Northampton, Mass., 2002)

Jules Tygiel, *Baseball's Great Experiment* (New York, 1983)

Jules Tygiel, *Past Time: Baseball as History* (New York, 2000)

Bill Veeck, with Ed Linn, *The Hustler's Handbook* (New York, 1965; reprint Durham, N.C., 1996)

Bill Veeck, with Ed Linn, *Veeck—As in Wreck* (New York, 1962)

David Quentin Voigt, *American Baseball, Volume I: From the Gentleman's Sport to the Commissioner's System* (Norman, Okla., 1966)

David Quentin Voigt, *American Baseball, Volume II: From the Commissioners to Continental Expansion* (Norman, Okla., 1970)

David Quentin Voigt, *American Baseball, Volume III: From Postwar Expansion to the Electronic Age* (University Park, Pa., 1983)

David Quentin Voigt, *The League That Failed* (Lanham, Md., 1998)

Paul Votano, *Stand and Deliver: A History of Pinch-Hitting* (Jefferson, N.C., 2003)

Glen Waggoner, Kathleen Moloney, and Hugh Howard, *Spitters, Beanballs, and the Incredible Shrinking Strike Zone: The Stories Behind the Rules of Baseball*, revised edition (Chicago, 2000)

John Montgomery Ward, *Base-Ball: How to Become a Player* (Philadelphia, 1888; reprint Cleveland, 1993)

Don Warfield, *The Roaring Redhead* (South Bend, Ind., 1987)

Ty Waterman and Mel Springer, *The Year the Red Sox Won the Series: A Chronicle of the 1918 Championship Season* (Boston, 1999)

Lonnie Wheeler and John Baskin, *The Cincinnati Game* (Wilmington, Ohio, 1988)

G. Edward White, *Creating the National Pastime: Baseball Transforms Itself, 1903–1953* (Princeton, N.J., 1996)

George F. Will, *Bunts* (New York, 1999)

George F. Will, *Men at Work* (New York, 1990)

Pete Williams, ed., *The Joe Williams Baseball Reader* (Chapel Hill, N.C., 1989)

Ted Williams, with John Underwood, *My Turn at Bat: The Story of My Life* (New York, 1969)

Craig R. Wright and Tom House, *The Diamond Appraised* (New York, 1990)

Marshall D. Wright, *The American Association: Year-by-Year Statistics for the Baseball Minor League, 1902–1952* (Jefferson, N.C., 1997)

Marshall D. Wright, *The National Association of Base Ball Players, 1857–1870* (Jefferson, N.C., 2000)

David W. Zang, *Fleet Walker's Divided Heart: The Life of Baseball's First Black Major Leaguer* (Lincoln, Nebr., 1995)

Joel Zoss and John Bowman, *Diamonds in the Rough: The Untold History of Baseball* (New York, 1989)

NEWSPAPERS AND MAGAZINES

This study relies upon an enormous number of articles and notes from newspapers, magazines, and journals, many of them untitled and having no bylines. In many cases the entire note has already been quoted, which would mean that a researcher would gain little by going back to the original. Rather than trying to list every single article, I have included some of the most valuable ones and those with scopes that go well beyond documenting a particular event or game, since these are the ones a researcher is most likely to benefit by consulting. The list of articles is followed by a list of all the periodicals I utilized.

Dr. Daniel L. Adams (early Knickerbocker), interview, *Sporting News*, February 29, 1896, 3

Melvin L. Adelman, "The First Baseball Game, the First Newspaper References to Baseball, and the New York Club: A Note on the Early History of Baseball," *Journal of Sport History* 7, No. 3 (Winter 1980), 132–135

William P. Akin, "Bare Hands and Kid Gloves: The Best Fielders, 1880–1899," *Baseball Research Journal* 10 (1981), 60–65

Thomas L. Altherr, "A Place Level Enough to Play Ball," reprinted in David Block, *Baseball Before We Knew It* (Lincoln, Nebr., 2005), 229–251

Thomas L. Altherr, "Know Them by Their Autographs," *National Pastime* 18 (1998), 29–31

Priscilla Astifan, "Baseball in the Nineteenth Century," *Rochester History* LII, No. 3 (Summer 1990); "Baseball in the Nineteenth Century, Part Two," *Rochester History* LXII, No. 2 (Spring 2000); "Baseball in the Nineteenth Century, Part Three: The Dawn of Acknowledged Professionalism and Its Impact on Rochester Baseball," *Rochester History* LXIII, No. 1 (Winter 2001); "Rochester's Last Two Seasons of Amateur Baseball: Baseball in the Nineteenth Century, Part Four," *Rochester History* LXIII, No. 2 (Spring 2001); "Baseball in the Nineteenth Century, Part Five: 1877–Rochester's First Year of Professional Baseball," *Rochester History* LXIV, No. 4 (Fall 2002)

Bob Bailey, "Hunting for the First Louisville Slugger," *Baseball Research Journal* 30 (2001), 96–98

Stan Baumgartner, "Signals," *Baseball Guide and Record Book 1947* (St. Louis, 1947), 124–135

Jay Bennett and Aryn Martin, "The Numbers Game: What Fans Should Know About the Stats They Love," in Eric Bronson, ed., *Baseball and Philosophy: Thinking Outside the Batter's Box*, 233–245

Mike Berardino, "Economic Climate Could Snuff Out Waiver Blocking," *Baseball America*, September 1–14, 2003

Gai Ingham Berlage, "Women Umpires as Mirrors of Gender Roles," *National Pastime* 14 (1994), 34–38

Charles W. Bevis, "Family Baseball Teams," *Baseball Research Journal* 26 (1997), 8–12

Charles W. Bevis, "Holiday Doubleheaders," *Baseball Research Journal* 33 (2004), 60–63

Charles W. Bevis, "A Home Run by Any Measure," *Baseball Research Journal* 21 (1992), 64–70

Dennis Bingham and Thomas R. Heitz, "Rules and Scoring," *Total Baseball*, 4th edition, 2426–2481

Peter Bjarkman, "Cuban Blacks in the Majors Before Jackie Robinson," *National Pastime* 12 (1992), 58–63

Hal Bodley, "Teams Obsess Too Much Over Pitch Counts," *USA Today*, September 17, 2004, 4C

Larry G. Bowman, "The Monarchs and Night Baseball," *National Pastime* 16 (1996), 80–84

Randall Brown, "How Baseball Began," *National Pastime* 24 (2004), 51–54

Bozeman Bulger, "Pitching, Past and Present: The Evolution of the Twirler's Art," *Baseball Magazine*, February 1912, 71–73

Pete Cava, "Baseball in the Olympics," *National Pastime* 12 (1992), 2–8

O. P. Caylor, "The Theory and Introduction of Curve Pitching," *Outing*, August 1891, 402–405

Henry Chadwick, "The Art of Pitching," *Outing*, May 1889, 119–121

Irwin Chusid, "The Short, Happy Life of the Newark Peppers," *Baseball Research Journal* 20 (1991), 44–45

Eddie Cicotte, "The Secrets of Successful Pitching," *Baseball Magazine*, July 1918, 267–268, 299

Robert Cole, "Ball, Bat and Ad," *Baseball Research Journal* 8 (1979), 77–79

T. Z. Cowles, multi-part series on early Chicago sports history, *Chicago Tribune*, May 26, June 2, June 16, and June 30, 1918

"Cummings Tells Story of Early Days of Curve Ball," *Sporting News*, December 29, 1921, 7

"Curved Balls," *Sporting News*, February 20, 1897, 2

Dan Daniel, "Batters Going Batty from Butterflies," *Sporting News*, June 12, 1946, 3

George S. Davis, "How to Bat," syndicated column, *Warren* (Pa.) *Evening Democrat*, May 26, 1894, 2

Bill Deane, "The Old Hidden Ball Trick: No Longer Banned in Boston," in Mark Kanter, ed., *The Northern Game and Beyond: Baseball in New England and Eastern Canada* (Cleveland, 2002), 69–72

Clarence Deming, "Old Days in Baseball," *Outing*, June 1902, 357–360

Joe Dittmar, "A Shocking Discovery," *Baseball Research Journal* 20 (1991), 52–53, 65

Walter C. Dohm, "College Baseball," *Los Angeles Times*, May 21, 1893, 10

Joseph Durso, "Slider Is the Pitch That Put Falling Batting Averages on the Skids," *New York Times*, September 22, 1968, 198

Stefan Fatsis, "Mystery of Baseball: Was William White Game's First Black?," *Wall Street Journal*, January 30, 2004, 1

"The First Detroit Base Ball Club Formed in the *Free Press* Office Twenty-Seven Years Ago," *Detroit Free Press*, April 4, 1884

Val J. Flanagan, "Rain-Check Evolved to Check Flood of Fence-Climbers, Says Originator, Now 83," *Sporting News*, April 8, 1943, 2

Russell Ford (as told to Don E. Basenfelder), "Russell Ford Tells Inside Story of the 'Emery' Ball After Guarding His Secret for Quarter of a Century," *Sporting News*, April 25, 1935, 5

John B. Foster, "Buckeye Boys," *Sporting News*, December 28, 1895, 3

John B. Foster, "The Evolution of Pitching" (part 1), *Sporting News*, November 26, 1931, 5; "The Evolution of Pitching" (part 2), *Sporting News*, December 10, 1931, 6; "The Evolution of Pitching" (part 3), *Sporting News*, December 24, 1931, 6; "The Evolution of Pitching" (part 4), *Sporting News*, January 7, 1932, 6

Duane Frazier, "Wellington Celebrates the Evening It Lit Up High School Football," *Wichita Eagle*, September 10, 2004, 1D, 6D

Larry R. Gerlach, "Death on the Diamond: The Cal Drummond Story," *National Pastime* 24 (2004), 14–16

Larry R. Gerlach and Harold V. Higham, "Dick Higham," *National Pastime* 20 (2000), 20–32

"The Great National Game in Dollars and Cents," *Washington Post*, May 9, 1909

Barbara Gregorich, "Jackie and the Juniors vs. Margaret and the Bloomers," *National Pastime* 13 (1993), 8–10

William Ridgely Griffith, *The Early History of Amateur Base Ball in the State of Maryland*; reprinted in *Maryland Historical Magazine* 87, No. 2 (Summer 1992), 201–208

John H. Gruber, multi-part series on baseball rules and customs under a variety of headings, weekly series in *Sporting News*, November 4, 1915–April 6, 1916

Bob Hoie, "The Farm System," *Total Baseball*, 2nd edition, 644–647

John Holway, "Willie Wells: A Devil of a Shortstop," *Baseball Research Journal* 17 (1988), 50–53

"How to Hit a Ball," *New York Sun*, reprinted in *Birmingham* (Ala.) *Evening News*, October 2, 1888

"Dan Irish," "System Is Bad: Ball Players Not Properly Trained," *Sporting News*, February 19, 1898, 2

Frederick Ivor-Campbell, "Extraordinary 1884," *National Pastime* 13 (1993), 16–23

Frederick Ivor-Campbell, "Postseason Play," *Total Baseball* IV, 281–282

Frederick Ivor-Campbell, "When Was the First? (Continued)," *Nineteenth Century Notes* 95:1 (Winter 1995), 1–2

Frederick Ivor-Campbell, "When Was the First? (Part 4)," *Nineteenth Century Notes* 95:3, 4 (Summer/Fall 1995), 10–12

Frederick Ivor-Campbell, "When Was the First Match Game Played by the Knickerbocker Rules?" *Nineteenth Century Notes* 93:4 (Fall 1993), 1–2

Bill James, "A History of the Beanball," *The Bill James Baseball Abstract 1985*, 131–140

Willis E. Johnson, "The Player's Life in the Major Leagues," *Sporting Life*, March 4, 1916

Gene Karst, "Ready for the New Asterisk War?," *Baseball Research Journal* 26 (1997), 66–67

Seamus Kearney, "Bill Thompson, Pioneer," *National Pastime* 16 (1996), 67–68

Maclean Kennedy, "Charley Bennett, Former Detroit Catcher, Inventor of Chest Pad," *Detroit Free Press*, August 2, 1914

Al Kermisch, "Umpire Used Hand Signals in 1883," *Baseball Research Journal* 21 (1992), 111

Gene Kessler, "Deacon White, Oldest Living Player, at 92 Recalls Highlights of Historic Career That Started in 1868," *Sporting News*, June 22, 1939, 19

Bill Kirwin, "The Mysterious Case of Dick Brookins," *National Pastime* 19 (1999), 38–43

J. C. Kofoed, "Early History of Curve Pitching," *Baseball Magazine*, August 1915, 55–57

Leonard Koppett, "The Ex-National Sport Looks to Its Image," *New York Times*, December 20, 1964, SM18

Dan Krueckeberg, "Take-Charge Cy," *National Pastime* 4, No. 1 (Spring 1985), 7–11

F. C. Lane, "The Emery Ball Strangest of Freak Deliveries," *Baseball Magazine*, July 1915, 58–72

R. M. Larner, "Old-Time Baseball in the White Lot," *Washington Post*, June 26, 1904, S4

R. M. Larner, "Beginning of Professional Baseball in Washington," *Washington Post*, July 3, 1904, S3

Hal Lebovitz, "Zimmer, Oldest Catcher, Leafs Memory Book," *Sporting News*, January 12, 1949, 11

Larry Lester, "Only the Stars Come Out at Night!: J. L. Wilkinson and His Lighting Machine," Lloyd Johnson, Steve Garlick and Jeff Magalif, eds., *Unions to Royals: The Story of Professional Baseball in Kansas City* (Cleveland, 1996), 8–10

Frederick G. Lieb, "A Man Who Has Made Millions from By-Products of Sport," *Sportlife*, December 1925, 94

Joseph F. Lowry, "Baseball's Magic-Mud Man," *Family Weekly*, September 5, 1965

Connie Mack, "How to Play Ball," multi-part series, *Washington Post*, March 13, March 20, March 27, April 3, April 10, April 17, 1904

Connie Mack, "Memories of When the Game Was Young," *Sporting Life* (monthly), June 1924

Jerry Malloy, "Out at Home," in John Thorn, ed., *The National Pastime* (New York, 1988), 209–244

David Mandell, "Reuben Berman's Foul Ball," *National Pastime* 25 (2005), 106–107

Larry Marthey, "Park Tampering Is Old Custom," *Detroit News*, April 7, 1959, T-15

Beth Martin, "Hey, Blue!," *National Pastime* 18 (1998), 36–46

Andy McCue, "The King of Coolie Hats," *National Pastime* 19 (1999), 24–27

David McDonald, "The Senators' Diamond Dynasty," *Ottawa Citizen*, March 25, 2003

E. L. McDonald, "The National Game of Base Ball Was Born in Fort Wayne," *St. Louis Republican*, reprinted in *Fort Wayne Journal Gazette*, January 26, 1902

P. A. Meaney, "Who Invented the Spit Ball," *Baseball Magazine*, May 1913, 59–60

Leigh Montville, "Field of Screams," *Sports Illustrated*, May 22, 2000

Peter Morris, "'Attaboy!' Originated from the Dynamic Managing Style of Hughie Jennings (Detroit Tigers) in 1907," *Comments on Etymology* 33, No. 1 (October 2003), 2–4

Peter Morris, "Baseball Term 'Bunt' Was Originally Called 'Baby Hit'; Popular 19c. Lullaby 'Bye, Baby Bunting' May Have Produced 'Baby Bunting Hit,' Shortened to 'Bunt,'" *Comments on Etymology* 34, No. 1 (October 2004), 2–4

Edgar Munzel, "Daily Workouts Put Shaw in Pink for Comeback Pitch," *Sporting News*, November 16, 1960, 9

"Jim Nasium" [Edgar Wolfe], "'Ted' Sullivan, Baseball Pioneer," *Sporting Life* (monthly), January 1923

Tom Nawrocki, "Captain Anson's Platoon," *National Pastime* 15 (1995), 34–37

Amy Ellis Nutt, "Swinging for the Fences," in Lissa Smith, ed., *Nike Is a Goddess: The History of Women in Sports* (New York, 1998)

Robert A. Nylen, "Frontier Baseball," *Nevada*, Volume 50, Number 2 (March/April 1990), 27–29, 56

James O'Rourke, "Forty Two Years of Base Ball: Wonderful Life Story of Jim O'Rourke" (multi-part series), *Kalamazoo Evening Telegraph*, February 24, 25, 26, March 1, 2, 3, 1910

Steve Orr, "MSU Police Get Radar Gun," *State News*, October 10, 1974

Joseph M. Overfield, "The Richards-Jethroe Caper: Fact or Fiction?," *Baseball Research Journal* 16 (1987), 33–35

Joseph M. Overfield, "You Could Look It Up," *National Pastime* 10 (1990), 69–71

Ev Parker, "The Supreme Compliment," *National Pastime* 17 (1997), 138–139

Ted Patterson, "Jack Graney, The First Player-Broadcaster," *Baseball Research Journal* 2 (1973), 80–86, reprinted in *Baseball Historical Review* 1981, 52–57

William Perrin, "Line Drives Then and Now," originally published in 1928 in an unknown source, reprinted in James Charlton, ed., *Road Trips* (Cleveland, 2004), 81–91

William A. Phelon, "Shall We Have a Third Big League?," *Baseball Magazine*, March 1912, 10–12, 92

Deacon Phillippe, "Phillippe of Pittsburg Team Discusses Requirements of Successful Pitchers," *Syracuse Post Standard*, March 27, 1904, 10

David Pietrusza, "The Cahill Brothers' Night Baseball Experiments," *Baseball Research Journal* 23 (1994), 62–66

David Pietrusza, "The Continental League of 1921," *National Pastime* 13 (1993), 76–78

David Pietrusza, "Famous Firsts," *Total Baseball* VI, 2507

Bill Plott, "The Southern League of Colored Base Ballists," *Baseball Research Journal* 3 (1974), 91–95, reprinted in *Baseball Historical Review* 1981, 75–78

Barry Popik and Gerald Cohen, "Material on the Origin of the Spitball Pitch," *Comments on Etymology* 32:8 (May 2003), 21–28

Robert Pruter, "Youth Baseball in Chicago, 1868–1890: Not Always Sandlot Ball," *Journal of Sport History*, Spring 1999, 6

Chris Rainey, "A Cincy Legend: A Narrative of Bumpus Jones' Baseball Career," in Dick Miller and Mark Stang, eds., *Baseball in the Buckeye State* (Cleveland, 2004), 3–7

Bob Rives, "Good Night," *National Pastime* 18 (1998), 21–24

Emil H. Rothe, "History of the Chicago City Series," *Baseball Research Journal* 8 (1979), 15–24

Robert H. Schaefer, "The Lost Art of Fair-Foul Hitting," *National Pastime* 20 (2000), 3–9

John Schwartz, "From One Ump to Two," *Baseball Research Journal* 30 (2001), 85–86

Alan Schwarz, "Real-time Broadcasts Lead to Copyright Questions," *Baseball America*, September 15–28, 2003

Charley Scully, "'Father of the Catching Glove' Admits Split Finger Fifty Years Ago, with Twin Bill Ahead, Was 'Mother,'" *Sporting News*, February 23, 1939, 9

Peter Segroie, "Reuben's Ruling Helps You 'Have a Ball,'" *Baseball Research Journal* 20 (1991), 85

Tom Shieber, "The Earliest Baseball Photography," *National Pastime* 17 (1997), 101–104

Tom Shieber, "The Evolution of the Baseball Diamond," originally printed in the *Baseball Research Journal* 23 (1994), 3–13; reprinted in an expanded version in *Total Baseball* IV, 113–124

Herbert Simons, "Life of an Ump," *Baseball Magazine*, April 1942; reprinted in Sidney Offit, ed., *The Best of Baseball*, 156–162

Duane Smith, "Dickey Pearce: Baseball's First Great Shortstop," *National Pastime* 10 (1990), 38–42

Deron Snyder, "A Stat Worth Saving," *USA Today Baseball Weekly*, July 21–27, 1999

Fred Stein, "Managers and Coaches," *Total Baseball*, 2nd edition, 452–463

Bucky Summers, "Still Baseball on TV," *Frederick* (Md.) *Post*, April 20, 1965, 9

Scott S. Taylor, "Pure Passion for the Game: Albany Amateur Baseball Box Scores from 1864," *Manuscripts* LIV, No. 1 (Winter 2002), 5–13

Dick Thompson, "Matty and His Fadeaway," *National Pastime* 17 (1997), 93–96

George A. Thompson, Jr., "New York Baseball, 1823," *National Pastime* 21 (2001), 6–8

Ken Tillman, "The Portable Batting Cage," *Baseball Research Journal* 28 (1999), 23–26

E. H. Tobias, sixteen-part history of baseball in St. Louis up to 1876, *Sporting News*, November 2, 1895–February 15, 1896

M. E. Travaglini, "Olympic Baseball 1936: Was Es Das?," *National Pastime* (Winter 1985), 46–55

"Tri-Mountain," three-part series on early baseball in Boston, *Boston Journal*, February 20 and 22, March 6, 1905

John (Dasher) Troy, "Reminiscences of an Old-Timer," *Baseball Magazine*, June 1915, 93–94

Gary Waddingham, "Irish Bob O'Regan: A Bespectacled Ump in the Bush Leagues," *Minor League History Journal* 1:1, 33–36

William J. Weiss, "The First Negro in Twentieth Century O.B.," *Baseball Research Journal* 8 (1979), 31–35

H. H. Westlake, "The First Box Score Ever Published," *Baseball Magazine*, March 1925; reprinted in Sidney Offit, ed., *The Best of Baseball*, 156–162

William Wheaton (early Knickerbocker), interview, *San Francisco Examiner*, November 27, 1887

Tim Wiles, "The Joy of Foul Balls," *National Pastime* 25 (2005), 102–105

Bob Wolf, "Controversy Like Screaming at Danforth 40 Years Ago," *Sporting News*, May 1, 1957, 15

James Leon Wood, Sr. (as told to Frank G. Menke), "Baseball in By-Gone Days," syndicated series, *Indiana* (Pa.) *Evening Gazette*, August 14, 1916; *Marion* (Ohio) *Star*, August 15, 1916; *Indiana* (Pa.) *Evening Gazette*, August 17, 1916

ADDITIONAL PERIODICALS CONSULTED

Adrian (Mich.) *Press, Adrian Times and Expositor, American Chronicle of Sports and Pastimes, Atlanta Constitution, Atlanta Journal, Aurora* (Ill.) *Beacon-News, The Ball Player's Chronicle, Baltimore Sun, Baseball America, Baseball Magazine, Baseball Research Journal, Bay City* (Mich.) *Journal, Boston Globe, Brooklyn Eagle, Canton* (Ohio) *Repository, Chicago Inter-Ocean, Chicago Tribune, Christian Science Monitor, Cincinnati Enquirer, Cincinnati News-Journal, Cincinnati Times-Star, Cleveland Herald, Cleveland Leader, Cleveland Leader and Herald, Cleveland Plain Dealer, Colorado Daily Chieftain* (Pueblo), *Columbus* (Ohio) *Dispatch, Columbus* (Ohio) *Post, Columbus* (Ohio) *Press, Columbus* (Ohio) *Sunday Morning News, Comments on Etymology, Coshocton* (Ohio) *Tribune, Danville* (Va.) *Bee, Dayton Journal, Decatur Review, Delphos* (Ohio) *Herald, Detroit Advertiser and Tribune, Detroit Evening News, Detroit Free Press, Detroit News, Detroit Post, Detroit Post and Tribune, Detroit Tribune, Elyria* (Ohio) *Chronicle Telegram, Family Weekly, Fort Wayne Gazette, Fort Wayne Journal Gazette, Fort Wayne News, Fort Wayne News and Sentinel, Fort Wayne Sentinel, Frederick* (Md.) *News, Frederick* (Md.) *Post, Fremont* (Mich.) *Indicator, Gettysburg Times, Grand Rapids* (Mich.) *Democrat, Grand Rapids* (Mich.) *Evening Press, Grand Rapids* (Mich.) *Herald, Grand Rapids* (Mich.) *Leader, Grand Rapids* (Mich.) *Times, Grand Rapids* (Wisc.) *Tribune, Grand Traverse* (Mich.) *Herald, Grand Valley* (Moab, Utah) *Times, Harper's Weekly, Hawaiian Gazette, Holland* (Mich.) *Evening Sentinel, Indiana* (Pa.) *Gazette, Indianapolis Sentinel and News, Indianapolis Star, Ionia* (Mich.) *Sentinel, Jackson* (Mich.) *Citizen, Jonesville* (Mich.) *Independent, Kalamazoo Gazette, Kalamazoo Telegraph, Lansing* (Mich.) *Journal, Lapeer* (Mich.) *Democrat, Lima* (Ohio) *News, Lincoln* (Nebr.) *Evening Journal, Lincoln* (Nebr.) *Evening State Journal, London* (Ont.) *Free Press, Los Angeles Times, Louisville Courier-Journal, M.A.C.* [Michigan Agricultural College] *Record, Manistee* (Mich.) *Advocate, Mansfield* (Ohio) *News, Manufacturer and Builder, Marion* (Ohio) *Star, Marshall* (Mich.) *Statesman, Michigan Argus* (Ann Arbor), *Milwaukee Journal, Minor League History Journal, Muskegon News and Reporter, Mutes Chronicle* (Ohio School for the Deaf, Columbus), *National Chronicle, National Pastime, Nevada* (Reno) *State Journal, Newark Advocate, New England Base Ballist, New York Clipper, New York Herald, New York Herald Tribune, New York Sun, New York Times, New York Tribune,*

New York World, Niles (Mich.) *Republican, Niles* (Mich.) *Times, Nineteenth Century Notes, North Adams* (Mass.) *Transcript, The Official Baseball Record, Ohio State Journal* (Columbus), *Oshkosh Northwestern, Ottawa Citizen, Ottumwa* (Iowa) *Courier, Outside the Lines, Owosso* (Mich.) *Press, Paw Paw* (Mich.) *True Northerner, Perry* (Iowa) *Chief, Perry* (Iowa) *Pilot, Philadelphia Inquirer, Portage Lake* (Houghton, Mich.) *Mining Gazette, Port Arthur* (Tex.) *News, Port Huron Times, Reno Evening Gazette, Rochester History, Rocky Mountain* (Denver) *News, Saginaw Courier, Salisbury* (Md.) *Times, San-dusky* (Ohio) *Star, Sandusky* (Ohio) *Star-Journal, San Francisco Examiner, Sheboygan* (Wisc.) *Press, South Haven Sentinel, Spirit of the Times, Sporting Life, Sporting News, Sportlife, Sports Illustrated, St. Joseph* (Mich.) *Herald Press, St. Louis Globe-Democrat, St. Louis Post-Dispatch, St. Louis Republican, State News* (Michigan State University), *Steubenville Herald Star, Stevens Point* (Wisc.) *Journal, Syracuse Herald, Syracuse Her-ald Journal, Syracuse Post Standard, Tecumseh* (Mich.) *Herald, Titusville* (Pa.) *Morning Herald, Toledo Blade, Toronto Globe, Trenton Times, Troy* (N.Y.) *Times Record, USA To-day, USA Today Baseball Weekly, USA Today Sports Weekly, Virgin Island News, Warren Evening Times, Washington Evening Star, Washington Post, Wellsboro Agitator, Wichita Eagle, Williamsport Gazette-Bulletin, Williamsport Sunday Grit, Winnipeg Times, Wis-consin Northwestern, Wisconsin Rapids Tribune, Woodstock* (Ont.) *Review, Woodstock* (Ont.) *Sentinel Review, Youngstown Vindicator, Zanesville Signal, Zanesville Times-Recorder, Zanesville Times Signal*

SPECIAL COLLECTIONS AND ARCHIVAL SOURCES

Allen County (Indiana) Public Library; Chadwick Scrapbooks; Bentley Library, University of Michigan; Burton Collection, Detroit Public Library; Cincinnati Reds Collection, Cincinnati Historical Society; Michigan Pioneer and Historical Collec-tions; Michigan State University Library; Library of Michigan; Ohio Historical So-ciety; William Rankin Scrapbooks; Peter Tamony Collection, University of Missouri; University of Michigan Library; Wazoo Records, East Lansing

ON-LINE RESOURCES

While on-line resources are always prone to disappearing, a few websites seem well enough established and were valuable enough in my research that it would be inex-cusable not to mention them. The Baseball Index (http://www.baseballindex.org), compiled by the Bibliographic Committee of SABR, is an invaluable tool for tracking down sources. The wonderful Retrosheet website (http://www.retrosheet.org) has also been a constant aid in my research. The websites of the Vintage Base Ball As-sociation (http://www.vbba.org) and the National Baseball Hall of Fame (http://www.baseballhalloffame.org) also have considerable relevant material. The early card mentioned in entry 15.4.3 can be viewed at the website of Frank Ceresi and Associates (http://www.fcassociates.com/ntearlybb.htm).

I have also benefited greatly from the free on-line archives of the *Brooklyn Eagle* (http://www.brooklynpubliclibrary.org/eagle/index.htm), the newspapers of Utah (http://www.lib.utah.edu/digital/unews), Missouri (http://newspapers.umsystem.edu) and Colorado (http://www.cdpheritage.org/newspapers/index.html), and the diverse offerings of the Amateur Athletic Foundation of Los Angeles (http://www.aafla.org). My work has also been made easier by the subscription-based archives of ProQuest (available to SABR members at http://www.sabr.org), newspaperarchive.com and Cold North Wind (http://www.paperofrecord.com).

Index

A NOTE ON THE AUTHOR

Peter Morris was born in Birmingham, England, and studied English at the University of Toronto and Michigan State University. His first book, *Baseball Fever: Early Baseball in Michigan*, received the coveted Seymour Medal from the Society for American Baseball Research as the best book on baseball history published in 2003. A former world Scrabble® champion, Mr. Morris is now a researcher for the Michigan Public Health Institute and lives in Haslett, Michigan.